SAT 2005

Satisfiability Research in the Year 2005

T0138135

SAT 2005

Satisfiability Research in the Year 2005

Edited by

ENRICO GIUNCHIGLIA

Università di Genova, Italy

and

TOBY WALSH

*National ICT Australia and University of New South Wales,
Sydney, Australia*

Reprinted from *Journal of Automated Reasoning*, Vol. 35, Nos. 1–3, 2005

 Springer

A C.I.P. Catalogue record for this book is available from the Library of Congress.

ISBN-10 94-007-8715-4 (HB)
ISBN-13 978-94-007-8715-5 (HB)
ISBN-10 1-4020-5571-3 (eBook)
ISBN-13 978-1-4020-5571-3 (eBook)

Published by Springer,
P.O. Box 17, 3300 AA Dordrecht, The Netherlands.

www.springer.com

Printed on acid-free paper

All Rights Reserved
© 2006 Springer
Softcover re-print of the Hardcover 1st edition 2006
No part of this work may be reproduced, stored in a retrieval system, or transmitted
in any form or by any means, electronic, mechanical, photocopying, microfilming, recording
or otherwise, without written permission from the Publisher, with the exception
of any material supplied specifically for the purpose of being entered
and executed on a computer system, for exclusive use by the purchase of the work.

TABLE OF CONTENTS

J Autom Reasoning (2005) 35: 1–2
DOI 10.1007/s10817-006-9041-2

Satisfiability in the Year 2005

Enrico Giunchiglia · Toby Walsh

Published online: 31 August 2006
© Springer Science + Business Media B.V. 2006

Welcome to 'SAT 2005,' three special numbers of the *Journal of Automated Reasoning* devoted to Satisfiability in the Year 2005. This initiative follows on from SAT 2000, three special numbers of the journal (and an accompanying book) that were published back in 2000. Five years seemed the right amount of time to us and to Deepak Kapur, the editor in chief of the journal, to review the rapid progress being made in propositional satisfiability (SAT). This area has continued to flourish over the past decade and a half, with major advances in both theory and practice.

Propositional reasoning itself has had a long and distinguished history. In 1869, William Stanley Jevon's Logic Machine became the first machine to solve Boolean logic problems faster than was possible by hand. In 1957, Allen Newell and Herb Simon introduced the Logic Theory Machine to prove problems from Whitehead and Russel's *Principia mathematica*. In 1960, Martin Davis and Hillary Putnam introduced their eponymous decision procedure for SAT (though, for space reasons, it was quickly superseded by the modified procedure proposed by Martin Davis, George Logemann, and Donald Loveland two years later). In 1971, Stephen Cook's proof that SAT is NP-complete placed SAT as the cornerstone of complexity theory. More recently, SAT has been applied to solve practical problems in hardware verification and elsewhere using highly optimized solvers.

The papers in SAT 2005 fall (not entirely neatly) into the following categories: complete methods, local and stochastic search methods, random problems, applications, and extensions beyond the propositional. SAT 2005 is not a single special issue, because of the large response we received to our call for papers. We received

E. Giunchiglia (✉)
Dipartimento di Informatica, Sistemistica e Telematica, Università di Genova,
16145 Genova, Italy
e-mail: giunchiglia@unige.it

T. Walsh
National ICT Australia and Department of Computer Science and Engineering,
University of New South Wales, Sydney, NSW 2052, Australia
e-mail: tw@cse.unsw.edu.au

🎄 Springer

24 submissions totaling more than 500 pages. As papers were judged entirely on their quality (and not on any space considerations), we decided to accept 11 papers.

We thank again Deepak Kapur and Gail Pieper of *JAR* for inviting us to edit the special issue and for all their help along the way. We also thank the authors of all the submitted papers, and the many reviewers we called upon. We look forward to speaking to you again in 2010.

Journal of Automated Reasoning (2005) 35: 3–24
DOI: 10.1007/s10817-005-9005-y

© Springer 2005

Heuristic-Based Backtracking Relaxation for Propositional Satisfiability

ATEET BHALLA*, INÊS LYNCE, JOSÉ T. DE SOUSA
and JOÃO MARQUES-SILVA
Technical University of Lisbon, IST/INESC-ID, Rua Alves Redol 9, 1000-029, Lisbon, Portugal.
e-mail: {ateet.bhalla, ines.lynce, jts, jpms}@inesc-id.pt

Abstract. In recent years backtrack search algorithms for propositional satisfiability (SAT) have been the subject of dramatic improvements. These improvements allowed SAT solvers to successfully solve instances with thousands or tens of thousands of variables. However, many new challenging problem instances are still too hard for current SAT solvers. As a result, further improvements to SAT technology are expected to have key consequences in solving hard real-world instances. This paper introduces a new idea: choosing the backtrack variable using a heuristic approach with the goal of diversifying the regions of the space that are explored during the search. The proposed heuristics are inspired by the heuristics proposed in recent years for the decision branching step of SAT solvers, namely, VSIDS and its improvements. Completeness conditions are established, which guarantee completeness for the new algorithm, as well as for any other incomplete backtracking algorithm. Experimental results on hundreds of instances derived from real-world problems show that the new technique is able to speed SAT solvers, while aborting fewer instances. These results clearly motivate the integration of heuristic backtracking in SAT solvers.

1. Introduction

Propositional satisfiability is a well-known NP-complete problem, with theoretical and practical significance and with extensive applications in many fields of computer science and engineering, including artificial intelligence and electronic design automation.

Current state-of-the-art SAT solvers incorporate sophisticated pruning techniques as well as new strategies for organizing the search. Effective search pruning techniques are based, among others, on no-good learning and dependency-directed backtracking [24] and back-jumping [8], whereas recent effective strategies introduce variations on the organization of backtrack search. Examples of such strategies are weak-commitment search [25], search restarts [12], and random backtracking [15, 20].

Advanced techniques applied to backtrack search SAT algorithms have achieved remarkable improvements [2, 11, 18, 19], having been shown to be

---

* Author for correspondence.

crucial for solving hard instances of SAT obtained from real-world applications. Moreover, and from a practical perspective, the most effective algorithms are *complete* and so are able to prove unsatisfiabiltiy. Indeed, this is often the objective in a large number of significant real-world applications.

Nevertheless, it is also widely accepted that local search has some advantages compared to backtrack search. Although it is debatable which are the real advantages of local search (e.g., see [7]), one of them seems to be the use of search restarts. Search restarts prevent the search form *getting stuck* in a locally optimal partial solution. The advantage of search restarts has motivated the study of approaches for relaxing backtracking conditions (while still ensuring completeness). The key idea is to *unrestrictedly* choose the point to backtrack to, in order to avoid thrashing, that is, exploring useless portions of search space corresponding to very similar conflicting sets of assignments. Moreover, one can think of combining different forms of relaxing the identification of the backtrack point.

In this paper, we propose to use heuristic knowledge to select the backtrack point. Besides describing the generic heuristic backtracking search strategy, we establish backtracking heuristics inspired by the most effective branching heuristics proposed in recent years, namely, the VSIDS heuristic used by Chaff [19] and the BerkMin's branching heuristic [11].

Simply replacing deterministic backtracking with heuristic backtracking in SAT algorithms has two major drawbacks: (1) the resulting algorithm is no longer complete, and (2) an algorithm applying heuristic backtracking for every backtrack step becomes very unstable.

To eliminate these drawbacks, we introduce the concept of unrestricted backtracking algorithms. Each backtrack step is either a complete form of backtracking (i.e., chronological or nonchronological backtracking) or an incomplete form of backtracking (e.g., heuristic backtracking). Clearly an unrestricted backtracking algorithm applying heuristic backtracking after every k steps (with $k > 1$) and nonchronological backtracking every other steps is more stable than an unrestricted backtracking algorithm applying heuristic backtracking for every backtrack step. Moreover, we establish completeness conditions for unrestricted backtracking algorithms. These conditions guarantee completeness for *any* instantiation of the unrestricted backtracking algorithm.

This paper extends previous work. We first introduced our heuristic backtracking ideas in [3], where we showed that heuristic backtracking is superior to other forms of unrestricted backtracking such as search restarts and random backtracking. In [4], we introduced the completeness conditions and modified the algorithm accordingly to make it complete. Some preliminary and promising results have been presented in [3] and in [4]. This paper gives a more comprehensive description of the different forms of backtracking and integrates heuristic backtracking within the framework of unrestricted backtracking. In addition, we present improved experimental results that show that the benefits of heuristic backtracking increase for hard-to-solve problem instances.

We summarize the contributions of this paper as follows: (1) we introduce heuristic backtracking algorithms; (2) we show that heuristic backtracking is a special case of unrestricted backtracking, and we describe different approaches for guaranteeing completeness of unrestricted backtracking; and (3) we give experimental results that indicate that the proposed heuristic backtracking algorithm is a competitive approach for solving real-world instances of SAT.

The remainder of this paper is organized as follows. The next section presents definitions used throughout the paper. In Section 3 we briefly survey backtrack search SAT algorithms. In Section 4 we introduce heuristic backtracking. Section 5 describes unrestricted backtracking algorithms for SAT and explains how heuristic backtracking can be regarded as a special case or unrestricted backtracking. In addition, we address completeness issues. Section 6 gives experimental results, and Section 7 describes related work. In Section 8, we conclude the paper and give directions for future research work.

2. Definitions

This section introduces the notational framework used throughout the paper. Propositional variables are denoted $x_1, \ldots, x_n$ and can be assigned truth values 0 (or F) or 1 (or T). The truth value assigned to a variable x is denoted by $v(x)$. (When clear from context we use $x = v_x$, where $v_x \in \{0,1\}$). A literal l is either a variable x_i or its negation $\neg x_i$. A clause ω is a disjunction of literals and a CNF formula φ is a conjunction of clauses. A clause is said to be *satisfied* if at least one of its literals assume value 1, *unsatisfied* if all of its literals assume value 0, *unit* if all but one literal assume value 0 and *unresolved* otherwise. Literals with no assigned truth value are said to be *free literals*. A formula is said to be *satisfied* if all its clauses are satisfied, and is *unsatisfied* if at least one clause is unsatisfied. A *truth assignment* for a formula is a set of pairs of variables and their corresponding truth values. The SAT problem consists of deciding whether there exists a truth assignment to the variables such that the formula becomes satisfied.

SAT algorithms can be characterized as being either *complete* or *incomplete*. Complete algorithms can establish unsatisfiablity if given enough CPU time; incomplete algorithms cannot. Examples of complete and incomplete algorithms are backtrack search and local search algorithms, respectively. In a search context, complete algorithms are often referred to as *systematic*, whereas incomplete algorithms are referred to as *nonsystematic*.

3. Backtrack Search SAT Algorithms

Over the years a large number of algorithms have been proposed for SAT, from the original Davis–Putnam procedure [6], to recent backtrack search algorithms [2, 11, 18, 19] and local search algorithms [23], among many others.

The vast majority of backtrack search SAT algorithms are built on the original backtrack search algorithm of Davis, Logemann, and Loveland [5]. The backtrack search algorithm is implemented by a *search process* that implicitly enumerates the space of 2^n possible binary assignments to the n variables of the problem. Each different truth assignment defines a *search path* within the search space. A *decision level* is associated with each variable selection and assignment. (The notation $x@d$ is used to denote that variable x has been assigned at decision level d.) The first variable selection corresponds to decision level 1, and the decision level is incremented by 1 for each new decision assignments.[*] In addition, and for each decision level, the *unit clause rule* [6] is applied. The iterated application of the unit clause rule is often referred to as Boolean constraint propagation (BCP). If a clause is unit, then the sole free literal must be assigned value 1 for satisfying the formula. In this case, the values of the literal and of the associated variable are said to be *implied*. Thus, assigned variables can be distinguished as *decision variables* and *implied variables*.

In chronological backtracking, the search algorithm keeps track of which decision assignments have been toggled. Given an unsatisfied clause (i.e., a *conflict* or a *dead end*) at decision level d, the algorithm checks whether at the current decision level the corresponding decision variable x has already been toggled. If not, the algorithm erases the variable assignments that are implied by the assignment on x, including the assignment on x, assigns the opposite value to x, and marks decision variable x as toggled. In contrast, if the value of x has already been toggled, the search backtracks to decision level $d - 1$.

Recent state-of-the-art SAT solvers utilize different forms of nonchronological backtracking [2, 18, 19]. In these algorithms each identified conflict is analyzed to identify the variable assignments that caused it, and a new clause (*no-good*) is created to explain and prevent the identified conflicting conditions from happening again. The created clause is then used to compute the backtrack point as the *most recent* decision assignment represented in the recorded clause; moreover, some of the (larger) recorded clauses are eventually deleted. Clauses can be deleted opportunistically whenever they are no longer *relevant* for the current search path [18].

Figure 1 illustrates the differences between chronological backtracking (CB) and the nonchronological backtracking (NCB). On the top of the figure appears a generic search tree (either possible in the context of CB or NCB). The search is performed according to a depth-first search, and therefore the non-dashed branches define the search space explored so far. On the one hand, and when a conflict is found, the chronological backtracking algorithm makes the search backtrack to the most recent, yet untoggled decision variable (see CB(a)). On the

---

[*] All assignments made before the first decision assignment correspond to decision level 0, a preprocessing step.

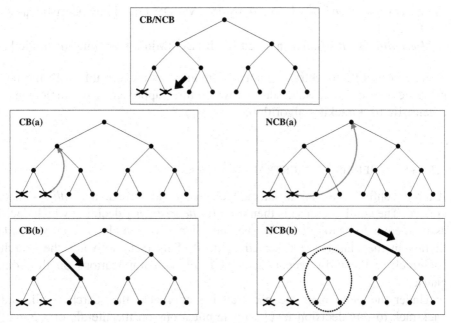

Figure 1. Chronological backtracking (CB) vs nonchronological backtracking (NCB).

other hand, when nonchronological backtracking is applied, the backtrack point is computed as the *most recent* decision assignment from all the decision assignments represented in the recorded clause. In this case the search backtracks to a higher level in the search tree (NCB(a)), skipping portions of the search tree that are found to have no solution (see NCB(b)). From the final figures (CB(b) and NCB(b)) it is plain to conclude that the number of nodes explored by NCB is always equal or smaller than the number of nodes explored by CB.[*] (Observe that no-goods can also reduce the search space because *similar* conflict paths of the search space are avoided in the future).

4. Heuristic Backtracking

Heuristic backtracking consists of selecting the backtrack point in the search tree using a heuristic function of the variables in the most recently recorded clause. Different heuristic functions can be envisioned for applying heuristic backtracking. In this work we implemented three heuristics:

1. *Plain heuristic*: uses a simple heuristic function.

---

[*] Assuming that a fixed-order branching heuristic is used.

2. *VSIDS-like heuristic*: inspired by the VSIDS branching heuristic used by Chaff [19].
3. *BerkMin-like heuristic*: inspired by the BerkMin's branching heuristic [11].

In all cases the backtrack point is computed as the variable with the largest heuristic metric. Next, we describe how the three approaches are implemented in a heuristic backtracking algorithm.

4.1. PLAIN HEURISTIC BACKTRACKING

After a conflict (i.e., an unsatisfied clause) is identified, a *conflict clause* is created. The conflict clause is then used for *heuristically* deciding which decision assignment is to be toggled. Observe that when a conflict clause is created, all the literals in the clause are assigned value 0. This fact motivates the search to backtrack to the most recent decision level with implications on the conflict clause.

Under the plain heuristic backtracking approach, the search is allowed to backtrack to *any* decision level with implications on the literals of the conflict clause. The backtrack point (i.e., decision level) is computed by selecting the decision level with the largest number of occurrences (assigned or implied literals) in the newly recorded clause. In addition, ties are broken randomly. This approach contrasts with the usual nonchronological backtracking approach, in which the most recent decision variable with implications on the conflict is selected as backtrack point.

EXAMPLE 1. Suppose that plain heuristic backtracking is to be applied after recording clause $\omega = (x_1 \lor x_3 \lor \neg x_5 \lor \neg x_9 \lor x_{12})$. Also, suppose that each literal in ω has been assigned at a given decision level: $\omega = (x_1@10 \lor x_3@7 \lor \neg x_5@8 \lor \neg x_9@7 \lor x_{12}@2)$. Clearly, the decision level with the largest number of occurrences (in this case 2 occurrences) is decision level 7. Hence, plain heuristic backtracking makes the search backtrack to level 7.

4.2. VSIDS-LIKE HEURISTIC BACKTRACKING

The second approach to heuristic backtracking is based in the variable-state independent decaying sum (VSIDS) branching heuristic. The heuristic [19]. VSIDS was the first of a new generation of decision heuristics. This heuristic has been used in *Chaff*, a highly optimized SAT solver. More than to develop a well-behaved heuristic, the motivation in Chaff has been to design a fast heuristic. In fact, one of the key properties of this strategies is the low computational overhead, due to being independent of the variable state. As a result, the variable metrics are updated only when there is a conflict.

Similarly to Chaff, in our VSIDS-like backtracking heuristic we have a counter for each literal. Each counter is initialized with the number of occurrences of the literal in the formula. Moreover, each counter is incremented when a new conflict clause containing the literal is added to the clause database. In addition, after every 255 decisions, the metric values are divided by a constant factor of 2, to give preference to variables occurring in the latest conflict clauses. With our VSIDS-like backtracking heuristic, whenever a conflict occurs, the literal in the just recorded clause with the highest metric is used to select the backtrack point.

EXAMPLE 2. Suppose that the VSIDS-like heuristic backtracking is to be applied after recording clause $\omega = (x_1@10 \lor x_3@7 \lor \neg x_5@8 \lor \neg x_9@7 \lor x_{12}@2)$. In addition, suppose that the VSIDS metric for a given variable x is given by $vsids(x)$ and that $vsids(x_1) = 45$, $vsids(x_3) = 5$, $vsids(x_5) = 94$, $vsids(x_9) = 32$ and $vsids(x_{12}) = 41$. The literal in the just recorded clause with the highest metric is x_5. Hence, the VSIDS-like backtracking heuristic makes the search backtrack to level 8, that is, the level where x_5 was assigned.

4.3. BERKMIN-LIKE HEURISTIC BACKTRACKING

The third approach for implementing heuristic backtracking is inspired by the BerkMin's branching heuristic [11], which, in turn, has been inspired by the VSIDS heuristic used in Chaff. In the BerkMin's branching heuristic, the process for updating the metrics of the literals is different. On the one hand, in Chaff the current activity of a variable x is computed by counting the number of occurrences of x in the conflict clause. On the other hand, in BerkMin a wider set of clauses involved in causing the conflict is taken into account for computing each variable's activity. This procedure avoids overlooking some variables that do not appear in the conflict clause, while actively contributing to the conflict.

In our BerkMin-like backtracking heuristic, we increment the metrics of the literals in all clauses that are directly involved in producing the conflict. The metrics are updated during the process of conflict analysis, which can find all clauses involved in producing the conflict by traversing an implication graph data structure. This process finishes with the creation of the conflict clause. As in the case of the VSIDS-like backtracking heuristic, the literal in the conflict clause with the highest metric is used to select the backtrack point.

EXAMPLE 3. Consider again the clause given in Example 2: $\omega = (x_1@10 \lor x_3@7 \lor \neg x_5@8 \lor \neg x_9@7 \lor x_{12}@2)$. Also, suppose that the values given for the BerkMin's metric are given by function $berkmin$ and that $berkmin(x_1) = 31$, $berkmin(x_3) = 38$, $berkmin(x_5) = 2$, $berkmin(x_9) = 15$ and $berkmin(x_{12}) = 53$. The literal in the just recorded clause with the highest metric is x_{12}. Hence,

BerkMin-like heuristic backtracking makes the search backtrack to level 2, that is, the level where x_{12} has been assigned.

5. Unrestricted Backtracking

Heuristic backtracking can be viewed as a special case of unrestricted backtracking [16]. While in unrestricted backtracking any form of backtrack step can be applied, in heuristic backtracking the backtrack point is computed from heuristic information, obtained from the current and past conflicts.

Unrestricted backtracking algorithms allow the search to *unrestrictedly* backtrack to *any* point in the current search path whenever a conflict is reached. Besides the freedom for selecting the backtrack point in the decision tree, unrestricted backtracking allows the application of different types of backtrack steps. Each backtrack step can be selected among chronological backtracking, nonchronological backtracking, (e.g., search restarts, weak-commitment search, random backtracking, or heuristic backtracking). More formally, unrestricted backtracking (UB) allows the application of a sequence of backtrack steps $\{BSt_1, BSt_2, BSt_3, \ldots\}$ such that each backtrack step BSt_i can be a chronological (CB), a nonchronological (NCB), or an incomplete form of backtracking (IFB). This formalism allows capturing the backtracking search strategies used by state-of-the-art SAT solvers [2, 11, 18, 19]. Indeed, if the backtracking sequence consists of always applying chronological backtracking steps or always applying nonchronological backtracking steps, then we capture the chronological and nonchronological backtracking search strategies, respectively.

Unrestricted backtracking gives a unified representation for different backtracking strategies, which allows establishing general completeness conditions for *classes* of backtracking strategies. This is more convenient than analyzing each individual strategy, as has been done in [22, 25]. In what follows, we establish general completeness conditions for unrestricted backtracking, which are valid for any special case of unrestricted backtracking; this includes heuristic backtracking, the main thrust of this paper.

Figure 2 exemplifies how an incomplete form of backtracking can lead to incompleteness, by providing possible sequels to the search process shown in Figure 1. Three backtracking strategies are illustrated: chronological (CB), nonchronological (NCB) and incomplete form of backtracking (IFB). The search path that leads to the solution is marked with the letter **S**. For CB and NCB the solution is found by orderly exploring the search space. With IFB the search backtracks to *any* point, which may cause skipping the search subspace that leads to the solution. Hence, something must be done to ensure the correctness and completeness of an unrestricted backtracking algorithm that includes incomplete backtracking steps. First, and similar to local search, we have to assume that variable toggling in unrestricted backtracking is *reversible*.

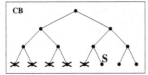 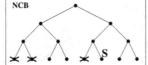 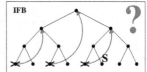

Figure 2. Comparing chronological backtracking (CB), nonchronological backtracking (NCB) and incomplete forms of backtracking (IFB).

This means that the solution can be found later, even if the solution is skipped during the search. Irreversible variable toggling would yield an incorrect or incomplete algorithm. Second, with reversible variable toggling, we must ensure that the algorithm terminates or otherwise it may loop forever in the search space.

A number of techniques can be used to ensure the completeness of unrestricted backtracking algorithms. These techniques are analyzed in [16] and reviewed in the remainder of this section. Completeness techniques for unrestricted backtracking can be organized in two classes:

− Marking recorded clauses as nondeletable. This solution may yield an exponential growth in the number of recorded clauses.★
− Increasing a given constraint (e.g., the number of nondeletable recorded clauses) in between applications of different backtracking schemes. This solution can be used to guarantee a polynomial growth of the number recorded clauses.

5.1. COMPLETENESS ISSUES

It has been explained above how unrestricted backtracking can yield incomplete algorithms. Hence, it is important to be able to apply conditions that guarantee the completeness for each newly devised SAT algorithm that utilizes IFB Steps.

The results presented in this section generalize completeness results that have been proposed in the past (for specific backtracking relaxations) to UB. We start by establishing a few already known results, and then we establish additional results for UB.

In what follows we assume the organization of a backtrack search SAT algorithm as described earlier in this paper. The main loop of the algorithm consists of selecting a decision variable, assigning the variable, and propagating the assignment by using BCP. If an unsatisfied clause occurs (i.e., a *conflict*) the

---

★ In practice an exponential growth in the number of recorded clauses hardly ever arises.

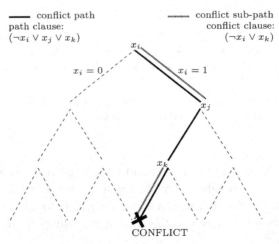

Figure 3. Search tree definitions.

algorithm backtracks to a decision assignment that can be toggled.★ Each time a conflict is identified, all the current decision assignments define a *conflict path* in the search tree. (We restrict the definition of conflict path solely with respect to the decision assignments.) After a conflict is identified, we may apply a *conflict analysis* procedure [2, 18, 19] to identify a subset of the decision assignments that represent a sufficient condition for producing the same conflict. The subset of decision assignments that is declared to be associated with a given conflict is referred to as a *conflict subpath*. A straightforward conflict analysis procedure consists of construction a clause with *all* the decision assignments in the conflict path. In this case the created clause is referred to as a *path-clause*. Figure 3 illustrates these definitions. We can now established a few general results that will be used throughout this section.

PROPOSITION 1. *If an unrestricted backtracking search algorithm does not repeat conflict paths, then it is complete.*

Proof. Assume a problem instance with n variables. Observe that there are 2^n possible conflict paths. If the algorithm does not repeat conflict paths, then it must necessarily terminate.

PROPOSITION 2. *If an unrestricted backtracking search algorithm does not repeat conflict subpaths, then it does not repeat conflict paths.*

Proof. If a conflict subpath is not repeated, then no conflict path can contain the same subpath, and so no conflict path can be repeated.

★ Without loss of generality, we assume that NCB uses irreversible variable toggling after backtracking. In some recent algorithms this happens as an implication caused by the newly derived conflict clause [19].

PROPOSITION 3. *If an unrestricted backtracking search algorithm does not repeat conflict subpaths, then it is complete.*

Proof. Given the two previous results, if no conflict subpaths are repeated, then no conflict paths are repeated, and so completeness is obtained.

PROPOSITION 4. *If the number of times an unrestricted backtracking search algorithm repeats conflict paths or conflict subpaths is upperbounded by a constant, then the backtrack search algorithm is complete.*

Proof. We prove the result for conflict paths; the proof for conflict subpaths is similar. Let M be a constant denoting an upper bound on the number of times a given conflict path can be repeated. Since the total number of distinct conflict paths is 2^n, and since each can be repeated at most M times, then the total number of conflict paths the backtrack search algorithm can enumerate is $M \times 2^n$, and so the algorithm is complete.

PROPOSITION 5. *For an unrestricted backtracking search algorithm following holds:*

1. If the algorithm creates a path clause for each identified conflict, then the search algorithm repeats no conflict paths.
2. If the algorithm creates a conflict clause for each identified conflict, then the search algorithm repeats no conflict subpaths.
3. If the algorithm creates a conflict clause (or a path clause) after every M identified conflicts, then the number of times an unrestricted backtracking search algorithm repeats conflict sub-paths (or conflict paths) is upper-bounded.

In all of the above cases, the search algorithm is complete.

Proof. Recall that the search algorithm always applies BCP after making a decision assignment. Hence, if a clause describing a conflict has been recorded and not deleted, BCP may trigger the same conflict with a different set of decision assignments. As a result, conflict paths are not repeated. The same holds true for conflict sub-paths. Since neither conflict paths nor conflict subpaths are repeated, the search algorithm is complete (form Propositions 1 and 3). With respect to creating (and recording) a conflict clause (or a path clause) after every M identified conflicts, clearly the number of times a given conflict subpath (or conflict path) is repeated is upper-bounded. Hence, using the results of Proposition 4 completeness is guaranteed.

Observed that Proposition 5 holds *independently* of which backtrack step is take each time a conflict is identified. Hence, as long as we record a conflict for each identified conflict, *any* form of unrestricted backtracking yields a complete algorithm. Less general formulations of this result have been proposed in the recent past [9, 22, 25].

The results established so far guarantee completeness at the cost of recording (and keeping) a clause for each identified conflict. Next, we propose and analyze conditions for relaxing this requirement. As a result, we allow for some clauses to be deleted during the search process and require only some specific recorded clauses to be kept.[*] (We note that clause deletion does not apply to chronological backtracking strategies and that existing clause deletion policies for nonchronological backtracking strategies do not compromise the completeness of the algorithm [18].) We also propose other conditions that do not require specific recorded clauses to be kept.

PROPOSITION 6. *An unrestricted backtracking algorithm is complete if it records (and keeps) a conflict-clause for each identified conflict for which an IFB step is taken.*

Proof. At most 2^n IFB steps can be taken because a conflict clause is recorded for each identified conflict after an IFB step is taken. Hence, conflict subpaths due to IFB steps cannot be repeated. Moreover, additional backtrack steps that may be applied (CB and NCB) also ensure completeness. Hence, the resulting algorithm is complete.

PROPOSITION 7. *Given an integer constant M, an unrestricted backtracking algorithm is complete if it records (and keeps) a conflict-clause after every M identified conflicts for which an IFB step is taken.*

Proof. The result immediately follows from the Propositions 5 and 6.

Under the conditions above, the number of recorded clauses grows linearly with the number of conflicts after IFB steps. Thus the number of recorded clauses is worst-case exponentially in the number of variables.

Other approaches to guarantee completeness involve increasing the value of some constraint associated with the search algorithm. The following results illustrate these approaches.

PROPOSITION 8. *Suppose that an unrestricted backtracking strategy applies a sequence of backtrack steps. If for this sequence the number of conflicts between IFB steps is allowed to increase strictly after each IFB step, then the resulting algorithm is complete.*

Proof. If only CB or NCB steps are taken, then the resulting algorithm is complete. When the number of conflicts in between IFB steps reaches 2^n, the algorithm is guaranteed to terminate.

We note that this result can be viewed as a generalization of the completeness condition used in search restarts, which consists of increasing the backtrack

---

[*] We say that a recorded clause is *kept* provided it is prevented from being deleted during the subsequent search.

cutoff value after search restart [1].[*] Also observe that in this situation the growth in the number of clauses can be made polynomial, provided clause deletion is applied on clauses recorded form NCB and IFB steps.

The next result establishes conditions for guaranteeing completeness in algorithms that opportunistically delete recorded clauses (as a result of an IFB step). The idea is to increase the size of the recorded clauses that are kept after each IFB step. Another approach is to increase the life-span of large recorded clauses, by increasing the relevance-based learning threshold [2].

PROPOSITION 9. *Suppose that an unrestricted backtracking strategy applies a specific sequence of backtrack steps. If, for this sequence, either the size of the largest recorded clause kept or the size of the relevance-based learning threshold is strictly increased after each IFB step is taken, then the resulting algorithm is complete.*

Proof. When either the size of the largest recorded clause reaches value n or the relevance-based learning threshold reaches value n, all recorded clauses will be kept, and so completeness is guaranteed from Proposition 5.

Observe that for this last result the number of clauses can grow exponentially with the number of variables. Moreover, we note that the observation regarding the increase of the relevance-based learning threshold was first suggested in [19].

One final result addresses the number of times conflict paths and conflict subpaths can be repeated.

PROPOSITION 10. Under the conditions of Proposition 8 and Proposition 9, the number of times a conflict path or a conflict subpath is repeated is upper-bounded.

Proof. The resulting algorithms are complete and thus known to terminate after a maximum number of backtrack steps (which is constant for each instance). Hence, the number of times a conflict path (or conflict subpath) can be repeated is necessarily upper-bounded.

5.2. HEURISTIC BACKTRACKING UNDER THE UNRESTRICTED BACKTRACKING FRAMEWORK

Unrestricted backtracking provides a framework for combining different forms of backtracking. These forms of backtracking may be complete, incomplete, or a combination of both. The completeness conditions established for unrestricted backtracking hold regardless of the comprised forms of backtracking.

We have noted before that applying heuristic backtracking at every backtrack step may lead to very unstable algorithms. Conversely, keeping all the recorded clauses to avoid this instability may lead to a significant memory overhead.

---

[*] Given this condition, the resulting algorithm resembles iterative-deepening.

Hence, the solution adopted for this problem is to combine heuristic backtracking with other complete forms of backtracking.

In what follows we refer to heuristic backtracking as an instantiation of unrestricted backtracking where incomplete heuristic backtracking steps are combined with complete nonchronological backtracking steps. For each algorithm, we will specify the frequency of the heuristic backtracking steps and the heuristic used. As mentioned before, we have developed three backtracking heuristics: the plain, VSIDS-like, and BerkMin-like backtracking heuristics.

6. Experimental Results

This section presents experimental results of applying heuristic backtracking to different classes of problem instances. We compare heuristic backtracking with nonchronological backtracking and nonchronological backtracking combined with search restarts [12], one of the most effective backtracking relaxation schemes known to date. Search restarts are now part of the most competitive backtrack search SAT algorithms [19, 11], and our goal here has been to demonstrate that heuristic backtracking is a more competitive form of backtracking relaxation.

The algorithms have been experimentally evaluated by using the JQuest2 SAT solver [17]. JQuest2 is a competitive solver and has been ranked among the top solvers in the industrial category in the SAT 2003 competition.* JQuest2 has been implemented in Java for providing an integrated framework for rapid prototyping of SAT algorithms.

It offers a significantly faster development time for testing new ideas in SAT algorithms, but its overall performance is slower than a C or C++ implementation because of the overhead associated with the Java virtual machine. It has been demonstrated that JQuest2 is slower than Chaff by an average factor of 2 [17]. The CPU time limit for each instance was set to 10^4 s. All experiments were run on the same P4/1.7 Ghz/1 GByte of RAM Linux machine.

Different SAT algorithm prototypes have been implemented and compared. The algorithms differ only in the unrestricted backtracking strategy applied. Five backtracking strategies are compared:

1. Plain heuristic backtracking.
2. VSIDS-like heuristic backtracking.
3. BerkMin-like heuristic backtracking.
4. Search restarts.
5. Nonchronological backtracking.

All algorithms use the VSIDS decision branching heuristic. In choosing a decision or backtrack variable, a slight randomization is used to select among the

---
* http://www.satlive.org/SATCompetition/2003/.

variables with the best metrics provided by the different heuristics. Combining the values of the metrics with a certain degree of randomization is known to produce good results.

The algorithms have been applied to 14 classes of problem instances containing 320 problem instances in total. In NCB, a nonchronological backtrack step is performed every step. In the other algorithms is defined as follows: an incomplete form of backtracking step (HB or restarts) is performed after every $10^4 + i \times 10^3$ backtracks, where i is incremented every time an IFB step is performed. The increase of constant i and the fact that conflict derived clauses are marked undeletable guarantee the completeness of the algorithms.

Table I shows the results obtained for each class of instances. *#I* denotes the number of problem instances, *Dec* denotes the average number of decision nodes per instance, *Time* denotes the average CPU time per instance, and X denotes the number of aborted instances. In addition, each column indicates a different form of backtracking relaxation:

- HB(P) indicates the plain heuristic backtracking algorithm is applied after $10^4 + i \times 10^3$ backtracks, where i is incremented every time a HB step is taken.
- HB(V) indicates the VSIDS-like heuristic backtracking algorithm is applied after $10^4 + i \times 10^3$ backtracks, where i is incremented every time a HB step is taken.
- HB(B) indicates the BerkMin-like heuristic backtracking algorithm is applied after $10^4 + i \times 10^3$ backtracks, where i is incremented every time a HB step is taken.
- RST indicates that search restarts are applied after $10^4 + i \times 10^3$ backtrack, where i is incremented every time a search restart is taken.
- NCB indicates nonchronological backtracking is applied in every backtrack step.

From the results in Table I several observations and comments can be made.

HB algorithms abort fewer instances. An instance is aborted whenever the memory or CPU time constraint is reached. In these experiments all instance abortions have been caused by memory exhaustion, which shows that fewer clauses using HB as compared to search restarts. A possible explanation is that our heuristics are more likely to reuse information provided by earlier conflicts than is the search restarts algorithm, which is more prone to encounter new conflict clauses after each restart. Equivalently, one can say that HB favors a more local search rather than search restarts.

The nonchronological backtracking algorithm is not a competitive approach, in terms of both decisions and CPU time. This is true when compared with any of the other four algorithms. In addition, the search restarts algorithm seems to be the second worst approach, although more competitive than the nonchronological backtracking algorithm. The computed average speedup against the nonchronological backtracking algorithm for the set of instances used is $1.95\times$.

Table I. Performance of different algorithms.

Benchmarks	#	HB(P)			HB(V)			HB(B)			RST			NCB		
		Dec	Time	X	Dec	Time	X	Dec	Time	X	Dec	Time	X	Dec	Time	X
bmc-barrel	8	1307492	4070.22	0	1013787	1819.11	0	584680	735.61	0	1031297	2397.81	0	1339798	4789.36	0
bmc-queueinvar	10	84784	33.02	0	85666	42.04	0	69758	25.86	0	66713	20.93	0	117823	69.34	0
bmc-longmult	16	1112467	5868.87	3	937649	3088.83	3	946813	4276.77	3	1177463	7873.19	3	1490667	8156.69	5
sss-sat-1.0	100	3470750	3018.83	0	3005868	1785.38	0	1486274	877.58	0	3142078	2425.27	0	3527717	4029.94	0
sss-1.0	48	939535	658.87	0	681025	199.68	0	467650	93.97	0	736851	408.56	0	945588	1167.82	0
sss-1.0a	9	191838	230.4	0	176227	108.77	0	98217	37.5	0	198363	459.68	0	260389	858.87	0
fvp-unsat.1.0	4	191300	180.93	1	196671	217.28	1	102657	38.94	1	167714	109.31	1	222725	395.18	1
qg	22	402257	1762.75	0	381790	1344.69	0	236258	577.63	0	283459	950.08	0	494616	2829.94	0
Bejing	16	522884	5055.56	2	509764	4063.42	2	517462	4906.94	2	523849	5284.38	2	585194	5653.04	2
equiv-checking	25	2317494	2035.26	2	2355508	2282.49	2	913835	1101.26	2	2853280	3467.24	2	3307203	4163.99	2
par16	10	74641	41.12	0	72607	27.8	0	56619	18.1	0	111228	79.95	0	122614	106.59	0
des-encryption	32	533520	3801.09	2	512640	3194.06	2	480812	2885.39	2	578128	5005.26	2	784206	9055.62	2
satplan_sat	11	78777	79.45	0	47403	33.1	0	28682	27.05	0	58412	71.42	0	127017	102.39	0
satplan_unsat	9	39042	65.5	0	27371	41.2	0	10021	24.3	0	51502	89.54	0	56780	95.68	0

The plain heuristic backtracking algorithm performed slightly better on average than the search restarts algorithm. Although these results are not very conclusive, they seem to indicate that using some heuristic information when performing backtracking is better than not using any information at all, as is the case of search restarts. Moreover, in the next table it is shown that, when applied to some instances, the plain backtracking heuristic is significantly superior to search restarts and nonchronological backtracking.

The VSIDS-like heuristic backtracking algorithm performed better than the search restarts algorithm for most of the instances, in terms of both the number of decisions and CPU time, even though slower in performance on some test instances. Its computed average speedup against the search restarts algorithm for the set of instances used is $1.77\times$. (Note that this is a lower bound of the average speedup, since the instances aborted by the search restarts algorithm are a superset of the instances aborted by the VSIDS-like heuristic backtracking algorithm; the aborted instances have not been taken into account in computing the average speedup).

The BerkMin-like heuristic backtracking algorithm performed better than the VSIDS-like heuristic backtracking algorithm. This result is consistent with the fact that the BerkMin decision branching heuristic is generally superior to the VSIDS decision backtracking heuristic. Its computed average speedup against the search restarts algorithm for the set of instances used is $3.32\times$.

Given the large number of instances tested, these results clearly demonstrate the backtracking heuristic can speed up execution time for the classes of problems tested. It is also remarkable that their effect is similar to the effect of decision branching heuristic: if a heuristic A is better than a heuristic B for decision branching, then A is also better than B for backtracking.

The result presented in Table I are significantly better than the preliminary results previously presented in [4]. The reason is that we eliminated many easy-to-solve instances from each problem class. These instances do not benefit from heuristic backtracking or search restarts because they can be solved quickly before a significant number of IFB steps are applied, if any. Large instances do benefit from HB or restarts because these techniques help get out of dead-ends in the search tree. Hence, they should be applied infrequently. In our studies we concluded that, similar to search restarts, HB is best when applied once in every 10^4 backtracks. More frequent applications cause the algorithms to wander without focusing in regions of search space that need a more thorough exploration. When applied infrequently, HB allows finding a solution or proving unsatisfiability using a significantly lower number of decisions.

To show that the performance of the heuristics improve with the hardness of the problem instances, we manually selected a set of 18 harder-to-solve instances.

The results in Table II show that for the set of harder-to-solve instances the benefits of heuristic backtracking are more visible. The three HB algorithms performs better than the search restarts algorithm and nonchronological backtracking, which aborted two of the instances (marked with *).

Clearly, the search restarts algorithm performs better than the nonchronological backtracking algorithm, in terms of both the number of decisions and CPU time.

The plain heuristic backtracking algorithm performed better than both the search restarts algorithm and the nonchronological backtracking algorithm for most of the instances. This is true both in terms of the number of decisions and CPU time.

The VSIDS-like heuristic backtracking algorithm performed better than the search restarts algorithm, both in terms of the number of decisions and CPU time. Its average speed-up has been computed as greater than 2.62×.

The BerkMin-like heuristic backtracking algorithm was again the best of the three backtracking algorithms. Its average speed-up against the search restarts algorithm has been computed as greater than 9.63×.

As can be concluded from the experimental results, heuristic backtracking can yield significant savings in CPU time, allows significant reductions in the number of decision nodes and also allows for a smaller number of instances to be aborted. This is true for several of the classes of problem instances analyzed.

7. Related Work

Dependency-directed backtracking and no-good learning were originally proposed by Stallman and Sussman in [24] in the area of truth maintenance systems. In the area of constraints satisfaction problems (CSPs), the topic was independently studied by J. Gaschnig [8] and others (see, e.g., [21]) as different forms of backjumping.

The introduction of relaxations in the backtrack steps is also related to dynamic backtracking [9]. Dynamic backtracking establishes a method by which backtrack points can be moved deeper in the search tree. This avoids the unneeded erasing of the amount of search that has been done thus far. The objective is to find a way to directly "erase" the value assigned to a variable as opposed to backtracking to it, moving the backjump variable to the end of the partial solution in order to replace its value without modifying the values of the variables that currently follow it. More recently, Ginsberg and McAllester combined local search and dynamic in an algorithm that enables arbitrary search movement [10], starting with *any complete assignment* and evolving by flipping values of variables obtained from the conflicts.

Local search and dynamic backtracking have also been combined by Prestwich in the Constrained Local Solver (CLS) [20]. CLS is constructed by randomizing the backtracking component of a systematic algorithm: that is, allowing backtracking to occur on *arbitrarily chosen* variables. The new algorithm has the drawback of being incomplete.

Table II. Performance of different algorithms on individual instances

Benchmarks	Instance	HB(P)		HB(V)		HB(B)		RST		NCB	
		Dec	Time	Dec	Time	Dec	Time	Dec	Time	Dec	Time
bmc	barrel9	869896	3332.68	780650	2542.17	238566	391.1	707033	1903.58	790029	266051
bmc	longmult10	229373	1720.57	220432	1234.4	188654	573.41	*	*	*	*
bmc	longmult15	284658	2500.61	175422	672.68	219087	1487.77	*	*	*	*
sss-sat-1.0	2dlx_...bug056	56197	34.88	55240	31.86	24565	19.48	60345	48.23	63303	56.32
sss.1.0a	dlx2_...bug54	29744	36.71	24466	33.21	2304	11.60	36596	58.94	35018	53.01
sss.1.0	dlx2_cl	17144	9.65	12882	4.92	13206	6.95	33244	14.13	36781	15.98
fvp-unsat.1.0	2dlx_ca_...bp_f	36156	30.36	32294	19.24	31181	15.42	42027	40.47	47982	83.67
qg	qg2-08	137102	762.72	36265	47.48	41455	278.52	58271	554.23	67954	608.59
qg	qg5-13	97086	298.67	103891	771.32	77634	186.81	51839	116.46	80370	217.36
equiv-checking	c7552	198240	95.92	243101	145.48	151021	75.93	313592	293.61	318831	461.34
equiv-checking	c7552-s	295689	158.52	400875	347.84	175070	58.91	411626	594.24	444888	867.96
equiv-checking	c3540_bug	2211	1.34	2560	2.69	557	0.38	3378	4.95	8472	15.24
des-encryption	cnf-r3-b1-k1.1	9943	6.25	10937	9.3	4716	1.11	13068	18.75	13960	21.65
des-encryption	cnf-r3-b1-k2.2	2275	1.18	5566	2.82	1220	0.76	7792	3.36	8042	4.76
par16	par16-1-c	8866	3.65	8019	2.70	7273	1.3	11143	18.8	21773	25.74
par16	par16-4	1964	2.4	1117	1.65	887	0.4	3378	3.55	3386	4.48
satplan_sat	bw-large.d	34890	62.13	22438	27.84	18805	17.09	30855	53.37	49110	82.55
satplan_unsat	logistics.c	5458	3.9	5018	2.61	4211	1.02	5334	3.4	5754	6.49

In weak-commitment search [25], the algorithm constructs a consistent partial solution but commits to the partial solution *weakly*. In weak-commitment search, whenever a conflict is reached, the *whole* partial solution is abandoned, in explicit contrast to standard backtracking algorithm where the most recently added variable is removed form the partial solution.

Moreover, search restarts have been proposed and shown effective for hard instances of SAT [12]. The search is repeatedly restarted whenever a cutoff value is reached. In [1], search restarts were jointly used with learning for solving hard real-world instances of SAT. This latter algorithm is complete because the backtrack cutoff value increases after each restart. One additional example of backtracking relaxation is described in [22], which is based on attempting to construct a complete solution, that restarts each time a conflict is identified. More recently, highly optimized complete SAT solvers [11, 19] have successfully combined nonchronological backtracking and search restarts, again obtaining remarkable improvements in solving real-world instances of SAT.

Other algorithms are known for performing an overall local search while using systematic search to prune the search space. For example, Jussien and Lhomme introduced the path-repair algorithm for CSP [14], which adds domain filtering techniques and no-good learning to local search. Furthermore, Hirsch and Kojevnikov introduced the UnitWalk SAT solver [13], which combines the iterative application of the unit clause rule with local search.

8. Conclusions and Future Work

This paper proposes the utilization of heuristic backtracking in backtrack search SAT solvers. The proposed algorithm, based on heuristic knowledge, is presented in the context of a backtracking-based SAT algorithm, which is currently the most successful class of general-purpose SAT algorithms especially for real-world applications. The most well-known branching heuristic used in state-of-the-art SAT solvers were adapted to the backtrack step of SAT solvers. The experimental results illustrate the usefulness of heuristic backtracking and realize the potential of this technique on practical examples, especially those coming from real-world applications.

The main contributions of this paper can be summarized as follows:

1. A new heuristic backtracking search SAT algorithm is proposed that heuristically selects the point to backtrack to.
2. The proposed algorithm is shown to be a special case of unrestricted backtracking, and different approaches for ensuring completeness are described.
3. Experimental results indicate that significant savings in search effort can be obtained for different organizations of the proposed heuristic backtrack search algorithm.

In fact, hundreds of problems instances have been analyzed in this paper, where heuristic backtracking algorithms have been compared to a state-of-the-art SAT solver algorithm. The only difference between the new algorithms and the reference SAT solver is the backtracking step: the new algorithms apply heuristic backtracking steps instead of search restarts, the best form of incomplete backtracking known to date.

Three backtracking heuristics have been tested: a plain heuristic that uses information from the conflict-clause, a VSIDS-like heuristic, and a BerkMin-like heuristic. Our results show that the better the heuristic is for decision branching, the more useful it is for backtracking, which is a consistent result.

In a set of 320 instances, the best backtracking heuristic (BerkMin's) shows an average speedup of about $3.5\times$ as compared with the search restarts algorithm. For a set of 18 harder-to-solve instances, the heuristic backtracking algorithms have been able to solve all of them, while the search restarts algorithm and nonchronological backtracking aborted two instances.

The heuristic backtracking procedure developed in this work is now ready to be incorporated in SAT solvers, with guaranteed performance improvement.

For future work, a more comprehensive experimental evaluation is required for combining different forms of decision heuristics and backtracking relaxation algorithms, thus motivating the utilization of multiple search strategies in backtrack search SAT algorithms.

Acknowledgements

This work is partially supported by the European research project IST-2001-34607 and by Fundação para a Ciência e Tecnologia under research projects POSI/CHS/34504/2000, POSI/SRI/41926/2001 and POSI/EIA/61852/2004.

References

1. Baptista, L. and Marques-Silva, J. P.: Using randomization and learning to solve real-world instances of satisfiablility, in R. Dechter (ed.), *Proceedings of the International Conference of Principles and Practice of Constraint Programming*, Vol. 1894 of Lecture Notes in Computer Science, 2000, pp. 489–494.

2. Bayardo Jr., R. and Scharg, R.: Using CSP look-back techniques to solve real-world SAT instances, in *Proceedings of the National Conference on Artificial Intelligence*, 1997, pp. 203–208.

3. Bhalla, A., Lynce, I., de Sousa, J. and Marques-Silva, J.: Heuristic backtracking algorithms for SAT, in *Proceedings of the International Workshop of Microprocessor Test and Verification*, 2003, pp. 69–74.

4. Bhalla, A., Lynce, J., de Sousa, J. and Marques-Silva, J. P.: Heuristic-based backtracking for propositional satisfiability, in F. Moura-Pires and S. Abreu (eds.), *Proceedings of the Portuguese Conference on Artificial Intelligence*, Vol., 1894 of Lecture Notes in Artificial Intelligence, 2003, pp. 116–130.

5. Davis, M., Logemann, G. and Loveland, D.: A machine program for theorem proving, *Commun. Assoc. Comput. Mach.* **5** (1962), 394–397.
6. Davis, M. and Putnam, H.: A computing procedure for quantification theory, *J. Assoc. Comput. Mach.* **7** (1960), 201–215.
7. Freuder, E. C., Dechter, R., Ginsberg, M. L., Selman, B. and Tsang, E.: Systematic versus stochastic constraint satisfaction, in *Proceedings of the International Joint Conference on Artificial Intelligence*, 1995, pp. 2027–2032.
8. Gaschnig, J.: Performance Measurement and Analysis of Certain Search Algorithms, PhD thesis, Carnegie-Mellon University, Pittsburgh, PA.
9. Ginsberg, M. L.: Dynamic backtracking, *J. Artif. Intell. Res.* **1** (1993), 25–46.
10. Ginsberg, M. L. and McAllester, D.: GSAT and dynamic backtracking, in *Proceedings of the International Conference of Principles of Knowledge and Reasoning*, 1994, pp. 226–237.
11. Goldberg, E. and Nonikov, Y.: BerkMin: A Fast and Robust SAT-Solver, in *Proceedings of the Design and Test in Europe Conference*, 2002, pp. 142–149.
12. Games, C. P., Selman, B. and Kautz, H.: Boosting combination search through randomization, in *Proceedings of the National Conference on Artificial Intelligence*, 1998, pp. 431–437.
13. Hirsch, E. A. and Kojevnikov, A.: Solving Boolean satisfiability using local search guided by unit clause elimination, in *Proceedings of the International Conference on Principles and Practice of Constraint Programming*, 2001, pp. 605–609.
14. Jussien, N. and Lhomme, O.: Local search with constraint propagation and conflict-based heuristics, in *Proceedings of the National Conference on Artificial Intelligence*, 2000, pp. 169–174.
15. Lynce, I., Baptista, L. and Marques-Silva, J. P.: Stochastic systematic search algorithm for satisfiability, in *Proceedings of the LICS Workshop on Theory and Applications of Satisfiability Testing*, 2001, pp. 1–7.
16. Lynce, I. and Marques-Silva, J. P.: Complete unrestricted backtracking algorithms for satisfiability, in *Proceedings of the International Symposium on Theory and Applications of Satisfiability Testing*, 2002, pp. 214–221.
17. Lynce, I. and Marques-Silva, J. P.: On implementing more efficient SAT data structures, in *Proceedings of the International Symposium on Theory and Applications of Satisfiability Testing*, 2003, pp. 510–516.
18. Marques-Silva, J. P. and Sakallah, K. A., GRASP—A search algorithm for propositional satisfiability, *IEEE Trans. Comput.* **48**(5) (1999), 506–521.
19. Moskewicz, M., Madigan, C., Zhao, Y., Zhang, L. and Malik, S.: Engineering an efficient SAT solver, in *Design Automation Conference*, 2001, pp. 530–535.
20. Prestwich, S.: A hybrid search architecture applied to hard random 3-SAT and low-autocorrelation binary sequences, in R. Dechter (ed.), *Proceedings of the International Conference on Principles and Practice of Constraint Programming*, Vol. 1894 of Lecture Notes in Computer Science, 2000, pp. 337–352.
21. Prosser, P.: Hybrid algorithms for the constraint satisfaction problems, *Comput. Intell.* **9**(3) (1993), 268–299.
22. Richards, E. T. and Richards, B.: Non-systematic search and no-good learning, *J. Autom. Reason.* **24**(4) (2000), 483–533.
23. Selman, B. and Kautz, H.: Domain-independent extensions to GSAT: Solving large structured satisfiability problems, in *Proceedings of the International Joint Conference on Artificial Intelligence*, 1993, pp. 290–295.
24. Stallman, R. M. and Sussman, G. J.: Forward reasoning and dependency-directed backtracking in a system for computer-aided circuit analysis, *Artif. Intell.* **9** (1977), 135–196.
25. Yokoo, M.: Weak-commitment search for solving satisfaction problems, in *Proceedings of the National Conference on Artificial Intelligence*, 1994, pp. 313–318.

Journal of Automated Reasoning (2005) 35: 25–50
DOI: 10.1007/s10817-005-9009-7

© Springer 2005

Symbolic Techniques in Satisfiability Solving*

GUOQIANG PAN and MOSHE Y. VARDI
Department of Computer Science, Rice University, Houston, TX, USA.
e-mail: {gqpan, vardi}@cs.rice.edu

Abstract. Recent work has shown how to use binary decision diagrams for satisfiability solving. The idea of this approach, which we call *symbolic quantifier elimination*, is to view an instance of propositional satisfiability as an existentially quantified proposition formula. Satisfiability solving then amounts to quantifier elimination; once all quantifiers have been eliminated, we are left with either **1** or **0**. Our goal in this work is to study the effectiveness of symbolic quantifier elimination as an approach to satisfiability solving. To that end, we conduct a direct comparison with the DPLL-based ZChaff, as well as evaluate a variety of optimization techniques for the symbolic approach. In comparing the symbolic approach to ZChaff, we evaluate scalability across a variety of classes of formulas. We find that no approach dominates across all classes. While ZChaff dominates for many classes of formulas, the symbolic approach is superior for other classes of formulas. Once we have demonstrated the viability of the symbolic approach, we focus on optimization techniques for this approach. We study techniques from constraint satisfaction for finding a good plan for performing the symbolic operations of conjunction and of existential quantification. We also study various variable-ordering heuristics, finding that while no heuristic seems to dominate across all classes of formulas, the maximum-cardinality search heuristic seems to offer the best overall performance.

Key words: satisfiability, binary decision diagram, symbolic decision procedure.

1. Introduction

Propositional-satisfiability solving has been an active area of research throughout the past 40 years, starting from the resolution-based algorithm in [24] and the search-based algorithm in [23]. The latter approach, referred to as the DPLL approach, has since been the method of choice for satisfiability solving. In the past ten years, much progress has been made in developing highly optimized DPLL solvers, leading to efficient solvers such as ZChaff [45] and BerkMin [33], all of which use advanced heuristics in choosing variable splitting order, in performing efficient Boolean constraint propagation, and in conflict-driven learning to prune unnecessary search branches. These solvers are so effective that they are used as generic problem solvers, where problems such as bounded

---

* A preliminary version of the paper was presented in SAT'04. Supported in part by NSF grants CCR-9988322, CCR-0124077, CCR-0311326, IIS-9908435, IIS-9978135, EIA-0086264, ANI-0216467, and by BSF grant 9800096.

model checking [8], planning [39], and scheduling [20] are typically solved by reducing them to satisfiability problems.

Another successful approach to propositional reasoning is that of decision diagrams, which are used to represent propositional functions. An instance of the approach is that of ordered binary decision diagrams (BDDs) [12], which are used successfully in model checking [14] and planning [17]. A BDD representation also enables easy satisfiability checking, which amounts to deciding whether it is different from the empty BDD [12]. Since decision diagrams usually represent the set of all satisfying truth assignments, they incur a significant overhead over search techniques that focus on finding a single satisfying assignment [19]. Thus, published comparisons between search and BDD techniques [40, 55] used search to enumerate all satisfying assignments. The conclusion of that comparison is that no approach dominates; for certain classes of formulas search is superior, and for other classes of formulas BDDs are superior.

Recent work has shown how to use BDDs for satisfiability solving rather than enumeration [50]. The idea of this approach, which we call *symbolic quantifier elimination*, is to view an instance of propositional satisfiability as an existentially quantified propositional formula. Satisfiability solving then amounts to quantifier elimination; once all quantifiers have been eliminated, we are left with either 1 or 0. This enables us to apply ideas about existential quantifier elimination from model checking [49] and constraint satisfaction [26]. The focus in [50] is on expected behavior on random instances of 3-SAT rather than on efficiency. In particular, only a minimal effort is made to optimize the approach, and no comparison to search methods is reported. Nevertheless, the results in [50] show that BDD-based algorithms behave quite differently from search-based algorithms, which makes them worthy of further investigation. (Other recent approaches reported using decision diagrams in satisfiability solving [15, 22, 29, 46]. We discuss these works later).

Our goal in this paper is to study the effectiveness of symbolic quantifier elimination as an approach to satisfiability solving. To that end, we conduct a direct comparison with the DPLL-based ZChaff, as well as evaluate a variety of optimization techniques for the symbolic approach. In comparing the symbolic approach to ZChaff we use a variety of classes of formulas. Unlike, however, the standard practice of comparing solver preformance on benchmark suites [42], we focus here on *scalability*. That is, we focus on scalable classes of formulas and evaluate how performance scales with formula size. As in [55] we find that no approach dominates across all classes. While ZChaff dominates for many classes of formulas, the symbolic approach is superior for other classes of formulas.

Once we have demonstrated the viability of the symbolic approach, we focus on optimization techniques. The key idea underlying [50] is that evaluating an existentially quantified propositional formula in conjunctive-normal form requires performing several instances of conjunction and of existential quantification. The goal is to find a good plan for these operations. We study two approaches to this problem. The first is Bouquet's method (BM) of [50], and the second is the *bucket-elimination* (BE) approach of [26]. BE aims at reducing the size of the support set of the generated BDDs through quantifier elimination. It has the theoretical advantage of being, in principle, able to attain optimal support set size, which is the *treewidth* of the input formula [28]. Nevertheless, we find that for certain classes of formulas, BM is superior to BE.

The key to good performance in both BM and BE is in choosing a good variable order for quantification and BDD order. Finding an optimal order is by itself a difficult problem (computing the treewidth of a given grah is NP-hard [4]), so one has to resort to various heuristics; cf. [41]. No heuristic seems to dominate across all classes of formulas, but the maximal-cardinality search (MCS) heuristic seems to offer the best overall performance.

We contrast our symbolic solvers with two other solvers, using the MCS variable order. We reimplemented ZRes, the ZDD-based multiresolution aproach of [15], and ZChaff, the DPLL-based solver of [45] to use the MCS variable order. The goal is to have a comparison of the different techniques, using the same variable order. See further discussion below.

We start the paper with a description of symbolic quantifier elimination as well as the BM approach in Section 2. We then describe the experimental setup in Section 3. In Section 4 we compare ZChaff with BM and show that no approach dominates across all classes of formulas. In Section 5 we compare BM with BE and study the impact of various variable-ordering heuristics. In Section 6 we compare our BDD-based algorithm with a ZDD-based algorithm based on ZRes [15] and compare the dynamic variable decision order used in ZChaff with a structural-guided static variable order. We conclude with a discussion in Section 7.

2. Background

A binary decision diagram is a rooted directed acyclic graph that has only two terminal nodes, labeled **0** and **1**. Every nonterminal node is labeled with a Boolean variable and has two outgoing edges labeled 0 and 1. An ordered binary decision diagram (BDD) is a BDD with the constraint that the input variables are ordered and every path in BDD visits the variables in ascending order. We assume that all BDDs are reduced, which means that every node represents a distinct logic function. BDDs constitute an efficient way to represent and manipulate Boolean functions [12], in particular, for a given variable order, BDDs offer a canonical representation. Checking whether a BDD is satisfiable is also easy; it requires checking that it differs from the predefined constant 0 (the empty BDD). We used the CUDD package for managing BDDs [53]. The *support set* of a BDD is the set of variables labeling its internal nodes.

In [19, 55], BDDs are used to construct a compact representation of the set of all satisfying truth assignments of CNF formulas. The input formula φ is a conjunction $c_1 \wedge \ldots \wedge c_m$ of clauses. The algorithm constructs BDD A_i for each clause c_i. (Since a clause excludes only one assignment to its variables, A_i is of linear size.) A BDD for the set of satisfying truth assignments is then constructed incrementally; B_1 is A_1, while B_{i+1} is the result of APPLY $(B_i, A_i, \wedge)$, where APPLY $(A, B, \circ)$ is the result of applying a Boolean operator $\circ$ to two BDDs A and B. The resulting BDD B_m represents all satisfying assignments of the input formula.

We can apply existential quantification to a BDD B:

$$(\exists x)B = \text{APPLY}(B|_{x \leftarrow 1}, B|_{x \leftarrow 0}, \vee),$$

where $B|_{x \leftarrow c}$ restricts B to truth assignments that assign the value c to the variable x. Note that quantifying x existentially eliminates it from the support set of B. The satisfiability problem is to determine whether a given formula $c_1 \wedge \dots \wedge c_m$, is satisfiable. In other words, the problem is to determine whether the existential formula $(\exists x_1) \dots (\exists x_n) (c_1 \wedge \dots \wedge c_m)$ is true. Since checking whether the final BDD B_m is equal to 0 can be done by CUDD in constant time, it makes little sense to apply existential quantification to B_m. Suppose, however, that a variable x_j does not occur in the clauses $c_{i+1}, \dots, c_m$. Then the existential fomula can be rewritten as

$$(\exists x_1) \dots (\exists x_{j-1})(\exists x_{j+1}) \dots (\exists x_n)\left((\exists x_j)(c_1 \wedge \dots \wedge c_1) \wedge (c_{i+1} \wedge \dots \wedge c_m)\right).$$

Pursuing this rewriting strategy as aggressively as possible, we process the clauses in the order $c_1, \dots, c_n$, quantifying variables existentially as soon as possible (that is, a variable is quantified as soon as it does not occur anymore in the unprocessed clauses). We refer to this as *early quantification* of variables. Note that different clause orders may induce different orders of variable quantification. Finding a good clause order is a major focus of this paper.

This motivates the following change in the earlier BDD-based satisfiability-solving algorithm [50]: after constructing the BDD B_i, quantify existentially variables that do not occur in the clauses $c_{i+1}, \dots, c_m$. In this case we say that the quantifier $\exists x$ has been *eliminated*. The computational advantage of quantifier elimination stems from the fact that reducing the size of the support set of a BDD typically (though not necessarily) results in a reduction of its size; that is, the size of $(\exists x)B$ is typically smaller than that of B. In a nutshell, this method, which we describe as *symbolic quantifier elimination*, eliminates all quantifiers until we are left with the constant BDD 1 or 0. Symbolic quantifier elimination was first applied to SAT solving in [34] (under the name of *hiding functions*) and tried on random 3-SAT instances. The work in [50] studies this method further, and considered various optimizations. The main interest here, however, is in the behavior of the method on random 3-SAT instances, rather in its comparison to DPLL-based methods.★

★ Note that symbolic quantifier elimination provides *pure* satisfiability solving; the algorithm returns 0 or 1. To find a satisfying truth assignment when the formula is satisfiable, one can use the technique of self-reducibility; cf. [5].

So far we have processed the clauses of the input formula in a linear fashion. Since the main point of quantifier elimination is to eliminate variables as early as possible, reordering the clauses may enable us to do more aggressive quantification. That is, instead of processing the clauses in the order $c_1, \ldots, c_m$, we can apply a permutation π and process the clauses in the order $c_{\pi(1)}, \ldots, c_{\pi(m)}$. the permutation π should be chosen so as to minimize the number of variables in the support sets of the intermediate BDDs. This observation was first made in the context of symbolic model checking; cf [9, 13, 32, 36]. Unfortunately, finding an optimal permutation π is by itself a difficult optimization problem, motivating heuristic approaches.

A particular heuristic proposed in the context of symbolic model checking in [49] was that of *clustering*. In this approach, the clauses are not processed one at a time; instead, several clauses are first partitioned into several clusters. For each cluster C we first apply conjunction to all the BDDs of the clauses in the C to obtain a BDD B_C. The clusters are then combined, together with quantifier elimination, as described earlier. Heuristics are required both for clustering the clauses and for ordering the clusters. Bouquet proposed the following heuristics in [11] (the focus there is on enumerating prime implicants). Consider some order of the variables. Let the *rank* (form 1 to n) of a variable x be $rank(x)$, let the rank $rank(\ell)$ of a literal ℓ be the rank of its underlying variable, and let the rank $rank(c)$ of a clause c be the maximum rank of its literals. The clusters are the equivalence classes of the relation $\sim$ defined by: $c \sim c'$ iff $rank(c) = rank(c')$. The rank of a cluster is the rank of its clauses. The clusters are then ordered according to increasing rank. For example, given the set of clauses $\{x_1 \lor \neg x_2, x_1 \lor x_3, \neg x_2 \lor x_3, x_3 \lor x_4\}$, the clusters are $C_1 = \{\}$, $C_2 = \{x_1 \lor \neg x_2\}$, $C_3 = \{x_1 \lor x_3, \neg x_2 \lor x_3\}$, and $C_4 = \{x_3 \lor x_4\}$.

Satisfiability solving using symbolic quantifier elimination is a combination of clustering and early quantification. We keep a set of *active* variables as we conjoin clusters in order $C_1, \ldots, C_n$. Starting from an empty set, after each cluster C_i is processed, we add all the variables that occur in C_i to the active set. Then, a variable that does not occur in all C_js, where $j > i$, can be removed from the active set and eliminated by means of early quantification. Hence, we are computing $\exists X_n \ldots (\exists X_2(((\exists X_1)C_1) \land C_2) \ldots \land C_n)$, where the quantified variable set X_i consists of the active variables that can be quantified early after C_i is processed. (CUDD allows quantifying several variables in function call.) When we use Bouquet's clustering, the method is referred to in [50] as *Bouquet's method*, which we abbreviate here as BM. For the example above, the BM quantification schedule is $\exists x_3 x_4((\exists x_1 x_2((C_1 \land C_2) \land C_3)) \land C_4)$.

We still have to choose a variable order. An order that is often used in constraint satisfaction [25] is the "maximum cardinality search" (MCS) order of [54], which is based on the graph-theoretic structure of the formula. The graph associated with a CNF formula $\varphi = \land_i c_i$ is $G_\varphi = (V, E)$, where V is the set of variables in φ and an edge $\{x_i, x_j\}$ is in E if there exists a clause c_k such that x_i

and x_j occur in c_k. We refer to G_φ as the *Gaifman graph* of φ. MCS ranks the vertices from 1 to n in the following way: as the next vertex to rank, select the vertex adjacent to the largest number of previously ranked vertices (ties can be broken in various ways). The variable order used for the BDDs in the comparisons unless otherwise mentioned is the inverse of the MCS order[★] (see Section 5.2 for exceptions).

3. Experimental Setup

We compare symbolic quantifier elimination to ZChaff across a variety of classes of formulas. Unlike the standard practice of comparing solver performance on benchmark suites [42], our focus here is not on simple time comparison, but rather on *scalability*. That is, we focus on scalable classes of formulas and evaluate how performance *scales* with formula size. We are interested in seeing which method scales better, that is, polynomial vs. exponential scalability, or different degrees of exponential scalability. Our test includes both random and non-random formulas (for random formulas we took 60 samples per case and reported median time). Experiments were performed by using x86 emulation on the Rice Terascale Cluster,[★★] which is a large Linux cluster of Itanium II processors with 4 GB of memory each.

Our test suite includes the following classes of formulas:

- Random 3-CNF: We choose uniformly k 3-clauses over n variables. The *density* of an instance is defined as k/n. We generate instances at densities 1.5, 6, 10, and 15, with up to 200 variables, to allow comparison for both under-constrained and over-constrained cases. (it is known that the satisfiability threshold of such formulas is around 4.25 [52]).
- Random affine 3-CNF: Affine-3-CNF formulas belongs to a polynomial class as classified by Schaefer [51]. Here, they are generated in the same way as random 3-CNF formulas except that the constraints are not 3-clauses but are parity equations in the form of $l_1 \oplus l_2 \oplus l_3 = 1$.[‡] Each constraint is then converted into four clauses, $l_1 \vee l_2 \vee l_3$, $\neg l_1 \vee \neg l_2 \vee l_3$, $\neg l_1 \vee l_2 \vee \neg l_3$, and $l_1 \vee \neg l_2 \vee \neg l_3$, yielding CNF formulas. The satisfiability threshold of such formula is found empirically to be around density (number of equations divided by number of variables) 0.95. We generate instances of density 0.5 and 1.5, with up to 400 variables.
- Random biconditionals: Biconditional formulas, also known as Urquhart formulas, form a class of affine formulas that have provably exponential

---

[★] Using the MCS order or its inverse as the BDD variable order exhibits little performance difference, so the inverse is preferred because the BE approach presented in Section 5.1 is easier to implement on the inverse order.

[★★] http://www.citi.rice.edu/rtc/

[‡] This is equivalent to just choosing three variables and generating $x_1 \oplus x_2 \oplus x_3 = p$ where $p = 0$ or $p = 1$ with equal probability.

resolution proofs. A biconditional formula has the form $l_1 \leftrightarrow (l_2 \leftrightarrow (\ldots(l_{k-1} \leftrightarrow l_k)\ldots))$, where each l_i is a positive literal. Such a formula is valid if either all variables occur an even number of times or all variables occur an odd number of times [56]. We generate valid formulas with up to 100 variables, where each variable occurs three times on average.

- Random chains: The classes described so far all have an essentially uniform random Gaifman graph, with no underlying structure. To extend our comparison to structured formulas, we generate random chains [27]. In a random chain, we form a long chain of random 3-CNF formulas, called *subtheories*. (The chain structure is reminiscent of the structure typically seen in satisfiability instances obtained from bounded model checking [8] and planning [39]). We use similar generation parameters as in [27], where there are 5 variables per subtheory and 5–23 clauses per subtheory, but we generate instances with a much bigger number of subtheories, scaling up to >20,000 variables and >4,000 subtheories.

- Nonrandom formulas: As in [55], we considered a variety of formulas with very specific scalable structure:

  - The n-Rooks problem (satisfiable).
  - The n-Queens problem (satisfiable for $n > 3$).
  - The pigeon-hole problem with $n + 1$ pigeons and n holes (unsatisfiable).
  - The mutilated-checkerboard problem, where an $n \times n$ board with two diagonal corner tiles removed is to be tiled with 1×2 tiles (unsatisfiable).

4. Symbolic vs. Search Approaches

Our goal in this section is to address the viability of symbolic quantifier elimination. To that end we compare the performance of BM against ZChaff,[*] a

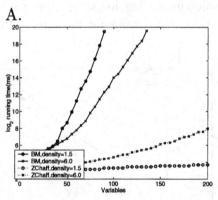
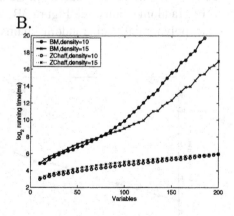

Figure 1. Random 3-CNF.

---

[*] ZChaff version 2004.5.13.

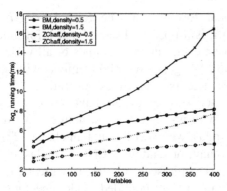

Figure 2. Random 3-Affine.

leading DPLL-based solver across the classes of formulas described above, with a focus on scalability. For now, we use the MCS variable order.

In Figure 1A and B, we can see that BM is not very competitive for random 3-CNF formulas. At density 1.5, ZChaff scales polynomially, while BM scales exponentially. At density 6.0 and at higher densities, both methods scale exponentially, but ZChaff scales exponentially better. (Note that above density 6.0 both methods scale better as the density increases. This is consistent with the experimental results in [19] and [50].) A similar pattern emerges for random affine formulas; see Figure 2. Again, ZChaff scales exponentially better than BM. (Note that both methods scale exponentially at the higher density, while it is known that affine satisfiability can be determined in polytime by using Gaussian elimination [51]).

The picture changes for biconditional formulas, as shown in Figure 3A. Again, both methods are exponential, but BM scales exponentially better than ZChaff. (This result is consistent with the finding in [15], which compares search-based methods methods to ZDD-based multiresolution).

For random chains, see Figure 3B, which uses a log–log scale. Both methods scale polynomially on random chains. (Because density for the most difficult

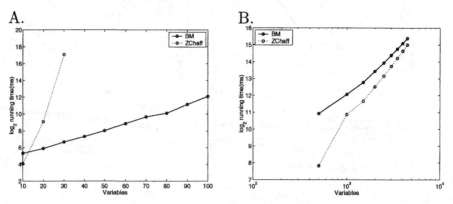

Figure 3. A) Random Biconditionals, B) Random Chains.

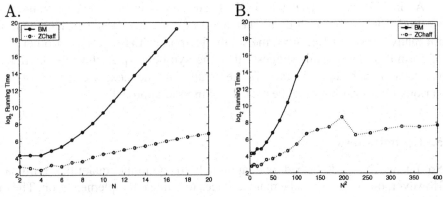

Figure 4. A) n-Rooks B) n-Queens.

problems changes as the size of the chains scales, we selected here the hardest density for each problem size.) Here BM scales polynomially better than ZChaff. Note that for smaller instances ZChaff outperforms BM, thereby justifying our focus on scalability rather than on straightforward benchmarking.

In addition, we compare BM with ZChaff on the nonrandom formulas of [55]. The *n*-Rooks problem is a simpler version of *n*-Queens problem, where the diagonal constraints are not used. For *n*-Rooks, the results are as in Figure 4A. This problem has the property of being globally *consistent*; that is, any consistent partial solution can be extended to a solution [25]. Thus, the problem is trivial for search-based solvers because no backtracking is needed. In contrast BM scales exponentially on this problem. For *n*-Queens (see Figure 4B), BM scales exponentially in n^2, while ZChaff seems to have better scalability. Again, a different picture emerges when we consider the pigeon-hole problem and the mutilated-checkerboard problem; see Figure 5A and B. On both problems both BM and ZChaff sclae exponentially, but BM scales exponentially better than ZChaff.

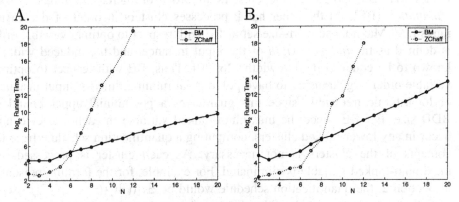

Figure 5. A) Pigeon-Hole, B) Mutilated Checkerboard.

As in [55], where BDDs and DPLL are compared for solution enumeration, we find that no approach dominates across all classes. While ZChaff dominates for many classes of formulas, the symbolic approach is superior for other classes of formulas. This result suggests that the symbolic quantifier elimination is a viable approach and deserves further study. In the next section we focus on various optimization strategies for the symbolic approach.

5. Optimizations

So far we have described one approach to symbolic quantifier elimination. However, one needs to make many choices to guide an implementation. The order of variables is used to guide clustering and quantifier elimination, as well as to order the variables in the underlying BDDs. Both clustering and cluster processing can be performed in several ways. In this section, we investigate the impact of choices in clustering, variable order, and quantifier elimination in the implementation of symbolic algorithms. Our focus here is on measuring the impact of variable order on BDD-based SAT solving; thus, the running time for variable ordering, which is polynomial for all algorithms, is not counted in our figures.

5.1. CLUSTER ORDERING

As argued earlier, the purpose of quantifier elimination is to reduce support-set size of intermediate BDDs. What is the best reduction one can hope for? This question has been studied in the context of constraint satisfaction. It turns out that the optimal schedule of conjunctions and quantifier eliminations reduces the support-set size to one plus the *treewidth* of the Gaifman graph of the input formula [21]. The treewidth of a graph is a measure of how close this graph is to being a tree [28]. Computing the treewidth of a graph is known to be NP-hard, which is why heuristic approaches are employed [41]. It turns out that by processing clusters in a different order we can attain the optimal support-set size. Recall that BM processes the clusters in order of increasing ranks. *Bucket elimination* (BE), on the other hand, processes clusters in order of decreasing ranks [26]. Maximal support-size set of BE with respect to optimal variable order is defined as the *induced width* of the input instance, and the induced width is known to be equal to the treewidth [26, 30]. Thus, BE with respect to optimal variable order is guaranteed to have polynomial running time for input instances of logarithmic treewidth, since this guarantees a polynomial upper bound on BDD size. For BE, since the maximum-ranked variable in each cluster cannot occur in any lower-ranked clusters, computing a quantification schedule from the contents of the clusters is not necessary. As each cluster is processed, the maximum-ranked variable is eliminated. For example, for the formula presented in Section 2, the quantification schedule would be $\exists x_1((\exists x_2((\exists x_3((\exists x_4 C_4) \wedge C_3)) \wedge C_2)) \wedge C_1)$, with one variable eliminated per cluster processed. As shown,

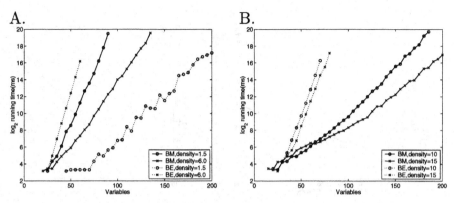

Figure 6. Clustering Algorithms – Random 3-CNF.

using the inverse of variable rank as the BDD variable order allows us to always eliminate the top variable in the BDD.

We now compare BM and BE with respect to MCS variable order (MCS is the preferred variable order also for BE).

The results for the comparison on random 3-CNF formulas are plotted in Figure 6A and B. We see that the difference between BM and BE is density dependent, where BE excels in the low-density cases, which have low treewidth, and BM excels in the high-density cases, which have high treewidth. A similar density-dependent behavior is shown for the affine case in Figure 7. The difference of the two schemes on biconditional formulas is quite small, as shown in Figure 8A. For chains, see Figure 8B. Because the number of variables for these formulas is large, the cost of computing the quantification schedule gives BE an edge over BM.

On most constructed formulas, the picture is similar to the high-density random cases, where BM dominates, except for mutilated-checkerboard formulas, where BE has a slight edge. (Note that treewidth for mutilated checkerboard problems grows only at $O(n)$, compared to $O(n^2)$ for other constructed problems.) We plot the performance comparison for n-rook formulas

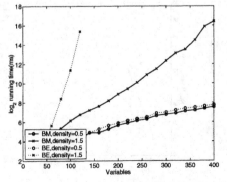

Figure 7. Clustering Algorithms – Random Affine.

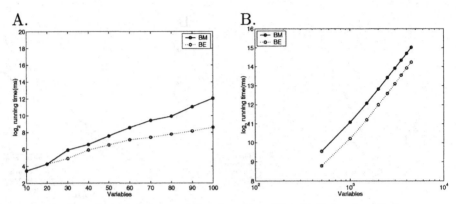

Figure 8. Clustering Algorithms – A) Random Biconditionals, B) Random Chains.

in Figure 9A, n-queens formulas in Figure 9B, pigeon-hole formulas in Figure 10A, and mutilated-checkerboard problems in Figure 10B.

To understand the difference in performance between BM and BE, we study their effect on intermediate BDD size. BDD size for a random 3-CNF instance depends crucially on both the number of variables and the density of the instance. Thus, we compare the effect of BM and BE in terms of these measures for the intermediate BDDs. We apply BM and BE to random 3-CNF formulas with 50 variables and densities 1.5 and 6.0. We then plot the density vs. the number of variables for the intermediate BDDs generated by the two cluster-processing schemes. The results are plotted in Figure 11A and B. Each plotted point corresponds to an intermediate BDD, which reflects the clusters processed so far.

As can be noted from the figures, BM increases the density of intermediate results much faster than does BE. This difference is quite dramatic for high-density formulas. The relation between density of random 3-CNF instance and BDD size has been studied in [19], where it is shown that BDD size peaks at around density 2.0 and is lowest when the density is close to 0 or the satisfiability threshold. This enables us to offer an possible explanation to the superiority of

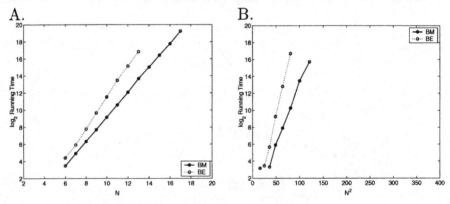

Figure 9. Clustering Algorithms – A) n-Rooks, B) n-Queens.

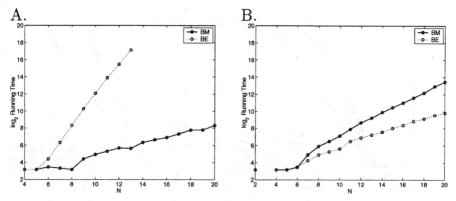

Figure 10. Clustering Algorithms – A) Pigeon-Hole, B) Mutilated Checkerboard.

BE for low-density instances and the superiority of BM for high-density instances. For formulas of density 1.5, the density of intermediate results is smaller than 2.0, and BM's increased density results in larger BDDs. For formulas of density 6.0, BM crosses the threshold density 2.0 using a smaller number of variables, and then BM's increased density results in smaller BDDs.

The general superiority of BM over BE suggests that minimizing support-set size ought not to be the dominant concern. BDD size is correlated with, but not dependent on, support-set size. More work is required in order to understand the good performance of BM. Our explanation argues that, as in [3], BM first deals with the most constrained subproblems, therefore reducing BDD-size of intermediate results. While the performance of BE can be understood in terms of treewidth, however, we still lack a fundamental theory to explain the performance of BM.

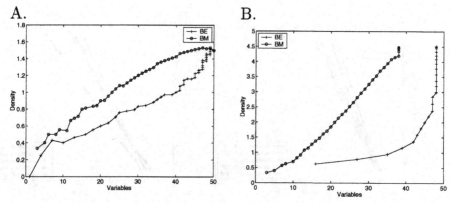

Figure 11. Clustering Algorithms A) Density = 1.5, B) Density = 6.0.

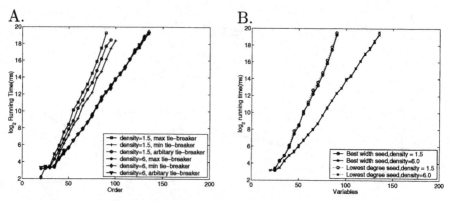

Figure 12. A) Variable Ordering Tie-Breakers B) Initial Variable Choice.

5.2. VARIABLE ORDERING

In this section, we study the effects of the variable order on the performance of symbolic algorithms. We present results only for BM because the picture is similar for BE. The variable order for the BDD representation is again the inverse of the variable order for clustering. As mentioned earlier, when selecting variables, MCS has to break ties, a situation that happens quite often. One can break ties by choosing (form those variables that have the maximum cardinality to ranked variables as MCS requires) the variable with minimal degree to unselected variables [50] or the variable with the maximal degree to unselected variables [6]. (Another choice is to break ties uniformly at random, but this choice is expensive to implement because it is difficult to choose an element uniformly at random from a heap). We compare these two heuristics with an arbitrary tie-breaking heuristic, in which we simply select the top variable in the heap. The results are shown in Figure 12A for random 3-CNF formulas. For high-density formulas, tie breaking makes no significant difference, but least-degree tie breaking is markedly better for the low-density formulas. This

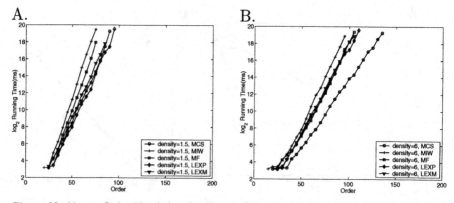

Figure 13. Vertex Order Heuristics: Random 3-CNF – A) Density = 1.5, B) Density = 6.

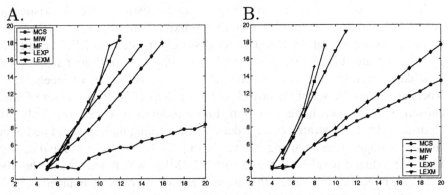

Figure 14. Vertex Order Heuristics – A) Pigeon-Hole, B) Mutilated Checkerboard.

situation seems to be applicable across a variety of class of formulas and even for different orders and algorithms.

MCS typically has many choices for the lowest-rank variable. In Koster et al. [41], it is recommended to start from every vertex in the graph and choose the variable order that leads to the lowest treewidth. This approach is easily done for instances of small size, that is, random 3-CNF or affine problems; but for structured problems, which could be much larger, the overhead is too expensive. Since min-degree tie-breaking worked quite well, we used the same idea for initial variable choice. In Figure 12B, we see that our assumption is well founded; that is, the benefit of choosing the best initial variable compared to choosing a min-degree variable is negligible. For larger problems like the chains or the bigger constructed problems, the additional overhead of trying every initial variable would be prohibitive, so we used the low-degree seed in all cases.

Algorithms for BDD variable ordering in the model-checking systems are often based on circuit structures, for example, some form of circuit traversal [31, 43] or graph evaluation [16]. These techniques are not applicable here because the formulas are provided in CNF and the original circuit structure is lost.

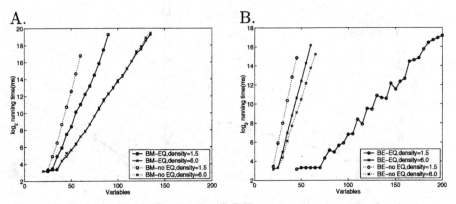

Figure 15. Quantifier Elimination-Random 3-CNF.

MCS is just one possible vertex-ordering heuristics. Other heuristics have been studied in the context of treewidth approximation. In [41] two other vertex-ordering heuristics that are based on local search are studied: LEXP and LEXM. Both LEXP and LEXM are based on *lexicographic breadth-first search*, where candidate variables are lexicographically ordered with a set of labels, and the labels are either the set of already chosen neighbors (LEXP) or the set of already chosen vertices reachable through lower-ordered vertices (LEXM). Both algorithms try to generate vertex orders where a triangulation would add a small amount of edges, thus reducing treewidth. In [25], Dechter also studied heuristics like min-induced-width (MIW) or min-fill (MF), which are greedy heuristics based on choosing the vertex that have the least number of induced neighbors (MIW) or the vertex that would add the least number of induced edges (MF).

In Figure 13A and B, we compare variable orders constructed from MCS, LEXP, LEXM, MIW, and MF for random 3-CNF formulas. For high-density cases, MCS is clearly superior. For low-density formulas, LEXP has a small edge, although the difference is minimal. Across the other problem classes (for example, pigeon-hole formulas as in Figure 14A and mutilated checkerboard as in Figure 14B), MCS uniformly appears to be the best order, being the most consistent and generally the top performer. Interesting, while other heuristics like MF often yield better treewidth, MCS still yields better runtime performance. This indicates that minimizing treewidth need not be the dominant concern; the dominant concern is minimizing BDD size. (BDD size seems more closely related to *pathwidth* [10], rather than treewidth. We speculate that MCS is a better order for pathwidth minimization).

5.3. QUANTIFIER ELIMINATION

So far we have argued that quantifier elimination is the key to the performance of the symbolic approach. In general, reducing support-set size does result in

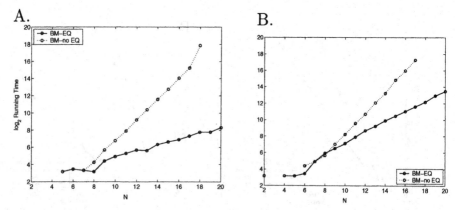

Figure 16. Quantifier Elimination – A) Pigeon-Hole, B) Mutilated Checkerboard.

smaller BDDs. It is known, however, that quantifier elimination may incur nonnegligible overhead and may not always reduce BDD size [12]. To understand the role of quantifier elimination in the symbolic approach, we reimplemented BM and BE without quantifier elimination. Thus, we do not construct a BDD that represent all satisfying truth assignments, but we do that according to the clustering and cluster processing order of BM and BE.

In Figures 15A and B, we plotted the running time of both BM and BE, with and without quantifier elimination on random 3-CNF formulas. We see that there is a trade-off between the cost and benefit of quantifier elimination. For low-density instances, where there are many solutions, the improvement from quantifier elimination is clear, but for high-density instances, quantifier elimination results in no improvement (while not reducing BDD size). For BE, where the overhead of quantifier elimination is lower, quantifier elimination improves performance very significantly at low density, although at high density there is a slight slowdown. On the other hand, quantifier elimination is important for the constructed formulas, for example, for the pigeon-hole formulas in Figure 16A and the mutilated checkerboard formulas in Figure 16B.

6. Comparison with Other Approaches

In the previous section, we conducted a comprehensive comparison of the impact of different parameters on the BDD-based symbolic approach. Next, we expand our focus to other approaches, first by comparing the BDD-based symbolic quantifier elimination with ZDD-based multiresolution, then by comparing the structural variable order we used with the default dynamic variable order in the context of ZChaff.

6.1. BDDS VS. ZDDS

So far we have used symbolically represented sets of truth assignments. An alternative approach is to use decision diagrams to represent sets of clauses instead of sets of assignments. ZRes [15] is a symbolic implementation of the directional resolution alogrithm in [24, 27]. The approach is also referred to as *multiresolution* because the algorithm carries out all resolutions over a variable in one symbolic step. Since individual clauses are usually sparse with respect to the set of variables, ZRes [15] used ZDDs [44], which typically offer a higher compression ratio than BDDs for the sparse spaces. Each propositional literal ℓ is represented by a ZDD variable v_ℓ (thus a propositional variable can be represented by two ZDD variables), and clause sets are represented as follows:

- The empty clause ε is represented by the terminal node 1.
- The empty set $\emptyset$ is represented by the terminal node 0.

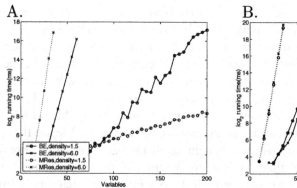

Figure 17. Random 3-CNF.

— Given a set C of clauses and a literal ℓ whose ZDD variable v_ℓ is lowest in a given variable order, we split C into two subsets: $C_\ell = \{c|c \in C, \ell \in c\}$ and $C' = C - C_\ell$. Given ZDDs representing C would be rooted at v_ℓ and have ZDDs for C'' and C' as its left and right children.

This representation is the dual of using ZDDs to represent irredundant sum of products (ISOPs) of Boolean functions [44].

We use two set operations on sets of clauses: (1) $\times$ is the crossproduct operator, where for two clause sets C and D, $C \times D = \{c \mid \exists c' \in C, \exists c'' \in D, c = c' \cup c''\}$, and (2) $+$ is subsumption-free union, so if both C and D are subsumption-free, and $c \in C + D$, then there is no $c' \in C + D$ where $c' \subset c$. Multiresolution is implemented by using $\times$ on cofactors: given a ZDD f, f_{x+} (resp. f_{x-}) is the ZDDs corresponding to the positive cofactor on ZDD variable v_x (resp. $v_{\neg x}$, so $f_{x+} = \{a|a \vee x \in f\}$ and $f_{x-} = \{a|a \vee \neg x \in f\}$. Now $f_{x+} \times f_{x-}$ (after removing tautologies) represents the set of all resolvents of f and x, which has to be combined by using $+$ with $f_{x'}$, which is the ZDD for the clauses not containing x. ZRes eliminates variables by using multiresolution one by one until either the

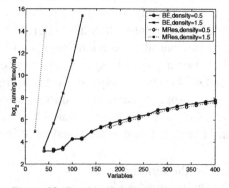

Figure 18. Random 3-Affine.

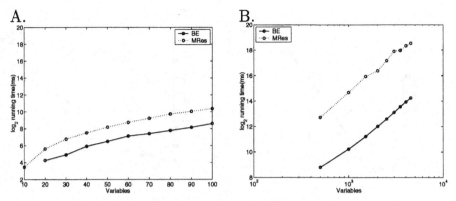

Figure 19. A) Random Biconditionals, B) Random Chains.

empty clause is generated, in which case the formula is unsatisfiable, or all variables have been eliminated, in which case the formula is satisfiable.

To facilitate a fair comparison between ZRes and our BDD-based solver, we used the multiresolution code used in [15] under our bucket elimination framework and used the same variable and elimination order as the BDD-based algorithms. This can be seen as a comparison of the compression capability of ZDD-based clause sets versus BDD-based solutions sets representations, since at comparable stages of the two algorithms (say, before variable x_i, is eliminated), the data structures represents the same Boolean function. As an optimization, a simple form of unit preference is implemented for the ZDD-based multi-resolution, since unit clauses can be easily detected in the ZDD-based clause set representation and resolved out-of-order.

The results for the 3-CNF and affine satisfiability cases are plotted in Figures 17A,B, and 18. We see that the differences between the two approaches are again density dependent. Just like the differences between BE and BM, ZDD-based multiresolution is more efficient at low density and less efficient at high density. This result can be related to the compression ratio achieved by the two

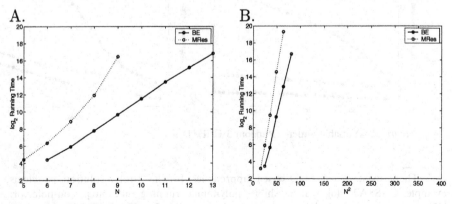

Figure 20. A) n-Rooks, B) n-Queens.

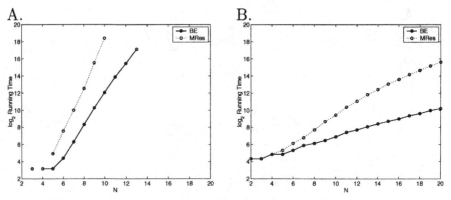

Figure 21. A) Pigeon-Hole, B) Multilated Checkerboard.

representations at different densities, where the clause set representation is far more efficient at low densities. For the high-density case, the clause set representation starts to show its shortcomings. High-density problems typically have a large number of clauses and few solutions: clause-set representation is less efficient in this case. This is especially evident for the unsatisfiable case where, if BDDs are used, unsatisfiability can be detected immediately, but if clause sets are used, detection is delayed until an empty clause is generated.

Next we examine the other classes of formulas in Figure 19A,B, Figure 20A,B, Figure 21A, and B. In all cases, the BDD-based approach is superior to the ZDD-based approach.[*]

An explanation for the superiority of the BDD-based approach can be provided in terms of the cost of the quantifier-elimination operation. Complexity of decision-diagram algorithms can be measured in the number of cache lookups

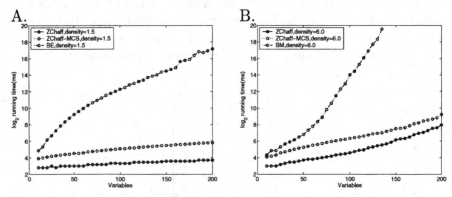

Figure 22. Variable Order – Random 3-CNF (1).

---

[*] There exist other ZDD-based approaches for hard-for-resolution problems, for example, CASSAT [46], which exhibits polynomial running time on pigeon-hole formulas [47]. A comparison with these approaches would be a future direction of this research.

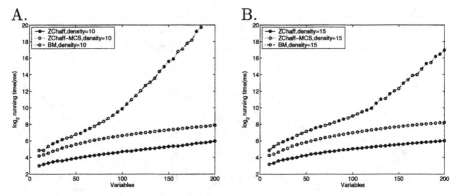

Figure 23. Variable Order – Random 3-CNF (2).

that the algorithm performs. Quantifying out a single variable uses the BDD "or" operation, which has a proven $O(n^2)$ upper bound on the number of cache look-ups [12]. The same cannot be said for the ZDD multiresolution operation used to quantify out a single variable, where the number of cache look-ups can be exponential in the width of the input ZDDs. Empirically, the number of cache lookups can be 1–2 orders of magnitude larger than the size of the output ZDD. This is the main contribution to the performance hit taken by the ZDD-based algorithm.

In [48] we compared BDD-based and ZDD-based approaches to QBF solving, showing that ZDD-based multiresolution has a clear edge. Since QBF problems are required to be underconstrained propositionally (otherwise they would be easily unsatisfiable because of the universal quantifiers), the extra compression of the ZDD-based clause-set representation would apply, explaining the superiority of the ZDD-based approach.

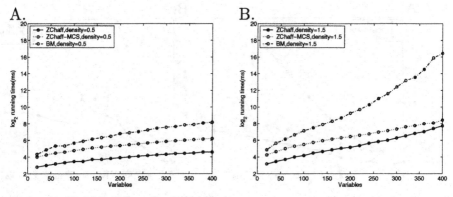

Figure 24. Variable Order – Random Affine.

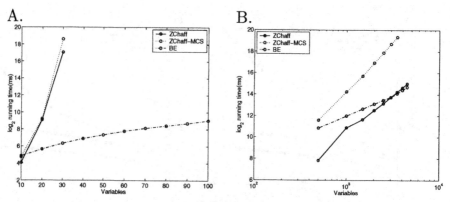

Figure 25. Variable Order – A) Random Biconditional, B) Random Chains.

6.2. STRUCTURE-GUIDED VARIABLE ORDER FOR SEARCH

In Section 5, we showed that the choice of variable order is important to the performance of BDD-based satisfiability solvers. We showed that MCS variable order offers good algorithmic performance across a variety of input formulas. In contrast, most search-based algorithms use a dynamic variable order, based on the clauses visited or generated during the search procedure, for example, the VSIDS heuristic used in ZChaff [45]. To offer a more direct comparison between search-based and symbolic methods, we reimplemented ZChaff with the MCS variable order and compared its performance with ZChaff and with the symbolic solvers. (See [1, 37] for earlier work on structure-guided variable order for search-based methods.) We compared here the performance of ZChaff with the default (VSIDS) variable order, ZChaff with MCS variable order, and the BDD-based sovers (for each formula class we chose the best solver between BM and BE).

The results for random formulas are shown in Figure 22A,B, Figure 23A,B, Figure 24A,B, Figure 25A and B, and the results for constructed formulas are shown in Figures 26A,B, Figure 27A and B. In general, the structure-guided

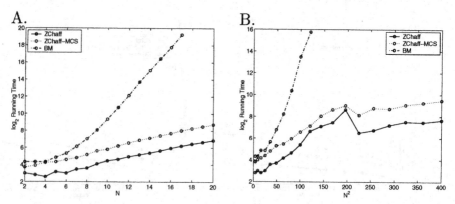

Figure 26. Variable Order – A) n-Rooks, B) n-Queens.

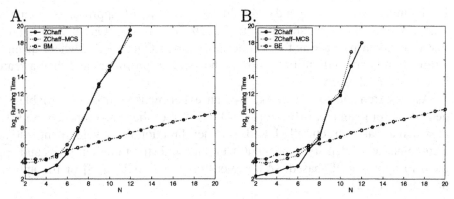

Figure 27. Variable Order – A) Pigeon-Hole, B) Multi Checkerboard.

variable order is inferior in terms of performance to dynamic variable order (VSIDS). For easy problems, the overhead of precomputing the variable order is quite significant. The performance loss should not be entirely attributed to the overhead, though, since we also observed an increase in the number of implications performed. Thus, dynamic variable order is, in general, a better algorithmic choice. Nevertheless, for most formulas, these is no exponential gap in scaling between the two variable-order heuristics.

Also, replacing VSIDS by MCS did not change the relationship between ZChaff and the BDD-based solvers. The difference in performance between search-based and symbolic approaches is larger than the difference between static and dynamic decision order for ZChaff. In none of the cases did the static variable order change the relative picture between search and symbolic approaches. This shows that the general superiority of search-based vs. symbolic techniques cannot be attributed to the use of dynamic variable order.

7. Discussion

Satifiability solvers have made tremendous progress over the past few years, partly driven by frequent competitions; cf. [42]. At the same time, our understanding of why extant solvers perform so well is lagging. Our goal in this paper is not to present a new competitive solver but rather to call for a broader research agenda in satisfiability solving. We showed that a symbolic approach can outperform a search-based approach in certain cases, but more research is needed before we can have robust implementations of the symbolic approach. Recent works have suggested other symbolic approaches to satisfiability solving, for example, compressed BFS search in [46] and BDD representation for non-CNF constraints in the framework of DPLL search in [22, 29, 38]. These works bolster our call for a broader research agenda. Such an agenda should build connections with two other successful areas of automated reasoning, namely, model checking [18] and constraint satisfaction [25].

Furthermore, such an agenda should explore *hybrid* approaches combining search and symbolic techniques; cf. [22, 29, 35, 38, 46]. One hybrid approach that has shown promise is that of the QBF solver Quantor [7], where quantifier elimination is applied until the formula become propositional and then a search-based solver takes olver.

As an extension to this work, we can experiment with other variable-order heuristics, for example, MINCE [1], FORCE [2], or the ones proposed in [37], all of which are also structurally based. Another direction for development is to take a combination of density-dependent heuristics and structural heuristics and apply them to hybrid BDD-based SAT solvers such as CirCUs [38] or the approach presented in [22].

Acknowledgement

We thank Enrico Giunchiglia for proposing the experiments on structural-guided variable order for search.

References

1. Aloul, F., Markov, I. and Sakallah, K.: MINCE: a static global variable-ordering for SAT and BDD, in *Proc. IEEE 10th International Workshop on Logic and Synthesis*, 2001, pp. 281–286.

2. Aloul, F., Markov, I. and Sakallah, K.: FORCE: a fast and easy-to-implement variable-ordering heuristic, in *Proc. of the 13th ACM Great Lakes Symposium on VLSI 2003*, 2003, pp. 116–119.

3. Amir, E. and McIlraith, S.: Solving satisfiability using decomposition and the most constrained subproblem, in *LICS Workshop on Theory and Applications of Satisfiability Testing (SAT 2001)*, June 2001.

4. Arnborg, S., Corneil, D. and Proskurowski, A.: Complexity of finding embeddings in a k-tree, *SIAM J. Algebr. Discrete Math.* **8** (1987), 277–284.

5. Balcazar, J.: Self-reducibility, *J. Comput. Syst. Sci.* **41**(3) (1990), 367–388.

6. Beatty, D. and Bryant, R.: Formally verifying a microprocessor using a simulation methodology, in *Proc. 31st Design Automation Conference*, 1994, pp. 596–602.

7. Biere, A.: Resolve and expand, in: *Proc. 7th Conf. on Theory and Applications of Satisfiability Testing (SAT 2004)*, 2004, pp. 238–246.

8. Biere, A., Clarke, C. A. E., Fujita, M. and Zhu, Y.: Symbolic model checking using SAT procedures instead of BDD, in *Proc. 36th Conf. on Design Automation*, 1999, pp. 317–320.

9. Block, M., Gröpl, C., Preuß, H., Proömel, H. L. and Srivastav, A.: Efficient ordering of state variables and transition relation partitions in symbolic model checking. Technical report, Institute of Informatics, Humboldt University of Berlin, 1997.

10. Bodlaender, H. and Kloks, T.: Efficient and constructive algorithms for the pathwidth and treewidth of graphs, *J. Alogorithms* **21** (1996), 358–402.

11. Bouquet, F.: Gestion de la dynamicite et enumeration d'implicants preniers, une approche fondee sur les Diagrammes de Decision Binaire. Ph.D. thesis, Universite de Privence, France, 1999.

12. Bryant, R.: Graph-based algorithms for Boolean function manipulation, *IEEE Trans. Comput*, **C35**(8) (1986), 677–691.

13. Burch, J., Clarke, E. and Long, D.: Symbolic model checking with partitioned transition relations, in *VLSI 91, Proc. IFIP TC10/WG 10.5 International Conference on Very Large Scale Integration, Edinburgh, Scotland*, 20–22 August, 1991, pp. 49–58

14. Burch, J., Clarke, E., McMillan, K., Dill, D. and Hwang, L.: Symbolic model checking: 10^{20} states and beyond, *Inf. Comput.* **98**(2) (1992), 142–170.

15. Chatalic, P. and Simon, L.: Multi-resolution on compressed sets of clauses, in *Twelfth International Conference on Tools with Artificial Intelligence (IXTAI'00)*, 2000, pp. 2–10.

16. Chung, P., Hajj, I. and Patel, J.: Efficient variable ordering heuristics for shared ROBDD, in *Proc. 1993 IEEE Int. Symp. on Circuits and Systems (ISCA93)*, 1993, pp. 1690–1693.

17. Cimatti, A. and Roveri, M.: Conformant planning via symbolic model checking, *J. Artif. Intell. Res.* **13** (2000), 305–338

18. Clarke, E., Grumberg, O. and Peled, D.: *Model Checking*, MIT Press, 1999.

19. Coarfa, C., Demopoulos, D. D., San Miguel Aguirre, A., Subramanian, D. and Vardi, M.: Random 3-SAT: the plot thickens, *Constraints* (2003), 243–261.

20. Crawford, J. and Baker, A.: Experimental results on the application of satisfiability algorithms to scheduling problems, in *Proc. 12th Nat. Conf. on Artificial Intelligence*, Vol. 2, 1994, pp. 1092–1097.

21. Dalmau, V., Kolaitis, P. and Vardi, M.: Constraint satisfaction, bounded treewidth, and finite-variable logics, in *Proceedings of 8th Int. Conf. on Principles and Practice of Constraint Programming (CP 2002)*, 2002, pp. 310–326.

22. Damiano, R. F. and Kukula, J. H.: Checking satisfiability of a conjunction of BDDs, in: *Proc. 40th Design Automation Conference (DAC 2003)*, 2003, pp. 818–823.

23. Davis, M., Logemann, G. and Loveland, D.: A machine program for theorem proving. *J. ACM* **5** (1962), 394–397.

24. Davis, S. and Putnam, M.: A computing procedure for quantification theory, *J. ACM* **7** (1960), 201–215.

25. Dechter, R.: *Constraint Processing*, Morgan Kaufmann, 2003.

26. Dechter, R. and Pearl, J.: Network-based heuristics for constraint-satisfaction problems. *Artif. Intell.* **34** (1987), 1–38.

27. Dechter, R. and Rish, I.: Directional resolution: the Davis–Putnam procedure, revisited, in *KR'94: Principles of Knowledge Representation and Reasoning*, 1994, pp. 134–145.

28. Downery, R. and Fellows, M.: *Paraetrized Complexity*, Springer-Verlag, 1999.

29. Franco, J., Kouril, M., Schlipf, J., Ward, J., Weaver, S., Dransfield, M. and Vanfleet, W.: SBSAT: a state-based, BDD-based satisfiability solver, in *Proc. 6th Int. Conf. on Theory and Applications of Satisfiability Testing (SAT 2003)*, 2003, pp. 398–410.

30. Freuder, E.: Complexity of k-tree structured constraint satisfaction problems, in *Proc. 8th Nat. Conf. on Artificial Intelligence*, 1990, pp. 4–9.

31. Fujita, M., Fujisawa, H. and Kawato, N.: Evaluation and improvements of Boolean comparison method based on binary decision disgrams, in *Proc. IEEE/ACM Int. conf. on Computer-Aided Design (ICCAD-88)*, 1988, pp. 2–5.

32. Geist, D. and Beer, H.: Efficient model checking by automated ordering of transition relation partitions, in *Proc. 6th Int. Conf. on computer Aided Verification (CAV 1994)*, 1994, pp. 299–310.

33. Goldberg, E. and Novikov, Y.: BerkMin: a fast and robust SAT solver, in *Proc. Design Automation and Test in Europe (DATE 2002)*, 2002, pp. 142–149.

34. Groote, J. F.: Hiding propositional constants in BDDs, *FMSD* **8** (1996), 91–96.

35. Gupta, A., Yang, Z., Ashar, P., Zhang, L. and Malik, S.: Partition-based decision heuristics for image computation using SAT and BDDs, in: *Proc. IEEE/ACM Int. Conf. on Computer-Aided Design (ICCAD-01)*, 2001, pp. 286–292.

36. Hojati, R., Krishman, S.C. and Brayton, R.K.: Early quantification and partitioned transition relations, in *Proc. 1996 Int. Conf. on Computer Design (ICCD'96)*, 1996, pp. 12–19.

37. Huang, J. and Darwiche, A.: A structure-based variable ordering heuristic for SAT, in *Proc. 18th Int. Joint Conf. on Artificial Intelligence (IJCAI 2003)*, 2003, 1167–1172.

38. Jon, H. and Somenzi, F.: CirCUs: hybrid satisfiability solver, in *Proc. of the 7th Int. Conf. on Theory and Applications of Satisfiability Testing (SAT 2004)*, 2004, pp. 47–55.

39. Kautz, H. and Selman, B.: Planning as satisfiability, in *Proc. 10th Eur. conf. on AI (ECAI 92)*, 1992, pp. 359–363.

40. Khurshid, S., Marinov, D., Shlyyakhter, I. and Jackson, D.: A case for efficient solution enumeration, in *Proc. 6th Int. Conf. on Theory and Applications of Satisfiability Testing (SAT 2003)*, 2001, pp. 272–286.

41. Koster, A., Bodlaender, H. and van Hoesel, S.: Treewidth: computational experiments. Technical report, Konrad-Zuse-Zentrum für Informationstechnik Berlin.

42. Le Berre, D. and Simon, L.: The essentials of the SAT'03 competition, in *Proc. 6th Int. Conf. on Theory and Applications of Satisfiability Testing (SAT 2003)*, 2003, pp. 452–467.

43. Malik, S., Wang, A., Brayton, R. and Sangiovanni Vincentelli, A.: Logic verification using binary decision diagrams in a logic synthesis environment, in: *Proc. IEEE/ACM Int. Conf. on Computer-Aided Design (ICCAD-88)*, 1988, pp. 6–9.

44. Minato, S.: *Binary Decision Diagrams and Applications to VLSI CAD*. Kluwer, 1996.

45. Moskewicz, M., Madigan, C., Zhao, Y., Zhang, L. and Malik, S.: Chaff: engineering an efficient SAT solver, in *Proc. of 39th Design Automation Conference (DAC 2001)*, 2001, pp. 530–535.

46. Motter, D.B. and Markov, I.L.: A compressed breadth-first search for satisfiability, in *Proc. 4th Int. Workshop on Algorithm Engineering and Experiments (ALENEX 2002)*, Vol. 2409 of *Lecture Notes in Computer Science*, 2002, pp. 29–42.

47. Motter, D.B. and Markov, I.L.: On proof systems behind efficient SAT solvers, in *Proc. of 5th Int. Symp. on the Theory and Applications of Satisfiability Testing (SAT 2002)*, 2002, pp. 206–213.

48. Pan, G. and Vardi, M.Y.: Symbolic decision procedures for QBF, in *Proceedings of 10th Int. Conf. on Principles and Practice of Constraint Programming (CP 2004)*, 2004, pp. 453–467.

49. Ranjan, R., Aziz, A., Brayton, R., Plessier, B. and Pixley, C.: Efficient BDD algorithms for FSM synthesis and verification, in *Proc. of IEEE/ACM Int. Workshop on Logic Synthesis*, 1995.

50. San Miguel Aguirre, A. and Vardi, M.Y.: Random 3-SAT and BDDs: the plot thickens further, in *Proc. of the 7th Int. Conf. Principles and Practice of Constraint Programming (CP 2001)*, 2001, pp. 121–136.

51. Schaefer, T.: The Complexity of satisfiability problems, in *Proc. of the 10th annual ACM symposium on Theory of Computing (STOC'78)*, 1978, pp. 216–226.

52. Selman, B., Mitchell, D. G. and Levesque, H. J.: Generating hard satisfiability problems, *Artif. Intell.* **81**(1–2) (1996), 17–29.

53. Somenzi, F.: 'CUDD: CU Decision Diagram package'. http://vlsi.colorado.edu/~fabio/CUDD/, 1998.

54. Tarjan, R. E. and Yannakakis, M.: Simple linear-time algorithms to test chordality of graphs, tests acyclicity of hypergraphs, and selectively reduce acyclic hypergraphs, *SIAM J. Comput.* **13**(3) (1984), 566–579.

55. Uribe, T.E. and Stickel, M.E.: Ordered binary decision diagrams and the Davis–Putnam procedure, in *1st Int. Conf. on Constraints in Computational Logics*, 1994, pp. 34–39.

56. Urquhart, A.: The complexity of propositional proofs, *Bull. Symb. Log.* **1** (1995), 425–467.

Journal of Automated Reasoning (2005) 35: 51–72
DOI: 10.1007/s10817-005-9006-x

© Springer 2006

Exponential Lower Bounds for the Running Time of DPLL Algorithms on Satisfiable Formulas[*]

MICHAEL ALEKHNOVICH[1,†], EDWARD A. HIRSCH[2,‡]
and DMITRY ITSYKSON[3,§]

[1]*Institute for Advanced Study, Princeton, NJ, USA. e-mail: misha@ias.edu*
[2]*St. Petersburg Department of Steklov, Institute of Mathematics, St. Petersburg, 191011, Russia.*
e-mail: hirsch@pdmi.ras.ru
[3]*Faculty of Mathematics and Mechanics, St. Petersburg State University, St. Petersburg, Russia.*
e-mail: dmitrits@mail.ru

Abstract. DPLL (for *Davis*, *Putnam*, *Logemann*, and *Loveland*) algorithms form the largest family of contemporary algorithms for SAT (the propositional satisfiability problem) and are widely used in applications. The recursion trees of DPLL algorithm executions on unsatisfiable formulas are equivalent to treelike resolution proofs. Therefore, lower bounds for treelike resolution (known since the 1960s) apply to them. However, these lower bounds say nothing about the behavior of such algorithms on satisfiable formulas. Proving exponential lower bounds for them in the most general setting is impossible without proving $P \neq NP$; therefore, to prove lower bounds, one has to restrict the power of branching heuristics. In this paper, we give exponential lower bounds for two families of DPLL algorithms: *generalized myopic* algorithms, which read up to $n^{1-\epsilon}$ of clauses at each step and see the remaining part of the formula without negations, and *drunk* algorithms, which choose a variable using any complicated rule and then pick its value at random.

Key words: satisfiability, DPLL algorithms.

1. Introduction

SAT solving heuristics. The propositional satisfiability problem (*SAT*) is one of the most well-studied NP-complete problems. In this problem, one is asked whether a Boolean formula in conjunctive normal form (a conjunction of *clauses*, which are disjunctions of *literals*, which are variables or their negations) has an

---

[*] Extended abstract of this paper appeared in *Proceedings of ICALP 2004*, LNCS 3142, Springer, 2004, pp. 84–96.
[†] Supported by CCR grant $\mathcal{N}$CCR-0324906.
[‡] Supported in part by Russian Science Support Foundation, RAS program of fundamental research "Research in principal areas of contemporary mathematics," and INTAS grant $\mathcal{N}$ 04-77-7173.
[§] Supported in part by INTAS grant $\mathcal{N}$04-77-7173.

assignment that satisfies all its clauses. Despite the P ≠ NP conjecture, there are numerous algorithms for SAT (motivated, in particular, by its importance for applications). DPLL algorithms (defined below) are based on the most popular approach that originates in the papers by Davis, Putnam, Logemann, and Loveland [9, 10]. Very informally, these algorithms use a 'divide-and-conquer' strategy: they split a formula into two subproblems by fixing a value of some literal, and then they recursively process the arising formulas. These algorithms received much attention of researchers both from theory and practice and are heavily used in the applications.

Lower bounds for resolution and the running time of DPLL algorithms. Propositional proof systems form one of the simplest and the most studied model in propositional calculus. Given a formula F, a propositional proof system allows to show that F is unsatisfiable. For example, using the well-known $\frac{x \vee C_1; \; \neg x \vee C_2}{C_1 \vee C_2}$, one can nondeterministically build a *resolution refutation of F*, which may be used as a certificate of unsatisfiability for the formula F. The size of the minimum tree-like resolution refutation and the running time of DPLL algorithms are related by the following well-known statement.

FACT 1. *For each unsatisfiable formula the shortest treelike resolution proof is at most polynomially longer than the smallest recursion tree of a DPLL algorithm, and vice versa.*

Therefore, (sub)exponential lower bounds for treelike resolution (starting with Tseitin's bounds [16] and finishing with quite strong bounds of [14]) imply that any DPLL algorithm should take exponentially long to prove that the corresponding formulas are unsatisfiable. However, these results say nothing in the case of *satisfiable* formulas. There are several reasons why the performance may differ on satisfiable and unsatisfiable instances:

− Experiments show that contemporary SAT solvers are able to solve much larger satisfiable formulas than unsatisfiable ones [15].
− Randomized one-sided error algorithms fall out of scope because they do not yield proofs of unsatisfiability.
− If a DPLL algorithm is provably efficient (i.e., takes polynomial time) on some class of formulas, then one can interrupt the algorithm running on a formula from this class after a sufficiently large number of steps if it has not found a satisfying assignment. This will result in a certificate of unsatisfiability that can be much smaller than the minimum treelike resolution refutation.

Previously known lower bounds for satisfiable formulas. Despite the importance of this problem, only few works have addressed the question of the worst-case running time of SAT algorithms on satisfiable formulas. There have been two papers [4, 11] on (specific) local search heuristics; as to DPLL algorithms, all we know are the bounds of [1, 2, 13].

In the work of Nikolenko [13] exponential lower bounds are proved for two specific DPLL algorithms (called GUC and Randomized GUC) on specially tailored satisfiable formulas.

Achlioptas, Beame, and Molloy [1] prove the hardness of random formulas in 3-CNF with n variables and cn ($c < 4$) clauses for three specific DPLL algorithms (called GUC, UC, and ORDERED-DLL). It is an open problem to prove that these formulas are satisfiable (though it is widely believed they are). Recently, the same authors [2] have proved an *unconditional* lower bound on satisfiable random formulas in 4-CNF for ORDERED-DLL. The latter result states that ORDERED-DLL takes exponential time with *constant* (rather than exponentially close to 1) probability.

Our contribution. Proving such bounds for DPLL algorithms in a greater generality is the ultimate goal of the present paper. We design two families of satisfiable formulas and show lower bounds for two general classes of algorithms (see Section 2.1 for precise definitions).

The first class of formulas simply encodes a linear system $Ax = b$ that has a unique solution over $\mathbb{GF}_2$, where A is a 'good' expander. We prove that any *generalized myopic* DPLL algorithm that has a local access to the formula (i.e., can read up to $n^{1-\epsilon}$ clauses at every step) with high probability has to make an exponential number of steps before it finds a satisfying assignment.

In our second result we describe a general way to cook a satisfiable formula out of any unsatisfiable formula hard for treelike resolution so that the resulting formula is hard for any *drunk* DPLL algorithm that chooses a variable in an arbitrarily complicated way and then tries both its values in a random order.

Both classes of algorithm that we consider are classical DPLL backtracking algorithms and, in general, are much less restricted than those studied before.

Organization of the paper. Section 2 contains basic notation and the rigorous definitions of DPLL algorithms that we consider. In the subsequent two sections we present our two main results. We discuss their possible extensions and open questions in Section 5.

2. Preliminaries

Let x be a Boolean variable, that is, a variable that ranges over the set $\{0, 1\}$. A *literal* of x is either x or $\neg x$. A *clause* is a disjunction of literals (considered as a set). A *formula* in this paper refers to a Boolean formula in conjunctive normal form, that is, a conjunction of clauses (a formula is considered as a multiset). A formula in k-CNF contains clauses of size at most k. We use the notation $\text{Vars}(\Phi)$, $\text{Vars}(Ax = b)$ to denote the set of variables occurring in a Boolean formula, in a system of equations, and so on.

An *elementary substitution* $v := \varepsilon$ just chooses a Boolean value, namely, $\varepsilon \in \{0, 1\}$, for a variable, namely, v. A *substitution* (also called a *partial assignment*) is a set of elementary substitutions for different variables. The result of applying a substitution ρ to a formula F (denoted by $F[\rho]$) is a new formula obtained from F by removing the clauses containing literals satisfied by ρ and removing the opposite literals from other clauses.

We say that an assignment α *satisfies* a Boolean function f if $f(\alpha) = 1$. For Boolean functions $f_1, \ldots, f_k$, g we say that $f_1, \ldots, f_k$ *semantically imply* g, (denoted $f_1, \ldots, f_k \vDash g$), if every assignment to the variables in $V = \text{Vars}(f_1) \cup \ldots \cup \text{Vars}(f_k) \cup \text{Vars}(g)$ satisfying $f_1, \ldots, f_k$, satisfies g as well (i.e., $\forall \alpha \in \{0, 1\}^V$ $(f_1(\alpha) = \cdots = f_k(\alpha) = 1 \Rightarrow g(\alpha) = 1)$).

For a nonnegative integer n, let $[n] = \{1, 2, \ldots n\}$. For a vector $v = (v_1, \ldots, v_m)$ and index set $I \subseteq [m]$ we denote by v_I the subvector with coordinates chosen according to I. For a matrix A and a set of rows $I \subseteq [m]$ we use the notation A_I for the submatrix of A corresponding to these rows. In particular, we denote the ith row of A by A_i and identify it with the set $\{j \mid A_{ij} = 1\}$. The cardinality of this set is denoted by $|A_i|$.

2.1. DPLL ALGORITHMS: GENERAL SETTING

A DPLL algorithm is a recursive algorithm. At each step, it simplifies the input formula F (without affecting its satisfiability), chooses a variable v in it, and makes two recursive calls for the formulas $F[v := 1]$ and $F[v := 0]$ in some order; it outputs 'Satisfiable' iff at least one of the recursive calls says so (there is no reason to make the second call if the first one was successful). The recursion proceeds until the formula trivializes, that is, it becomes empty (hence, satisfiable) or one of the clauses becomes empty (hence, the formula is unsatisfiable).

A DPLL algorithm is determined by its simplification rules and two heuristics: Heuristic A, which chooses a variable, and Heuristic B, which chooses its value to be examined first. A formal description is given in Figure 1. Note that if $\mathbf{P} = \mathbf{NP}$ and Heuristic B is not restricted, it can simply choose the correct values, and the algorithm will terminate quickly. Therefore, in order to prove unconditional lower bounds one has to restrict the simplification rules and heuristics and prove the result for the restricted model. In this paper, we consider two models: generalized myopic algorithms and drunk algorithms. Both models extend the original algorithm of [9], which uses the unit clause and pure literal rules and no nontrivial Heuristics A and B.

Drunk algorithms. Heuristic A of a drunk algorithm can be arbitrarily complicated (even nonrecursive). This feature is compensated by the simplicity

Algorithm $\mathcal{A}$.
Input: formula F in CNF.
Output: "Satisfiable" or "Unsatisfiable".

1. Simplify F using *simplification rules*.

2. If F is empty, return "Satisfiable".

3. If F contains the empty clause, return "Unsatisfiable".

4. Choose a variable v using *Heuristic A*.

5. Choose a Boolean value ε using *Heuristic B*.

6. If $\mathcal{A}(F[v := \varepsilon])$ returns "Satisfiable", return "Satisfiable".

7. If $\mathcal{A}(F[v := \neg\varepsilon])$ returns "Satisfiable", return "Satisfiable".

8. Return "Unsatisfiable".

Figure 1. A DPLL algorithm.

of Heuristic B: it chooses 0 or 1 at random. The simplification rules are as follows.

Unit clause elimination. If the formula F contains a clause that consists of a single literal l, replace F by $F[l := 1]$, where $l := 1$ denotes the elementary substitution that satisfies the literal l.

Pure literal elimination. If the formula F contains a literal l such that its negation does not occur in any clause,* replace F by $F[l := 1]$.

Subsumption. If the formula F contains a clause that contains another clause as a subset, delete the larger clause.

Note that `Randomized GUC` with pure literal elimination considered in [13] is a drunk algorithm (that does not use subsumption).

In Section 4 we prove an exponential lower bound on the running time of drunk algorithms on satisfiable formulas obtained by a simple construction that uses (known) hard unsatisfiable formulas.

Myopic algorithms. Both heuristics are restricted w.r.t. the parts of formula that they can read (this can be viewed as accessing the formula via an oracle). Heuristic A can read

- $K(n)$ clauses of the formula (where n is the number of variables in the original input formula and $K(n) = n^{1-\epsilon}$ is a function with $\epsilon > 0$);

---

* An occurrence of a positive literal is an occurrence of the corresponding variable *without* the negation.

- the formula with negation signs removed;
- the number of occurrences of each literal.

Heuristic B may use the information obtained by Heuristic A. The information revealed about the formula can be used in the subsequent recursive calls (but not in other branches of the recursion tree).

The only simplification rule is pure literal elimination. Also the unit clause elimination can be easily implemented by choosing the proper variable and value. In particular, heuristics ORDERED-DLL, GUC, and UC considered in [1] yield generalized myopic algorithms. Note that our definition generalizes the notion of myopic algorithms introduced in [3].

Formally, the heuristics are unable to read all clauses containing a variable if this variable is too frequent. However, it is easy to see that we can restrict our hard formulas (that we use for proving our exponential lower bound) so that every variable occurs $O(\log n)$ times; see Remark 1.

In Section 3 we prove an exponential lower bound on the running time of myopic algorithms on satisfiable formulas based on expanders.

2.2. DPLL RECURSION TREE

A DPLL *recursion tree* is a binary tree (a node may have zero, one, or two children) in which nodes correspond to the intermediate subproblems that arise after the algorithm makes a substitution, and edges correspond to the recursive calls on the resulting formulas. The computation of a DPLL algorithm thus can be considered as a depth-first traversal of the recursion tree from the left to the right; in particular, the rightmost leaf always corresponds to the satisfying assignment (if any). The overall running time is proportional to the size of the tree.

For a node v in the computation tree by ρ_v we denote the partial assignment that was set prior to visiting v. Thus the algorithm at v works on the subformula $F[\rho_v]$.

2.3. EXPANDERS

An expander is a bounded-degree graph that has many neighbors for every sufficiently small subset of its nodes. Similarly to [5], we use a more general notion of expander as an $m \times n$ matrix. There are two notions of expanders: expanders and boundary expanders. The latter notion is stronger as it requires the existence of unique neighbors. However, every good expander is also a boundary expander.

DEFINITION 1. For a set of rows $I \subseteq [m]$ of an $m \times n$ matrix A, we define its boundary $\partial_A I$ (or just ∂I) as the set of all $j \in [n]$ (called boundary elements) such that there exists exactly one row $i \in I$ that contains j. We say that A is an (r, s, c)-boundary expander if

1. $|A_i| \leq s$ for all $i \in [m]$, and
2. $\forall I \subseteq [m] \left(|I| \leq r \Rightarrow |\partial I| \geq c \cdot |I|\right)$.

Matrix A is an (r, s, c)-expander if condition 2 is replaced by

2′. $\forall I \subseteq [m] \left(|I| \leq r \Rightarrow |\cup_{i \in I} A_i| \geq c \cdot |I|\right)$.

We define the boundary and boundary elements of equation(s) in a linear system $Ax = b$ similarly to those of rows in a matrix A.

LEMMA 1. *Any $(r, 3, c)$ -expander is an $(r, 3, 2c-3)$ -boundary expander.*

Proof. Assume that A is $(r, 3, c)$-expander. Consider a set of its rows I with $|I| \leq r$. Since A is an expander, $|\cup_{i \in I} A_i| \geq c|I|$. On the other hand we may estimate separately the number of boundary and nonboundary variables, which will give $|\cup_{i \in I} A_i| \leq E + (3|I| - E)/2$, where E is the number of boundary variables. This implies $E + (3|I| - E)/2 \geq c|I|$ and $E > (2c - 3)|I|$.   □

3. An Exponential Lower Bound for Myopic Algorithms

In this section, we prove an exponential lower bound on the running time of generalized myopic algorithms (described in Section 2.1) on satisfiable formulas. The proof strategy is as follows. We take a full-rank $n \times n$ 0/1-matrix A having certain expansion properties and construct a uniquely satisfiable Boolean formula Φ expressing the statement $Ax = b$ (modulo 2) for some vector b. Then we prove that if one obtains an unsatisfiable formula from Φ using a reasonable substitution, the resulting formula is hard for treelike resolution (the proof is similar to that of [8]). Finally, we show that changing several bits in the vector b, while changes the satisfying assignment, does not affect the behavior of a generalized myopic algorithm that did not reveal these bits, which implies it encounters a hard unsatisfiable formula on its way to the satisfying assignment.

In what follows, we prove the existence of appropriate expanders (Section 3.1) and examine their properties (Section 3.2). Then we give the construction of the corresponding Boolean formulas (Section 3.3) and prove the statement concerning the behavior of a generalized myopic algorithm on unsatisfiable formulas (Section 3.4). Finally, we prove our main result of this section (Section 3.5).

3.1. THE EXISTENCE OF APPROPRIATE EXPANDERS

We now prove the existence of expanders that we use to construct satisfiable formulas hard for myopic DPLL algorithms.

THEOREM 1. *For every sufficiently large n, there exists an $n \times n$ nondegenerate matrix $A^{(n)}$ such that $A^{(n)}$ is an $(n/\log^{14} n, 3, 25/13)$-expander.*

Let $\binom{[n]}{3}$ be the set of all $\{0, 1\}^n$-vectors of Hamming weight 3 (i.e., containing exactly three 1's). We use a probabilistic construction. The rows of a larger matrix are drawn at random from the set of all vectors of Hamming weight 3; then we choose a submatrix of the appropriate size. In order to establish the goal, we prove two lemmas.

LEMMA 2. *Let A be a $\Delta n \times n$ matrix (Δ may depend on n) in which each row is randomly chosen from $\binom{[n]}{3}$. Assume that $c < 2$ is a constant and $r = 0\left(\frac{n}{\Delta^{1/(2-c)}}\right)$. Then with probability $1-o(1)$ the matrix A is an $(r, 3, c)$-expander.*

Proof. The probability p_t of the event that there exists a subset of rows I of size $t \le r$ and a subset of columns $J \supseteq A_I$ of size $\lfloor ct \rfloor$ is upper bounded as

$$
p_t \le \binom{\Delta n}{t}\binom{n}{\lfloor ct \rfloor}\left(\frac{ct}{n}\right)^{3t}
$$

$$
\le \left(\frac{e\Delta n}{t}\right)^t \left(\frac{en}{ct}\right)^{ct}\left(\frac{ct}{n}\right)^{3t} = \left[e^{1+c}c^{3-c}\Delta\left(\frac{n}{t}\right)^{c-2}\right]^t
$$

$$
\le \left[e^{(1+c)/(2-c)}c^{(3-c)/(2-c)}r\frac{\Delta^{1/(2-c)}}{n}\right]^{(2-c)t}.
$$

Clearly, $p_1 = o(1)$. Since for sufficiently large n, $\sum_{t=1}^{r} p_t \le 2p_1$, the lemma follows. ☐

LEMMA 3. *Let L be a linear subspace of $\{0, 1\}^n$ of codimension k. Let vector v be chosen uniformly at random from $\binom{[n]}{3}$. Then $Pr[v \notin L] = \Omega\left(\frac{k}{n}\right)$.*

Proof. L can be specified as a kernel of a $k \times n$ matrix M of full rank (i.e., $L = \{u \mid Mu = 0\}$). The product Mu is distributed as a sum of three columns randomly chosen (without replacement) from the matrix M; we need to estimate the probability that this sum equals zero. Let $M_{i_1}, M_{i_2}, M_{i_3}$ be the three randomly chosen columns of M. ☐

Case 1: $k \ge 3$. In this case, consider the vector $u = M_{i_1} + M_{i_2}$. Since $\mathrm{rk}\, M = k$, there are at least $k - 2$ other columns in M different from u. Thus, $M_{i_3} \ne u$ with probability at least $\frac{k-2}{n}$.

Case 2: $k < 3$.

Case 2a: $\exists j_1 j_2 \forall j \, (j \notin \{j_1, j_2\} \Rightarrow M_j = M_{j_1} + M_{j_2})$. Since $\mathrm{rk}\, M > 0$, either M_{i_1} or M_{i_2} is nonzero. With probability $1/n$ the nonzero the first column. If this happens, then with probability at least $\frac{n-2}{n-1} \cdot \frac{n-3}{n-2}$ the second and the third column are chosen from those equal to $M_{i_1} + M_{i_2}$. Thus, with probability at least $\frac{1}{n} \cdot \frac{n-2}{n-1} \cdot \frac{n-3}{n-2} \ge \frac{1}{2n}$ $M_{i_1} + M_{i_2} + M_{i_3} \ne 0$.

Case 2b: The condition of case 2a does not hold. Consider the vector $u = M_{i_1} + M_{i_2}$. By our assumption, there is at least one column $j \notin \{i_1, i_2\}$ different from u. With probability at least $\frac{1}{n-2}$ this column will be chosen as the third one.

Proof of Theorem 1. The estimation of the number Δn of random vectors that suffices to obtain a $\Delta n \times n$ matrix of full rank resembles the analysis of the well-known 'coupon collector' problem. Let $S_0 = \emptyset, S_{i+1} = S_i \cup \{v_i\}, v_i \in_U \left(\frac{[n]}{3}\right)$. Let T be the first step when the vector system S_T is complete. One can easily see that the expectation of T is $O(n \log n)$: Lemma 3 shows that if the dimension of $\text{Span}(S_k)$ is t, then $\dim \text{Span}(S_{k+1}) = t + 1$ with probability $\Omega\left(\frac{n-t}{n}\right)$. Thus $O\left(\frac{n}{n-t}\right)$ steps suffice on average to increase the dimension from t to $t + 1$. By linearity of expectation,

$$\mathbf{E}T \leq O\left(\frac{n}{n} + \frac{n}{n-1} + \frac{n}{n-2} + \ldots + \frac{n}{1}\right) = O(n \log n).$$

Let a' be the constant in the $O(\cdot)$ notation above, that is, $\mathbf{E}T \leq a'n \log n$. Let $a'' = \frac{a'}{\epsilon}$ (we will choose ϵ later). By Markov inequality,

$$\Pr\{T > a''n \log n\} < \epsilon.$$

Let us choose ϵ and ϵ' so that $\epsilon + \epsilon' < 1$. For sufficiently large n, Lemma 2 guarantees that A is an $(n/\log^{14} n, 3, 25/13)$-expander with probability at least $1 - \epsilon'$. By the above reasoning, also $\text{rk } A = n$ with a positive probability. Thus, we can choose n linear independent rows of A; the resulting $n \times n$ matrix is an $(n/\log^{14} n, 3, 25/13)$-expander. $\qquad\qquad\square$

Remark 1. It is easy to see that one can add an additional requirement: for every column j, there is only $O(\log n)$ rows A_i such that $A_{ij} = 1$. Using such expanders would result in hard formulas with only $O(\log n)$ occurrences of every variable.

3.2. CLOSURE OPERATORS

Throughout this section, A denotes an $(r, 3, c)$-boundary expander. We need two operations of taking closure of a set of columns w.r.t. matrix A. The first was defined in [7].

DEFINITION 2. Let $A \in \{0, 1\}^{m \times n}$. For a set of columns $J \subseteq [n]$ define the following inference relation $\vdash_J$ on the sets $[m]$ of rows of A:

$$I \vdash_J I_1 \Leftrightarrow |I_1| \leq r/2 \wedge \partial_A(I_1) \subseteq \left[\bigcup_{i \in I} A_i \cup J\right]. \tag{1}$$

That is, we allow rows of A to be derived from already derived rows. We can use these derived rows in further derivations (for example, derive new rows from

$I \cup I_1$). Let the closure $\mathrm{Cl}(J)$ of J be the set of all rows which can be inferred via $\vdash_J$ from the empty set.

The following lemma was proved in ([7], Lemma 3.16).

LEMMA 4. *For any set J with $|J| \le (cr/2)$, $|\mathrm{Cl}(J)| \le r/2$.*

We also need another (stronger) closure operation the intuitive sense of which is to extract a good expander out of a given matrix by removing rows and columns.

DEFINITION 3.   For an $A \in \{0, 1\}^{m \times n}$ and a subset of its columns $J \subseteq [n]$ we define an inference relation $\vdash'_J$ on subsets of rows of A:

$$I \vdash'_J I_1 \Leftrightarrow |I_1| \le r/2 \wedge \left| \partial_A(I_1) \backslash \left[\bigcup_{i \in I} A_i \cup J \right] \right| < c/2|I_1|. \tag{2}$$

Given a set of rows I and a set of columns J, consider the following cleaning step:

− If there exists a nonempty subset of rows I_1 such that $I \vdash'_J I_1$, then

• Add I_1 to I.
• Remove all rows corresponding to I_1 from A.

Repeat the cleaning step as long as it is applicable. Fix any particular order on the sets to exclude ambiguity, initialize $I = \emptyset$, and denote the resulting content of I at the end by $\mathrm{Cl}^e(J)$.

LEMMA 5. *Assume that A is an arbitrary matrix and J is a set of its columns. Let $I' = \mathrm{Cl}^e(J)$, $J' = \bigcup_{i \in \mathrm{Cl}^e(J)} A_i$. Denote by $\hat{A}$ the matrix that results from A by removing the rows corresponding to I' and columns to J'. If $\hat{A}$ is nonempty, then it is an $(r/2, 3, c/2)$-boundary expander.*
Proof. Follows immediately from the definition of Cl^e.   □

LEMMA 6. *If $|J| < cr/4$, then $|\mathrm{Cl}^e(J)| < 2c^{-1}|J|$.*
Proof. Assume that $|\mathrm{Cl}^e(J)| \ge 2c^{-1}|J|$. Consider the sequence $I_1, I_2, \dots,$ I_t appearing in the cleaning procedure; that is,

$$I_1 \cup I_2 \cup \dots \cup I_k \vdash'_J I_{k+1}.$$

Note that $I_i \cap I_{i'} = \emptyset$ for $i \ne i'$ because we remove the implied set of rows from A at each cleaning step. Denote by $C_t = \bigcup_{k=1}^t I_k$ the set of rows derived in t steps.

Let T be the first t such that $|C_t| \geq 2c^{-1}|J|$. Note that $|C_T| \leq 2c^{-1}|J| + r/2 \leq r$, hence $|J| < cr/4 \leq c|C_T|/4$. Because of the expansion properties of A, $\partial C_T \geq c|C_T|$, which implies

$$|\partial C_T \backslash J| \geq c|C_T| - |J| > c|C_T|/2. \tag{3}$$

On the other hand, every time we add some I_{t+1} to C_t during the cleaning procedure, only $c/2\,|I_{t+1}|$ new elements can be added to $\partial C_t \backslash J$ (of those elements that have never been there before). This implies

$$|\partial C_T \backslash J| \leq c|C_T|/2,$$

which contradicts (3).   □

3.3. HARD FORMULAS BASED ON EXPANDERS

Let A be an $n \times n$ matrix provided by Theorem 1; let also $r = n/\log^{14} n$, $c' = 25/13$ be the parameters of the theorem. Denote $c = 2c' - 3$ (thus A is an $(r, 3, c)$-boundary expander).

DEFINITION 4. Let b be a vector from $\{0, 1\}^n$. Then $\Phi (b)$ is the formula expressing the equality $Ax = b$ (modulo 2); in other words, every equation $a_{ij_1}x_{j_1} + a_{ij_2}x_{j_2} + a_{ij_3}x_{j_3} = b_i$ is transformed into the 4 clauses on $x_{j_1}, x_{j_2}, x_{j_3}$ satisfying all its solutions. Sometimes we identify an equation with the corresponding clauses.

Remark 2. The formula $\Phi(b)$ has several nice properties that we use in our proofs. First, note that $\Phi(b)$ has exactly one satisfying assignment (since rk $A = n$). It is also clear that a myopic DPLL algorithm has no reasonable chance to apply pure literal elimination to it because, for any substitution ρ, the formula $\Phi(b)[\rho]$ never contains a pure literal unless this pure literal is contained in a unit clause. Moreover, the number of occurrences of a literal in $\Phi(b)[\rho]$ always equals the number of occurrences of the opposite literal (recall that a formula is a *multi*set of clauses); again the only exception is literals occurring in unit clauses.

To the abuse of notation we identify $j \in J$ (where J is a set of columns of A) with the variable x_j.

3.4. BEHAVIOR OF MYOPIC ALGORITHMS ON UNSATISFIABLE FORMULAS

DEFINITION 5.   A substitution ρ is said to be locally consistent w.r.t. the linear system $Ax = b$ if and only if ρ can be extended to an assignment on X that satisfies the equations corresponding to $\text{Cl}(\rho)$:

$$A_{\text{Cl}(\rho)}x = b_{\text{Cl}(\rho)}.$$

LEMMA 7. *Assume that A is (r, 3, c)-boundary expander. Let $b \in \{0, 1\}^m$; ρ is a locally consistent partial assignment. Then for any set $I \subset [m]$ with $|I| \leq r/2$, ρ can be extended to an assignment x that satisfies the subsystem $A_I x = b_I$.*

Proof. Assume for the contradiction that there exists set I for which ρ cannot be extended to satisfy $A_I x = b_I$; choose the minimal such I. Then $\partial_A(I) \subseteq \text{Vars}(\rho)$; otherwise one could remove an equation with boundary variable in $\partial_A(I)\backslash\text{Vars}(\rho)$ from I. Thus, $\text{Cl}(\rho) \supseteq I$, which contradicts Definition 5. $\square$

The *width* [8] of a resolution proof is the maximal length of a clause in the proof. We need the following lemma, which is a straightforward generalization of ([8], Theorem 4.4).

LEMMA 8. *For any matrix A that is an (r, 3, c)-boundary expander and any vector $b \notin \text{Im}(A)$, any resolution proof of the system*

$$Ax = b \tag{4}$$

must have width at least cr/2.

Proof. For a clause C define Ben-Sasson–Wigderson measure as

$$\mu(C) = \min_{(A_I x = b_I) \models C} |I|.$$

Similar to the proof of ([8], Theorem 4.4), μ is a subadditive measure, for any D appearing in the translation* of Equation (4) to CNF $\mu(D) = 1$ and $\mu(\emptyset) \geq r$ (the latter inequality follows from the fact that any set I' ($I' \models \emptyset$) with $|I'| < r$ has a nonempty boundary, and an equality containing a boundary variable can be removed from the subsystem $A_{I'} x = b_{I'}$, leaving it still contradictory).

It follows that any resolution refutation of the system (4) contains a clause C s.t. $r/2 \leq \mu(C) < r$. Consider a minimal I s.t. $(A_I x = b_I) \models C$. As in [8] we claim that C has to contain all variables corresponding to $\partial_A(I)$. Indeed, if there exists a boundary variable in the equation $A_i x = b_i$ ($i \in I$) not included in C, then we may remove this equation so that $(A_{[I\backslash i]} x = b_{[I\backslash i]}) \models C$. Thus, C contains all boundary variables of I, and there are at least $c|I| \geq cr/2$ of them. $\square$

We also need the following lemma from [8].

LEMMA 9 ([8], *Corollary 3.4). The size of any treelike resolution refutation of a formula Ψ is at least 2^{w-w_Ψ}, where w is the minimal width of a resolution refutation of Ψ, and w_Ψ is the maximal length of a clause in Ψ.*

---

* See Definition 4.

LEMMA 10. *If a locally consistent substitution ρ s.t. $\left| \text{Vars}(\rho) \right| \leq cr/4$ results in an unsatisfiable formula $\Phi(b)[\rho]$, then every generalized myopic DPLL algorithm will take $2^{\Omega(r)}$ time on $\Phi(b)[\rho]$.*

Proof. The work of any DPLL algorithm on an unsatisfiable formula can be translated to treelike resolution refutation so that the size of the refutation is the working time of the algorithm. Thus, it is sufficient to show that the minimal treelike resolution refutation size of $\Phi(b)[\rho]$ is large.

Denote by $I = \text{Cl}^e(\rho)$, $J = \cup_{i \in I} A_i$. By Lemma 6 $\left| I \right| \leq r/2$. By Lemma 7 ρ can be extended to another partial assignment ρ' on variables x_J, s.t. ρ' satisfies every linear equation in $A_I x = b_I$. The restricted formula $(Ax = b) |_{\rho'}$ still encodes an unsatisfiable linear system, $A' x = b'$, where matrix A' results from A by removing rows corresponding to I and variables corresponding to J. By Lemma 5, A' is an $(r/2, 3, c/2)$-boundary expander. Lemmas 8 and 9 now imply that the minimal treelike resolution refutation of the Boolean formula corresponding to the system $A'x = b'$ has size $2^{\Omega(r)}$.   □

3.5. BEHAVIOR OF MYOPIC ALGORITHMS ON SATISFIABLE FORMULAS

We fix A, r, c, c' of Section 3.3 and $m = m(n) = n$ throughout this section.

THEOREM 2. *For every deterministic generalized myopic DPLL algorithm $\mathcal{A}$ that reads at most $K = K(n)$ clauses per step, $\mathcal{A}$ stops on $\Phi(b)$ in $2^{o(r)}$ steps with probability $2^{-\Omega(r/K)}$. The probability is taken over b uniformly distributed on $\{0, 1\}^n$.*

COROLLARY 1. *Let $\mathcal{A}$ be any (randomized) generalized myopic DPLL algorithm that reads at most $K = K(n)$ clauses per step. $\mathcal{A}$ stops on $\Phi(b)$ (a satisfiable formula in 3-CNF containing n variables and 4n clauses, described in Section 3.3) in $2^{o\left(n \log^{-14} n\right)}$ steps with probability $2^{-\Omega\left(K^{-1} n \log^{-14} n\right)}$ (taken over random bits used by the algorithm and over b uniformly distributed on $\{0, 1\}^n$).*

Proof. [Proof of Theorem 2]. The proof strategy is to show that during its very first steps the algorithm does not get enough information to guess a correct substitution with nonnegligible probability. Therefore, the algorithm chooses an incorrect substitution and has to examine an exponential-size subtree by Lemma 10.

Without loss of generality, we assume that our algorithm is a *clever myopic* algorithm. We define a clever myopic algorithm w.r.t. matrix A as a generalized myopic algorithm (defined as in Section 2.1) that

- has the following ability: whenever it reveals occurrences of the variables x_J (at least one entry of each), it can also read all clauses in $\text{Cl}(J)$ for free and reveal the corresponding occurrences;

— never asks for a number of occurrences of a literal (syntactical properties of our formula imply that $\mathcal{A}$ can compute this number itself: the number of occurrences outside unit clauses does not depend on the substitutions that $\mathcal{A}$ has made; all unit clauses belong to $Cl(J)$);
— always selects one of the revealed variables;
— never makes stupid moves: whenever it reveals the clauses $\overrightarrow{C}$ and chooses the variable x_j for branching, it makes the right assignment $x_j = \epsilon$ in the case when $\overrightarrow{C}$ semantically imply $x_j = \epsilon$ (this assumption can save only the running time).   □

PROPOSITION 1. *After the first $\lfloor \frac{cr}{6K} \rfloor$ steps a clever myopic algorithm reads at most $r/2$ bits of b.*

Proof. At each step the algorithm makes K clause queries, asking for $3K$ variable entries. This will sum up to $3K \, (cr/(6K))$ variables, which will result by Lemma 4 in at most $r/2$ revealed bits of b.   □

Recall that an assignment ρ is locally consistent if it can be extended to an assignment that satisfies $A_{Cl(\rho)}x = b_{Cl(\rho)}$.

PROPOSITION 2. *During the first $\lfloor \frac{cr}{6K} \rfloor$ steps the current partial assignment made by a clever myopic algorithm is locally consistent (in particular, the algorithm does not backtrack).*

Proof. The statement follows by repeated application of Lemma 7. Note that the definition of clever myopic algorithm requires that it choose a locally consistent assignment if possible.

Formally we prove the proposition by induction. In the beginning of the execution the current partial assignment is empty; hence it is locally consistent. By the definition of a clever myopic algorithm, whenever it makes a step t (where $t < \lfloor \frac{cr}{6K} \rfloor$) having a locally consistent partial assignment ρ_t it extends this assignment to an assignment ρ_{t+1} that is also locally consistent if possible. By Lemma 7 it can always do so as long as $\left| Cl(Vars(\rho_t) \cup \{x_j\}) \right| \leq r/2$ for the newly chosen variable x_j.   □

Assume now that b chosen at random is hidden from $\mathcal{A}$. Whenever an algorithm reads the information about a clause corresponding to the linear equation $A_i x = b_i$, it reveals the ith bit of b. Let us observe the situation after the first $\lfloor \frac{cr}{6K} \rfloor$ steps of $\mathcal{A}$, that is, the $\lfloor \frac{cr}{6K} \rfloor$-th vertex v in the leftmost branch in the DPLL tree of the execution of $\mathcal{A}$. By Proposition 1 the algorithm reads at most $r/2$ bits of b. Denote by $I_v \subset [m]$ the set of the revealed bits and by R_v the set of the assigned variables, $|R_v| = \lfloor \frac{cr}{6K} \rfloor$. The idea of the proof is that $\mathcal{A}$ cannot guess the true values of x_{R_v} by observing only r bits of b. Denote by ρ_v the partial assignment to the variables in R_v made by $\mathcal{A}$. Consider the event

$$E = \left\{ (A^{-1}b)R_v = \rho_v \right\}$$

(recall that our probability space is defined by the 2^m possible values of b). This event holds if and only if the formula $\Phi(b)\big|_{\rho_v}$ is satisfiable. For $I \subset [m], R \subset [n], \vec{\epsilon} \in \{0,1\}^I, \rho \in \{0,1\}^R$ we want to estimate the conditional probability

$$\Pr\left[E | I_v = I, \ R_v = R, \ b_{I_v} = \vec{\epsilon}, \ \rho_v = \rho \right]. \tag{5}$$

If we show that this conditional probability is small (irrespective of the choice of I, R, $\vec{\epsilon}$, and ρ), it will follow that the probability of E is small.

We use the following lemma (and delay its proof for a moment).

LEMMA 11. *Assume that an $m \times n$ matrix A is an $(r, 3, c')$-expander, $X = \{x_1, \ldots, x_n\}$ is a set of variables, $\hat{X} \subseteq X$, $|\hat{X}| < r, b \in \{0,1\}^m$, and $\mathcal{L} = \{\ell_1, \ldots \ell_k\}$ (where $k < r$) is a tuple of linear equations from the system $Ax = b$. Denote by L the set of assignments to the variables in $\hat{X}$ that can be extended to X to satisfy $\mathcal{L}$. If L is not empty, then it is an affine subspace of $\{0,1\}^{\hat{X}}$ of dimension greater than $|\hat{X}| \cdot \left(\frac{1}{2} - \frac{14-7c'}{2(2c'-3)} \right)$.*

Choose $\mathcal{L} = \{A_i x = \epsilon_i\}_{i \in I}$, $X = \text{Vars}(\mathcal{L})$, $\hat{X} = R$, $|\hat{X}| = \lfloor cr/(6K) \rfloor$. Recall that $c' = 25/13$. Then Lemma 11 says that $\dim L > \frac{2}{11}|R|$, where L is the set of locally consistent assignments to the variables in R. Let

$$(\hat{b})_i = \begin{cases} \epsilon_i, & i \in I, \\ b_i, & \text{otherwise.} \end{cases}$$

Note that $\hat{b}$ has the distribution of b when we fix $I_v = I$ and $b_I = \vec{\epsilon}$. The vector $\hat{b}$ is independent from the event $E_1 = [I_v = I \wedge R_v = R \wedge b_{I_v} = \vec{\epsilon} \wedge \rho_v = \rho]$. This is because in order to determine whether E_1 holds, it is sufficient to observe the bits b_I only. Clearly, $(A^{-1}\hat{b})_R$ is distributed uniformly on L (note that A is a bijection). Thus

$$\Pr\left[E | I_v = I, \ R_v = R, \ b_{I_v} = \vec{\epsilon}, \ \rho_v = \rho \right]$$

$$= \Pr\left[(A^{-1}\hat{b})_R = \rho | I_v = I, R_v = R, b_{I_v} = \vec{\epsilon}, \rho_v = \rho \right]$$

$$= \Pr\left[(A^{-1}\hat{b})_R = \rho \right]$$

$$\leq 2^{-\dim L} < 2^{-\frac{2}{11}|R|} \leq 2^{-\frac{cr}{1000 K}}.$$

If E does not happen, however, then by Lemma 10 it takes time $2^{\Omega(r)}$ for $\mathcal{A}$ to refute the resulting unsatisfiable system (note that by Proposition 2 the assignment ρ_v is locally consistent).

Proof of Lemma 11. First we repeatedly eliminate variables and equations from $\mathcal{L}$ until we get rid of

- equations containing boundary variables not from $\hat{X}$; and
- equations containing more than one boundary variable.

We do so by repeating the following two procedures (in any order) as long as at least one of them is applicable.   □

PROCEDURE 1. *If $\mathcal{L}$ contains an equation ℓ with boundary element $j \in \partial\mathcal{L}$ s.t. $x_j \notin \hat{X}$, then remove ℓ from $\mathcal{L}$.*

Note that Procedure 1 does not change L and $\hat{X}$. Therefore, if the claim of our lemma holds for the new system and new $\hat{X}$, it holds for the original one as well.

PROCEDURE 2. *If $\mathcal{L}$ contains an equation ℓ with at least two boundary elements j_1, j_2 s.t. $x_{j_1}, x_{j_2} \in \hat{X}$, then remove ℓ from $\mathcal{L}$ and all these (two or three) boundary elements from $\hat{X}$.*

This procedure decreases $|\hat{X}|$ by 2 (or by 3) and decreases dim L by 1 (resp., by 2). Therefore, if the claim of our lemma holds for the new system and new $\hat{X}$, it holds for the original one as well.

Thus, it is enough to prove the claim of our lemma for the case where none of the procedures above is applicable to $\mathcal{L}$. Then $\partial\mathcal{L}$ is covered by $\hat{X}$; in particular,

$$k(2c' - 3) \le |\partial\mathcal{L}| \le |\hat{X}|,$$

which implies

$$k \le \frac{|\hat{X}|}{2c' - 3}. \tag{6}$$

(Note that we have used Lemma 1 here.) Denote by $\mathcal{L}' \subseteq \mathcal{L}$ the subset of equations that contain at least one variable from $\hat{X}$. Since none of them contains two boundary variables and there are at least $k(2c'-3)$ such boundary variables,

$$|\mathcal{L}'| \ge k(2c' - 3).$$

Let $\bar{\mathcal{L}} = \mathcal{L}\backslash\mathcal{L}'$. We have

$$|\bar{\mathcal{L}}| \le k(1 - (2c' - 3)) = k(4 - 2c').$$

Finally, since A is an $(r, 3, c')$-expander, $|\text{Vars}(\mathcal{L})| \ge c'k$. On the other hand, $|\text{Vars}(\bar{\mathcal{L}})| \le 3|\bar{\mathcal{L}}| \le k(12 - 6c')$. Thus, the number of variables in $\mathcal{L}'$ is at least $k(c' - (12 - 6c')) = k(7c' - 12)$.

We now apply Gaussian elimination to the set $\mathcal{L}'$. Namely, we subsequently consider variables $y \in \text{Vars}(\mathcal{L}')\backslash\hat{X}$ and make substitutions $y = \ldots$ with the corresponding linear forms. Clearly, during this process every equation in (the modified) $\mathcal{L}'$ still contains at most two variables not from $\hat{X}$. Also, each substitution decreases the number of variables in $\mathrm{Vars}(\mathcal{L}')\backslash\hat{X}$ at most by two. Thus the Gaussian elimination has to make at least $(k(7c'-12)-|\hat{X}|)/2$ substitutions before all variables in $\mathrm{Vars}(\mathcal{L}')\backslash\hat{X}$ are eliminated.

After this, the values of variables in $\hat{X}$ are determined by the remaining system that contains at most

$$k - \frac{k(7c'-12)-|\hat{X}|}{2} = \frac{14k - 7kc' + |\hat{X}|}{2}$$

linear equations (containing only variables in $\hat{X}$); hence, the dimension of L is lower bounded by

$$|\hat{X}| - \frac{14k - 7kc' + |\hat{X}|}{2} \geq |\hat{X}|\left(\frac{1}{2} - \frac{14 - 7c'}{2(2c'-3)}\right)$$

(here we used (6)).

4. An Exponential Lower Bound for Drunk Algorithms

In this section, we prove an exponential lower bound on the running time of drunk algorithms (described in Section 2.1) on satisfiable formulas. The proof strategy is as follows. We take a known hard unsatisfiable formula G and construct a new satisfiable formula that turns into G if the algorithm chooses a wrong value for some variable. Since for several tries the algorithms errs at least once with high probability, the recursive procedure is likely to be called on G and hence will take an exponential time.

In what follows, we give the construction of our hard satisfiable formulas (citing the construction of hard unsatisfiable formulas), then prove two (almost trivial) formal statements for the behavior of DPLL algorithms on hard unsatisfiable formulas, and finally prove the main result of this section.

Since the size of recursion tree for an unsatisfiable formula does not depend on the random choices of a drunk algorithm, we can assume that our algorithm has the smallest possible recursion tree for every unsatisfiable formula. We call such an algorithm an 'optimal' drunk algorithm.

4.1. HARD SATISFIABLE FORMULAS BASED ON HARD UNSATISFIABLE FORMULAS

Our formulas are constructed from known hard unsatisfiable formulas. For example, we can take hard unsatisfiable formulas from [14].

THEOREM 3 ([14], Theorem 1). *For each $k \geq 3$ there exist a positive constant $c_k = O(k^{-1/8})$, a function $f(x) = \Omega(2^{x(1-c_k)})$, and a sequence of unsatisfiable formulas G_n in k-CNF (for each l, G_l uses exactly l variables) such that all treelike resolution proofs of G_n have size at least $f(n)$.*

COROLLARY 2. *The recursion tree of the execution of a drunk DPLL algorithm on the formula G_n from Theorem 3 (irrespective of the random choices made by the algorithm) has at least $f(n)$ nodes.*

Proof. It is well known that treelike resolution proofs and DPLL trees are equivalent. Note that the subsumption rule cannot reduce the size of a DPLL tree.   □

Remark 3. We do not use other facts about these formulas; therefore, our construction works for any sequence of formulas satisfying a similar statement.

DEFINITION 6. Let us fix n. We call an unsatisfiable formula F (we do not assume that F contains n variables) hard if the recursion tree of the execution of (every) 'optimal' drunk algorithm on F has at least $f'(n) = (f(n) - 1)/2$ nodes, where f is the function appearing in Theorem 3.

DEFINITION 7. We consider formulas of the form⋆ $H_n = G^{(1)} \wedge G^{(2)} \wedge \ldots \wedge G^{(n)}$, where $G^{(i)}$ is the formula in CNF of n variables⋆⋆ $x_1^{(i)}, \ldots, x_n^{(i)}$ (for all $i \neq j$, the sets of variables of the formulas $G^{(i)}$ and $G^{(j)}$ are disjoint) defined as follows. Take a copy of the hard formula from Theorem 3; call its variables $x_j^{(i)}$ and the formula $\widetilde{G}^{(i)}$. Then change the signs of some literals in $\widetilde{G}^{(i)}$ (this is done by replacing all occurrences of a positive literal l with $\neg l$ and, simultaneously, of the negative literal $\neg l$ with l) so that the recursion tree of the execution of (every) 'optimal' drunk algorithm on $\widetilde{G}^{(i)}[x_j^{(i)}]$ is not smaller than that on $\widetilde{G}^{(i)}[x_j^{(i)}]$ (hence, $\widetilde{G}^{(i)}[\neg x_j^{(i)}]$ is hard). Use the (modified) formula $\widetilde{G}^{(i)}$ to construct the formula† $(\widetilde{G}^{(i)} \vee x_1^{(i)}) \wedge (\widetilde{G}^{(i)} \vee x_2^{(i)}) \wedge \ldots \wedge (\widetilde{G}^{(i)} \vee x_n^{(i)})$ and simplify it using the simplification rules; the obtained formula is $G^{(i)}$.

Remark 4. We change signs of literals only to simplify the proof of our result; one can think that the algorithm is actually given the input formula without the change.

Remark 5. Clearly, H_n has size polynomial in n (and hence in the number of variables).

⋆ Note that the subscript in H_n does *not* denote the number of variables.

⋆⋆ It is possible that some of these variables do not appear in the formula; therefore, formally, a formula is a pair: a formula and the number of its variables.

† We use $G \vee x$ to denote a formula in CNF: x is added to each clause of G, and the clauses containing $\neg x$ are deleted.

4.2. BEHAVIOR OF DRUNK ALGORITHMS ON UNSATISFIABLE FORMULAS

LEMMA 12. *Let G be a hard formula. Let F be a formula having exactly one satisfying assigment. Let the sets of variables of F and G be disjoint. Then the formula $F \wedge G$ is hard.*

Proof. The statement is easy to see (note that hardness does not depend on the number of variables in the formula): a recursion tree for the formula $F \wedge G$ corresponds to a recursion tree for the formula G.   □

LEMMA 13. *The formula $G^{(i)}[\neg x_j^{(i)}]$ is hard.*

Proof. For each formula F by Simplify(F) we denote the result of applying the simplification rules to F (the rules are applied as long as at least one of them is applicable). One can easily see that this formula is uniquely defined (note that our simplification rules commute with each other). By our definition of a DPLL algorithm, F is hard if and only if Simplify(F) is hard. Note that

Simplify $(G^{(i)}[\neg x_j^{(i)}]) =$
Simplify $((\widetilde{G}^{(i)}[\neg x_j^{(i)}] \vee x_1^{(i)}) \wedge \ldots \wedge (\widetilde{G}^{(i)}[x_j^{(i)}]) \wedge \ldots \wedge (\widetilde{G}^{(i)}[\neg x_j^{(i)}] \vee x_n^{(i)})) =$
Simplify $(\widetilde{G}^{(i)}[\neg x_j^{(i)}]).$

(The last equality is obtained by applying the subsumption rule.) The formula Simplify $(\widetilde{G}^{(i)}[\neg x_j^{(i)}])$ is hard because $(\widetilde{G}^{(i)}[\neg x_j^{(i)}])$ is hard.   □

4.3. BEHAVIOR OF DRUNK ALGORITHMS ON SATISFIABLE FORMULAS

THEOREM 4. *The size of the recursion tree of the execution of a drunk DPLL algorithm on input H_n is less than $f'(n)$ with probability at most 2^{-n}.*

Proof. The unique satisfying assignment to H_n is $x_j^{(i)} = 1$. Note that $H_n[\neg x_j^{(i)}]$ contains an unsatisfiable subformula $G^{(i)}[\neg x_j^{(i)}]$.   □

Consider the splitting tree of our algorithm on input H_n. It has exactly one leaf corresponding to the satisfying assignment. We call node w on the path corresponding to the satisfying assignment *critical* if Heuristic A chooses a variable $x_m^{(i)}$ for this node and this is the first time a variable from the subformula $G^{(i)}$ is chosen along this path. A *critical subtree* is the subtree corresponding to the unsatisfiable formula resulting from substituting a 'wrong' value in a critical node.

By Lemmas 12 and 13 the size of a critical subtree is at least $f'(n)$ (note that the definition of a critical node implies that the corresponding subformula $G^{(i)}$ is untouched in it and hence its child contains a hard subformula $G^{(i)}[\neg x_j^{(i)}]$; it is clear that the simplification rules could not touch $G^{(i)}$ before the first assignment to its variables).

The probability of choosing the value $x_j^{(i)} = 0$ equals $\frac{1}{2}$. There are n critical nodes on the path leading to the satisfying assignment; therefore the probability that the algorithm does not go into any critical subtree equals 2^{-n}. Note that if it ever goes into a critical subtree, it has to examine all its nodes, and there are at least $f'(n)$ of them.

COROLLARY 3. *For each $k \geq 3$ there exist a positive constant $c_k = O(k^{-1/8})$, a function $g(x) = \Omega(2^{x(1-c_k)})$, and a sequence of unsatisfiable formulas H_n in $(k + 1)-CNF$ (H_n uses m variables, where $n \leq m \leq n^2$) such that the size of recursion tree of the execution of any drunk DPLL algorithm on input H_n is less than $g(n)$ with probability at most 2^{-n}.*

5. Recent Developments and Remaining Open Questions

Since the publication of the preliminary version of this paper, our results were developed and generalized in [6] (see the section on Satisfiability). First, [6] constructed a sequence of full rank matrices that are $(\epsilon n, 3, \delta)$-expanders for some constant ϵ, δ. With our Theorem 2 this implies that no generalized myopic DPLL algorithm may find a solution for a satisfiable formula in 3-CNF in time $2^{\Omega(n)}$ in the worst case (as opposed to our $2^{n/\log^{O(1)} n}$ bound).

Unfortunately, this newer bound as well as the bound of Pudlák and Impagliazzo [14] for unsatisfiable formulas is still far from upper bounds for 3-SAT (the currently best one is $O(1.324^n)$ [12]). However, Pudlák and Impagliazzo prove that for unsatisfiable k-CNF formulas the lower bound converges to $\Omega(2^n)$ as k goes to the infinity. Does the corresponding result hold for satisfiable formulas, for example, if we replace $(r, 3, \delta)$-expanders by (r, k, δ)-expanders?

Second, [6] generalized our DPLL lower bounds for a wide class of algorithms called BT (which stands for 'backtracking'). The latter model for solving satisfiability combines the greedy methods with backtracking, it is similar to DPLL-style algorithms, although formally, two models are incomparable.

The 'difficult' formulas used in our proof in Section 3 encode a linear system over $\mathbb{GF}_2$ and thus are solvable in polynomial time by Gaussian elimination procedure. Therefore, it may be interesting to prove an exponential lower-bound analogous result for some difficult formulas, for example, random formulas generated near the 3-SAT phase transition or w.r.t. even more complicated distributions (like hgen2; see [15]) that are empirically hard for contemporary SAT solvers.

Various generalizations of the notions of myopic and drunk algorithms would guide natural extensions of our results. Note, however, that merging the notions is not easy: if Heuristic A is not restricted, it can feed information to Heuristic B even if it is not enabled directly (for example, it can choose variables that are to be assigned one while they persist). Therefore, Heuristic B must have oracle access that would hide syntactical properties of the formula so that Heuristic B would not gain any other information from Heuristic A except for "branching on the variable v is nice." For example, the oracle must randomly rename variables, (consistently) negate some of them, and change the order of clauses. It is also interesting to consider models that would cover heuristics that apply to recursion tree as a whole rather than to one branch (for example, learning).

Acknowledgement

We are grateful to Eli Ben-Sasson for helpful discussions and to anonymous referees for numerous comments that improved the quality of this paper.

References

1. Achlioptas, D., Beame, P. and Molloy, M.: A sharp threshold in proof complexity, *J. Comput. Syst. Sci.* (2003).
2. Achlioptas, D., Beame, P. and Molloy, M.: Exponential bounds for DPLL below the satisfiability threshold, in *Proceedings of the Fifteenth Annual ACM-SIAM Symposium on Discrete Algorithms, SODA'04*, 2004, pp. 139–140.
3. Achlioptas, D. and Sorkin, G. B.: Optimal myopic algorithms for random 3-SAT, in *Proceedings of the 41st Annual IEEE Symposium on Foundations of Computer Science, FOCS'00*, 2000.
4. Alekhnovich, M. and Ben-Sasson, E.: Analysis of the random walk algorithm on random 3-CNFs, Manuscript, 2002.
5. Alekhnovich, M., Ben-Sasson, E., Razborov, A. and Wigderson, A.: Pseudorandom generators in propositional complexity, in *Proceedings of the 41st Annual IEEE Symposium on Foundations of Computer Science, FOCS'00*, Journal version is to appear in *SIAM Journal on Computing*, 2000.
6. Alekhnovich, M., Borodin, A., Buresh-Oppenheim, J., Impagliazzo, R., Magen, A. and Pitassi, T.: Toward a model for backtracking and dynamic programming, in *Proceedings of the 20th Annual Conference on Computational Complexity*, 2005, pp. 308–322.
7. Alekhnovich, M. and Razborov, A.: Lower bounds for the polynomial calculus: Non-binomial case, in *Proceedings of the 42nd Annual IEEE Symposium on Foundations of Computer Science*, 2001.
8. Ben-Sasson, E. and Wigderson, A.: Short proofs are narrow – resolution made simple, *J. ACM* **48**(2) (2001), 149–169.
9. Davis, M., Logemann, G. and Loveland, D.: A machine program for theorem-proving, *Commun. ACM* **5** (1962), 394–397.
10. Davis, M. and Putnam, H.: A computing procedure for quantification theory, *J. ACM* **7** (1960), 201–215.
11. Hirsch, E. A.: SAT local search algorithms: Worst-case study, *J. Autom. Reason.* **24**(1/2) (2000), 127–143. Also reprinted in "Highlights of Satisfiability Research in the Year 2000", Volume 63 in Frontiers in Artificial Intelligence and Applications, IOS.
12. Iwama, K. and Tamaki, S.: Improved upper bounds for 3-SAT, in *Proceedings of the Fifteenth Annual ACM–SIAM Symposium on Discrete Algorithms, SODA'04*, 2004, pp. 328–328.

13. Nikolenko, S. I.: Hard satisfiable formulas for DPLL-type algorithms, *Zap. Nauc. Semin. POMI* **293** (2002), 139–148. English translation is to appear in Journal of Mathematical Sciences: Consultants Bureau, N.Y., March 2005, Vol. 126, No. 3, pp. 1205–1209.
14. Pudlák, P. and Impagliazzo, R.: A lower bound for DLL algorithms for k-SAT, in *Proceedings of the 11th Annual ACM–SIAM Symposium on Discrete Algorithms, SODA'00*, 2000.
15. Simon, L., Le Berre, D. and Hirsch, E. A.: The SAT 2002 Competition, *Ann. Math. Artif. Intell.* **43** (2005), 307–342.
16. Tseitin, G. S.: On the complexity of derivation in the propositional calculus, *Zap. Nauc. Semin. LOMI* **8** (1968), 234–259. English translation of this volume: Consultants Bureau, N.Y., 1970, pp. 115–125.

Journal of Automated Reasoning (2005) 35: 73–88
DOI: 10.1007/s10817-005-9007-9

© Springer 2006

Backdoor Sets for DLL Subsolvers

STEFAN SZEIDER
Department of Computer Science, Durham University, DH1 3LE, Durham, England, UK.
e-mail: stefan.szeider@durham.ac.uk

Abstract. We study the parameterized complexity of detecting small *backdoor sets* for instances of
the propositional satisfiability problem (SAT). The notion of backdoor sets has been recently
introduced by Williams, Gomes, and Selman for explaining the 'heavy-tailed' behavior of backtracking algorithms. If a small backdoor set is found, then the instance can be solved efficiently by
the propagation and simplification mechanisms of a SAT solver. Empirical studies indicate that
structured SAT instances coming from practical applications have small backdoor sets. We study
the worst-case complexity of detecting backdoor sets with respect to the simplification and
propagation mechanisms of the classic Davis–Logemann–Loveland (DLL) procedure. We show
that the detection of backdoor sets of size bounded by a fixed integer k is of high parameterized
complexity. In particular, we determine that this detection problem (and some of its variants) is
complete for the parameterized complexity class W[P]. We achieve this result by means of a
generalization of a reduction due to Abrahamson, Downey, and Fellows.

Key words: satisfiability, unit propagation, pure literal elimination, backdoor sets, parameterized
complexity, W[P]-completeness.

1. Introduction

The propositional satisfiability problem (SAT) is the first problem shown to be NP-
complete. It holds a central role in the theory of computational complexity and is of
practical relevance for applied areas such as verification or planning. SAT instances with n variables can be solved by brute force, checking all 2^n truth
assignments; no algorithm is known that runs in time $2^{o(n)}$ in the worst case.
However, SAT instances arising from applications often impose a 'hidden structure' that allows significantly faster SAT decision than by brute force search.

One example of such a hidden structure is based on the concept of
backdoor sets of variables, recently introduced by Williams, Gomes, and Selman
[11, 12]. A *weak backdoor set* of a SAT instance is a set B of variables such that
for at least one truth assignment to the variables in B, simplifying the instance
according to that assignment yields a satisfiable instance that can be decided in
polynomial time by a 'subsolver.' A subsolver is an incomplete polynomial-time
algorithm that uses the propagation and simplification mechanisms of a SAT-

solver. A *strong backdoor set* of a SAT instance is a set B of variables such that for *every* truth assignment to the variables in B, the resulting simplified SAT instance can be decided by the subsolver (exact definitions are given in Sections 3 and 4 below). As reported by Williams, Gomes, and Selman [12], highly structured problem instances have small weak backdoor sets; for example, for a logistics planning benchmark instance with about 7,000 variables, a weak backdoor set of size 12 could be found. However, the minimum size of backdoor sets of nonstructured instances, such as random 3-SAT, appears to be a constant fraction (about 30%) of the total number of variables (Interian [7]). The dependency among the variables of minimal weak backdoor set is studied by Ruan, Kautz, and Horvitz [10]. It is observed that SAT-solvers may heuristically be quite capable of exploiting the existence of small weak backdoor sets in practice, without necessarily identifying the backdoor sets explicitly [10, 12].

In the sequel we address the worst-case time complexity of deciding whether a given SAT instance has a weak or strong backdoor set of size bounded by some integer k. We study this problem with respect to subsolvers of the standard Davis–Logemann–Loveland (DLL) algorithm, that is, subsolvers that are based on *unit propagation* and *pure literal elimination*, or on one of these two principles.

We can detect a weak/strong backdoor set of size at most k by considering all sets B of k or fewer variables of the given instance and by checking whether one or all of the $2^{|B|}$ assignments to the variables in B yield an instance that can be decided by the subsolver under consideration. Thus a backdoor set can be detected in time $O(2^k n^{k+\alpha})$, where $O(n^\alpha)$ is the worst-case time complexity of the subsolver. However, such a trivial approach becomes impractical for large n even if the parameter k, the maximum size of a backdoor set, is chosen small. In this paper we tackle the question of whether, in general, a small backdoor set can be found significantly faster than by brute force search.

The framework of parameterized complexity (Downey and Fellows [5]) provides an excellent framework for studying this question. A parameterized problem is a set $L \subseteq \Sigma^* \times \Sigma^*$ for some fixed alphabet Σ. For a problem instance $(x, k) \in L$, we refer to x as the main part, and to k as the parameter. Typically (and for all problems considered in the sequel), the parameter is a positive integer (presented in unary). XP denotes the class of parameterized problems that can be solved in polynomial time whenever the parameter is considered as a constant; the above considerations show that the detection of a backdoor set is in XP. If a parameterized problem L can be solved in time $O(f(k)n^c)$, where f is any computable function of the parameter and c is a constant (independent from k), then L is called *fixed-parameter tractable*; FPT denotes the class of all fixed-parameter tractable problems. Parameterized complexity classes are defined as equivalence classes of parameterized problems under a certain parameterized reduction. This parameterized reduction is an extension of the polynomial-time many–one reduction where a parameter for one problem maps into a parameter for another. More specifically, a parameterized problem L reduces to a parameterized problem L' if we can transform an instance (x, k) of L into an instance $(x', g(k))$ of L' in time $f(k) \cdot |x|^{O(1)}$ (f, g are arbitrary computable functions), such that (x, k) is a yes-instance of L if and only if $(x', g(k))$ is a yes-instance of L'. The class XP contains a hierarchy of parameterized complexity classes

$$\text{FPT} \subseteq \text{W}[1] \subseteq \text{W}[2] \subseteq \ldots \subseteq \text{W}[P] \subseteq \text{XP}.$$

All inclusions are assumed to be proper; FPT $\neq$ XP is known [5]. The higher a problem is located in this hierarchy, the more unlikely it is fixed-parameter tractable. The canonical W[P]-complete problem is the following (cf. [5]).

WEIGHTED CIRCUIT SATISFIABILITY
Input: A decision circuit D.
Parameter: A positive integer k.
Question: Does D accept an input assignment of weight k?

If a W[P]-complete problem turns out to be fixed-parameter tractable, then the n-variable SAT problem can be solved in time $2^{o(n)}$ (Abrahamson, Downey, and Fellows [1]); a recent treatment of the relationship between parameterized complexity classes and SAT upper bounds can be found in Flum and Grohe [6]. The parameterized problem WEIGHTED MONOTONE CIRCUIT SATISFIABILITY arises from WEIGHTED CIRCUIT SATISFIABILITY by restricting the instances to *monotone* circuits. Surprisingly, WEIGHTED MONOTONE CIRCUIT SATISFIABILITY remains W[P]-hard [1, 5]. Furthermore, the problems remain W[P]-complete if we ask for an accepted input assignment of weight *at most k* (see Section 2).

In this paper we completely classify the parameterized complexity of the problem of whether a SAT instance has a weak or strong backdoor set of size not exceeding a parameter k w.r.t. subsolvers that arise from the DLL procedure. In particular, we determine that detection of weak and strong backdoor sets is W[P]-complete for the considered subsolvers. Thus we provide strong theoretical evidence that these problems are not fixed-parameter tractable. We generalize the proof technique used by Abrahamson, Downey, and Fellows [1] for k-INDUCED SATISFIABILITY and other problems by introducing a certain parameterized problem on *cyclic monotone circuits* (see, e.g., Malik [8]). We show that this new problem, CYCLIC MONOTONE CIRCUIT ACTIVATION, is W[P]-complete. Parameterized reductions of this problem provide the base for our W[P]-hardness results. We think that CYCLIC MONOTONE CIRCUIT ACTIVATION is interesting on its own as its W[P]-hardness proof is conceptually simple, and it provides a means for several other W[P]-hardness proofs.

2. Notation and Preliminaries

We assume an infinite supply of propositional *variables*. A *literal* is a variable x with an assigned parity $\varepsilon \in \{0, 1\}$ and is denoted by x^ε. We also write $x = x^1$ and

$\bar{x} = x^0$. A set S of literals is *tautological* if it contains both x and $\bar{x}$ for some variable x. A *clause* is a finite nontautological set of literals. We consider a finite set of clauses as a *CNF formula* (or *formula*, for short). Clauses of size one are called *unit clauses*. The set of variables occurring (negated or unnegated) in a formula F is denoted by var(F). A literal x^ε is a *pure literal* of a formula F if $x \in$ var(F) and no clause of F contains $x^{1-\varepsilon}$.

A *truth assignment* (or *assignment*, for short) is a map $\tau : X_\tau \rightarrow \{0, 1\}$ defined on some set X_τ of variables. If X_τ is a singleton $\{x\}$ with $\tau(x) = \varepsilon$, then we denote τ simply by $x = \varepsilon$. An assignment τ is *total* for a formula F if $X_\tau =$ var(F). For $x \in X_\tau$ we define $\tau(\bar{x}) = 1 - \tau(x)$. For an assignment τ and a formula F, $F[\tau]$ denotes the formula obtained from F by removing all clauses that contain a literal x with $\tau(x) = 1$ and removing literals y with $\tau(y) = 0$ from the remaining clauses. An assignment τ *satisfies* a formula F if $F[\tau] = \emptyset$. A formula is *satisfiable* if it is satisfied by some assignment; otherwise it is *unsatisfiable*. Let F be a formula and $(x, \varepsilon) \in$ var(F) $\times \{0, 1\}$. If F contains the unit clause $\{x^\varepsilon\}$ (or x^ε is a pure literal of F), then we say that the assignment $x = \varepsilon$ can be inferred (in one step) by *unit propagation* (or *pure literal elimination*, respectively). If both $x = 0$ and $x = 1$ can be inferred, then F is unsatisfiable (F contains both $\{x\}$ and $\{\bar{x}\}$).

A *decision circuit* (or *circuit*, for short) D is a triple (G, E, λ), where (G, E) is an acyclic digraph (the *underlying digraph* of D) and λ is a mapping from G to $\{$AND, OR, NOT$\}$. The elements of G are the *gates* and the elements of E are the *lines* of D. A gate $g \in G$ is called $\lambda(g)$-gate. D is *monotone* if it contains no NOT-gates. The *fanin* (*fanout*) of a gate $g \in G$ is its in-degree (out-degree) in the underlying digraph. We assume that NOT-gates have fanin 1 and that AND/OR-gates have fanin at least one. Gates with fanin 2 are *binary* gates. If E contains the line (g, h), then we say that g is a *predecessor* of h and that h is a *successor* of g. Gates with fanin 0 are the *input gates* of the circuit and gates with fanout 0 are the *output gates* of the circuit. We assume that every circuit has exactly one output gate. If the underlying digraph of a circuit D is a tree, then D can be identified with a Boolean formula. An *input assignment* ν for a circuit D is a mapping from the set of input gates of D to $\{0, 1\}$. An *input assignment* ν propagates through the circuit in the natural way; for example, for an AND-gate g with predecessors $g_1, \ldots, g_n$, we have $\nu(g) = \min_{i=1}^{n} \nu(g_i)$. A circuit D *accepts* an input assignment ν if $\nu(u) = 1$ holds for the output gate u of D. The *weight* of an input assignment is the number of input gates that are assigned to 1.

Note that a monotone circuit with n input gates accepts an input assignment of weight at most k for some $k \leq n$ if and only if it accepts an input assignment of weight exactly k. If D is nonmonotone, then we can still obtain in polynomial time a circuit D' with nk input gates such that D accepts an input assignment of weight at most k if and only if D' accepts an input assignment of weight exactly k (D' can be obtained from D by adding an OR-gate of fanin k in front of each input gate). Furthermore, by means of a standard construction, we can transform a circuit D into a circuit D_2 (D_2 has the same input gates as D) by replacing gates of fanin greater than 2 by several binary gates. The construction of D_2 from D can be carried out in polynomial time, and both circuits accept the same input assignments.

3. Subsolvers

The Davis–Putnam (DP) procedure [4] and the related Davis–Logemann–Loveland (DLL) procedure [3] are certainly the best known complete algorithms for solving the satisfiability problem. Complete state-of-the-art SAT-solvers are typically based on variants of the DLL procedure. A concise description of these procedures can be found in Cook and Mitchell [2]. Both procedures, DP and DLL, search for a satisfying assignment, applying first *unit propagation* and *pure literal elimination* as often as possible. Then, DLL makes a case distinction on the truth value of a variable, and DP eliminates a variable x by replacing the clauses in which x occurs by all the clauses that can be obtained by resolving on x. The DLL procedure is sketched in Figure 1.

If we use only unit propagation and pure literal elimination, then we get an incomplete algorithm that decides satisfiability for a subclass of CNF formulas. (Whenever the algorithm reaches the branching step, it halts and outputs 'give up.') This incomplete algorithm is an example of a 'subsolver' as considered by Williams et al. [11]; a polynomial-time algorithm S is called a *subsolver* if it either correctly decides satisfiability of the given formula F or it gives up. Moreover, it is required that if the subsolver S decides that F is satisfiable, it also returns

---

Procedure DLL(F)

Input: A CNF formula F.

Output: Either a truth assignment which satisfies F or "unsatisfiable".

1. *Trivial Decision:* If $F = \emptyset$, then return the empty satisfying assignment; if F contains the empty clause, then return "unsatisfiable."

2. *Unit Propagation:* If F contains a unit clause $\{x^\varepsilon\}$, then call DLL($F[x = \varepsilon]$). If a satisfying assignment τ for $F[x = \varepsilon]$ is returned, then return $\tau \cup \{x = \varepsilon\}$; otherwise return "unsatisfiable."

3. *Pure Literal Elimination:* If F contains a pure literal x^ε, then call DLL($F[x = \varepsilon]$). If a satisfying assignment τ for $F[x = \varepsilon]$ is returned, then return $\tau \cup \{x = \varepsilon\}$; otherwise return "unsatisfiable."

4. *Branching:* Choose a variable $x \in var(F)$.

   a) Call DLL($F[x = 0]$). If a satisfying assignment τ for $F[x = 0]$ is returned, then return $\tau \cup \{x = 0\}$.

   b) Otherwise, call DLL($F[x = 1]$). If a satisfying assignment τ for $F[x = 1]$ is returned, then return $\tau \cup \{x = 1\}$.

   c) Otherwise return "unsatisfiable."

Figure 1. The Davis–Logemann–Loveland (DLL) procedure.

a satisfying assignment and that S satisfies the following basic conditions: first, that it decides the empty formula as being satisfiable and a formula containing the empty clause as being unsatisfiable, and second, that if it decides the satisfiability of a formula F, then it does so for $F[x = \varepsilon]$ for any $(x, \varepsilon) \in \mathrm{var}(F) \times \{0, 1\}$.

The DLL procedure gives rise to three nontrivial subsolvers: UP + PL (unit propagation and pure literal elimination are available), and UP (only unit propagation is available), PL (only pure literal elimination is available).

4. Backdoor Sets

The power of a subsolver can be enhanced by taking an assignment τ to a few variables of the given formula F and inputting $F[\tau]$ to the subsolver. This idea leads to the concept of backdoor sets (cf. [11, 12]).

A set B of variables is a *weak backdoor set* of a formula F w.r.t. a subsolver S if $B \subseteq \mathrm{var}(F)$ and there exists an assignment $\tau : B \to \{0, 1\}$ such that S returns a satisfying assignment for the input $F[\tau]$; we also say that B is a *weak S-backdoor set*. The set B is a *strong backdoor* set of F w.r.t. S if $B \subseteq \mathrm{var}(F)$ and for every assignment $\tau : B \to \{0, 1\}$, the subsolver S decides whether $F[\tau]$ is satisfiable; we also say that B is a *strong S-backdoor set*.

Similarly one can define backdoor sets with respect to a class C of formulas where membership in C and satisfiability of formulas in C can be decided in polynomial time.

Note that by definition, unsatisfiable formulas do not have weak backdoor sets and that $B = \mathrm{var}(F)$ is always a weak backdoor set of any satisfiable formula F. Moreover, if F is satisfiable, then every strong backdoor set of F is also a weak backdoor set of F w.r.t. any subsolver S, but the converse does not hold in general.

For a subsolver S we consider the following two parameterized problems.

WEAK S-BACKDOOR
Input: A formula F.
Parameter: A positive integer k.
Question: Does F have a weak S-backdoor set B of size at most k?

STRONG S-BACKDOOR
Input: A formula F.
Parameter: A positive integer k.
Question: Does F have a strong S-backdoor set B of size at most k?

In the next section we formulate an intermediate problem on cyclic monotone circuits that will allow us to determine the complexity of backdoor set detection for the nontrivial subsolvers UP + PL, UP, and PL.

5. Cyclic Monotone Circuits

A *cyclic monotone circuit* is a monotone circuit whose underlying digraph may contain directed cycles. Cyclic circuits have been considered by several authors; see, for example, Malik [8] for references. We assume that a cyclic monotone circuit may have no input or output gates.

Consider a set A of gates of a cyclic monotone circuit D (we think of the gates in A to be *activated*). The *successor set* $s(A)$ of A contains all gates g of D for which at least one of the following holds:

 − $g \in A$;
 − g is an AND-gate and all predecessors of g are in A;
 − g is an OR-gate and at least one predecessor of g is in A.

If we take iteratively successor sets of A (i.e., we compute a sequence of sets $A^0 \subseteq A^1 \subseteq A^2 \subseteq \ldots$ with $A^0 = A$ and $A^{i+1} = s(A^i)$), then we end up with a set A^* such that $s(A^*) = A^*$. We call A^* the *closure* of the starting set A. Since $A^i \subseteq s(A^i)$ holds always by monotonicity, the closure of A for a cyclic monotone circuit D with n gates is obtained after at most n iterations. We say that A *activates* D if the closure A^* contains all gates of D.

Consider, for example, the cyclic monotone circuit exhibited in Figure 2. The set $\{g_1\}$ activates the circuit, since we have $s(s(\{g_1\})) = s(\{g_1, g_2\}) = \{g_1, g_2, g_3\}$. However, the set $\{g_2\}$ does not activate the circuit, since $s(\{g_2\}) = \{g_2\} = \{g_2\}^* \neq \{g_1, g_2, g_3\}$.

We are interested in finding a small set of gates that activates a given cyclic monotone circuit. To this end, we define the following parameterized problem.

CYCLIC MONOTONE CIRCUIT ACTIVATION
Instance: A cyclic monotone circuit D.
Parameter: A positive integer k.
Question: Does some starting set A containing at most k gates activate D?

LEMMA 1. CYCLIC MONOTONE CIRCUIT ACTIVATION *is* W[P]-*complete. The problem remains* W[P]-*complete for instances without input or output gates.*

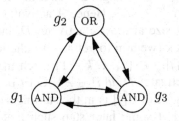

Figure 2. A cyclic monotone circuit.

Proof. We show membership in W[P] by reducing the problem to WEIGHTED CIRCUIT SATISFIABILITY. Given a cyclic monotone circuit D with n gates, we construct an acyclic monotone circuit C as follows. For every $\circ$-gate g of D, $\circ \in \{$AND, OR$\}$, with predecessors $g_1, \ldots, g_r$ and $0 \le t \le n$, we add a gate $g[t]$ to C as follows. For $t = 0$, the gate $g[0]$ is an input gate of C, and for $t > 0$, we put

$$g[t] = g[t-1] \vee \left(\bigcirc_{i=1}^{r} g_i[t-1] \right).$$

Finally, we add the output gate

$$u = \bigwedge_{g \in D} g[n].$$

It is straightforward to verify that C accepts a weight k input assignment if and only if some starting set of size k activates D. Hence CYCLIC MONOTONE CIRCUIT ACTIVATION is in W[P].

To show W[P]-hardness, we reduce from WEIGHTED MONOTONE CIRCUIT SATISFIABILITY, using ideas from Abrahamson, Downey, and Fellows [1]. Let C be a monotone circuit with n input gates $x_1, \ldots, x_n$ and the output gate u. We construct a cyclic monotone circuit D as follows. We take $k + 1$ copies of C, say $C[1], \ldots, C[k+1]$, and denote the copy of a gate g in $C[j]$ by $g[j]$. We add n identical AND-gates $h_1, \ldots, h_n$, each defined by

$$h_i = \bigwedge_{j=1}^{k+1} u[j].$$

We 'feed back' the gates h_i to the input gates of the circuits $C[1], \ldots, C[k+1]$, adding all the lines $(h_i, x_i[j])$ for $j = 1, \ldots, k+1$ and $i = 1, \ldots, n$. This concludes the construction of D. Observe that D has no input or output gates.

We show that C accepts an input assignment of weight at most k if and only if a starting set of size at most k activates D.

Assume that C accepts an input assignment ν of weight k. We take $A = \{h_i : 1 \le i \le n, \nu(x_i) = 1\}$ and put $A^0 = A$ and $A^i = s(A^{i-1})$ for $i > 0$. Let d be the length of a longest path in the underlying digraph of C from some input gate x_i to the output gate u (i.e., d is the 'depth' of C). Since C accepts ν, it follows that after $d + 1$ iterations all output gates $u[j]$ are activated, that is, $\{u[1], \ldots, u[k+1]\} \subseteq A^{d+1}$. Hence $\{h_1, \ldots, h_n\} \subseteq A^{d+2}$. In the next step *all* input gates of the circuits $C[i]$ are activated. After d more iterations, going through the circuits $C[i]$ a second time, finally all gates of D belong to $A^{2d+2} = A^*$. Hence A activates D.

Conversely, assume that a starting set A of size at most k activates D, but C accepts no input assignment of weight at most k (we aim to get a contradiction). Since $|A| \le k$, there must be at least one $C[j], j \in \{1, \ldots, k+1\}$, such that A does not contain any gate of $C[j]$. Since A activates D, $u[j] \in A^*$. Let t be the smallest integer such that $u[j] \in A^t$. Since no gate of $C[j]$ is in the starting set A, some of the input gates of $C[j]$ are activated at some later step such that the activation of the input gates propagates through $C[j]$ to $u[j]$. In other words, we have $X' \subseteq \{x_1[j], \ldots, x_n[j]\} \in A^s$ for some $s < t$ such that $C[j]$ accepts the input assignment ν' of $C[j]$ with $\nu'(x_i[j]) = 1$ if and only if $x_i[j] \in A^s$. By assumption, $|X'| > k$ follows. Consequently, $|\{h_1,\ldots,h_n\} \cap A^s| > k$. This is only possible if all $u[i]$, $1 \leq i \leq n$, are in A^{s-1}. In particular, $u[j] \in A^{s-1}$ and so $t \leq s - 1$, a contradiction to $s < t$. Hence C accepts some input assignment of weight at most k. This completes the proof of the lemma. $\qquad\qquad\square$

It is easy to verify that some starting set of size k activates a cyclic monotone circuit D if and only if some starting set of size k activates the corresponding circuit D_2 that contains only binary gates (see Section 2). Consequently, CYCLIC MONOTONE CIRCUIT ACTIVATION remains W[P]-hard for cyclic monotone circuits that contain only binary gates.

6. Backdoor Sets for Nontrivial Subsolvers;

LEMMA 2. WEAK S-BACKDOOR *is in* W[P] *for any* $S \in \{$UP + PL, UP, PL$\}$.

Proof. We reduce WEAK UP + PL-BACKDOOR to WEIGHTED CIRCUIT SATISFIABILITY. Let F be an instance of UP + PL-BACKDOOR with n variables. We construct an acyclic circuit C with $2n$ input gates that accepts a weight k input assignment if and only if F has a weak UP + PL-backdoor set of size k.

We describe C as consisting of $n + 1$ layers, $L_0,\ldots, L_n$. Each layer L_t has input gates $x^0[t]$ and $x^1[t]$ for every $x \in \mathrm{var}(F)$. We think of the values of $x^0[t]$ and $x^1[t]$ under some assignment ν as representing the value of the variable x under some assignment τ of F after t propagation steps. That is, $\nu(x^0[t]) = \nu(x^1[t]) = 0$ means that $\tau(x)$ is not defined at step t; $\nu(x^\varepsilon[t]) = 1$ means that $\tau(x) = \varepsilon$ at step t. The construction of C will guarantee that $\nu(x^0[t]) = \nu(x^1[t]) = 1$ cannot be the case for any input assignment ν accepted by C. The input gates of the first layer are the input gates of the whole circuit C. A layer L_t, $t < n$, contains gates that are connected to the input gates of the next layer L_{t+1}. The last layer L_n defines the output gate u of C. Next we describe the construction of C in detail.

For $x \in \mathrm{var}(F)$, $\varepsilon \in \{0, 1\}$, and $t \in \{0,\ldots, n-1\}$, we put

$$x^\varepsilon[t + 1] = x^\varepsilon[t] \vee \tag{1}$$

$$\left(\bigwedge_{C \in F \text{ with } x^{1-\varepsilon} \in C} \left(\bigvee_{y^\eta \in C} y^\eta[t] \right) \right) \vee \tag{2}$$

$$\left(\bigvee_{C \in F \text{ with } x^\varepsilon \in C} \left(\bigwedge_{y^\eta \in C \setminus \{x^\varepsilon\}} y^{1-\eta}[t] \right) \right). \tag{3}$$

The disjunctive term in (1) ensures that once an assignment to a variable is made it is not changed at a later step. The circuits defined in (2) express pure literal elimination: we set x^ε to 1 at step $t + 1$ if all clauses that contain the complementary literal $x^{1-\varepsilon}$ are satisfied at step t. The circuits defined in (3) express unit propagation: we set x^ε to 1 at step $t + 1$ if there is some clause in F containing x^ε and all other literals in the clause are set to 0 at step t. It remains to ensure that two input gates $x^\varepsilon[t]$ and $x^{1-\varepsilon}[t]$, representing complementary literals, are never both set to 1, and that finally, at step n, all clauses of F are satisfied. Hence we define the output gate u as

$$
u = \left(\bigwedge_{\substack{x \in \mathrm{var}(F) \\ 0 \le t \le n}} \neg\left(x^\varepsilon[t] \wedge x^{1-\varepsilon}[t]\right) \right) \wedge \bigwedge_{C \in F} \bigvee_{y^\eta \in C} y^\eta[n].
$$

It is straightforward to verify that C accepts an input assignment of weight k if and only if F has a weak UP + PL-backdoor set of size k. Hence WEAK UP + PL-BACKDOOR is in W[P]. For the problems WEAK UP-BACKDOOR and WEAK PL-BACKDOOR we proceed similarly, omitting the constructions (2) or (3), respectively.   □

LEMMA 3. STRONG S-BACKDOOR *is in* W[P] *for any* $S \in \{\text{UP} + \text{PL}, \text{UP}, \text{PL}\}$.

Proof. We reduce STRONG UP + PL-BACKDOOR TO WEIGHTED CIRCUIT SATISFIABILITY, extending the construction of the proof of Lemma 2. Let F be an instance of STRONG UP + PL-BACKDOOR with n variables. We construct a circuit D with $2^k n$ input gates that accepts a weight $2^k k$ input assignment if and only if F has a strong UP + PL-backdoor set of size k.

For $i = 1, \ldots, 2^k$ we construct circuits D_i as in the proof of Lemma 2; each D_i consists of $n + 1$ layers and has input gates $x_i^\varepsilon[t]$ for $\varepsilon \in \{0, 1\}$, $x \in \mathrm{var}(F)$, and $t \in \{0, \ldots, n\}$. The layers of D_i consist of gates as defined in (2) and (3). The output gate u_i of D_i is defined by

$$
u_i = \left(\bigwedge_{x \in \mathrm{var}(F)} \neg\left(x^\varepsilon[0] \wedge x^{1-\varepsilon}[0]\right) \right) \wedge
$$
$$
\left(\bigwedge_{C \in F} \bigvee_{y^\eta \in C} y^\eta[n] \vee \bigvee_{C \in F} \bigwedge_{y^\eta \in C} y^{1-\eta}[0] \vee \bigvee_{\substack{x \in \mathrm{var}(F) \\ 1 \le t \le n}} \left(x^\varepsilon[t] \wedge x^{1-\varepsilon}[t]\right) \right).
$$

The difference to the construction in the proof of Lemma 2 is that we also allow the detection of unsatisfiability. We use the fact that unsatisfiability of a formula can be detected by unit propagation and pure literal elimination if and only if the formula contains the empty clause, or both $x = 0$ and $x = 1$ can be inferred.

We combine the circuits $D_1, \ldots, D_{2^k}$ and define the output gate u of D by setting

$$u = \bigwedge_{i=1}^{2^k} u_i \wedge \tag{4}$$

$$\left(\bigwedge_{1 \leq i < j \leq 2^k} \bigvee_{x \in \mathrm{var}\,(F)} x_i^0[0] \not\equiv x_j^0[0] \right) \wedge \tag{5}$$

$$\left(\bigwedge_{\substack{x \in \mathrm{var}(F) \\ 1 \leq i < j \leq 2^k}} \left(x_i^0[0] \vee x_i^1[0] \right) \equiv \left(x_j^0[0] \vee x_j^1[0] \right) \right) \tag{6}$$

where $p \not\equiv q$ abbreviates $(p \wedge \neg q) \vee (\neg p \wedge q)$, and $p \equiv q$ abbreviates $(p \wedge q) \vee (\neg p \wedge \neg q)$. Part (4) ensures that all the circuits D_i accept the input assignment. Part (5) ensures that the input assignment to different copies D_i, D_j, differ in at least one position. Part (6) ensures that all circuits D_i, $1 \leq i \leq 2^k$, receive input assignments that correspond to the same set B of variables of F. We claim that F has a strong UP + PL-backdoor set B of size k if and only if D accepts an input assignment of weight k.

Assume that $B \subseteq \mathrm{var}(F)$ is a strong UP + PL-backdoor set of F with $|B| = k$. Let $\{\tau_1, \ldots, \tau_{2^k}\}$ be the set of all assignments $\tau_i : B \to \{0, 1\}$. We define an input assignment ν of D by setting for all $(x, \varepsilon) \in \mathrm{var}(F) \times \{0, 1\}$

$$\nu\left(x_i^\varepsilon[0]\right) = \begin{cases} 1 \text{ if } x \in B \text{ and } \tau_i(x) = \varepsilon; \\ 0 \text{ otherwise.} \end{cases}$$

We observe that for each D_i, τ sets exactly k input gates to 1; hence the weight of τ is $2^k k$. Since B is a strong UP + PL-backdoor set, it follows by construction of D that D accepts ν.

Conversely, assume that D accepts an input assignment ν of weight $2^k k$. For $i = 1, \ldots, 2^k$ let $B_i = \{x \in \mathrm{var}(F) : \nu(x_i^0[0]) = 1 \text{ or } \nu(x_i^1[0]) = 1)\}$, and define an assignment $\tau_i : B_i \to \{0, 1\}$ such that $\tau_i(x) = 1$ if and only if $\nu(x_i^1[0]) = 1$. Part (6) of the definition of D implies $B_i = B_j$ for all $1 \leq i < j \leq 2^k$, and part (5) implies $|\{\tau_1, \ldots, \tau_{2^k}\}| = 2^k$. Thus $\tau_1, \ldots, \tau_{2^k}$ are all possible assignments for the set $B = B_1 = \ldots = B_{2^k}$. Since D accepts ν, it follows that for every $i \in \{1, \ldots, 2^k\}$, the UP + PL-subsolver decides whether $F[\tau_i]$ is satisfiable. In summary, B is a strong UP + PL-backdoor set of size k.

Hence we have shown that STRONG UP + PL-BACKDOOR is in W[P]. This holds as well for STRONG UP-BACKDOOR and STRONG PL-BACKDOOR, as we can modify the above construction by omitting (2) or (3), respectively, in the definitions of the circuits D_i. □

LEMMA 4. *The problems* WEAK UP + PL-BACKDOOR *and* WEAK UP-BACKDOOR *are* W[P]-*hard. The problems remain* W[P]-*hard for CNF formulas that have exactly one satisfying total assignment.*

Proof. We reduce CYCLIC MONOTONE CIRCUIT ACTIVATION. Let $D = (G, E, \lambda)$ be a cyclic monotone circuit without input or output gates. We may assume that all gates of D are binary (see the discussion at the end of Section 5).

For each gate $g \in G$ we define a set of clauses F_g, and we obtain a formula F by taking the union of all sets F_g with $g \in G$. For an AND-gate $g = x_1 \wedge x_2$, the set F_g contains the clauses

$$\{x_1, y_1\}, \{\overline{x_1}, y_1\}, \{x_1, \overline{y_1}\},$$
$$\{x_2, y_2\}, \{\overline{x_2}, y_2\}, \{x_2, \overline{y_2}\},$$
$$\{\overline{x_1}, \overline{y_1}, \overline{x_2}, \overline{y_2}, g\};$$

the variables y_1, y_2 are new variables not occurring outside of these seven clauses (we call the variables y_1, y_2 *private*). Similarly, for an OR-gate $g = x_1 \vee x_2$, the set F_g contains the clauses

$$\{x_1, y_1\}, \{\overline{x_1}, y_1\}, \{x_1, \overline{y_1}\},$$
$$\{x_2, y_2\}, \{\overline{x_2}, y_2\}, \{x_2, \overline{y_2}\},$$
$$\{\overline{x_1}, \overline{y_1}, z\}, \{\overline{x_2}, \overline{y_2}, g\};$$

again, y_1, y_2 are private variables. By construction, $G \subseteq \mathrm{var}(F)$, and since D has no input gates, $\mathrm{var}(F) \backslash G$ is the set of all private variables of F. Evidently, each F_g is satisfied by assigning 1 to all its variables; however, if 0 is assigned to at least one variable, at least one clause of F_g is not satisfied. Hence the assignment τ_1 that sets all variables to 1 is the only satisfying total assignment of F. Consequently, for any subsolver $\mathcal{S}$, a set $B \subseteq \mathrm{var}(F)$ is a weak $\mathcal{S}$-backdoor set of F if and only if $\mathcal{S}$ extends the assignment $\tau_0 : B \to \{1\}$ to the satisfying assignment τ_1.

From $y_i = 1$ for a private variable y_i we can infer $x_i = 1$ by means of unit propagation, since the clause $\{x_i, \overline{y_i}\}$ is contained in F. Consequently, if B is a weak UP-backdoor set of F, then replacing private variables y_i of B with x_i, yields a weak UP-backdoor set $B' \subseteq G$ with $|B'| \leq |B|$. Moreover, unit propagation on a set F_g behaves exactly as the activation process on the gate g in D. For example, consider F_g for an AND-gate $g = x_1 \wedge x_2$. By unit propagation, we infer from $x_1 = 1$ and $x_2 = 1$ the assignments $y_1 = 1$ and $y_2 = 1$, and, in turn, $g = 1$. (However, setting $g = 1$ does not propagate 'upward' to y_i or x_i.) Thus, a set B of gates of D activates D if and only if for $\tau_0 : B \to \{1\}$, all clauses of $F[\tau_0]$ can be satisfied using several steps of unit propagation; that is, B is a weak UP-backdoor set of F. Hence we have shown that some starting set of size at most k activates D if and only if F has a weak UP-backdoor set of size at most k. Consequently, W[P]-hardness of WEAK UP-BACKDOOR follows from Lemma 1.

Next we show that W[P]-hardness also holds for WEAK UP + PL-BACKDOOR by proving that every weak UP + PL-backdoor set of F is a weak UP-backdoor set. Consider $\emptyset \neq B \subseteq \text{var}(F)$ and $\tau_0 : B \to \{1\}$. First we observe that for any variable $x \in \text{var}(F)$, the negative literal $\bar{x}$ cannot be pure in $F[\tau_0]$, since otherwise we could infer $x = 0$ by means of pure literal elimination, but then $F[\tau_0]$ would be unsatisfiable. Since the circuit D has no output gates, every variable of F occurs as x_i or y_i in some set F_g. However, for every pair of variables x_i, y_i, some F_g contains the binary clauses $\{x_i, \bar{y_i}\}$ and $\{\bar{x_i}, y_i\}$. Thus, for x_i being a pure literal of $F[\tau_0]$, $y_i \in B$ must prevail. Then, however, $F[\tau_0]$ contains the unit clause $\{x_i\}$, and so $x_i = 1$ can be inferred by unit propagation, and pure literal elimination is not needed. Similarly, if y_i is a pure literal of $F[\tau_0]$, then $F[\tau_0]$ contains the unit clause $\{y_i\}$, and again $y_i = 1$ can be inferred by unit propagation. We conclude that pure literal elimination is redundant for $F[\tau_0]$. Thus, it follows by induction on $|\text{var}(F)\backslash B|$ that B is a weak UP + PL-backdoor set of F if and only if B is a weak UP-backdoor set of F. Hence WEAK UP + PL-BACKDOOR is W[P]-hard. □

LEMMA 5. *The problems* STRONG UP + PL-BACKDOOR *and* STRONG UP-BACKDOOR *are* W[P]-*hard.*

Proof. Let $S \in \{\text{UP} + \text{PL}, \text{UP}\}$. We reduce WEAK S-BACKDOOR. Let F be a formula with exactly one satisfying total assignment τ; w.l.o.g., we assume that τ assigns 1 to each variable of F. We obtain a formula F^* from F by taking for every $x \in \text{var}(F)$ a new variable x^* and adding the clauses $\{x, x^*\}$ and $\{x, \overline{x^*}\}$ to F. Note that τ also satisfies F^* and that every satisfying assignment τ^* of F^* extends τ.

We show that F has a weak S-backdoor set of size at most k if and only if F^* has a strong S-backdoor set of size at most k.

Let B be a weak S-backdoor set of F. Thus, with input $F[\tau_0]$, $\tau_0 : B \to \{1\}$, the subsolver S finds the assignment τ that satisfies F. Since the presence of clauses $\{x, x^*\}$ and $\{x, \overline{x^*}\}$ does not prevent any application of unit propagation or pure literal elimination, the subsolver S finds the assignment τ also with input $F^*[\tau_0]$. Hence B is a weak S-backdoor set of F^*. The set $B^* = \{x^*: x \in B\}$ is evidently a weak S-backdoor set of F^* and we have $|B| = |B^*|$. However, B^* is also a strong S-backdoor set of F^*, since, by symmetry, it does not matter whether a variable x^* is set to 0 or set to 1.

Conversely, let B^* be a strong S-backdoor set of F^*. Since F^* is satisfiable, B^* is also a weak S-backdoor set of F^*; thus S extends $\tau_0^*: B^* \to \{1\}$ to a satisfying assignment of F^*. Since $\{x, \overline{x^*}\} \in F^*$, $x^* = 1$ yields $x = 1$ by unit propagation. Hence we can replace each $x^* \in B^*$ by x and still have a weak S-backdoor set $B := \{x \in \text{var}(F) : x \in B^* \text{ or } x^* \in B^*\}$ with $|B| \leq |B^*|$. Thus, the subsolver S extends $\tau_0 : B \to \{1\}$ to a satisfying assignment of F^*. The clauses in $F^* \backslash F$ are irrelevant for such extension, since as early as a variable $x \in \text{var}(F)$ gets the value 1 under some extension of τ_0, the clauses $\{x, x^*\}$ and $\{x, \overline{x^*}\}$ are removed. Consequently B is also a weak S-backdoor set of F. □

LEMMA 6. WEAK PL-BACKDOOR *is* W[P]-*hard and remains* W[P]-*hard for CNF formulas that have exactly one satisfying total assignment.*

Proof. We reduce CYCLIC MONOTONE CIRCUIT ACTIVATION as in Lemma 4. Again, let $D = (G, E, \lambda)$ be a cyclic monotone circuit without input or output gates and where all gates are binary. For each gate $g \in G$ we define a set F_g of clauses , and we obtain a formula F by taking the union of all sets F_g with $g \in G$. For an AND-gate $g = x_1 \wedge x_2$, the set F_g contains the clauses

$$\{x_1, y_1\}, \{x_1, \overline{y_1}\},$$
$$\{x_2, y_1\}, \{x_2, \overline{y_1}\},$$
$$\{y_1, \overline{g}\};$$

for an OR-gate $g = x_1 \vee x_2$, the set F_g contains the clauses

$$\{x_1, x_2, y_1\},$$
$$\{x_1, x_2, \overline{y_1}\},$$
$$\{y_1, \overline{g}\};$$

the variables y_i are *private* variables. We have $G \subseteq \mathrm{var}(F)$, and since D has no input gates, $\mathrm{var}(F) \backslash G$ is the set of private variables. We show that F has a weak PL-backdoor set of size at most k if and only if some starting set of size at most k activates D. As in the proof of Lemma 4 it follows from the definition of the sets F_g, that the only satisfying total assignment of F sets all variables to 1. Pure literal elimination on F_g behaves exactly as the activation process on the corresponding gate: for example, for an AND-gate $g = x_1 \wedge x_2$, if $\tau_0(x_1) = \tau_0(x_2) = 1$, then the clauses $\{x_1, y_1\}$, $\{x_1, \overline{y_1}\}$, $\{x_2, y_1\}$, and $\{x_2, \overline{y_1}\}$ are removed from the formula and g becomes a pure literal; thus $g = 1$ follows. Hence a set $B \subseteq G$ of gates activates D if and only if B is a weak PL-backdoor set of F. By replacing private variables y_i by x_i, we can find for every weak PL-backdoor set B of F a weak PL-backdoor set $B' \subseteq G$ with $|B'| \leq |B|$. Hence F has a weak PL-backdoor set of size at most k if and only if some starting set of size at most k activates D. Thus we have reduced CYCLIC MONOTONE CIRCUIT ACTIVATION to WEAK PL-BACKDOOR, and the lemma follows.   □

LEMMA 7. *The problem* STRONG PL-BACKDOOR *is* W[P]-*hard.*

Proof. We reduce WEAK PL-BACKDOOR. Let F be a formula with exactly one satisfying total assignment τ; w.l.o.g., we assume that τ assigns 1 to each variable of F. We obtain a formula F^* from F by adding the unit clause $\{x\}$ for every variable x of F; that is,

$$F^* = F \cup \{\{x\} : x \in \mathrm{var}(F)\}.$$

Evidently, τ is also the unique satisfying total assignment of F^*. Let $\emptyset \neq B \subseteq \mathrm{var}(F)$ and $\tau_0 : B \to \{1\}$. We observe that a variable is pure in $F[\tau_0]$ if and only if it is pure in $F^*[\tau_0]$. Hence, it follows by induction on $|\text{var}(F)\backslash B|$ that B is a weak PL-backdoor set of F if and only if B is a weak PL-backdoor set of F^*. On the other hand, let $\tau_0' : B \rightarrow \{0, 1\}$ be any assignment different from τ_0. There is at least one $x \in \text{var}(F)$ such that $\tau_0'(x) = 0$. Since $\{x\} \in F^*$, $F^*[\tau_0']$ contains the empty clause, and so the unsatisfiability of $F^*[\tau_0']$ can be decided by any subsolver. Thus, if B is a weak PL-backdoor set of F, B is also a strong PL-backdoor set of F. Since F^* is satisfiable, every strong PL-backdoor set of F^* is also a weak PL-backdoor set of F^*. In summary, F has a weak PL-backdoor set of size at most k if and only if F^* has a strong PL-backdoor set of size at most k. Hence W[P]-hardness of STRONG PL-BACKDOOR follows from Lemma 6. □

In view of the above lemmas we conclude that all the considered problems are W[P]-complete.

THEOREM 1. *The problems* WEAK S-BACKDOOR *and* STRONG S-BACKDOOR *are* W[P]-*complete for each subsolver* $S \in \{$UP + PL, UP, PL$\}$.

7. Final Remarks

In this paper we have determined the parameterized complexity of the backdoor set detection problem for subsolvers that arise from the DLL/DP procedures. Our results indicate that these problems are computationally hard; it is very unlikely that, in the worst case, smallest backdoor sets for DLL subsolvers can be found more efficiently than by brute force search. Complementary to the findings of the present paper are the results of Nishimura, Ragde, and Szeider [9] on the parameterized complexity of backdoor set detection with respect to the syntactically defined classes HORN and 2-CNF. It turns out that, although weak backdoor set detection with respect to these classes is W[P]-hard, the detection of strong backdoor sets is fixed-parameter tractable! The identification of further polynomial-time classes of SAT instances that allow fixed-parameter tractable backdoor set detection is a challenging new direction of research. For example, it would be interesting to know whether the detection of strong backdoor sets w.r.t. the class RHORN of renamable Horn formulas is fixed-parameter tractable. It is well known that RHORN properly contains the class of all Horn formulas, and RHORN is itself a proper subclass of the class of formulas decidable by unit propagation.

References

1. Abrahamson, K. A., Downey, R. G. and Fellows, M. R. (1995) Fixed-parameter tractability and completeness. IV. On completeness for W[P] and PSPACE analogues, *Ann. Pure Appl. Logic* **73**(3), 235–276.

2. Cook, S. A. and Mitchell, D. G. (1997) Finding hard instances of the satisfiability problem: A survey, in *Satisfiability problem: theory and applications (Piscataway, NJ, 1996)*, American Mathematical Society, pp. 1–17.

3. Davis, M., Logemann, G. and Loveland, D. (1962) A machine program for theorem-proving, *Commun. ACM* **5**, 394–397.

4. Davis, M. and Putnam, H. (1960) A computing procedure for quantification theory, *J. ACM* **7**(3), 201–215.

5. Downey, R. G. and Fellows, M. R. (1999) *Parameterized Complexity*, Monographs in Computer Science. Springer.

6. Flum, J. and Grohe, M. (2004) Parameterized complexity and subexponential time, *Bull. Eur. Assoc. Theor. Comput. Sci.* **84**, 71–100.

7. Interian, Y. (2003) Backdoor sets for random 3-SAT, in *Sixth International Conference on Theory and Applications of Satisfiability Testing, S. Margherita Ligure, Portofino, Italy, May 5–8, 2003, (SAT 2003), informal proceedings*, pp. 231–238.

8. Malik, S. (1994) Analysis of Cyclic Combinatorial Circuits, *IEEE Trans. Comput.-Aided Des.* **13**(7), 950–956.

9. Nishimura, N., Ragde, P. and Szeider, S. (2004) Detecting backdoor sets with respect to horn and binary clauses, in H. Hoos and D. G. Mitchell (eds.), *Seventh International Conference on Theory and Applications of Satisfiability Testing, 10–13 May, 2004, Vancouver, BC, Canada (SAT 2004), informal proceedings*, pp. 96–103.

10. Ruan, Y., Kautz, H. A. and Horvitz, E. (2004) The backdoor key: A path to understanding problem hardness, in D. L. McGuinness and G. Ferguson (eds.), *Proceedings of the 19th National Conference on Artificial Intelligence, 16th Conference on Innovative Applications of Artificial Intelligence*, pp. 124–130.

11. Williams, R., Gomes, C. and Selman, B. (2003a) Backdoors to typical case complexity, in G. Gottlob and T. Walsh (eds.), *Proceedings of the Eighteenth International Joint Conference on Artificial Intelligence, IJCAI 2003*, pp. 1173–1178.

12. Williams, R., Gomes, C. and Selman, B. (2003b) On the connections between backdoors, restarts, and heavy-tailedness in combinatorial search, in *Sixth International Conference on Theory and Applications of Satisfiability Testing, S. Margherita Ligure, Portofino, Italy, May 5–8, 2003 (SAT 2003), informal proceedings*, pp. 222–230.

Journal of Automated Reasoning (2005) 35: 89–95
DOI: 10.1007/s10817-005-9008-8

© Springer 2005

The Complexity of Pure Literal Elimination

JAN JOHANNSEN
Institut für Informatik, Ludwig-Maximilians-Universität München, München, Germany

Abstract. The computational complexity of eliminating pure literals is calibrated for various classes of CNF formulas. The problem is shown to be P-complete in general, NL-complete for 2-CNF, and SL-complete for CNF formulas with at most two occurrences of each variable.

Key words: pure literal, completeness, computational complexity.

1. Introduction and Preliminaries

A literal a is *pure* in a CNF formula F if $\bar{a}$ does not occur in F. Pure literals can always be set to true without affecting satisfiability, which amounts to the same as removing clauses containing them. Since this can lead to other literals becoming pure, the process needs to be iterated to obtain a satisfiability equivalent formula without any pure literals. This process is known as pure literal elimination.

The elimination of pure literals is a common heuristic used in many satisfiability algorithms. It was part of the original DLL algorithm (Davis et al., 1962), and it is still employed by those DLL-type backtracking algorithms that achieve the best theoretical worst-case upper bounds for 3-SAT (Kullmann, 1999; Schiermeyer, 1996). The currently most efficient implementations of DLL-type SAT solvers, like Chaff (Moskewicz et al., 2001) or Berkmin (Goldberg and Novikov, 2002), use a data structure that is optimized for unit propagation, and therefore sacrifice the pure literal heuristic, while other contemporary solvers, like OKsolver (Kullmann, 2002), still use the heuristic.

On another note, pure literal elimination becomes essential again for the efficient implementation of solvers for quantified Boolean formulas (QBF): it appears to be crucial (according to Letz (2004), personal communication) for the performance of Semprop (Letz, 2002), currently one of the most efficient QBF solvers, and is indeed employed by most of the QBF solvers that participated in the 2003 QBF solver evaluation (Le Berre et al., 2003).

We will determine precisely the computational complexity of pure literal elimination for different classes of formulas. Next to the complexity class P of problems computable in polynomial time, we will consider classes defined by logarithmic space-bounded algorithms employing different forms of nondeterminism. Among these, the classes L of deterministic and NL of nondeterministic logarithmic space are the most familiar ones.

Less known perhaps is the class SL defined by *symmetric* nondeterministic logarithmic space (Lewis and Papadimitriou, 1982), which lies between L and NL. Just as NL exactly captures the complexity of the reachability problem in directed graphs, SL is the precise complexity of reachability in undirected graph, since this problem (UGAP) is complete for SL (Jones et al., 1976). It was shown recently by Reingold (2005) that UGAP is in L, and hence SL = L. Nevertheless, we still think there is some significance to the class SL, as will be explained below.

Our main result shows that the elimination of pure literals is *inherently sequential*; technically, this means that it is complete for P. Hence, there is no hope for efficient parallel or small-space implementations of the heuristic.

For a formula F in CNF, let $pl(F)$ be the formula obtained from F by deleting all clauses that contain a pure literal. Let F^* denote the least fixed point of this operation, that is, define

$$F_0 := F$$
$$F_{i+1} := pl(F_i)$$
$$F^* := F_r \quad \text{where } r \text{ is the least } i \text{ s.t. } F_i = F_{i+1}.$$

This algorithm computes F^* in polynomial time, since the operation $pl()$ is computable in logarithmic space (even in the much smaller class AC^0), and the number r of iterations is bounded by n.

The following decision problem PL is obviously equivalent to the problem of computing F^*:

Given a formula $F = C_1 \wedge \ldots \wedge C_m$ in CNF, and $1 \leq i \leq m$, does the clause C_i occur in F^*?

Therefore, we concentrate on the complexity of this decision problem. By the above algorithm, PL is in P. We will study the complexity of the problem PL for various classes of formulas.

For $k, \ell \in \mathbb{N}$, let k-CNF and CNF(ℓ) denote the classes of formulas in CNF having at most k literals per clause and at most ℓ occurrences of each variable, respectively. k-CNF(ℓ) denotes the class of formulas obeying both restrictions.

The complexity of the satisfiability problem for these classes is well known: it is NP-complete already for 3-CNF(3), but NL-complete for 2-CNF (Jones et al., 1976) and L-complete for CNF(2) (Johannsen, 2004). We will completely classify the complexity of the problem PL for these formula classes.

We show that as in the case of satisfiability, the problem PL for 3-CNF(3) is already as hard as possible, in this case P-complete. For 2-CNF formulas, PL is exactly as hard as satisfiability, namely, NL-complete.

The most unexpected case, which was the starting point of this whole investigation, is that of CNF(2). It was suggested to the author several times that the algorithm showing that satisfiability for these formulas is in L (Johannsen, 2004) could be simplified by first eliminating pure literals. This way the algorithm would only need to work with ordinary graphs instead of the *tagged* graphs (see definition below.) We show here that this is not an option, since removing pure literals from a CNF(2)-formula is actually more complex than testing its satisfiability: the problem PL for these formulas is SL-complete.

Even though we know now from Reingold (2005) that SL = L, we think there is still a conceptual difference in difficulty between a typical logarithmic space algorithm and Reingold's algorithm: where the former uses only constantly many pointers into the input data structure, the latter also needs logarithmically many registers storing a constant amount of information each. This distinction is blurred by the Turing machine model, and it remains to be seen whether it can be made precise, or whether a "typical" logarithmic space algorithm for UGAP can be found. Until this question is resolved, it still makes sense to regard an SL-completeness result as indicating that a problem is harder than one in L.

2. The General Case

We first show that for general formulas in CNF, the problem is P-complete. Later we will verify that the reduction still works if the numbers of literals per clause and occurrences of variables are bounded by 3.

The following problem AGAP, the alternating graph accessibility problem, is well known to be P-complete (cf. Greenlaw et al., 1995):

> Given a directed graph $G = (V, E)$ with a partition $V = \forall \uplus \exists$, and vertices s, t $\in V$, does APATH(s, t) hold, where the predicate APATH(x, y) is inductively defined by
>
> — $x = y$, or
> — $y \in \exists$, and there is a z with $(z, y) \in E$ and APATH(x, z), or
> — $y \in \forall$, and APATH(x, z) holds for all z with $(z, y) \in E$?

THEOREM 1. *PL is complete for* P.

Proof. As remarked above, the problem is in P. To show it is hard for P, we reduce AGAP to PL as follows:

For a given instance (G, s, t) of AGAP, we construct a formula $F(G, s)$. The variables of $F(G, s)$ are y_e for every edge $e \in E$, a variable x_v for every vertex $v \in \forall$, and variables $x_v^1, \ldots, x_v^k$ for every vertex $v \in \exists$ of in-degree k, plus one more variable z.

Let v be a vertex with ingoing edges $e_1, \ldots, e_k$ and outgoing edges $e_1', \ldots, e_\ell'$. If $v \in \forall$, then there is a clause

$$C_v = x_v \vee \bar{y}_{e_1'} \vee \ldots \vee \bar{y}_{e_\ell'}$$

and for each of the edges e_j for $1 \leq j \leq k$, the clauses

$$\bar{x}_v \vee y_{e_j} \text{ and } y_{e_j}.$$

If $v \in \exists$, then there is a clause

$$C_v = x_v^1 \vee \ldots \vee x_v^k \vee \bar{y}_{e_1'} \vee \ldots \vee \bar{y}_{e_\ell'}$$

and for each of the edges e_j for $1 \leq j \leq k$, the clauses

$$\bar{x}_v^j \vee y_{e_j} \text{ and } y_{e_j}.$$

Additionally, the clause C_s contains the variable z, i.e., if $v = s$, the clause C_s is

$$x_s^1 \vee \ldots \vee x_s^k \vee \bar{y}_{e_1'} \vee \ldots \vee \bar{y}_{e_\ell'} \vee z.$$

Note that the variable z does not occur in any other clause.

LEMMA 2. *For every $v \in V$, if* APATH(s, v) *holds, then* $C_v \notin F(G, s)^*$.

Proof. We prove by induction along the definition of APATH(s, v) that for every v with APATH(s, v) there is an i such that $v \notin F_i$.

For $v = s$, the clause C_s does not occur in $F_1 = \text{pl}(F)$, since it contains the pure literal z.

Now let v have predecessors $u_1, \ldots, u_k$ joined to v by edges $e_j = (u_j, v)$ for $1 \leq j \leq k$.

If $v \in \forall$, and APATH(s, u_j) holds for every j, then by the induction hypothesis there is an i_j such that $C_{u_j} \notin F_{i_j}$ for every j. Thus in F_{i_j}, the literal y_{e_j} is pure, and thus the clause $y_{e_j} \vee \bar{x}_v$ does not occur in F_{i_j+1}. Thus for $r = \max_{1 \leq j \leq k} i_j + 1$, the literal x_v is pure in F_r, and hence C_v does not occur in F_{r+1}.

Similarly, if $v \in \exists$, and APATH(s, u_j) holds for some j, then by the induction hypothesis there is an i such that $C_{u_j} \notin F_i$. By the same reasoning as in the previous case, x_v^j is pure in F_{i+1}, and hence $C_v \notin F_{i+2}$.   □

LEMMA 3. *For every $v \in V$, if* $C_v \notin F(G, s)^*$, *then* APATH(s, v) *holds.*

Proof. Let $C_v \notin F(G, s)^*$. We prove the claim by induction on i such that $v \in F_i \backslash F_{i+1}$. For $i = 0$, the only clause in $F_0 \backslash F_1$ is C_s, and APATH(s, s) holds by definition, which gives the base case.

Let again v have predecessors $u_1, \ldots, u_k$ joined to v by edges $e_j = (u_j, v)$ for $1 \leq j \leq k$, and let $C_v \in F_i \setminus F_{i+1}$.

If $v \in \forall$, then x_v must be pure in F_i, since due to the unit clauses y_{f_v}, the literals $\bar{y}_{f_v}$ cannot become pure as long as C_v is present. Thus for each edge e_j, the clause $y_{e_j} \vee \bar{x}_v$ does not occur in F_i, and thus for some $i_j < i$, it is in $F_{i_j} \backslash F_{i_j+1}$. Therefore, y_{e_j} is pure in F_{i_j}, and hence $C_{u_j} \in F_{i_j'} \backslash F_{i_j'}$ for some $i_j' < i_j$. By the induction hypothesis, APATH(s, u_j) holds for every j, and consequently APATH(s, v) holds as well.

The case where $v \in \exists$ is similar.   □

It follow that APATH(s, t) holds iff $C_t \notin F(G, s)^*$, and thus the construction reduces AGAP to PL.

For a vertex v in a directed graph, let the in-degree in-deg(v) denote the number of edges going into and the out-degree out-deg(v) the number of edges leaving v, so that deg v = in-deg v + out-deg v. Observe that the width of the clause C_v is 1 + out-deg v for $v \in \forall$, and in-deg v + out-deg v for $v \in \exists$. Also, the number of occurrences of the variables x_v for $v \in \forall$ is 1 + in-deg v, and all other variables occur at most three times.

Thus the reduction yields a formula in 3-CNF(3) if the graph G has the following properties:

- every vertex v has deg $v \leq 3$,
- every vertex v has in-deg $v \leq 2$ and out-deg $v \leq 2$.

It is easily verified that the problem AGAP remains complete for P for such graphs. We can reduce the general case to this special case by replacing each vertex v with ingoing edges $e_1, \ldots, e_k$ and outgoing edges $e'_1, \ldots, e'_\ell$ by a gadget as shown in Figure 1. All the $k + \ell - 2$ new vertices are of the same type as v: if $v \in \exists$, then they all are in $\exists$, and if $v \in \forall$, they all are in $\forall$. Moreover, in the new graph the vertex s will be the $k - 1$st vertex (marked by a dot in the figure) of the chain corresponding to s in the original graph, and similarly for t.

COROLLARY 4. *PL for 3-CNF(3) formulas is complete for* P.

3. The Case of CNF(2)

A *tagged graph* $G = (V, E, T)$ is an undirected multigraph (V, E) with a distinguished set $T \subseteq V$ of vertices. We refer to the vertices in T as the *tagged* vertices.

From a formula $F \in$ CNF(2), we construct a tagged graph $G(F)$ as follows:

- $G(F)$ has a vertex v_C for every clause C in F.
- If clauses C and D contain a pair of complementary literals x and $\bar{x}$, then there is an edge e_x between v_C and v_D.
- If C contains a pure literal, then v_C is tagged.

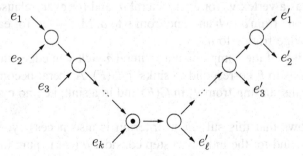

Figure 1. Reduction of AGAP to the special case.

THEOREM 5. *PL for formulas in CNF(2) is complete for* SL.

Proof. Consider a formula F. The graph $G(\text{pl}(F))$ is obtained from $G(F)$ by removing the tagged vertices and tagging the remaining vertices that used to be their neighbors. Thus, by iterating we see that $G(F^*)$ is obtained by removing all connected components from $G(F)$ that contain tagged vertices.

Therefore the following algorithm decides PL: given F and a the number i of a clause C_i in F, loop through all tagged vertices in $G(F)$ and verify for each of them whether it is connected to v_{C_i}. This is a logarithmic space algorithm with an oracle for UGAP; thus PL is in L^{SL}, which is known to be the same as SL (Nisan and Ta-Shma, 1995).

To show hardness for SL, we reduce UGAP to PL as follows: For an un-directed graph $G = (V, E)$, we construct a formula $F(G)$ as follows: we introduce one variable x_e for every edge $e \in E$, and for each vertex $v \in V$, we construct a clause C_v that contains one literal for each edge e incident to v. This literal is x_e, if e connects v to a higher numbered vertex, and $\bar{x}_e$ otherwise. Finally we add an additional variable y_s to the clause C_s. Obviously, $C_t \in F(G)^*$ if and only if t is reachable from s. □

4. The Case of 2-CNF

Let RC denote the following decision problem:

> Given a directed graph G and vertex s in G, is there a cycle in G reachable from s?

This problem is NL-complete, since it is easily seen to be in NL by the following algorithm: guess a vertex v, and verify nondeterministically that v is reachable from s and that v is reachable from itself by a nontrivial path. On the other hand, the NL-complete problem of deciding whether G contains a cycle (Jones, 1975) can be reduced to RC by adding a new source s and edges from s to every vertex in G.

THEOREM 6. *PL for 2-CNF formulas is* NL-*complete*.

Proof. We consider the same directed graph $G(F)$ that is also used in the NL-algorithm for 2-SAT. It has a vertex v_a for every literal a, and for every clause $a \vee b$, there are two edges, one from $\bar{a}$ to b and one from $\bar{b}$ to a. Moreover, for each unit clause a there is an edge from $\bar{a}$ to a.

Note that each occurrence of the complementary literal $\bar{a}$ yields an edge out of v_a, therefore the pure literals in F correspond to sinks in $G(F)$. A literal becomes a pure in some F_i if all paths starting from v_a in $G(F)$ end in a sink, i.e., no cycle is reachable from a.

An induction on i shows that this sufficient criterion is also necessary: the base case $i = 0$ is obvious, and for the induction step consider a that is pure in F_i for $i > 0$. Then all literals b occurring together with $\bar{a}$ in a clause must be pure in some F_j for $j < i$. By the induction hypothesis, every path starting from any of the vertices v_b for these literals b ends in a sink. Since these v_b are all the successors of v_a, all paths starting from v_a end in a sink as well.

Therefore, a clause C does occur in F^* iff no literal in C is pure in some F_i iff for every literal a in C, a cycle is reachable from v_a in $G(F)$. This can be tested in nondeterministic logarithmic space; thus the problem is in NL.

To show it is NL-hard, we reduce RC to PL. To this end, we build a formula $F(G)$ from a directed graph $G = (V, E)$ and $s \in V$, where w.l.og. we assume that s is a source, as follows: There is a variable x_v for every vertex $v \in V$, and for every edge $(u, v) \in E$ we add a clause $\bar{x}_u \vee x_v$. Moreover, we add a unit clause x_u for every source u in G. Thus the only pure literals in $F(G)$ are x_v for the sinks v in G. As above, it follows that the unit clause x_s occurs in $F(G)^*$ if and only if a cycle is reachable from s in G.   □

References

Davis, M., Logemann, G. and Loveland, D. (1962) A machine program for theorem proving, *Commun. ACM* **5,** pp. 394–397.

Goldberg, E. and Novikov, Y. (2002) BerkMin: a fast and robust SAT-solver, in *Design, Automation, and Test in Europe* (DATE '02), pp. 142–149.

Greenlaw, R., Hoover, H. J. and Ruzzo, W. L. (1995) *Limits to Parallel Computation*, Oxford University Press.

Johannsen, J. (2004) Satisfiability problems complete for deterministic logarithmic space, in V. Diekert and M. Habib (eds.), *21st International Symposium on Theoretical Aspects of Computer Science (STACS 2004)*, pp. 317–325.

Jones, N. D. (1975) Space bounded reducibility among combinatorial problems, *J. Comput. Syst. Sci.* **11**, pp. 65–85.

Jones, N. D., Lien, Y. E. and Laaser, W. T. (1976) New problems complete for nondeterministic log space, *Math Syst. Theory.* **10**, pp. 1–17.

Kullmann, O. (1999) New methods for 3-SAT decision and worst-case analysis, *Theor. Comp. Sci.* **223**(1–2), pp. 1–72.

Kullmann, O. (2002) Investigating the behaviour of a SAT solver on random formulas, Submitted.

Le Berre, D., Simon, L. and Tacchella, A. (2003) Challenges in the QBF arena: the SAT'03 evaluation of QBF solvers, in *Proceedings of the Sixth International Conference on Theory and Applications of Satisfiability Testing (SAT2003)*, pp. 468–485, Springer LNCS 2919.

Letz, R. (2002) Lemma and model caching in decision procedures for quantified Boolean formulas, in U. Egly and C. G. Fermüller (eds.), *TABLEAUX 2002*, pp. 160–175.

Letz, R. (2004) personal communication.

Lewis, H. R. and Papadimitriou, C. H. (1982) Symmetric space-bounded computation, *Theor. Comp. Sci.* **19**, pp. 161–187.

Moskewicz, M. W., Madigan, C. F., Zhao, Y., Zhang, L. and Malik, S. (2001) Chaff: Engineering an efficient SAT solver, in *Proceedings of the 38th Design Automation Conference (DAC'01)*.

Nisan, N. and Ta-Shma, A. (1995) Symmetric logspace is closed under complement, *Chic. J. Theor. Comput. Sci.*

Reingold, O. (2005) Undirected ST-connectivity in log-space, To appear in *Proceedings of the 37th ACM Symposium on Theory of Computing*.

Schiermeyer, I. (1996) Pure literal lookahead: an $O(1.497^n)$ 3-satisfiability algorithm, in J. Franco, G. Gallo, H. Kleine Büning, E. Speckenmeyer and C. Spera (eds.), *Workshop on the Satisfiability Problem*.

Journal of Automated Reasoning (2005) 35: 97–142
DOI: 10.1007/s10817-005-9010-1

© Springer 2006

Clause Weighting Local Search for SAT

JOHN THORNTON
Institute for Integrated and Intelligent Systems, Griffith University, PMB 50,
Gold Coast Mail Centre, Queensland 9726, Australia.
e-mail: j.thornton@griffith.edu.au

Abstract. This paper investigates the necessary features of an effective clause weighting local search algorithm for propositional satisfiability testing. Using the recent history of clause weighting as evidence, we suggest that the best current algorithms have each discovered the same basic framework, that is, to increase weights on false clauses in local minima and then to periodically normalize these weights using a decay mechanism. Within this framework, we identify two basic classes of algorithm according to whether clause weight updates are performed *additively* or *multiplicatively*. Using a state-of-the-art multiplicative algorithm (SAPS) and our own pure additive weighting scheme (PAWS), we constructed an experimental study to isolate the effects of multiplicative in comparison to additive weighting, while controlling other key features of the two approaches, namely, the use of pure *versus* flat random moves, deterministic *versus* probabilistic weight smoothing and multiple *versus* single inclusion of literals in the local search neighbourhood. In addition, we examined the effects of adding a threshold feature to multiplicative weighting that makes it indifferent to similar cost moves. As a result of this investigation, we show that additive weighting can outperform multiplicative weighting on a range of difficult problems, while requiring considerably less effort in terms of parameter tuning. Our examination of the differences between SAPS and PAWS suggests that additive weighting does benefit from the random flat move and deterministic smoothing heuristics, whereas multiplicative weighting would benefit from a deterministic/probabilistic smoothing switch parameter that is set according to the problem instance. We further show that adding a threshold to multiplicative weighting produces a general deterioration in performance, contradicting our earlier conjecture that additive weighting has better performance due to having a larger selection of possible moves. This leads us to explain differences in performance as being mainly caused by the greater emphasis of additive weighting on penalizing clauses with relatively less weight.

Key words: constraint satisfaction, satisfiability, local search.

1. Introduction and Background

Clause weighting algorithms for satisfiability testing have formed an important research area since their introduction in the early 1990s. Since then various improvements have been proposed, resulting in the two best-known recent algorithms: the discrete Lagrangian method (DLM) (Wu and Wah, 2000) and scaling and probabilistic smoothing (SAPS) (Hutter et al., 2002). While these methods differ in important aspects, both use the same underlying trap avoiding strategy: increasing weights on unsatisfied clauses in local minima and then periodically adjusting weights to maintain effective weight differentials during the search.

The earliest clause weighting algorithms, such as Breakout (Morris, 1993), repeatedly increased weights on unsatisfied clauses and so allowed unrestricted weight growth during the search. Flips were then chosen on the basis of minimizing the combined weight of the unsatisfied clauses. In 1997, Frank proposed a new weight decay algorithm that updated weights on unsatisfied clauses using a combination of a multiplicative decay rate and an additive weight increase. While Frank's work laid the ground for future advances, his decay scheme produced relatively small improvements over earlier weighting approaches. At this point, clause weighting algorithms proved competitive on many smaller problems but were unable to match the performance of faster and simpler heuristics, such as Novelty, on larger problem instances (McAllester et al., 1997). As a key reason for developing incomplete local search techniques is to solve problems beyond the reach of complete SAT solvers, the poor scalability of clause weighting was a major disadvantage.

It was not until the development of DLM that a significant performance gain was achieved. In its simplest form, DLM follows Breakout's weight increment scheme, but additionally decrements clause weights after a fixed number of increases. DLM also alters the point at which weight is increased by allowing *flat* moves that leave the weighted cost of the solution unchanged. These flat moves are in turn controlled by a tabu list and by a parameter that limits the total number of consecutive flat moves (Wu and Wah, 2000). In empirical tests DLM proved successful at solving a range of random and structured SAT problems and in particular was able to outperform the best nonweighting algorithms on many larger and more difficult problem instances.

In another line of research, Schuurmans and Southey (2000) developed a fully multiplicative weighting algorithm: smoothed descent and flood (SDF). SDF introduced a new method for breaking ties between equal cost flips by additionally considering the number of true literals in satisfied clauses. In situations where no improving moves are available, SDF multiplicatively increases weights on unsatisfied clauses and then normalizes (or *smooths*) clause weights so that the greatest cost difference between any two flips remains constant. SDF's reported flip performance was promising in comparison to DLM, but these results did not look at the more difficult problems for which DLM was especially suited. In addition, SDF's time performance did not compare well, due to the overhead of adjusting weights on all clauses at each local minimum.

In subsequent work, SDF evolved into the exponentiated subgradient algorithm (ESG) (Schuurmans et al., 2001), which in turn formed the basis of the scaling and probabilistic smoothing (SAPS) algorithm (Hutter et al., 2002). ESG and SAPS dispensed with SDF's augmented cost function, and SAPS further improved on the run-time performance of ESG by smoothing weights only periodically, and increasing weights only on violated clauses in a local minimum (rather than updating all clauses).

The basic idea of using weight penalties, or Lagrangian multipliers, to solve discrete optimization problems was originally developed in the operations research (OR) community (Everett, 1963), and has evolved into the area of subgradient optimization. These approaches have significant similarities to the weighting algorithms developed in the SAT community. However, as Schuurmans et al. (2001) pointed out, the crucial difference is that OR techniques use linear penalty functions, whereas SAT algorithms use nonlinear *hinge* penalty functions that do not explicitly reward features or clauses that remain satisfied. In their analysis of ESG, Schuurmans et al. further demonstrated that nonlinear penalty functions have the better performance in the SAT domain.

The important point for the current research is not only that the leading SAT clause weighting algorithms have converged on the same class of nonlinear hinge penalty functions, but also that they have converged on the same basic framework of weight control. One of the crucial steps from ESG to SAPS was the realization that weight normalization can be split into two phases: first penalizing false clauses in local minima and second periodically reducing weights according to a problem specific parameter. As the number of false clauses at any point during the search is relatively small compared to the total number of clauses, this splitting of the weight control allows for regular and fast weight increases, while the slower process of weight reduction occurs more infrequently, leading to significant gains in time performance. With this change, the weight update scheme of SAPS becomes almost identical in structure to the weight update scheme of DLM: both increase weight when a local minimum is identified (although using different identification criteria), and both periodically adjust weights according to a parameter value that varies for different problems. SAPS differs from DLM in using this parameter to probabilistically determine when weight is reduced, whereas DLM deterministically reduces weight after a fixed number of increases. Therefore, the remaining and crucial difference between the weighting mechanisms of SAPS and DLM is the use of multiplicative as opposed to additive weight updates.

It is of interest to note that a third clause weighting algorithm, GLSSAT (Mills and Tsang, 1999), employs a similar weight update scheme, additively increasing weights on the least weighted unsatisfied clauses and multiplicatively reducing weights whenever the weight on any one clause exceeds a predefined threshold. However, although GLSSAT performed well in comparison to Walksat, it could not match DLM on larger problems. Also, an earlier study (Thornton and Sattar, 1999) indicated that the basic approach of increasing weights on the least weighted false clauses is not as effective as increasing weights on all false clauses. For these reasons we decided to concentrate on SAPS and DLM and leave a GLS type approach for future work.

The main aim of the study is to investigate whether an additive or multiplicative weight update scheme is better for satisfiability testing. The secondary aim is to discover whether the various subheuristics used in the two approaches provide a useful contribution to performance. Given that SAPS and DLM both have some claim to be considered as the state of the art in local search for SAT and that both have separately hit upon the same underlying weighting structure, it now becomes possible to compare additive and multiplicative clause weighting without their relative performance being disguised by differing implementation details. To perform this comparison, we started with the authors' original version of SAPS and changed it in small steps until it became an effective additive clause weighting algorithm. By examining and empirically testing the effect of each step, we set out to isolate exactly those features that are crucial for the success of each approach. This resulted in the development of the pure additive weighting scheme (PAWS). As the published results for SAPS have looked only at relatively small problems, we also decided to evaluate SAPS and PAWS on an extended test set that includes a selection of the more difficult problems for which DLM was developed. In the remainder of the paper we describe in detail the development of PAWS from SAPS and DLM and then present the results and conclusions of our empirical study.

2. Clause Weighting Algorithms for SAT

Clause weighting local search algorithms for SAT follow the basic procedure of repeatedly flipping single literals that produce the greatest reduction in the sum of false clause weights. Typically, all literals are randomly initialized, and all clauses are given a fixed initial weight. The search then continues until no further cost reduction is possible, at which point the weight on all unsatisfied clauses is increased, and the search is resumed, punctuated with periodic weight reductions.

Clause weighting algorithms differ primarily in the schemes used to control the clause weights, and in the definition of the points where weight should be adjusted. Multiplicative methods, such as SAPS, generally adjust weights when no further improving moves are available in the local neighbourhood. This can be either when all possible flips lead to a worse cost or when no flip will improve cost, but some flips will lead to equal cost solutions. As multiplicative real-valued weights have much finer granularity, the presence of equal cost flips is much more unlikely than for an additive approach, where weight is adjusted in integer units. This means that additive approaches frequently have the choice between adjusting weight when no improving move is available, or taking an equal cost (flat) move.

Following the DLM literature (Shang and Wah, 1998), we consider a *local minimum* to be a point or a connected area of equal cost moves where no further cost improvement is possible (i.e., the area is *surrounded* by cost increasing moves, and no combination of equal cost moves can ever escape). In this model, a *plateau* is a connected area of equal cost moves that eventually lead to one or more cost improving moves. An additive weighting algorithm, like DLM, will continually encounter situations where both equal cost and cost increasing moves are available, but is unable to distinguish between a plateau (where it is worth continuing the search) and a local minimum (where weight should be increased in order to escape).

Considerable effort has gone into developing strategies to help guide additive weighting over potential plateau areas. While this is described as plateau searching, it should be noted that such techniques search plateaus and local minima indifferently. It should also be noted that the SAPS' authors have developed a different terminology to describe local search landscapes (see Hoos and Stützle, 2005).

2.1. DLM AND SAPS

DLM has been described as 'ad hoc' (Schuurmans et al., 2001) and criticized for requiring a large number of parameters to obtain optimum performance. However, DLM has evolved through several versions, the last of which was developed specifically to solve the larger towers of Hanoi and parity learning problems from the DIMACS benchmarks (Wu and Wah, 2000). As already discussed, the basic structure of DLM is similar to SAPS, except for the heuristic used to control the taking of flat moves. In addition, although the last version of DLM had 27 parameters, in practice only three of these require adjustment in the SAT domain.

Of particular interest is that DLM uses a single parameter to control the weighting process (corresponding to Max_{inc} in Figure 1), which determines when weights are to be reduced. In contrast, SAPS requires two further parameters (α and ρ) to determine the amount that weights are multiplicatively scaled or smoothed (in DLM, clause weight increases and decreases are implemented by adding or subtracting one). The other two DLM parameters (θ_1 and θ_2) are used to control the flat move heuristic: Using the terms from Figure 2, if $best < 0$, DLM will randomly select and flip any $x_i \in L$. Otherwise, if $best = 0$, and the number of immediately preceding consecutive flat moves is $< \theta_1$ and $L_t \neq \emptyset$, then DLM will randomly select and flip any $x_i \in L_t$, where L_t contains all flat move literals that have not been flipped in the last θ_2 moves. Otherwise, clause weights are additively updated, as per Figure 1.

Although SAPS implements a fairly 'pure' weighting algorithm, there are a few implementation details that distinguish it from DLM (see Figure 2). The first is the *wp* parameter that probabilistically controls whether a random flip is taken when no cost improving move is available. This acts as an alternative to DLM's flat move heuristic. The second is that the set of local neighbourhood moves for SAPS contains a single copy of each literal that can *make* a false clause (i.e., turn

```
procedure PAWS
begin
    generate random starting point
    for each clause c_i do: set clause weight w_i ← 1
    while solution not found and not timed out do
        best ← ∞
        for each literal x_ij in each false clause f_i do
            Δw ← change in summed weight of false clauses caused by flipping x_i
            if Δw < best then L ← x_ij and best ← Δw
            else if Δw = best then L ← L ∪ x_ij
        end for
        if best < 0 then randomly flip x_ij ∈ L
        else if best = 0 and probability ≤ P_flat then flip x_ij ∈ L
        else
            for each false clause f_i do: w_i ← w_i + 1
            if # times clause weights increased % Max_inc = 0 then
                for each clause c_j|w_j > 1 do: w_j ← w_j − 1
            end if
        end if
    end while
end
```

Figure 1. The pure additive weighting scheme (PAWS).

it from false to true). In DLM, the neighbourhood consists of all literals in all false clauses. This means that if a literal appears in more than one false clause, it will appear more than once in the local neighbourhood, thereby increasing the probability that it will be selected. Finally, as noted earlier, SAPS uses *probabilistic* smoothing when adjusting clause weights, that is, if P_{smooth} is set to 5% then there is a 1 in 20 chance that weight will be adjusted after an

```
procedure SAPS
begin
    generate random starting point
    for each clause c_i do: set clause weight w_i ← 1
    while solution not found and not timed out do
        best ← ∞
        for each literal x_i appearing in at least one false clause do
            Δw ← change in summed weight of false clauses caused by flipping x_i
            if Δw < best then L ← x_i and best ← Δw
            else if Δw = best then L ← L ∪ x_i
        end for
        if best < −0.1 then randomly flip x_i ∈ L
        else if probability ≤ wp then randomly flip any literal
        else
            for each false clause f_i do: w_i ← w_i × α
            if probability ≤ P_smooth then
                μ_w ← mean of current clause weights
                for each clause c_j do: w_j ← w_j × ρ + (1 − ρ) × μ_w
            end if
        end if
    end while
end
```

Figure 2. Scaling and probabilistic smoothing (SAPS).

increase. In contrast, DLM's third parameter fixes the exact number of increases before weight is decreased, and so represents a *deterministic* weight reduction scheme.

Overall, there is little difference between DLM and SAPS in terms of parameter tuning. While SAPS has four parameters (α, ρ, wp, and P_{smooth}) and a basic version of DLM has three, in practice at least one of the SAPS parameters can be treated as a constant and the others adjusted to suit (in this study wp is set at 1%). For both algorithms the process of parameter tuning is time consuming, as optimal performance is highly dependent on the correct settings. This compares poorly with simpler nonweighting algorithms, such as Walksat (Hoos, 2002), which generally require the tuning of only a single noise parameter. In order to address this, a version of SAPS called Reactive SAPS (RSAPS) was developed (Hutter et al., 2002) that automatically adjusts the P_{smooth} parameter during the search. However we found this algorithm did not perform as well as a properly tuned SAPS on our problem set, so we did not consider it further.

Hence, the main design criticism that can be levelled at DLM is that it relies on a somewhat *ad hoc* flat move heuristic, whereas SAPS can search purely on the basis of weight guidance (while taking the occasional random flip). From this it could be argued that multiplicative weighting is superior to additive weighting because it avoids the need for a flat move heuristic, that is, by making finer weight distinctions between moves, the search space for a multiplicative method will contain far fewer and smaller plateau areas. However, this assumes that the overall performance of SAPS is at least as good as DLM's and that the effectiveness of additive weighting depends on plateau searching, both issues we shall address later in the paper.

3. The Pure Additive Weighting Scheme (PAWS)

SAPS has demonstrated that effective local search guidance can be given by a reasonably simple manipulation of clause weights. It has also outperformed DLM on a range of SATLIB benchmark problems, in terms of both time and median number of flips (Hutter et al., 2002). From this work several questions arise: first how does SAPS perform on the larger DIMACS benchmark problems for which DLM was developed? Second, the SAPS code is based on a very efficient implementation of Walksat,[*] so to what extent is the superior time performance of SAPS based on the details of this implementation? Third, does the success of SAPS depend on multiplicative weighting? That is, can we obtain the same quality of guidance using additive weighting, avoiding the use of the

---

[*] http://www.cs.washington.edu/homes/kautz/walksat/walksat-dist.tar.Z.uu.

multiplicative update parameters α and ρ? And finally, does additive weighting require a plateau searching strategy, with the associated tabu list length and flat move parameters, to compensate for the coarser-grained nature of the additive weight updates?

To answer these questions we developed a pure additive weighting scheme (PAWS),[*] which we embedded directly into the SAPS source code[**] (so the same efficiencies were obtained), and tested PAWS on both the SATLIB benchmarks used for SAPS and a selection of the DIMACS benchmarks used for DLM.

PAWS takes a middle line between SAPS and DLM, first by doing away with DLM's plateau searching heuristic (and the associated θ_1 and θ_2 parameters) and replacing it with a random flip heuristic. Now, whenever PAWS encounters a situation where the best available move does not change the overall cost, it will either take this move with probability P_{flat} or it will increase weight. In contrast, DLM would always take the equal cost move unless it was on the tabu list (controlled by θ_2) or unless the maximum number of consecutive flat moves had already been taken (controlled by θ_1). PAWS retains DLM's preference for taking flat moves when no improving moves are available, by selecting random moves only from the domain of available flat moves. In contrast, when SAPS takes a random move (controlled by wp), it picks from the domain of all possible moves, regardless of cost. Finally, PAWS retains DLM's deterministic weight reduction scheme and the multiple inclusion of literals that appear in more than one false clause (whereas SAPS reduces weight probabilistically according to P_{smooth} and includes only unique literals in its candidate move list).

Figure 1 shows the complete PAWS procedure, which is now controlled by two parameters: P_{flat} which decides whether a randomly selected flat move will be taken (corresponding to wp in SAPS), and Max_{inc} which determines at which point weight will be decreased (corresponding to P_{smooth} in SAPS). As with wp in SAPS, we found that P_{flat} can be treated as a constant, and for all subsequent experiments it was set at 15%. Hence PAWS requires the tuning of only a single parameter, Max_{inc}, which we found to have roughly the same settings and sensitivity as the equivalent parameter in DLM. On all our test problems the optimum value of Max_{inc} was relatively easy to find, generally showing a similar concave-shaped relationship with local search cost as that observed for Walksat's noise parameter in (Hoos, 2002) (for example, see Figure 3b). The requirement to tune only a single parameter with a fairly stable relationship to cost gives PAWS a significant practical advantage over DLM and SAPS, which typically

---

[*] PAWS is a simplification and improvement over our earlier MAX-AGE algorithm, which was shown to be competitive with DLM on a range of larger SAT problems (Thornton et al., 2002).

[**] http://www.cs.ubc.ca/davet/dls4sat/software/saps-1.0.tar.gz.

need considerably more effort to set up for a particular set of problems (see Section 4.4 for a further discussion of parameter tuning).

3.1. DIFFERENCES BETWEEN SAPS AND PAWS

While PAWS comes close to being an additive version of SAPS, as discussed earlier, it differs in three aspects:

1. Multiple Inclusion (m): PAWS allows optimal cost flips that appear in n false clauses to also appear n times in its move list L (rather than exactly once).
2. Random Flat (r): PAWS probabilistically takes a random flat move when no improving move is available (rather than allowing cost increasing moves).
3. Deterministic Smoothing (d): PAWS reduces weight deterministically after Max_{inc} number of increases (rather than reducing weight with probability P_{smooth}).

In order to distinguish the essential from the inessential features of the two approaches, we developed four SAPS variants based on the inclusion of the above heuristics:

1. SAPS+m: includes the multiple inclusion heuristic from PAWS.
2. SAPS+r: replaces the pure random move selection of SAPS with a random flat move selection. Hence SAPS+r will (probabilistically) take a move in a local minimum only if there is at least one move available that does not increase the weighted solution cost.[★]
3. SAPS+d: replaces the probabilistic smoothing of SAPS with a deterministic weight reduction scheme that smooths weights after a fixed number of weight increases.
4. SAPS+a: uses all three heuristics at once, that is, multiple inclusion, random flat move and deterministic smoothing. Hence SAPS+a is equivalent to PAWS except for the use of multiplicative weighting.

We then developed four variants of PAWS that use the alternative SAPS heuristics:

1. PAWS-m: discards the multiple inclusion heuristic, and considers only distinct literals in move list L.
2. PAWS-r: discards the random flat move heuristic, and probabilistically selects a move in a local minimum without consideration of cost.

[★] In the original SAPS source code, the authors used a 0.1 threshold to distinguish an improving move from a zero cost move (see Figure 2). We therefore reused this value to define a flat move for SAPS+r as any move causing a weighted cost change within the range of ±0.1.

3. PAWS-d: uses probabilistic rather than deterministic weight reduction.
4. PAWS-a: uses all three of the above heuristics at once. Hence PAWS-a is equivalent to SAPS except for the use of additive weighting.

Finally, in our earlier work (Thornton et al., 2004), we observed that the average length of move list L for PAWS tends to be longer than for SAPS. The explanation for this difference is that multipliers create finer distinctions between clause weights: as multiplicative weights are real-valued, the previous history of clause weighting will be retained in small differences, even after smoothing. Hence, in longer term searches, we would expect clause weights to become more and more distinguished, making it increasingly unlikely that any two flips will evaluate to the same cost. Conversely, additive weighting changes clause weights by simply adding or subtracting one, and most weights are returned to a base weight of one at some point in the search. Hence longer term residual weight is eliminated, and the likelihood that different flips will evaluate to the same cost remains relatively high, meaning additive weighting will generally have a greater number of possible best cost moves to select from.

This led us to conjecture that differences in performance between SAPS and PAWS may be explained by differences in the number of moves available during the search. To test this, we developed a fifth variant of SAPS (SAPS+t) that includes a *threshold of indifference* between moves. This threshold is compared to an averaged flip cost, calculated by dividing the weighted cost change of a flip (Δw_{x_i} in Figure 2) by the current average clause weight. A flip is then included in list L if its cost change is within a threshold value of the best cost change available at that point in the search. This alters the SAPS move selection heuristic from Figure 2 to the heuristic shown in Figure 4.

In the following empirical study the threshold heuristic is added to the SAPS+a variant to make SAPS+t. Hence, SAPS+t is almost the same as PAWS, remaining indifferent to finer move distinctions but retaining a multiplicative clause weight ordering. In this way we can test our earlier conjecture that a

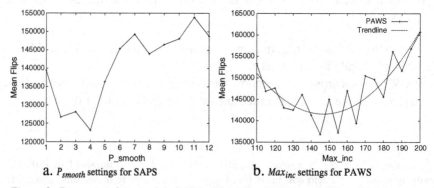

Figure 3. Parameter plots on the ais12 problem (for SAPS $\alpha = 1.25$, $\rho = 0.95$).

longer L has a positive impact on performance, all else being equal (Thornton et al., 2004).

4. Empirical Study

4.1. PROBLEM SET

To examine the relative performance of additive and multiplicative weighting, and the influences of the various SAPS and PAWS heuristics, we designed an experimental study using 29 benchmark problems that cover various dimensions of problem size, difficulty and structure.

First, we took the problem set reported in the original study on SAPS (Hutter et al., 2002), consisting of the median and hardest problems from several SATLIB problem classes. Second, to test performance on larger problem instances, we included the SATLIB ais12, logistics.d and bw-large.d blocks world problems, the two most difficult DIMACS graph colouring problems (g125.17 and g250.29) and the median and hardest DIMACS 16-bit parity learning problems (par16). We then generated two sets of random 3-SAT problems from the accepted hard region, each containing 20 instances, the first with 800 variables and the second with 1,600 variables. To these we added the f800 and f1600 DIMACS problems and selected the median and hardest problem from each set. Finally, we generated a range of random binary CSPs, again from the accepted hard region, and transformed them into SAT problems using the multivalued encoding described in (Prestwich, 2003). These problems were divided into four sets of five problems each, according to the number of variables (v), the domain size (d), and the constraint density (c) in the original CSP, giving the 30v10d40c (bin30-40), 30v10d80c (bin30-80), 50v15d40c (bin50-40) and 50v15d80c (bin50-80) problem sets from each of which the hardest problem was selected.[*]

4.2. COMPLETE *VERSUS* LOCAL SEARCH

One of the key motivations for the development of local search techniques for SAT is to solve problems beyond the reach of existing complete solvers. Complete solvers, even if slower on particular instances, have the advantage of unambiguously reporting if an instance is unsatisfiable. Hence, local search for SAT is most applicable to problems that are too difficult for complete search to solve in a reasonable time frame. This means that the scalability of local search is important and that evaluations on problems that can easily be solved by a complete solver are less decisive. To clarify this issue, we additionally tested our problem set using the well-known DPLL complete

---

[*] Note that for all the larger randomly generated problems satisfiability was determined using our own local search algorithms with a cut-off of 100 million flips. Hence we may have rejected some harder satisfiable instances.

solvers, Satz (version 214) (Li and Anbulagan, 1997) and zChaff (version 2004.11.15) (Moskewicz et al., 2001).

4.3. TESTING FOR SIGNIFICANCE

Local search run-times can vary significantly on the same problem instance, as determined by the initial starting point and any subsequent randomized decisions. For this reason empirical studies require the same problem to be solved multiple times, and at least for the mean, median, and standard deviation to be reported. However, it is still unclear exactly how much confidence we can have in the reported differences between algorithms. Standard deviation is informative for normally distributed data, but local search run-times are generally not normally distributed, often having the median to the left of the mean and a number of unpredictably distributed outliers. Hence standard comparisons that assume normality, such as a two-sample t-test, are not reliable, and the level of statistical confidence in differences between algorithms is rarely investigated.

However, nonparametric measures, such as the Wilcoxon rank–sum test, do not rely on normality and assume only that the distributions to be compared have a similar shape. To use the Wilcoxon test requires that the run-times (or number of flips) from two sets of observations, A and B, are sorted in ascending order. Then each observation is ranked (from $1 \ldots N$) and the sum of the ranks for distribution A is calculated. This value (w_A) can now be used to test the hypothesis that distribution A lies to the left of distribution B, i.e., $H_1 : A < B$, using the normal approximation to the Wilcoxon distribution (Gibbons and Chakraborti, 1992):[*]

$$z = \left(w_A - n_A(N+1)/2 - 0.5\right) \Big/ \sqrt{n_A n_B (N+1)/12},$$

where n_A and n_B are the number of observations in distributions A and B respectively and $N = n_A + n_B$. Using the standard $Z \sim \text{Normal}(0, 1)$ tables, z will give the probability P that the null hypothesis, $H_0 : A \geq B$, is true.

While the Wilcoxon test provides a good measure of overall performance, it can miss situations where one algorithm has a better probability of solving a problem within a certain time-range, even though its overall performance is relatively poor. In such circumstances a hybrid or portfolio approach (Gent et al., 1999) can produce better results, that is, using the algorithm that has the greater solution probability in a given time-range. Hence, to test whether one algorithm clearly dominates another, we produced run-time distributions (RTDs) (Hoos and Stützle, 1998) to compare the best performing algorithm variants for each problem. RTDs are used to analyze local search performance of multiple runs on the same problem instance. By calculating and graphing the cumulative

---

[*] Assuming $n_A > 12$, $n_B > 12$ and that no rank values are tied.

for each literal x_i in each false clause **do**
  $\Delta w_{x_i} \leftarrow \dfrac{\text{change in summed weight of false clauses caused by flipping } x_i}{\text{average clause weight}}$
  if $\Delta w_{x_i} \leq best + threshold$ **then**
    if $\Delta w_{x_i} < best$ **then**
      $best \leftarrow \Delta w_{x_i}$
      remove all x_j from L where $\Delta w_{x_j} - best > threshold$
    end if
    $L \leftarrow L \cup x_i$
  end if
end for

Figure 4. The SAPS+t move selection heuristic.

percentage of runs that have been solved over time, a picture of the overall behaviour of an algorithm on a problem can be obtained (see Figures 5 and 6). More important, if the RTD distribution of one algorithm dominates another on the same problem (i.e., at every time point it has solved a greater percentage of runs, as with the PAWS RTD of Figure 5a), then we can be more confident that the algorithm has the better performance. Conversely, if two RTD's cross (as in Figure 5b), then we cannot safely conclude that one is uniformly better than another.

We therefore used a combination of the Wilcoxon test and an RTD analysis to assess whether there is a significant difference in algorithm performance according to the following rule: if the Wilcoxon rank–sum test is significant for $P < 0.05$ *and* the RTD of the better algorithm dominates the other for all solution probabilities > 0.1 (as with the PAWS RTDs of Figure 6), then the algorithm is classed as significantly better on the problem instance.

4.4. PARAMETER SETTING

To make the empirical study feasible, we adopted a combination of exhaustive and local search strategies for setting the parameters of individual algorithm

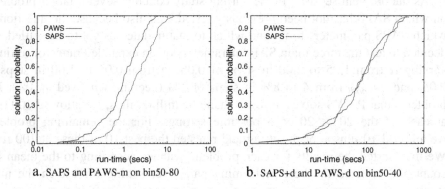

a. SAPS and PAWS-m on bin50-80   b. SAPS+d and PAWS-d on bin50-40

Figure 5. Comparative run-time distributions for the large binary CSPs.

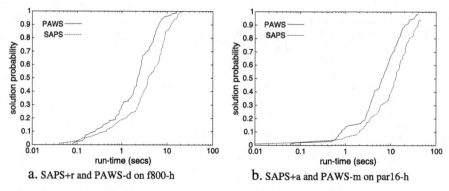

a. SAPS+r and PAWS-d on f800-h   b. SAPS+a and PAWS-m on par16-h

Figure 6. Comparative run-time distributions for f800-hard and par16-hard.

variants. In the exhaustive phase, we tested a range of parameter settings for the original SAPS and PAWS algorithms on each problem instance. As the issue of the number and sensitivity of parameters is important to our overall evaluation, we have taken a closer look at the parameter tuning process in the following two subsections.

4.4.1. *Tuning SAPS*

As discussed earlier (see Section 2), SAPS has four parameters: α, ρ, P_{smooth}, and wp. In the original study (Hutter et al., 2002), the SAPS authors fixed wp at 1% and P_{smooth} at 5% and manipulated α in the range of $1.1\ldots1.3$ and ρ in the range of $0.2\ldots0.9$. However, they acknowledge that "there are better parameter settings for almost all problem instances tested here. Determining these settings manually can be difficult and time-consuming." The attempt to reduce this difficulty led to the development of Reactive SAPS (RSAPS) (Hutter et al., 2002). Here, instead of fixing P_{smooth} and manipulating α and ρ, the authors fixed α, manually manipulated ρ, and set P_{smooth} using an automated reactive mechanism.

As the problem set used in the current study contains several larger problems on which SAPS has not been previously tested, and also because the question of which SAPS parameters to fix and which to manipulate has yet to be settled, we decided to test the three main SAPS parameters on an expanded range of settings, varying α from 1.05 to 2.00 in steps of 0.05, ρ from 0.05 to 1.00 in steps of 0.05, and P_{smooth} from 4 to 8% in steps of 1% (keeping wp fixed at 1%). For problems that PAWS solves in fewer than one million flips, we allowed 100 runs at each of the $20 \times 20 \times 5$ possible settings. For the remaining problems we allowed 10 runs at each setting and retested the best 10 of these at 100 runs. We then sorted the results for each problem instance according to the mean flip count and selected the best performing parameter setting for use in the main study.

We first allowed SAPS such a wide range of parameter values to ensure that the comparison with PAWS was not biased by a limited choice. Second, the experiment allows us to examine the range and sensitivity of the SAPS parameters. In Table I, we show the mean flip counts of the best parameter settings for SAPS on each test set problem, in comparison to the recommended default settings of $\alpha = 1.3$, $\rho = 0.8$ and $P_{smooth} = 5\%$, with 100 runs on each problem and a cut-off of 20 million flips (50 million for bin50-40). These results show that using default parameter settings is not a practical approach, particularly on the larger, more difficult problems. For instance, the default settings were unable to solve any run on the g250.29, f1600-med and f1600-hard problems, and could only solve one out of 100 runs on g125.17. The results also show that the best performing algorithms have exploited nearly the full range of parameter settings with α varying between 1.05 (bw_large.d) and 2.00 (par16-med), ρ varying between 0.05 (g125.17) and 1.00 (logistics.d), and P_{smooth} varying between 4% (ais10) and 7% (bw_large.c). However, the larger values for α appear only on nonstatistically significant results (par16-med and par16-hard[*]). Ignoring these two problems, α ranges more narrowly between 1.05 ... 1.40.

Although the results show that a wide range of parameter values was used to obtain the best performance, we have yet to consider the sensitivity of individual parameters. It could be the case that one SAPS parameter dominates the others to the extent that the variations in the dominated parameters do not significantly affect performance. We can first reject the hypothesis that α is insignificant from the bw_large.c result. Here α is the only parameter varied from the default, and the result is a significant difference in performance. There are several similar examples of a significant difference obtained by only manipulating ρ from the default (i.e., flat200-med, uf200-hard, uf400-med, uf400-hard, and logistics.c). Hence we can conclude that α and ρ are important parameters, with ρ showing a significant difference at a sensitivity of at least 0.1 (for logistics.c) and α showing a sensitivity of at least 0.15 (for bw_large.d).

However, as Table I does not show a significant difference arising from the manipulation of P_{smooth} alone, we decided to look at an individual problem (ais12) in more detail. From our initial parameter tests at 100 runs, the best setting for SAPS on ais12 was $\alpha = 1.25$, $\rho = 0.95$, and $P_{smooth} = 4\%$. In order to test sensitivity, we decided to manipulate P_{smooth} from 1% to 12% in steps of 1% at 1,000 runs per setting, keeping the other parameters fixed at their tuned values. The mean flip values for each of these settings are graphed in Figure 3a and show there is a relationship between P_{smooth} and performance on this problem. We performed a further Wilcoxon analysis between the 4% and 5% P_{smooth} settings and found a *nearly* significant time difference at $p = 0.06852$. A second comparison between the 4% and 6% settings did yield a significant difference at $p = 0.00013$.

---

[*] Although not statistically different on flips the tuned par16 runs had better success rates.

Table 1. SAPS parameter tuning comparison: SAPS defaults are α 1.30, ρ 0.80, and P_{smooth} 5%.

Problem	Tuned settings			Tuned results		Default results		Speed-up	Wilcoxon	
	α	ρ	P	Success (%)	Mean flips	Success (%)	Mean flips		p-value	Significant
bw_large.a	1.30	0.80	6	100	2,824	100	3,000	1.06	0.13066	×
bw_large.b	1.30	0.80	5	100	45,335	=	=	=	=	=
bw_large.c	1.10	0.60	7	100	2,103,352	75	7,034,958	3.34	0.00000	✓
bw_large.d	1.05	0.80	5	100	2,398,205	5	19,589,233	8.17	0.00000	✓
flat100-med	1.30	0.40	5	100	7,460	100	10,729	1.44	0.00000	✓
flat100-hard	1.30	0.80	6	100	31,812	100	29,906	0.94	0.86585	×
flat200-med	1.30	0.40	5	100	83,558	100	168,030	2.01	0.00000	✓
flat200-hard	1.30	0.40	5	100	3,397,088	100	3,837,537	1.13	0.15793	×
g125.17	1.20	0.05	5	97	4,187,750	1	19,953,867	4.76	0.00000	✓
g250.29	1.15	0.10	6	90	4,622,915	0	20,000,000	4.33	0.00000	✓
uf100-hard	1.30	0.80	5	100	4,250	=	=	=	=	=
uf250-med	1.30	0.40	6	100	7,050	100	13,584	1.93	0.00000	✓
uf250-hard	1.30	0.70	5	100	223,593	100	254,243	1.14	0.00710	✓
uf400-med	1.30	0.20	5	100	61,159	100	167,785	2.74	0.00000	✓
uf400-hard	1.30	0.20	5	100	1,446,987	98	3,901,415	2.70	0.00000	✓

f800-med	1.25	0.10	5	100	263,105	33	16,665,531	63.34	0.00000	✓
f800-hard	1.25	0.30	5	100	1,754,017	17	18,593,591	10.60	0.00000	✓
f1600-med	1.25	0.30	5	99	1,303,941	0	20,000,000	15.34	0.00000	✓
f1600-hard	1.25	0.30	5	94	7,777,980	0	20,000,000	2.57	0.00000	✓
ais10	1.30	0.90	4	100	18,085	100	20,339	1.12	0.00384	✓
ais12	1.25	0.95	4	100	123,099	100	186,402	1.51	0.00000	✓
logistics.c	1.30	0.90	5	100	8,436	100	9,399	1.11	0.00088	✓
logistics.d	1.20	1.00	4	100	21,248	100	57,151	2.69	0.00000	✓
par16-med	2.00	0.25	7	88	7,720,965	82	7,521,553	0.97	0.54918	×
par16-hard	1.40	0.90	4	86	9,725,495	78	9,825,138	1.01	0.12296	×
bin30-80	1.30	0.10	6	100	12,299	100	23,127	1.88	0.00000	✓
bin30-40	1.25	0.50	6	100	19,711	100	36,826	1.87	0.00000	✓
bin50-80	1.20	0.10	6	100	186,552	100	1,495,097	8.01	0.00000	✓
bin50-40	1.25	0.25	5	99	11,562,103	70	25,607,766	2.21	0.00000	✓

In the table P_{smooth} is abbreviated to P and rows with '=' values indicate the default and tuned settings were equal.

From the foregoing analysis we can conclude that each of the three main SAPS parameters can produce significant differences in performance on at least one of the test problems. However, this result must be qualified in several respects. First, fine tuning parameters is unnecessary when comparing with another algorithm, if a coarsely tuned version still dominates. As the subsequent results show, SAPS does not clearly dominate PAWS, and so the fine tuning of parameters can be justified. Second, while the individual parameters are sensitive in isolation, this does not mean that one or two parameters could be fixed, and the free parameter(s) adjusted to achieve optimal performance (this assumes that different combinations of parameter settings could produce the same optimal performance). The earlier study on RSAPS (Hutter et al., 2002) shows that holding α and ρ constant and manipulating P_{smooth} is not as effective as additionally allowing ρ to change. This indicates that at least two SAPS parameters need to be manipulated to achieve acceptable performance.

If we further consider the actual effects of α, ρ and P_{smooth}, it seems reasonable to assume that similar weighting behaviour could be achieved with combinations of different settings, that is, α determines the amount of weight increase, ρ determines the amount of decrease, and P_{smooth} determines how frequently a decrease occurs. Hence we could expect a smaller increase and larger decrease performed less frequently to behave similarly to a large increase and a smaller decrease performed more frequently. In this case we would prefer the setting that reduces weight more infrequently, as it would be more time efficient. But the question remains as to how infrequently weight can be reduced without degrading performance. Certainly we know performance will degrade eventually, as the limit would be to never reduce weight, and the more infrequently we reduce weight the more insensitive the search becomes to local conditions.

In summary, we conjecture there may be discoverable relationships between α, ρ, and P_{smooth} that could simplify the parameter tuning process. It may also be the case that a more fine grained tuning of one parameter could eliminate the need to tune another. We leave these questions for future research. In practical terms, the sensitivity of the SAPS parameters means we cannot be certain of obtaining the best performance without searching an extensive range of settings. While a particular parameter may not be sensitive on a particular problem, we are unfortunately unable to know this in advance.

4.4.2. *Tuning PAWS*

Tuning PAWS presented a relatively simpler problem. Keeping P_{flat} constant at 15%, we manipulated Max_{inc} from 5 to 100 in steps of 5, with 100 runs at each setting (as with SAPS we reduced the number of runs for the more difficult problems). We then graphed the mean flip performance against Max_{inc} and decided on an optimum setting by visual inspection. If the performance still appeared to be improving at $Max_{inc} = 100$, we tested PAWS with no weight decrease (i.e., $Max_{inc} = \infty$), and, if this proved better than $Max_{inc} = 100$, the ∞

value was accepted. Otherwise we continued with a further analysis from 105 to 200 in steps of five (this secondary analysis only proved necessary for the ais12 problem). Given an optimum point from graphical analysis, a final fine grained analysis was performed around this point, in the range of ±5 in steps of ±1. From this the best value was selected and used in the remainder of the study. As an example, the performance graph for PAWS on ais12 for the Max_{inc} range of 110 to 200 is shown in Figure 3b (with a trendline fitted). This gives a fairly typical picture of the behaviour of Max_{inc}, showing the presence of an unambiguous minimum flip value.

While Max_{inc} is sensitive to changes down to ±1, especially for $Max_{inc} < 20$, the tuning process is considerably simpler than for SAPS and contains less margin for error due to noise. This is because the single parameter allows for a simple graphical analysis and hence the identification of trends that are independent of noise. Conversely, tuning SAPS runs the risk of missing the best parameter settings, even when averaging over 100 runs.

4.4.3. *Tuning the Variant Algorithms*

After completing the above exhaustive parameter tuning exercise, we used the SAPS parameter settings to test the SAPS variants and the PAWS parameter settings to test the PAWS variants, with two qualifications:

1. Changing from deterministic to probabilistic smoothing or *vice versa* (i.e., for SAPS+d, SAPS+a, SAPS+t, PAWS-d, and PAWS-a) requires a conversion of the PAWS Max_{inc} and SAPS P_{smooth} parameters. This is achieved by dividing either parameter into 100. For example, if $Max_{inc} = 5$, this is converted to a P_{smooth} value of $100/5 = 20\%$, that is, reducing weight at every 5th local minimum is most closely approximated by a 20% chance of reducing weight at *each* local minimum. Similarly, P_{smooth} can be converted to a Max_{inc} value using the same procedure, that is, $100/20 = 5$.
2. Although SAPS is usually run with a fixed *wp* probability of 1% and PAWS is run with a fixed flat move probability of 15%, it was not clear which probability value to use when converting between the two random move selection heuristics. We therefore ran versions of SAPS+r, SAPS+a, PAWS-r, and PAWS-a using both settings and selected the best performing variant.

After these conversions, we tested all variants on the full problem set. The results of a similar experiment (excluding SAPS+a, SAPS+t, and PAWS-a) were informally described in (Thornton et al., 2004), where it was concluded that no particular variant produced an improvement over the base versions. For the current study, further parameter tuning was executed in the local neighbourhoods of the original conversions. From this we found that the α and ρ values for SAPS are fairly robust, as was P_{smooth} for SAPS+m and SAPS+d. However, our test showed that the Max_{inc}/P_{smooth} conversions did not necessarily produce the best performance on all problems. Also, on several problems, the optimal Max_{inc} settings for PAWS-m and PAWS-r differed slightly from the original PAWS setting. Using these more refined settings we were able to produce considerably better performance across the range of SAPS and PAWS variants, as the following results show.

4.5. RESULTS

Tables II–X divide the problem set results according to problem types, placing the instances in ascending order of size and/or difficulty within each table. For each problem we then report the performance of the original PAWS and SAPS algorithms and their variants, as described in Section 3.1. All results have a 20 million flip cut-off, except bin50-40, which has a 50 million cut-off, and the statistics refer to averages over 1,000 runs, except for those problems where at least one algorithm has an average flip cost greater than one million, in which case the average is over 100 runs.[★]

In all six tables, the Wilcoxon values give the probability that the null hypothesis $A \geq B$ is true, where A is the distribution of flips or run-times that has the *smaller* rank–sum value. We record P-values against distribution A and take $P < 0.05$ to indicate that A is significantly less than B, marking such results with '*'. The *intra* Wilcoxon column compares flips for the standard SAPS and SAPS+a heuristics for SAPS, and the standard PAWS and PAWS-a heuristics for PAWS. Hence the Wilcoxon intra column value of 0.3473f in the bw_large.a, SAPS+a row of Table II indicates that we can reject the hypothesis that SAPS+a has significantly better flip performance than SAPS on this problem (in all Wilcoxon statistics an 'f' refers to a comparison between flips and a 't' refers to a comparison between run-times). Conversely, the intra column value of *0.0283f in the bw_large.d, PAWS row of Table II indicates that we can accept the hypothesis that PAWS has significantly better performance than PAWS-a on this problem. Additionally, the Wilcoxon *inter* column compares the original SAPS and PAWS heuristics in terms of both flips and time. Hence the Wilcoxon inter column values of *0.0000f and *0.0000t in the bw_large.d, PAWS section of Table II indicate that we can accept the hypothesis that the basic PAWS heuristic has better flip and time performance than the basic SAPS heuristic on this problem. The additional RTD analysis described in Section 4.3 is shown in Table XI, where we present an overall comparison of the results.

Lastly, the table parameter column values for each variant are encoded using α, ρ, s and n, where α and ρ have their usual SAPS interpretation, but s and n

---

[★] All experiments were performed on a Sun supercomputer with $8 \times$ Sun Fire V880 servers, each with $8 \times$ UltraSPARC-III 900 MHz CPU and 8 GB memory per node.

have common definitions across both SAPS and PAWS variants, where s represents the smoothing parameter, which has a probabilistic interpretation for SAPS, SAPS+m, SAPS+r, PAWS-d, and PAWS-a and a deterministic interpretation for all other variants (see Section 4.4), and n represents a noise parameter that applies either as the probability of taking a pure random move for SAPS, SAPS+m, SAPS+d, PAWS-r, and PAWS-a or as the probability of taking a random flat move for all other variants.

In the following subsections we discuss the results for each of the six problem domains.

4.5.1. *Blocks World Results*

For the smaller bw_large.a and b problems (in Table II), the SAPS variants generally have the better flip performance. However, this advantage does not carry over into the time domain, where PAWS is not significantly different from SAPS on bw_large.a and dominates on the three other problems. PAWS further dominates SAPS in terms of flips for bw_large.c and d. Hence, as problem size and difficulty increase, the PAWS variants also improve relative to SAPS, meaning PAWS has the overall advantage for this problem set.

In terms of individual variants, SAPS+a dominates the original SAPS, being significantly better on problems b and d and slightly better on a and c. SAPS+a also challenges PAWS on bw_large.b, having a better flip count and roughly equal time performance. For the PAWS variants, there is a (nonsignificant) indication that PAWS-a does better on the smaller a and b problems, but standard PAWS becomes better on the larger problems and is significantly better on bw_large.d.

4.5.2. *Graph Colouring Results*

As with the blocks world problems, SAPS starts well on the smaller graph colouring problems, having significantly better flip and time performance on the two flat-100 problems (see Table III). However, as problem size increases, the relative performance of PAWS also improves, becoming significantly better than SAPS in terms of flips and time on flat200-med and on the larger g125.17 and g250.29 problems (see Table IV) and roughly equal on flat200-hard.

The SAPS+a variant again looks better than standard SAPS, being significantly better on flat100-med, flat-200-med, and g125.17 and *verging* on significantly better for the flat100-hard and flat200-hard problems. However, the situation is less clear for the largest g250.29 problem, where SAPS is significantly better than SAPS+a but has poorer success rate (90% *versus* 98%). For the PAWS variants, there is little difference on the smaller flat100 problems, but for all larger problems PAWS becomes significantly better.

Considering the standard SAPS and PAWS algorithms, we can conclude that PAWS has the better performance on this problem set, particularly as

Table II. Blocks world planning problem results.

Problem	Method	Parameters	Success (%)	Time (s)		Flips		Wilcoxon	
				Median	Mean	Median	Mean	Intra	Inter
bw_large.a	SAPS	$\alpha 1.3\rho 0.8 s6n1$	100	0.01	0.01	2,184	2,824		*0.0007f
	SAPS+m	$\alpha 1.3\rho 0.8 s6n1$	100	0.01	0.01	2,236	2,905		
	SAPS+r	$\alpha 1.3\rho 0.8 s6n1$	100	0.01	0.01	2,168	2,895		
	SAPS+d	$\alpha 1.3\rho 0.8 s16n1$	100	0.01	0.01	2,155	2,809		
	SAPS+a	$\alpha 1.3\rho 0.8 s16n1$	100	0.01	0.01	2,089	2,772	0.3473f	
	SAPS+t	$\alpha 1.3\rho 0.8 s16n15$	100	0.01	0.02	2,251	2,889		
	PAWS	$s34n15$	100	0.01	0.01	2,518	3,235		
	PAWS-m	$s34n15$	100	0.01	0.01	2,273	3,003		0.4570t
	PAWS-r	$s34n15$	100	0.01	0.01	2,403	3,067		
	PAWS-d	$s3n15$	100	0.01	0.01	2,369	3,169	0.2075f	
	PAWS-a	$s3n1$	100	0.01	0.01	2,453	3,118		
bw_large.b	SAPS	$\alpha 1.3\rho 0.8 s5n1$	100	0.20	0.26	34,488	45,335		0.4302f
	SAPS+m	$\alpha 1.3\rho 0.8 s5n1$	100	0.20	0.28	34,584	48,071		
	SAPS+r	$\alpha 1.3\rho 0.8 s5n1$	100	0.17	0.26	29,701	45,750		
	SAPS+d	$\alpha 1.3\rho 0.8 s30n1$	100	0.15	0.21	26,910	39,033		
	SAPS+a	$\alpha 1.3\rho 0.8 s30n1$	100	0.16	0.21	27,591	37,731	*0.0000f	
	SAPS+t	$\alpha 1.3\rho 0.8 s30n15$	100	0.19	0.27	26,508	38,524		
	PAWS	$s50n15$	100	0.16	0.21	33,480	45,501		
	PAWS-m	$s50n15$	100	0.15	0.20	30,832	43,418		*0.0000t
	PAWS-r	$s50n15$	100	0.16	0.21	32,977	44,635		
	PAWS-d	$s2n15$	100	0.15	0.21	32,104	44,458	0.2402f	
	PAWS-a	$s2n1$	100	0.15	0.21	32,133	44,109		

bw_large.c	SAPS	α1.1ρ0.6s7n1	100	17.63	26.45	1,366,319	2,103,352			
	SAPS+m	α1.1ρ0.6s7n1	100	18.53	30.96	1,448,924	2,370,600			
	SAPS+r	α1.1ρ0.6s7n1	100	21.21	30.02	1,669,114	2,264,986			
	SAPS+d	α1.1ρ0.6s20n1	100	13.80	16.68	1,366,083	1,671,323	0.1256f		
	SAPS+a	α1.1ρ0.6s20n15	100	12.72	17.20	1,224,860	1,664,822			
	SAPS+t	α1.1ρ0.6s20n15	82	15.00	29.34	1,471,762	4,665,851	0.3147f	*0.0001f	
	PAWS	s5n15	100	4.74	6.87	798,389	1,181,032		*0.0000t	
	PAWS-m	s5n15	100	4.64	6.67	786,344	1,143,014			
	PAWS-r	s5n15	100	5.84	7.40	957,610	1,247,581			
	PAWS-d	s30n15	100	7.26	9.04	1,246,342	1,581,417			
	PAWS-a	s30n1	100	4.41	6.96	742,669	1,206,099			
bw_large.d	SAPS	α1.05ρ0.8s5n1	100	29.22	37.87	1,868,733	2,398,205			
	SAPS+m	α1.05ρ0.8s5n1	100	25.11	36.64	1,512,079	2,213,055			
	SAPS+r	α1.05ρ0.8s5n1	100	30.92	47.27	1,884,327	2,819,920			
	SAPS+d	α1.05ρ0.8s20n1	100	21.68	29.00	1,210,114	1,660,640	*0.0002f		
	SAPS+a	α1.05ρ0.8s20n15	100	20.01	25.53	1,152,146	1,536,322			
	SAPS+t	α1.05ρ0.8s20n15	85	34.03	48.02	2,575,821	4,949,418	*0.0283f	*0.0000f	
	PAWS	s4n15	100	7.07	10.87	903,962	1,432,780		*0.0000t	
	PAWS-m	s4n15	100	7.50	10.13	1,007,744	1,324,650			
	PAWS-r	s4n15	100	8.24	10.45	1,058,403	1,349,599			
	PAWS-d	s35n15	100	7.72	12.67	930,462	1,594,599			
	PAWS-a	s35n15	100	9.65	15.75	1,175,815	1,956,037			

Table III. Small graph colouring problem results.

Problem	Method	Parameters	Success (%)	Time (s)		Flips		Wilcoxon	
				Median	Mean	Median	Mean	Intra	Inter
flat100-med	SAPS	$\alpha 1.3\rho 0.4s5n1$	100	0.01	0.01	5,415	7,460		*0.0004f
	SAPS+m	$\alpha 1.3\rho 0.4s5n1$	100	0.01	0.01	5,156	7,340		*0.0209t
	SAPS+r	$\alpha 1.3\rho 0.4s5n1$	100	0.01	0.01	5,314	7,532		
	SAPS+d	$\alpha 1.3\rho 0.4s20n1$	100	0.01	0.01	4,623	6,381		
	SAPS+a	$\alpha 1.3\rho 0.4s20n1$	100	0.01	0.01	4,684	6,527	*0.0056f	
	SAPS+t	$\alpha 1.3\rho 0.4s20n15$	100	0.01	0.02	5,182	7,425		
	PAWS	$s13n15$	100	0.01	0.01	6,402	8,628	0.4683f	
	PAWS-m	$s10n15$	100	0.01	0.01	5,747	7,883		
	PAWS-r	$s13n15$	100	0.01	0.01	6,078	8,117		
	PAWS-d	$s11n15$	100	0.01	0.02	6,409	9,024		
	PAWS-a	$s11n1$	100	0.01	0.02	6,207	8,676		
flat100-hard	SAPS	$\alpha 1.3\rho 0.8s6n1$	100	0.04	0.06	21,965	31,812		*0.0010f
	SAPS+m	$\alpha 1.3\rho 0.8s6n1$	100	0.04	0.06	20,938	30,288		*0.0164t
	SAPS+r	$\alpha 1.3\rho 0.8s6n1$	100	0.04	0.05	22,422	30,669		
	SAPS+d	$\alpha 1.3\rho 0.8s18n1$	100	0.04	0.05	21,449	30,026		
	SAPS+a	$\alpha 1.3\rho 0.8s18n1$	100	0.04	0.05	20,888	29,321	0.0649f	
	SAPS+t	$\alpha 1.3\rho 0.8s18n15$	100	0.05	0.08	19,828	29,952		
	PAWS	$s46n15$	100	0.05	0.06	26,065	36,178	0.2398f	
	PAWS-m	$s46n15$	100	0.04	0.06	25,626	37,882		
	PAWS-r	$s46n15$	100	0.05	0.07	27,191	39,825		
	PAWS-d	$s2n15$	100	0.04	0.06	25,039	35,993		
	PAWS-a	$s2n1$	100	0.04	0.06	27,046	37,880		

flat200-med	SAPS	$\alpha 1.3 \rho 0.4 s5 n1$	100	0.12	0.17	57,411	83,558		
	SAPS+m	$\alpha 1.3 \rho 0.4 s5 n1$	100	0.12	0.17	55,035	79,073		
	SAPS+r	$\alpha 1.3 \rho 0.4 s5 n1$	100	0.12	0.17	59,249	82,414		
	SAPS+d	$\alpha 1.3 \rho 0.4 s20 n1$	100	0.09	0.13	43,725	61,878	*0.0000f	
	SAPS+a	$\alpha 1.3 \rho 0.4 s20 n1$	100	0.09	0.12	40,900	57,946		
	SAPS+t	$\alpha 1.3 \rho 0.4 s20 n15$	100	0.16	0.23	48,850	71,190		
	PAWS	$s10 n15$	100	0.10	0.13	48,990	67,781	*0.0000f	*0.0002f
	PAWS-m	$s9 n15$	100	0.10	0.13	53,529	71,553		*0.0000t
	PAWS-r	$s11 n15$	100	0.11	0.15	56,983	78,090		
	PAWS-d	$s13 n15$	100	0.11	0.16	59,731	80,022		
	PAWS-a	$s13 n1$	100	0.12	0.17	64,818	88,593		
flat200-hard	SAPS	$\alpha 1.3 \rho 0.4 s5 n1$	100	4.86	6.38	3,173,188	3,397,088		
	SAPS+m	$\alpha 1.3 \rho 0.4 s5 n1$	100	3.75	5.64	1,801,981	2,714,483		
	SAPS+r	$\alpha 1.3 \rho 0.4 s5 n1$	100	3.63	5.11	1,791,686	2,532,616		
	SAPS+d	$\alpha 1.3 \rho 0.4 s20 n1$	100	3.02	4.50	1,526,524	2,283,598		
	SAPS+a	$\alpha 1.3 \rho 0.4 s20 n1$	100	3.34	4.95	1,634,472	2,417,211	0.0525f	
	SAPS+t	$\alpha 1.3 \rho 0.4 s20 n15$	93	5.83	9.76	1,949,826	3,445,606		
	PAWS	$s74 n15$	99	4.34	5.90	2,354,944	3,224,432	*0.0004f	0.3842f
	PAWS-m	$s74 n15$	99	4.34	6.68	2,414,031	3,748,207		0.2121t
	PAWS-r	$s74 n15$	100	5.58	6.70	3,009,177	3,621,447		
	PAWS-d	$s2 n15$	98	6.52	9.45	3,376,852	5,001,280		
	PAWS-a	$s2 n15$	99	7.83	9.93	4,245,350	5,425,641		

Table IV. Large graph colouring problem results.

Problem	Method	Parameters	Success (%)	Time (s)		Flips		Wilcoxon	
				Median	Mean	Median	Mean	Intra	Inter
g125.17	SAPS	$\alpha 1.2\rho 0.05s5n1$	97	55.59	81.65	2,772,017	4,187,750		
	SAPS+m	$\alpha 1.2\rho 0.05s5n1$	99	59.86	86.35	2,940,185	4,253,806		
	SAPS+r	$\alpha 1.2\rho 0.05s5n1$	99	54.59	81.10	2,683,624	3,998,689		
	SAPS+d	$\alpha 1.2\rho 0.05s25n1$	89	55.85	104.55	2,564,038	5,457,198		
	SAPS+a	$\alpha 1.2\rho 0.05s25n15$	100	35.10	52.35	1,845,627	2,641,413	*0.0104f	
	SAPS+t	$\alpha 1.2\rho 0.05s25n15$	73	55.80	111.66	2,696,440	7,259,569		
	PAWS	$s4n15$	100	7.91	10.89	596,447	841,063	*0.0245f	*0.0000f
	PAWS-m	$s4n15$	100	7.68	9.17	542,355	668,972		*0.0000t
	PAWS-r	$s5n15$	100	11.93	15.23	821,849	1,057,978		
	PAWS-d	$s40n15$	100	8.76	13.27	644,027	986,354		
	PAWS-a	$s40n15$	100	11.86	17.15	849,986	1,235,643		
g250.29	SAPS	$\alpha 1.15\rho 0.1s6n1$	90	100.14	219.92	563,152	4,622,915	*0.0000f	
	SAPS+m	$\alpha 1.15\rho 0.1s6n1$	92	102.70	201.86	595,098	3,876,035		
	SAPS+r	$\alpha 1.15\rho 0.1s6n1$	98	92.71	166.75	576,122	1,554,811		
	SAPS+d	$\alpha 1.15\rho 0.1s30n15$	99	107.15	182.17	845,374	1,727,007		
	SAPS+a	$\alpha 1.15\rho 0.1s33n15$	98	170.04	289.68	1,477,554	3,124,190		
	SAPS+t	$\alpha 1.15\rho 0.1s33n15$	86	285.47	429.94	2,661,027	5,313,553		
	PAWS	$s4n15$	100	19.73	21.89	275,188	315,937	*0.0000f	*0.0000f
	PAWS-m	$s4n15$	100	20.33	23.92	252,243	302,942		*0.0000t
	PAWS-r	$s5n15$	100	34.22	45.43	348,796	483,978		
	PAWS-d	$s36n15$	100	29.66	38.17	364,024	444,394		
	PAWS-a	$s36n1$	100	47.22	60.43	502,662	633,402		

problem size grows. However, if we include consideration of the SAPS variants, then SAPS further dominates on both flat200 problems, at least in terms of flips. This is examined in more detail when we look at the overall results in Table XI.

4.5.3. *Small and Medium Random 3-SAT Results*

Repeating the blocks world and graph colouring pattern, SAPS begins well on the smaller problems, with significantly better flip and time performance on uf250-hard and significantly better flip performance uf100-hard, but is overtaken by PAWS on uf250-med and both larger uf400 problems (see Tables V and VI).

Variant performance also follows the previous results, with PAWS consistently outperforming PAWS-a, and SAPS+a outperforming SAPS on all problems except uf100-hard. SAPS+a further dominates PAWS in terms of flips of uf400-hard (see Table VI), while achieving similar time performance (see Table XI for more details).

4.5.4. *Large Random 3-SAT Results*

These problems continue the 3-SAT results from Tables V and VI and show the dominance of PAWS growing as problem size increases, with significantly better performance compared to all SAPS variants for all problems in terms of both flips and time (see Table VII).

PAWS remains dominant over PAWS-a, but PAWS-d also performs well on the three larger and more difficult problems. More interesting, the previous dominance of SAPS+a over SAPS breaks down, with no significant difference on any problem except f1600-med where SAPS dominates.

4.5.5. *Structured DIMACS Results*

These less related problems show PAWS doing significantly better on the par16 and logistics instances but with SAPS pulling ahead on flip count for the ais problems (see Tables VIII and IX). However, as the ais problem difficulty increases, there are signs that PAWS scales better, particularly in terms of time performance.

SAPS+a returns to its position of relative dominance over SAPS, although it achieves a significant difference only on logistics.c and ais12. PAWS also continues to dominate or roughly equal the performance of PAWS-a and its other variants.

4.5.6. *Random CSP Results*

Table X shows the results for the random binary CSPs. These problems present a mixed picture, with SAPS showing better flip but equal time performance on bin30-40, and PAWS showing significantly better time and flip performance on bin30-80. For the larger problems, and unlike the other problem domains, SAPS

Table V. Small random 3-SAT problem results.

Problem	Method	Parameters	Success (%)	Time (s)		Flips		Wilcoxon		
				Median	Mean	Median	Mean	Intra	Intra	Inter
uf100-hard	SAPS	$\alpha 1.3 \rho 0.8 s5n1$	100	0.01	0.01	2,857	4,250	0.4726f		*0.0444f
	SAPS+m	$\alpha 1.3 \rho 0.8 s5n1$	100	0.01	0.01	3,041	4,344			*0.2460t
	SAPS+r	$\alpha 1.3 \rho 0.8 s5n1$	100	0.01	0.01	2,924	4,120			
	SAPS+d	$\alpha 1.3 \rho 0.8 s20n1$	100	0.01	0.01	2,833	4,095			
	SAPS+a	$\alpha 1.3 \rho 0.8 s20n1$	100	0.01	0.01	2,936	4,330			
	SAPS+t	$\alpha 1.3 \rho 0.8 s20n15$	100	0.01	0.01	3,222	4,455			
	PAWS	$s40n15$	100	0.01	0.01	3,282	4,579	*0.0280f		
	PAWS-m	$s40n15$	100	0.01	0.01	3,124	4,641			
	PAWS-r	$s40n15$	100	0.01	0.01	3,368	5,017			
	PAWS-d	$s3n15$	100	0.01	0.01	3,370	4,650			
	PAWS-a	$s3n1$	100	0.01	0.01	3,614	4,809			
uf250-med	SAPS	$\alpha 1.3 \rho 0.4 s6n1$	100	0.01	0.02	4,895	7,050			
	SAPS+m	$\alpha 1.3 \rho 0.4 s6n1$	100	0.01	0.02	4,799	6,939			
	SAPS+r	$\alpha 1.3 \rho 0.4 s6n1$	100	0.01	0.02	4,628	6,353			
	SAPS+d	$\alpha 1.3 \rho 0.4 s19n1$	100	0.01	0.01	4,282	5,972			
	SAPS+a	$\alpha 1.3 \rho 0.4 s19n1$	100	0.01	0.02	4,519	6,442	0.0503f		
	SAPS+t	$\alpha 1.3 \rho 0.4 s19n15$	100	0.02	0.02	4,647	6,197			
	PAWS	$s11n15$	100	0.01	0.01	3,795	5,040	*0.0000f		*0.0000f
	PAWS-m	$s11n15$	100	0.01	0.01	3,954	5,356			*0.0000t
	PAWS-r	$s11n15$	100	0.01	0.01	3,733	5,183			
	PAWS-d	$s12n15$	100	0.01	0.01	4,135	5,705			
	PAWS-a	$s12n1$	100	0.01	0.01	4,358	5,993			

uf250-hard								
SAPS	$\alpha1.3\rho0.7s5n1$	100	0.41	0.56	160,710	223,593	*0.0000f	*0.0000t
SAPS+m	$\alpha1.3\rho0.7s5n1$	100	0.39	0.58	149,149	223,794		
SAPS+r	$\alpha1.3\rho0.7s5n1$	100	0.39	0.55	156,802	220,161		
SAPS+d	$\alpha1.3\rho0.7s20n1$	100	0.34	0.53	140,166	215,087	*0.0412f	
SAPS+a	$\alpha1.3\rho0.7s20n1$	100	0.36	0.52	140,695	206,023		
SAPS+t	$\alpha1.3\rho0.7s20n15$	100	0.53	0.70	152,322	202,540	*0.0008f	
PAWS	$s18n15$	100	0.52	0.79	213,393	320,273		
PAWS-m	$s17n15$	100	0.63	0.94	262,147	394,199		
PAWS-r	$s18n15$	100	0.56	0.83	229,184	342,383		
PAWS-d	$s7n15$	100	0.55	0.78	222,563	316,954		
PAWS-a	$s7n1$	100	0.64	0.91	265,259	375,917		

Table VI. Medium random 3-SAT problem results.

Problem	Method	Parameters	Success (%)	Time (s) Median	Time (s) Mean	Flips Median	Flips Mean	Wilcoxon Intra	Wilcoxon Inter
uf400-med	SAPS	$\alpha1.3\rho0.2s5n1$	100	0.12	0.17	42,514	61,159		
	SAPS+m	$\alpha1.3\rho0.2s5n1$	100	0.12	0.17	41,799	59,483		
	SAPS+r	$\alpha1.3\rho0.2s5n1$	100	0.13	0.17	45,721	61,997		
	SAPS+d	$\alpha1.3\rho0.2s20n1$	100	0.09	0.14	33,420	50,452	*0.0000f	
	SAPS+a	$\alpha1.3\rho0.2s20n15$	100	0.09	0.13	31,938	47,701		
	SAPS+t	$\alpha1.3\rho0.2s20n15$	100	0.13	0.19	33,425	48,856		
	PAWS	$s9n15$	100	0.08	0.10	28,601	38,363	*0.0000f	*0.0000f
	PAWS-m	$s9n15$	100	0.07	0.10	27,945	39,660		*0.0000t
	PAWS-r	$s9n15$	100	0.08	0.11	29,027	42,359		
	PAWS-d	$s12n15$	100	0.09	0.12	32,760	44,729		
	PAWS-a	$s12n1$	100	0.09	0.13	35,277	49,865		
uf400-hard	SAPS	$\alpha1.3\rho0.2s5n1$	100	2.06	4.01	744,592	1,446,987		
	SAPS+m	$\alpha1.3\rho0.2s5n1$	100	2.92	4.10	102,8231	1,441,876		
	SAPS+r	$\alpha1.3\rho0.2s5n1$	100	2.15	3.33	779,638	1,207,029		
	SAPS+d	$\alpha1.3\rho0.2s20n1$	100	1.46	2.14	549,547	804,463		
	SAPS+a	$\alpha1.3\rho0.2s20n15$	100	1.31	1.98	479,088	726,173	*0.0001f	
	SAPS+t	$\alpha1.3\rho0.2s20n15$	96	2.09	5.13	555,764	1,496,309		
	PAWS	$s8n15$	100	1.71	2.28	699,892	929,791	*0.0036f	*0.0178f
	PAWS-m	$s8n15$	100	1.76	2.48	705,893	1,000,962		*0.0026f
	PAWS-r	$s8n15$	100	2.08	2.76	857,409	1,154,580		
	PAWS-d	$s17n15$	100	2.08	2.55	834,369	1,017,859		
	PAWS-a	$s17n1$	100	2.83	3.88	1,116,114	1,537,465		

and PAWS show roughly equivalent performance, with SAPS having an edge in terms of flips for bin50-40 and PAWS being significantly better in terms of time on bin50-80.

As with the large 3-SAT problems, the SAPS+a variant no longer clearly dominates SAPS, showing similar performance on bin50-40, slightly better performance on bin30-40, significantly better performance on bin30-80, but significantly worse performance on bin50-80. PAWS has roughly equivalent performance to PAWS-a, with PAWS dominating on the smaller bin30 problems, and PAWS-a matching PAWS on bin50-80 and dominating on bin50-40.

5. Analysis

Table XI gives an overall comparison of the results from Tables II–X, identifying the best variant for each algorithm on each problem, and giving a Wilcoxon and RTD analysis of the comparative time performance of these best variants. As discussed in Section 4.3, one variant is considered significantly better than another only if the Wilcoxon rank sum test is significant *and* it has a dominating RTD.

Table XI also provides statistics on the relative average lengths of list L for SAPS, SAPS+t, and PAWS and a comparison of the relative SAPS and PAWS flip rates. As the flip rates and list lengths remained stable across problem variants, we only report the statistics for the base versions of SAPS and PAWS (with the exception of SAPS+t list lengths, which were affected by the threshold heuristic). We also show the best Satz or zChaff solution time for each problem in seconds (as discussed in Section 4.2).

As there are considerable differences between the average flip rates for SAPS and PAWS on nearly all problem instances, in the following analysis we limit the comparison between SAPS and PAWS to their relative run-time distributions. However, as flip rates are fairly stable between variants of the same algorithm class, we generally consider flip distributions when comparing particular variants.

5.1. PAWS *VERSUS* SAPS

The first striking feature of Table XI is the dominance of the PAWS variants on the overall problem set. Of the 29 problem instances, PAWS is significantly better on 17 instances, SAPS is significantly better three instances, with no significant difference on the remaining nine instances. For the 17 instances on which PAWS is classed as better, in 13 cases the RTDs are clearly dominant, and in four cases there is some crossing at a solution probability of less than 10% (marked with a ‡ in Table XI). To give an idea of these distributions, Figure 6 shows two of the RTDs that cross at less than 10%, Figure 5a shows a clearly dominant RTD, and Figure 5b shows clearly crossing distributions.

Table VII. Large random 3-SAT problem results.

Problem	Method	Parameters	Success (%)	Time (s)		Flips		Wilcoxon	
				Median	Mean	Median	Mean	Intra	Inter
f800-med	SAPS	$\alpha 1.25\rho 0.1 s5 n1$	100	0.59	0.91	169,562	263,105	0.3358f	
	SAPS+m	$\alpha 1.25\rho 0.1 s5 n1$	100	0.74	0.96	207,760	270,976		
	SAPS+r	$\alpha 1.25\rho 0.1 s5 n1$	100	0.76	0.95	221,127	272,112		
	SAPS+d	$\alpha 1.25\rho 0.1 s30 n15$	100	0.54	1.02	160,086	307,293		
	SAPS+a	$\alpha 1.25\rho 0.1 s30 n15$	100	0.70	0.99	213,200	284,172		
	SAPS+t	$\alpha 1.25\rho 0.1 s30 n15$	100	1.11	1.39	228,023	282,938		
	PAWS	$s9 n15$	100	0.26	0.36	82,392	115,451	*0.0007f	*0.0000f
	PAWS-m	$s9 n15$	100	0.33	0.43	102,667	131,183		*0.0000t
	PAWS-r	$s9 n15$	100	0.29	0.49	91,693	172,521		
	PAWS-d	$s16 n15$	100	0.29	0.45	95,509	145,289		
	PAWS-a	$s16 n1$	100	0.42	0.54	129,184	171,549		
f800-hard	SAPS	$\alpha 1.25\rho 0.3 s5 n1$	100	4.88	6.12	1,414,621	1,754,017	0.2034f	
	SAPS+m	$\alpha 1.25\rho 0.3 s5 n1$	100	5.35	6.45	1,494,538	1,804,377		
	SAPS+r	$\alpha 1.25\rho 0.3 s5 n1$	100	3.92	5.54	1,113,578	1,576,366		
	SAPS+d	$\alpha 1.25\rho 0.3 s30 n1$	100	5.91	7.50	1,739,737	2,184,186		
	SAPS+a	$\alpha 1.25\rho 0.3 s30 n1$	100	5.49	7.25	1,557,723	2,039,950		
	SAPS+t	$\alpha 1.25\rho 0.3 s30 n15$	99	8.14	11.16	1,545,959	2,135,779		
	PAWS	$s10 n15$	100	2.58	3.18	897,696	1,087,076	0.2442f	*0.0011f
	PAWS-m	$s10 n15$	100	3.04	4.36	916,292	1,334,897		*0.0000t
	PAWS-r	$s10 n15$	100	3.53	4.40	1,199,636	1,607,297		
	PAWS-d	$s14 n15$	100	2.27	3.09	753,345	1,035,762		
	PAWS-a	$s14 n1$	100	2.80	4.11	867,340	1,277,586		

f1600-med	SAPS	α1.25ρ0.3s5n1	99	3.06	5.94	693,385	1,303,941	*0.0279f	*0.0000f
	SAPS-m	α1.25ρ0.3s5n1	100	2.58	4.96	538,407	1,033,478		*0.0000t
	SAPS-r	α1.25ρ0.3s5n1	100	3.30	5.12	715,152	1,098,818		
	SAPS-d	α1.25ρ0.3s30n15	99	4.80	8.11	1,086,758	1,920,641		
	SAPS+a	α1.25ρ0.3s30n15	100	4.49	8.07	1,036,529	1,810,566		
	SAPS+t	α1.25ρ0.3s30n15	92	5.64	16.70	896,631	2,742,393		
	PAWS	s10n15	100	0.98	1.74	284,591	5,483,22	*0.0006f	
	PAWS-m	s10n15	100	2.02	2.29	499,642	576,618		
	PAWS-r	s11n15	100	2.04	2.67	521,920	762,255		
	PAWS-d	s14n15	100	1.18	1.76	327,235	501,171		
	PAWS-a	s16n1	100	1.68	2.21	484,481	637,422		
f1600-hard	SAPS	α1.25ρ0.3s5n1	94	30.62	34.34	6,499,140	7,777,980	0.2850f	*0.0001f
	SAPS-m	α1.25ρ0.3s5n1	92	22.52	35.53	4,750,016	8,038,419		*0.0000t
	SAPS-r	α1.25ρ0.3s5n1	88	35.33	38.21	7,490,954	8,996,248		
	SAPS-d	α1.25ρ0.3s30n1	70	54.91	54.66	11,777,404	14,064,479		
	SAPS+a	α1.25ρ0.3s28n15	95	23.13	32.29	5,097,994	7,389,302		
	SAPS+t	α1.25ρ0.3s28n15	75	43.74	57.72	6,514,258	8,996,673		
	PAWS	s11n15	96	11.94	18.86	3,000,027	5,019,099	*0.0233f	
	PAWS-m	s9n15	94	11.72	17.15	3,764,003	5,826,437		
	PAWS-r	s11n15	95	16.37	21.59	4,778,339	6,348,370		
	PAWS-d	s14n15	100	9.35	16.02	2,709,427	4,711,993		
	PAWS-a	s16n1	95	16.20	19.86	4,651,466	6,053,078		

Table VIII. DIMACS logistics and all interval series problem results.

Problem	Method	Parameters	Success (%)	Time (s) Median	Mean	Flips Median	Mean	Wilcoxon Intra	Inter
logistics.c	SAPS	α1.3ρ0.9s5n1	100	0.04	0.05	6,954	8,436		
	SAPS+m	α1.3ρ0.9s5n1	100	0.04	0.05	6,687	8,246		
	SAPS+r	α1.3ρ0.9s5n1	100	0.04	0.05	6,512	8,328		
	SAPS+d	α1.3ρ0.9s20n1	100	0.04	0.04	6,450	8,071		
	SAPS+a	α1.3ρ0.9s20n1	100	0.04	0.05	6,397	8,028	*0.0378f	
	SAPS+t	α1.3ρ0.9s20n15	100	0.05	0.06	6,740	8,610		
	PAWS	s∞n15	100	0.02	0.03	5,229	6,771	*0.0280f	*0.0000f
	PAWS-m	s∞n15	100	0.02	0.03	5,144	6,611		*0.0000t
	PAWS-r	s∞n15	100	0.02	0.03	5,604	7,612		
	PAWS-d	s0n15	100	0.02	0.03	5,047	6,588		
	PAWS-a	s0n1	100	0.02	0.03	5,530	6,734		
logistics.d	SAPS	α1.2ρ1.0s4n1	100	0.18	0.19	19,202	21,248		
	SAPS+m	α1.2ρ1.0s4n1	100	0.19	0.20	18,269	20,904		
	SAPS+r	α1.2ρ1.0s4n1	100	0.18	0.20	19,199	21,486		
	SAPS+d	α1.2ρ1.0s23n1	100	0.18	0.19	18,721	21,384		
	SAPS+a	α1.2ρ1.0s23n1	100	0.20	0.21	18,869	21,355	0.3690f	
	SAPS+t	α1.2ρ1.0s23n15	100	0.36	0.38	21,794	24,005		
	PAWS	s∞n15	100	0.12	0.14	18,330	22,632		0.0707f
	PAWS-m	s∞n15	100	0.11	0.12	18,163	21,546		*0.0000t
	PAWS-r	s∞n15	100	0.12	0.13	18,316	21,777		
	PAWS-d	s0n1	100	0.12	0.13	17,584	21,351		
	PAWS-a	s0n1	100	0.11	0.12	17,867	21,236	*0.0519f	

ais10	SAPS	$\alpha1.3\rho0.9s4n1$	100	0.06	0.10	11,708	18,085		*0.0182f
	SAPS+m	$\alpha1.3\rho0.9s4n1$	100	0.07	0.11	13,197	19,692		
	SAPS+r	$\alpha1.3\rho0.9s4n1$	100	0.07	0.10	13,225	18,442		
	SAPS+d	$\alpha1.3\rho0.9s25n1$	100	0.07	0.10	12,516	18,755	0.3011f	
	SAPS+a	$\alpha1.3\rho0.9s25n1$	100	0.06	0.09	12,086	17,299		
	SAPS+t	$\alpha1.3\rho0.9s25n15$	100	0.08	0.11	13,207	18,670		
	PAWS	$s52n15$	100	0.06	0.09	13,661	19,594	0.0712f	0.4243t
	PAWS-m	$s52n15$	100	0.07	0.09	14,227	20,086		
	PAWS-r	$s52n15$	100	0.07	0.11	15,024	22,974		
	PAWS-d	$s2n15$	100	0.07	0.09	14,081	19,892		
	PAWS-a	$s2n1$	100	0.07	0.10	14,836	20,638		
ais12	SAPS	$\alpha1.25\rho0.95s4n1$	100	0.60	0.86	86,025	123,099		*0.0014f
	SAPS+m	$\alpha1.25\rho0.95s4n1$	100	0.67	0.96	93,867	133,992		
	SAPS+r	$\alpha1.25\rho0.95s4n1$	100	0.60	0.88	85,202	125,727		
	SAPS+d	$\alpha1.25\rho0.95s30n1$	100	0.60	0.86	88,482	127,737	*0.0000f	
	SAPS+a	$\alpha1.25\rho0.95s30n15$	100	0.53	0.81	78,086	117,774		
	SAPS+t	$\alpha1.25\rho0.95s30n15$	100	0.68	0.98	90,437	130,949		
	PAWS	$s148n15$	100	0.57	0.80	102,774	142,979	0.2565f	0.0792t
	PAWS-m	$s148n15$	100	0.52	0.79	94,512	143,541		
	PAWS-r	$s148n15$	100	0.64	0.94	111,792	164,807		
	PAWS-d	$s1n1$	100	0.60	0.85	102,253	145,982		
	PAWS-a	$s1n1$	100	0.60	0.87	102,275	149,958		

Table IX. DIMACS parity-learning problem results.

Problem	Method	Parameters	Success (%)	Time (s)		Flips		Wilcoxon	
				Median	Mean	Median	Mean	Intra	Inter
par16-med	SAPS	$\alpha 2\rho 0.25s7n1$	88	12.32	20.98	5,589,195	7,720,965		
	SAPS+m	$\alpha 2\rho 0.25s7n1$	90	12.73	19.90	5,563,752	7,667,145		
	SAPS+r	$\alpha 2\rho 0.25s7n1$	89	10.19	20.95	4,624,300	7,340,485		
	SAPS+d	$\alpha 2\rho 0.25s15n1$	96	10.68	15.22	4,985,909	6,677,620		
	SAPS+a	$\alpha 2\rho 0.25s15n15$	95	11.01	14.48	4,885,148	6,595,288	0.3181f	
	SAPS+t	$\alpha 2\rho 0.25s15n15$	40	n/a	54.53	n/a	12,899,759		
	PAWS	s36n15	97	5.32	8.77	2,646,531	4,496,763	0.0692f	*0.0000f
	PAWS-m	s36n15	100	6.00	8.14	3,116,219	4,216,251		*0.0000t
	PAWS-r	s36n15	99	6.70	8.98	3,316,710	4,517,832		
	PAWS-d	s3n15	97	8.16	10.36	4,081,225	5,320,932		
	PAWS-a	s3n15	98	7.30	10.31	3,835,814	5,512,200		
par16-hard	SAPS	$\alpha 1.4\rho 0.9s4n1$	86	13.78	18.71	6,454,597	9,725,495		
	SAPS+m	$\alpha 1.4\rho 0.9s4n1$	83	17.02	20.19	7,687,612	10,286,242		
	SAPS+r	$\alpha 1.4\rho 0.9s4n1$	87	12.34	17.37	5,781,604	8,950,757		
	SAPS+d	$\alpha 1.4\rho 0.9s30n1$	90	14.88	16.87	6,954,962	8,547,129		
	SAPS+a	$\alpha 1.4\rho 0.9s25n1$	94	12.86	16.11	5,751,190	7,597,764	0.0790f	
	SAPS+t	$\alpha 1.4\rho 0.9s25n15$	79	28.17	36.20	7,272,386	9,141,042		
	PAWS	s40n15	98	6.79	9.51	3,379,909	4,809,418	0.1057f	*0.0000f
	PAWS-m	s40n15	100	6.43	8.45	3,314,958	4,355,509		*0.0000t
	PAWS-r	s40n15	98	6.67	8.90	3,312,261	4,493,758		
	PAWS-d	s3n15	97	12.25	13.78	6,144,198	7,104,478		
	PAWS-a	s3n1	99	7.67	10.79	4,072,925	5,761,065		

The three instances on which SAPS does dominate are of relatively small size and can each be solved within 0.32 s by Satz or zChaff, and for those problems which the complete solvers find challenging (i.e., take longer than 1 s to solve), SAPS equals the performance of PAWS on only two instances: uf400-hard and bin50-40. In this context, bin50-40 presents an interesting case, as it has the longest solution times and highest flip count within the problem set, so any conclusion of the superiority of PAWS on larger problems must necessarily be qualified. Also, as with all empirical evaluations of stochastic local search algorithms, our conclusions cannot be reliably generalized beyond the given problem set. Having said this, the results do indicate that additive weighting has better general time performance than any of the multiplicative alternatives considered.

5.2. PAWS VARIANTS

An examination of the relative performance of each PAWS variant in Table XI shows that standard PAWS is better on 12 instances, PAWS-m is better on 11 instances, PAWS-d is better on five instances, and PAWS-a is better on one instance (but only marginally). This first indicates that PAWS-r and PAWS-a do not perform well, and by implication that the random flat move heuristic is playing an important role in the performance of PAWS (i.e., both PAWS-r and PAWS-a have had the random flat move heuristic removed).

Considering the flip count statistics of PAWS in relation to PAWS-d, there are several problems where PAWS-d has considerably worse performance, for example, bw_large.c, flat200-med, g250.29 and par16-hard, whereas on the five problems where PAWS-d has the best performance, the mean flip count in comparison to PAWS differs by less than 10%. A further run-*length* distribution (RLD) analysis (Hoos and Stützle, 1998) comparing flip performance on these problems confirmed that PAWS-d does not clearly dominate PAWS on any problem instance (an RLD analysis differs from the RTD analysis only in considering flip instead of time performance). Hence there is strong evidence suggesting that deterministic smoothing performs better than probabilistic smoothing for PAWS.

Lastly, the nearly equal first status of PAWS and PAWS-m (on a simple count of the problems on which they do better) suggests that they have roughly equal overall performance. However, a closer analysis of the flip counts for each problem shows there are several problems on which PAWS has considerably better mean flip performance (uf250-med, f800-hard, f1600-hard, and bin50-40) and a similar number on which PAWS-m appears to dominate (par16-med, par16-hard, and bin50-40). We therefore performed another RLD analysis on these problems, which showed a significant dominance only on bin50-40 (in favour of PAWS) and bin50-80 (in favour of PAWS-m). As there was no significant difference on any other problem, this suggests the multiple inclusion heuristic has a minimal effect on the overall performance of PAWS.

Table X. Random binary CSP problem results.

Problem	Method	Parameters	Success (%)	Time (s)		Flips		Wilcoxon	
				Median	Mean	Median	Mean	Intra	Inter
bin30-80	SAPS	$\alpha 1.3\rho 0.1 s6n1$	100	0.06	0.08	8,661	12,299		
	SAPS+m	$\alpha 1.3\rho 0.1 s6n1$	100	0.05	0.08	7,729	11,853		
	SAPS+r	$\alpha 1.3\rho 0.1 s6n1$	100	0.05	0.08	7,940	12,242		
	SAPS+d	$\alpha 1.3\rho 0.1 s20n1$	100	0.05	0.07	7,999	11,642		
	SAPS+a	$\alpha 1.3\rho 0.1 s20n1$	100	0.05	0.07	7,511	10,593	*0.0009f	
	SAPS+t	$\alpha 1.3\rho 0.1 s20n15$	100	0.05	0.08	7,652	10,594		
	PAWS	$s7n15$	100	0.04	0.06	7,576	10,633	*0.0449f	*0.0066f
	PAWS-m	$s7n15$	100	0.04	0.05	7,283	10,102		*0.0000t
	PAWS-r	$s9n15$	100	0.05	0.07	9,089	12,089		
	PAWS-d	$s15n15$	100	0.05	0.07	8,463	11,803		
	PAWS-a	$s17n1$	100	0.05	0.07	8,172	11,956		
bin30-40	SAPS	$\alpha 1.25\rho 0.5 s6n1$	100	0.08	0.12	13,716	19,711		*0.0101f
	SAPS+m	$\alpha 1.25\rho 0.5 s6n1$	100	0.09	0.12	14,470	20,149		0.4072t
	SAPS+r	$\alpha 1.25\rho 0.5 s6n1$	100	0.08	0.12	14,031	20,330		
	SAPS+d	$\alpha 1.25\rho 0.5 s17n1$	100	0.08	0.11	13,644	18,797		
	SAPS+a	$\alpha 1.25\rho 0.5 s15n1$	100	0.08	0.11	12,741	19,119	0.0091f	
	SAPS+t	$\alpha 1.25\rho 0.5 s15n15$	100	0.08	0.12	12,044	17,540		
	PAWS	$s7n15$	100	0.08	0.12	15,927	22,422	*0.0000f	
	PAWS-m	$s7n15$	100	0.08	0.13	15,779	24,321		
	PAWS-r	$s9n15$	100	0.10	0.14	18,746	27,309		
	PAWS-d	$s20n15$	100	0.08	0.12	15,798	23,287		
	PAWS-a	$s20n1$	100	0.10	0.14	19,432	27,610		

bin50-80	SAPS	$\alpha 1.2\rho 0.1 s6n1$	100	1.81	2.92	119,552	186,552	*0.0181f
	SAPS+m	$\alpha 1.2\rho 0.1 s6n1$	100	2.08	3.82	130,022	224,231	
	SAPS+r	$\alpha 1.2\rho 0.1 s6n1$	100	2.35	3.53	141,777	216,651	
	SAPS+d	$\alpha 1.2\rho 0.1 s30n15$	100	2.58	3.81	202,745	297,099	
	SAPS+a	$\alpha 1.2\rho 0.1 s30n1$	100	2.19	3.54	160,871	262,727	
	SAPS+t	$\alpha 1.2\rho 0.1 s25n15$	98	2.12	7.09	141,226	604,380	
	PAWS	$s5n15$	100	1.44	1.85	128,837	168,402	0.4011f 0.3574f
	PAWS-m	$s5n15$	100	0.99	1.42	90,567	130,162	*0.0062t
	PAWS-r	$s5n15$	100	1.73	2.60	165,065	266,514	
	PAWS-d	$s30n15$	100	1.63	1.99	147,552	182,763	
	PAWS-a	$s30n15$	100	1.44	2.14	134,187	198,013	
bin50-40	SAPS	$\alpha 1.25\rho 0.25 s5n1$	99	96.84	149.05	7,579,338	11,562,103	0.0735f
	SAPS+m	$\alpha 1.25\rho 0.25 s5n1$	92	114.69	165.67	8,961,133	11,552,914	0.2535t
	SAPS+r	$\alpha 1.25\rho 0.25 s5n1$	100	100.58	149.47	7,783,134	11,482,673	
	SAPS+d	$\alpha 1.25\rho 0.25 s20n1$	99	81.24	120.76	6,450,368	9,449,164	
	SAPS+a	$\alpha 1.25\rho 0.25 s20n1$	100	101.38	131.05	7,682,577	12,130,118	0.3305f
	SAPS+t	$\alpha 1.25\rho 0.25 s20n15$	37	n/a	334.81	n/a	32,454,528	
	PAWS	$s6n15$	98	121.12	169.55	10,866,838	14,848,547	
	PAWS-m	$s6n15$	91	155.61	209.73	13,644,648	17,170,359	
	PAWS-r	$s6n15$	100	114.85	194.17	10,487,116	17,164,797	
	PAWS-d	$s30n15$	100	84.64	119.13	7,591,267	13,659,181	*0.0419f
	PAWS-a	$s30n1$	99	100.44	126.90	8,923,186	14,874,496	

Table XI. Overall problem comparison.

Problem	Best time variant					List length			Flips per second	
	SAPS	PAWS	Overall	Wilcoxon	DPLL	SAPS	SAPS+t	PAWS	SAPS	PAWS
bw_large.a	SAPS+a	PAWS-m	PAWS	0.0021√	0.01z	1.4843	1.9527	2.8450	222,967	253,184
bw_large.b	SAPS+a	PAWS-m	not sig	0.2124×	†0.01z	1.1457	1.7786	3.1005	176,073	209,888
bw_large.c	SAPS+a	PAWS-m	PAWS	0.0000√	†0.53z	1.0185	3.2655	4.0911	79,529	171,719
bw_large.d	SAPS+a	PAWS-m	PAWS	0.0000√	†2.01z	1.0654	5.7542	4.9923	63,320	131,772
flat100-med	SAPS+d	PAWS-m	SAPS	0.0003√	0.01s	1.1612	2.0977	3.4890	546,523	578,702
flat100-hard	SAPS+a	PAWS-d	SAPS	0.0012√	†0.01z	1.0405	2.1411	3.0929	564,152	592,997
flat200-med	SAPS+a	PAWS	not sig	0.0355×	0.12s	1.0617	3.0782	5.2708	483,891	519,477
flat200-hard	SAPS+d	PAWS	not sig	0.2747×	†0.03s	1.0016	3.2044	3.4551	497,716	541,442
g125.17	SAPS+a	PAWS-m	PAWS	0.0000√	>1 hr	1.0045	3.2766	3.5996	51,289	77,222
g250.29	SAPS+r	PAWS-m	PAWS	0.0000√	>1 hr	1.0358	5.3512	4.7199	11,927	14,439
uf100-hard	SAPS+d	PAWS	not sig	0.0850√	0.01z	1.0269	1.4609	1.9685	433,712	454,314
uf250-med	SAPS+d	PAWS	PAWS	0.0002√	1.25s	1.0793	1.7371	3.1550	391,263	406,842
uf250-hard	SAPS+a	PAWS	SAPS	0.0000√	†0.32s	1.0027	1.7448	3.3338	397,796	407,566
uf400-med	SAPS+a	PAWS	PAWS	0.0000√	57.81s	1.2044	2.0989	4.0647	358,898	379,945
uf400-hard	SAPS+a	PAWS	not sig	0.1778×	178.92s	1.0011	2.0151	3.3460	361,168	407,892
f800-med	SAPS	PAWS	PAWS	0.0000√‡	>1 hr	1.0211	2.8490	5.2173	289,413	321,861

f800-hard	SAPS+r	PAWS-d	PAWS	0.0001/‡	>1 hr	1.0032	2.8492	4.1244	286,740	342,084
f1600-med	SAPS+m	PAWS	PAWS	0.0000/	>1 hr	1.0155	4.2052	4.2509	217,590	314,260
f1600-hard	SAPS+a	PAWS-d	PAWS	0.0000/	>1 hr	1.0030	4.2985	7.9250	215,021	257,173
logistics.c	SAPS+a	PAWS-d	PAWS	0.0000/	0.08z	2.5263	2.9066	3.7940	179,318	247,502
logistics.d	SAPS+m	PAWS-a	PAWS	0.0000/	0.19z	17.7148	17.8127	18.2289	110,813	167,203
ais10	SAPS+a	PAWS	not sig	0.3532×	0.06s	1.0130	1.2968	2.0533	187,028	209,968
ais12	SAPS+a	PAWS	not sig	0.3518×	0.17s	1.0036	1.3062	1.7517	143,347	179,228
par16-med	SAPS+a	PAWS-m	PAWS	0.0003/‡	†0.49z	1.0007	3.7710	5.3424	337,548	499,311
par16-hard	SAPS+a	PAWS-m	PAWS	0.0000/‡	†0.56s	1.0005	3.8163	5.6082	468,056	496,370
bin30-80	SAPS+a	PAWS-m	PAWS	0.0000/	0.26s	1.0363	1.6553	2.8070	153,169	187,080
bin30-40	SAPS+d	PAWS	not sig	0.1263×	†0.02z	1.0220	1.7828	3.3194	170,857	189,825
bin50-80	SAPS	PAWS-m	PAWS	0.0000/	>1 h	1.0091	1.6773	3.4783	63,909	90,890
bin50-40	SAPS+d	PAWS-d	not sig	0.4766×	>1 h	1.0002	1.4881	5.1387	78,822	89,409

Key: the DPLL column shows the best time in seconds for the Satz and zChaff DPLL methods, s indicates Satz dominated zChaff, z indicates zChaff dominated Satz and † indicates that the Satz or zChaff run-time dominates all other methods; / indicates the run-time distribution (RTD) of the overall best SAPS or PAWS variant dominates the other best variant; ‡ indicates the RTD domination is not perfect, some cross-over at solution probability < 0.1; × indicates significant cross-over of RTDs at solution probability > 0.1.

We therefore conclude, on the basis of the experimental evidence, that the PAWS deterministic smoothing and random flat move heuristics do contribute positively to the performance of additive weighting and that the multiple inclusion heuristic has no significant effect either positively or negatively.

5.3. SAPS VARIANTS

Again performing a count on Table XI gives 17 problems for which SAPS+a is better, six problems for which SAPS+d is better, two problems for which SAPS+r is better, two problems for which SAPS+m is better, and two problems for which SAPS is better. The counts certainly suggest that SAPS benefits from the inclusion of the PAWS heuristics. However, a closer examination of the problem flip counts shows that it is hard to draw a general conclusion that fits all problem instances.

First, SAPS+a and SAPS+d often clearly perform better than the other variants, while themselves having similar performance, that is, on bw_large.b, c and d, flat100-med, flat200-med and hard, uf400-med and hard, and par16-med and hard. However, there are other problems where SAPS does well and SAPS+a and SAPS+d do relatively worse, that is, on f800-med and hard, f1600-med, and bin50-80. Then there are problems where SAPS+d does badly relative to all other variants, that is, g125.17 and f1600-hard, and other problems where SAPS+d does well and SAPS+a does poorly, that is, g250.29 and bin50-40. Considering the other variants, SAPS+r stands out only on f800-hard and g250.29, and SAPS+m stands out only on f1600-med; otherwise their performance follows SAPS fairly closely. Hence, we consider that the +m and +r heuristics do not have a major effect on SAPS, at least in isolation. This result is further supported by the relatively insignificant effects that would be expected from these heuristics. First, although SAPS+m biases the move choice toward literals that appear more than once in the false clause list, it does not override the move cost. Also, removing this heuristic from PAWS has already been shown above to have little effect. Second, the SAPS+r heuristic is operational only in situations where no improving move is available, and then only for 1% of the time. At this point it simply reduces the domain of choice from all possible moves, to moves that have a zero cost (i.e., within the threshold of ±0.1). While this removes the chance of taking a cost increasing move, such moves will typically be quickly reversed in a local search. Also, in further work on SAPS, the removal of the random flip heuristic has been shown to have little noticeable effect (Tompkins and Hoos, 2004). Our results therefore support these findings.

This leaves SAPS+d and SAPS+a as the two candidate best SAPS variants. Of these SAPS+d has a slight advantage, first, because its worst performance is on problems for which SAPS is not competitive, and second because it represents a simpler change to SAPS, that is, switching from probabilistic to deterministic smoothing. However, uniformly adopting deterministic smoothing would definitely degrade the performance of SAPS on a range of the larger randomly generated CSP and 3-SAT problems. We therefore conclude that the best overall performance could be obtained by adding an additional SAPS parameter that switches between deterministic and probabilistic smoothing. This extends the results presented in (Tompkins and Hoos, 2004), where a deterministic version of SAPS was found not to differ from SAPS in performance on a range of the smaller problems already considered in this study.

5.4. THE SAPS THRESHOLD HEURISTIC

So far we have not considered the SAPS threshold variant, SAPS+t. The reason is that, while it can equal the flip performance of SAPS+a (on which it is based) for many smaller problems, it produced some of the highest failure rates of any variant on several of the larger problems (uf400-hard, f1600-med and hard, par16-med and hard, and bin50-40). Also, because of the additional overhead of calculating an averaged flip cost, the time performance of SAPS+t was uniformly worse than SAPS+a. Hence, we can conclude that adding a threshold, at least to SAPS+a, does not improve the performance of multiplicative weighting.

In relation to the effect of the threshold heuristic on the candidate list lengths, Table XI clearly shows the greater choice in candidate moves available to PAWS, and that, as solution times increase, the SAPS list length tends to one. For the SAPS+t experiments we set the threshold value to 0.1, producing SAPS+t list lengths somewhere between those of SAPS and PAWS. Further experiments with larger threshold values did produce longer list lengths, but these changes uniformly caused SAPS+t performance to degrade. Hence we have no evidence to suggest that the superior performance of PAWS can be explained by its greater choice of moves. If this were the case, we would expect SAPS+t to have improved over SAPS+a, as SAPS+a *is* PAWS except that it uses multiplicative weighting. This refutes our earlier conjecture (Thornton et al., 2004) and reopens the question of explaining the superior performance of PAWS, especially on the larger problems.

6. Conclusions

The aim of this study was to identify and analyze the key features required for an effective clause weighting local search algorithm. On the basis of the previous work, we observed that the best clause weighting algorithms use the same underlying strategy, that is, to increase clause weights in a local minimum and then to periodically reduce or smooth these weights to maintain a stable relative weight distribution that remains sensitive to local conditions in the search space. From this we identified the key distinguishing feature of current approaches, that is, the use of additive or multiplicative clause weighting. We therefore set out to systematically investigate the performance of additive and multiplicative clause weighting on a range of SAT benchmark problems, and using a range of subheuristics.

Overall, our results indicate that additive weighting tends to perform better than multiplicative weighting, particularly on larger and more difficult problems. From our investigation into the various additive and multiplicative subheuristics, we came to the following conclusions:

- The random flat move heuristic is useful for additive weighting. This is less relevant to multiplicative weighting, possibly because the finer weight distinctions caused by multiplicative updates produce smaller plateau areas.
- Deterministic weight reduction appears generally helpful for additive weighting but assists multiplicative weighting only on selected instances.
- The effect of the multiple inclusion heuristic is not significant. Overall it had little effect on multiplicative weighting, and made only a small difference, both positively and negatively, to additive weighting performance.
- The threshold heuristic caused a fairly uniform deterioration in the performance of multiplicative weighting. This means the superior performance of additive weighting cannot obviously be explained by the wider choice of moves afforded by additive weight updates.

As the threshold heuristic failed to produce any improvement, we were led to develop a new conjecture to explain the relatively better performance of the additive approach:

First, the study has shown that the differences in performance between the additive and multiplicative schemes cannot be explained by differences in the subheuristics used. If this were the case, we would expect the performance of SAPS and PAWS to become equivalent with the right application of heuristics. However, regardless of the choice of subheuristics, additive weighting has shown the generally superior performance.

Second, our experiments with SAPS+t indicate that there is no causative link between the coarser weight distinctions of additive weighting and its better performance.[*] Hence, the overall outcome of the study suggests there is something inherent in additive weight updates that can improve the performance of clause weighting algorithms. By a process of elimination, the remaining distinction is the essential geometric nature of multiplicative weight updates; that is, multiplicatively increasing weight will always cause those clauses with greater weight to have a greater relative increase in weight. Conversely, additive updates are more egalitarian, with each false clause getting an identical weight increase. The overall effect is that multiplicative weighting will raise the weight on a false clause more quickly, relative to other clauses with lesser weight, and

---

[*] This must be qualified by the understanding that there are other possible threshold heuristics that may have better performance.

will also reduce weight more quickly when a clause becomes true. Hence, a newly weighted clause will have less immediate effect on the search trajectory, and the basic ordering of clause weight importance will differ; that is, in a multiplicative scheme, clauses that have been false for longer will have greater importance.

In general, therefore, additive weighting is a 'blunter' instrument. For instance, most clause weights at any point in an additive search will have their weights set to one, whereas multiplicative weighting retains small real valued distinctions on nearly all clauses that have been false. Additive weighting is also less selective: it does not care how long a clause has been true or false, it still gets the same update. The conjecture of our study is therefore that this generally simpler behaviour explains the better performance of additive weighting on longer term searches. In particular, additive weighting provides a relatively greater emphasis on clauses that have recently become false and so is more responsive to the immediate situation. More generally, the efficiencies gained in performing simpler clause weight updates mean additive weighting can also dominate on smaller problems where multiplicative weighting otherwise has the advantage in terms of flips.

Overall the case for preferring additive over multiplicative weighting is compelling. First, the average flip performance of PAWS does not differ significantly from SAPS on smaller problems and strongly dominates SAPS on the more difficult problems (i.e., those beyond the reach of Satz or zChaff). Second, additive weighting is more time efficient than multiplicative due to using integer rather than real-valued clause weights. This is shown by the consistently faster flip rates for PAWS on most problems (remembering SAPS and PAWS are running within the same software architecture). And third, the search space of possible parameter settings is at least an order of magnitude less for PAWS than for SAPS.

In summary, this paper balances much of the recent work on clause weighting that has concentrated on multiplicative updates, showing that additive weighting can be faster, simpler in terms of parameter tuning, and more applicable to larger problems beyond the reach of complete search methods. However, multiplicative weighting still has the better performance in several problem domains, especially in terms of flips, and in future work it would be worth identifying the problem characteristics and search behaviours that favour a multiplicative approach.

References

Everett, H. (1963) Generalized Lagrange multiplier method for solving problems of the optimal allocation of resources, *Oper. Res.* **11**, 399–417.

Gent, I., Hoos, H., Prosser, P. and Walsh, T. (1999) Morphing: Combining structure and randomness, in *Proceedings of the Sixteenth National Conference on Artificial Intelligence (AAAI-99)*, pp. 654–660.

Gibbons, J. and Chakraborti, S. (1992) *Nonparametric Statistical Inference, Statistics: Textbooks and Monographs*, Marcel Dekker, Inc., New York, pp. 241–251.

Hoos, H. (2002) An adaptive noise mechanism for WalkSAT, in *Proceedings of the Nineteenth National Conference on Artificial Intelligence (AAAI-02)*, pp. 655–660.

Hoos, H. and Stützle, T. (1998) Evaluating Las Vegas algorithms: Pitfalls and remedies, in *Proceedings of the Fourteenth Conference of Uncertainty in Artificial Intelligence (UAI-98)*, pp. 238–245.

Hoos, H. and Stützle, T. (2005) *Stochastic Local Search: Foundations and Applications*, Elsevier, New York.

Hutter, F., Tompkins, D. and Hoos, H. (2002) Scaling and probabilistic smoothing: Efficient dynamic local search for SAT, in *Proceedings of the Eighth International Conference on the Principles and Practice of Constraint Programming (CP'02)*, pp. 233–248.

Li, C. and Anbulagan, A. (1997) Look-ahead *versus* look-back for satisfiability problems, in *Proceedings of the Third International Conference on the Principles and Practice of Constraint Programming (CP'97)*, pp. 341–355.

McAllester, D., Selman, B. and Kautz, H. (1997) Evidence for invariance in local search, in *Proceedings of the Fourteenth National Conference on Artificial Intelligence (AAAI-97)*, pp. 321–326.

Mills, P. and Tsang, E. (1999) Guided local search applied to the satisfiability (SAT) problem, in *Proceedings of the Fifteenth National Conference of the Australian Society for Operations Research (ASOR'99)*, pp. 872–883.

Morris, P. (1993) The Breakout method for escaping local minima, in *Proceedings of the Eleventh National Conference on Artificial Intelligence (AAAI-93)*, pp. 40–45.

Moskewicz, M., Madigan, C., Zhao, Y., Zhang, L. and Malik, S. (2001) Chaff: Engineering an efficient SAT solver, in *Proceedings of the Thirty-ninth Design Automation Conference (DAC2001)*, pp. 530–535.

Prestwich, S. (2003) Local search on SAT-encoded colouring problems, in *Proceedings of the Sixth International Conference on Theory and Applications of Satisfiability Testing (SAT-03)*, pp. 105–119.

Schuurmans, D. and Southey, F. (2000) Local search characteristics of incomplete SAT procedures, in *Proceedings of the Seventeenth National Conference on Artificial Intelligence (AAAI-00)*, pp. 297–302.

Schuurmans, D., Southey, F. and Holte, R. (2001) The exponentiated subgradient algorithm for heuristic Boolean programming, in *Proceedings of the Seventeenth International Joint Conference on Artificial Intelligence (IJCAI-01)*, pp. 334–341.

Shang, Y. and Wah, B. (1998) A discrete Lagrangian-based global search method for solving satisfiability problems, *J. Glob. Optim.* **12**, 61–99.

Thornton, J. and Sattar, A. (1999) On the behaviour and application of constraint weighting, in *Proceedings of the Fifth International Conference on the Principles and Practice of Constraint Programming, CP'99*, pp. 446–460.

Thornton, J., Pullan, W. and Terry, J. (2002) Towards fewer parameters for clause weighting SAT algorithms, in *Proceedings of the Fifteenth Australian Joint Conference on Artificial Intelligence, AI-2002*, pp. 569–578.

Thornton, J., Pham, D., Bain, S. and Ferreira Jr., V. (2004) Additive *versus* multiplicative clause weighting for SAT, in *Proceedings of the Nineteenth National Conference on Artificial Intelligence, AAAI-2004*, pp. 191–196.

Tompkins, D. and Hoos, H. (2004) Warped landscapes and random acts of SAT solving, in *Proceedings of the Eighth International Symposium on Artificial Intelligence and Mathematics, (AI&M-04)*.

Wu, Z. and Wah, B. (2000) An efficient global-search strategy in discrete Lagrangian methods for solving hard satisfiability problems, in *Proceedings of the Seventeenth National Conference on Artificial Intelligence (AAAI-00)*, pp. 310–315.

Journal of Automated Reasoning (2005) 35: 143–179
DOI: 10.1007/s10817-005-9011-0

© Springer 2006

Solving Non-Boolean Satisfiability Problems with Stochastic Local Search: A Comparison of Encodings

ALAN M. FRISCH*, TIMOTHY J. PEUGNIEZ, ANTHONY J. DOGGETT
and PETER W. NIGHTINGALE[†]
*Artificial Intelligence Group, Department of Computer Science, University of York, York,
YO10 5DD, UK. e-mail: frisch@cs.york.ac.uk, pn@dcs.st-and.ac.uk*

Abstract. Much excitement has been generated by the success of stochastic local search procedures at finding solutions to large, very hard satisfiability problems. Many of the problems on which these procedures have been effective are non-Boolean in that they are most naturally formulated in terms of variables with domain sizes greater than two. Approaches to solving non-Boolean satisfiability problems fall into two categories. In the direct approach, the problem is tackled by an algorithm for non-Boolean problems. In the transformation approach, the non-Boolean problem is reformulated as an equivalent Boolean problem and then a Boolean solver is used.

This paper compares four methods for solving non-Boolean problems: one direct and three transformational. The comparison first examines the search spaces confronted by the four methods, and then tests their ability to solve random formulas, the round-robin sports scheduling problem, and the quasigroup completion problem. The experiments show that the relative performance of the methods depends on the domain size of the problem and that the direct method scales better as domain size increases.

Along the route to performing these comparisons we make three other contributions. First, we generalize Walksat, a highly successful stochastic local search procedure for Boolean satisfiability problems, to work on problems with domains of any finite size. Second, we introduce a new method for transforming non-Boolean problems to Boolean problems and improve on an existing transformation. Third, we identify sufficient conditions for omitting at-least-one and at-most-one clauses from a transformed formula. Fourth, for use in our experiments we propose a model for generating random formulas that vary in domain size but are similar in other respects.

Key words: satisfiability, propositional logic, local search, encodings.

1. Introduction

Much excitement has been generated by the success of stochastic local search (SLS) procedures at finding satisfying truth assignments to large formulas of propositional logic. These procedures stochasticly search a space of all assignments for one that satisfies the given formula. Many of the problems on which

---

* Author for correspondence.
[†] Current address: School of Computer Science, University of St Andrews, Fife KY16 9SX, UK.

these methods have been effective are non-Boolean in that they are most naturally formulated in terms of variables with domain sizes greater than two. In order to tackle a non-Boolean problem with a Boolean procedure, the problem is first reformulated as an equivalent Boolean problem in which multiple Boolean variables are used in place of each non-Boolean variable.

This encode-and-solve approach often results in comparable, if not superior, performance to solving the problem directly. Because Boolean satisfiability (SAT) is conceptually simple, algorithms for it are often easier to design, implement, and evaluate. And because SLS algorithms for Boolean satisfiability have been studied intensively for more than a decade, highly optimized implementations are publicly available.

This paper proposes and studies a new approach to solving non-Boolean satisfaction (NB-SAT) problems: that of generalizing a Boolean SLS procedure to operate directly on a non-Boolean formula by searching through a space of assignments to non-Boolean variables. In particular, we have generalized Walksat (Selman et al., 1994), a highly successful SLS procedure for Boolean satisfiability problems, to a new procedure, NB-Walksat (first reported by Peugniez, 1998 and by Frisch and Peugniez, 1998), that works on formulas whose variables have domains of any finite size.[*] In this way we are able to apply highly refined SLS technology directly to non-Boolean problems without having to encode non-Boolean variables as Boolean variables.

The main question addressed by this paper is how the performance of the direct approach compares to that of the transformational (or encode and solve) approach. In particular we compare one direct method, NB-Walksat, and three transformational methods by empirically testing their ability to solve large random non-Boolean formulas, the round-robin tournament scheduling problem, and the quasi-group completion problem. Our three transformation methods consist of applying Walksat to the results of three transforms.

Boolean variables are merely a special case of non-Boolean variables, and, intuitively, the difference between the non-Boolean and Boolean variables grows as the domain size of the non-Boolean variable increases. Consequently, one would expect that in a comparison of encodings for non-Boolean problems that domain size would be the most important parameter to consider and that one would find that any difference in performance between the encodings would increase when domain size is increased. Ours is the first study to consider this.

We shall also see that the polarity of a non-Boolean formula – whether it is positive, negative or neither, as defined later – is another significant factor that affects its translation to a Boolean formula.

Our experimental results show NB-Walksat to be highly effective, demonstrating that the effectiveness of the Walksat strategies can be transferred from

---

[*] NB-Walksat and a suite of supporting programs are available at http://www.cs.york.ac.uk/~frisch/NB.

the Boolean case to the non-Boolean case. On problems with large domain sizes our direct method is often superior to the transformation methods, which in many cases are ineffective.

Besides introducing the generalization of Boolean formulas to non-Boolean formulas and Walksat to NB-Walksat, we make several other new contributions, including the following three. (1) Of the three non-Boolean to Boolean transformations we use, one is new and one is an enhanced version of a well-known transformation. (2) We identify sufficient conditions for omitting at-least-one and at-most-one clauses from a transformed formula. (3) To test the effect of domain size on problem solving performance we want a method for generating random formulas that vary in domain size but are similar in other respects. We propose such a method and use it in our experiments.

We conjecture that the transformation of non-Boolean SAT to Boolean SAT is an inherent component of using the encode-and-solve approach on any problem that is conceived of as having non-Boolean domains. More specifically, we put forward a hypothesis.

The SAT-Transform Hypothesis: Let P be a problem that we conceive of as having variables with finite domains of more than two elements. Let T be a SAT-effective transform for P; that is, P can be solved effectively by using a SAT solver on the result of applying transform T to P. Then T can be obtained by composing a transform from P to NB-SAT with a transform from NB-SAT to SAT.

Note that this is an empirical hypothesis and that it could be refuted by identifying a SAT-effective transform that cannot be decomposed in the stated manner. Such a transform might, for example, exploit some complex interaction between the encoding of the non-Boolean variables and the encoding of some other aspect of the problem. But in all uses of encode-and-solve known to us the hypothesis does hold, and thus every use embeds a transform from NB-SAT to SAT. This underscores the importance of studying the transformation of NB-SAT to SAT, as well as the alternative of generalizing SAT solvers to work directly on NB-SAT.

2. Non-Boolean Formulas

Syntactically, non-Boolean formulas are constructed from propositional variables, each of which is associated with a finite, nonempty domain. We refer to the domain of a variable X as $dom(X)$. Atomic non-Boolean formulas (or nb-atoms) are of the form X/d, where X is a variable and d is a member of its domain. Non-atomic non-Boolean formulas are constructed from atomic non-Boolean formulas with logical connectives in precisely the same manner as is used for Boolean formulas. As an example, if X and Y are variables both with domain $\{d_1, d_2, d_3\}$, then

$$X/d_1 \wedge (Y/d_2 \vee Y/d_3) \tag{1}$$

in a non-Boolean formula.

Now consider the semantics of non-Boolean formulas. A non-Boolean assignment maps every variable to a member of its domain. A non-Boolean assignment, A, satisfies an atomic non-Boolean formula X/d if and only if A maps X to d. The satisfaction of nonatomic non-Boolean formulas is determined from the satisfaction of atomic components in precisely the same manner as for Boolean formulas. So, an assignment that maps X to d_1 and Y to d_3 satisfies $X/1$, $Y/3$ and formula (1).

Walksat and many other Boolean SLS procedures operate on Boolean formulas in conjunctive normal form (CNF), and NB-Walksat, our generalization of Walksat, operates on non-Boolean formulas in CNF. A formula, Boolean or non-Boolean, is in CNF if it is a conjunction of disjunction of literals. A literal is either an atomic formula (called a positive literal) or its negation (called a negative literal). We say that a CNF formula is *positive* if all its literals are positive and *negative* if all its literals are negative. Thus, formula (1) is in CNF and it is positive.

Non-Boolean formulas generalize Boolean formulas because a Boolean formula can be transformed to a non-Boolean formula simply by replacing every Boolean atom P with the non-Boolean atom $P'/TRUE$, where P' is a variable whose domain is $\{TRUE, FALSE\}$.

We sometimes use terms such as "nb-atom" or "nb-formula" to emphasize that these syntactic objects are part of the non-Boolean language. Similar use is made of terms such as "b-atom" and "b-formula."

3. NB-Walksat

Walksat is a highly successful SLS procedure for finding satisfying assignments to Boolean formulas in clausal form. We have generalized Walksat to a new procedure, NB-Walksat, that operates similarly on non-Boolean formulas. Indeed when handling a Boolean formula, the two procedures perform the same search.[*] NB-Walksat was implemented by replacing the code of the core search procedure of Walksat version 19. Obtaining this generality required a complete reworking of the data structures that maintain formulas and assignments. This section describes the operation of NB-Walksat[**], and, since on Boolean

---

[*] We used this property to help test that NB-Walksat was correctly implemented.

[**] The description applies to NB-Walksat versions 4, 5, and 6. Version 6 is the most recent version at the time of writing this paper. Versions 1, 2, and 3 computed probability distributions in a subtly-different way – a difference that affects only some problem instances.

formulas NB-Walksat and Walksat perform the same search, this section implicitly describes the operation of Walksat.

The simplest way to understand the operation of NB-Walksat is to consider it as working on positive CNF nb-formulas. This can be achieved by considering NB-Walksat's first step to be the replacement of every negative literal $\neg X/d_i$ with $X/d_1 \vee \cdots \vee X/d_{i-1} \vee X/d_{i+1} \vee \cdots \vee X/d_n$, where X is a variable with domain $\{d_1, \ldots, d_n\}$.

Like many other SLS procedures for satisfiability, NB-Walksat operates by choosing a random assignment and then, until a satisfying assignment is found, repeatedly selecting a literal from an unsatisfied clause and modifying the assignment so as to satisfy that literal, and hence the clause in which it appears. Since the selected literal, X/d, occurs in an unsatisfied clause, the present assignment must map X to a value other than d. The present assignment is modified so that it maps X to d, and its mapping of all other variables is unmodified. We say that the literal X/d has been *flipped*.

What distinguishes NB-Walksat and Walksat from other procedures is the heuristic employed for choosing which literal to flip. Though recent versions of Walksat provide a range of user-selectable heuristics for choosing the literal, the original heuristic is the one called "best" or "SKC." As it has been used in many reported experiments (e.g., Selman et al., 1994; Kautz et al., 1997; Walser, 1997) it is the "best" version of Walksat that forms the basis for NB-Walksat and is the focus of this paper.

NB-Walksat with the "best" heuristic chooses a literal to flip by first randomly selecting a clause with uniform distribution from among all the clauses that are not satisfied by the current assignment. Let L be the set of literals in the selected clause. We say that flipping a literal *breaks* a clause if the clause is satisfied by the assignment before the flip but not after the flip. If L contains a literal such that flipping it would break no clauses, then the literal to flip is chosen randomly with uniform distribution from among all such literals. If L contains no such literals, then a literal is chosen either (i) randomly with uniform distribution from L or (ii) randomly with uniform distribution from among the literals in L that if flipped would break the fewest clauses. The decision to do (i) or (ii) is made randomly; with a user-specified probability, P_{noise}, the "noisy" choice (i) is taken. Figure 1 gives pseudo-code for the NB-Walksat procedure.

Experiments with Walksat (Selman et al., 1994) show that the incorporation of noisy choices dramatically improves its performance and that performance can vary greatly according to the value of P_{noise}. As one would expect, the same is true of NB-Walksat.

4. Transforming Non-Boolean Formulas

To transform NB-SAT to SAT, we map each nb-formula to a b-formula such that the satisfying assignments of the two formulas correspond, though not necessarily one to one. This paper presents three such transforms, called the

Input: F, a Non-Boolean formula in CNF; P_{noise}, the noise probability setting.
Output: A, an assignment that satisfies F.

(a) Transform F into a positive CNF formula.

(b) From among all assignments to the variables of F choose one at random with uniform distribution. Call it A.

(c) Repeat until A satisfies F:

   (d) From among the clauses of F that are not satisfied by A select one at random with a uniform distribution. Let L be the set of literals of this clause.

   (e) If there is a literal in L such that flipping it would break no clauses then set L to the set of all such literals in L.

   (f) Otherwise, with probability $1 - P_{noise}$ remove from L all literals that, if flipped, would break more clauses than would flipping another literal of L.

   (g) From among the literals of L select one at random with uniform distribution. Call it X/d.

   (h) Modify A by flipping X/d.

(i) Output A.

Figure 1. NB-Walksat with the "best" heuristic.

unary/unary, *unary/binary* and *binary* transforms. Each operates on an arbitrary formula, though our experiments apply the transforms only to CNF formulas. Each transform operates by replacing each nb-atom in the formula with a b-formula that, in a sense, encodes the nb-atom it replaces. The resulting formula is known as the *kernel* of the transformation. The transforms employ two core ways of producing a kernel; we call these two encodings "unary" and "binary."

If the unary encoding of the kernel is used, the transform also needs to conjoin two additional formulas to the kernel, known as the *at-least-one* formula (or ALO formula) and the *at-most-one* formula (or AMO formula). As with the kernel, two encodings can be used for the ALO and AMO formulas: unary and binary. The three transforms we use in this paper are *enhanced binary* (which uses a binary encoding for the kernel and no ALO or AMO formula), *unary/ unary* (which uses unary encodings for the kernel and for the ALO and AMO formulas), and *unary/binary* (which uses a unary encoding for the kernel and an enhanced binary encoding for the ALO and AMO formulas). The unary/binary transform is new, as is the enhanced version of the binary transform.

In the following presentation we discuss the size of the formula produced by each transform, where we take a formula's size to be the number of occurrences of atoms it contains. Throughout we assume that each transform is being applied to an nb-formula containing V variables each of which has a domain of size D, and we present the sizes of the resulting formulas in terms of these two parameters. The results of the discussion are summarized in Figure 2.

4.1. THE UNARY/UNARY TRANSFORM

The unary/unary transform produces a kernel by transforming each nb-atom X/d to a distinct propositional variable, which we shall call $X:d$. The idea is that a

	Unary/Unary	Enhanced Binary Positive	Negative	Unary/Binary
kernel variables	VD	$V\lceil \lg D\rceil$	$V\lceil \lg D\rceil$	VD
kernel size	L	$\leq L\lceil \lg D\rceil$	$\leq L\lceil \lg D\rceil$	L
kernel CNF size	L	$\leq L\lceil \lg D\rceil^J$	$\leq L\lceil \lg D\rceil$	L
at-least-one variables	VD	0	0	$V(D + \lceil \lg D\rceil)$
at-least-one size	VD	0	0	$\leq VD(\lceil \lg D\rceil + 1)$
at-least-one CNF size	VD	0	0	$\leq VD(\lceil \lg D\rceil + 1)$
at-most-one variables	VD	0	0	$V(D + \lceil \lg D\rceil)$
at-most-one size	$VD(D-1)$	0	0	$\leq VD(\lceil \lg D\rceil + 1)$
at-most-one CNF size	$VD(D-1)$	0	0	$\leq 2VD\lceil \lg D\rceil$

Figure 2. Size of the Boolean formulas produced by each of the three transformations applied to a non-Boolean formula of size L that has V variables, each with domain size D. The "CNF size" rows give the size of the formula when put into CNF form. It is assumed that the non-Boolean formula is in CNF and its clauses each have J literals. The size of the enhanced binary transformation is divided into two cases: a positive kernel and a negative kernel.

Boolean assignment maps $X{:}d$ to *TRUE* if and only if the corresponding non-Boolean assignment maps X to d. Thus, the role of an nb-variable with domain $\{d_1,\ldots, d_n\}$ is played by n b-variables.

Furthermore, one must generally add additional formulas to the Boolean encoding to represent the constraint that a satisfying assignment must satisfy exactly one of $X{:}d_1,\ldots, X{:}d_n$. This constraint is expressed as a conjunction of one formula (known as the ALO formula) asserting that at least one of the variables is true and another (known as the AMO formula) asserting that at most one of the variables is true.

To state that at *least* one of $X{:}d_1,\ldots, X{:}d_n$ must be satisfied we simply use the clause $X{:}d_1 \vee \cdots \vee X{:}d_n$. The entire ALO formula is a conjunction of such clauses, one clause for each nb-variables. Thus, the ALO formula consists of a conjunction of V clauses each with D literals, giving it a total size of $V D$.

To say that at *most* one of $X{:}d_1,\ldots, X{:}d_n$ must be satisfied we add the clause $\neg X{:}d_i \vee \neg X{:}d_j$, for all i and j such that $1 \leq i < j \leq n$. The entire AMO formula is a conjunction of such clauses, $\frac{1}{2}D(D-1)$ clauses for each nb-variable. Thus, the AMO formula consists of a conjunction of $\frac{1}{2}VD(D-1)$ clauses, each containing two literals, giving it a total size of $VD(D-1)$.

Notice that these ALO and AMO formulas are in CNF. And since the transform produces a kernel whose form is identical to that of the original formula, the entire b-formula produced by the unary/unary transform is in CNF if and only if the original nb-formula is.

4.2. THE BINARY TRANSFORM

The unary/unary transform uses D b-variables to encode a single nb-variable of domain size D and, hence, uses a base 1 encoding. By using a base 2 encoding, the binary transformation requires only $\lceil \lg D\rceil$ b-variables to encode the same nb-variable.[*] If X is a variable with domain $\{d_1,\ldots, d_n\}$, the binary transform maps an nb-literal of the form X/d_i by taking the binary representation of $i-1$ and encoding this in $\lceil \lg n \rceil$ Boolean variables. For example, if n is 4, then

X/d_1 is mapped to $\neg X_2 \wedge \neg X_1$,
X/d_2 is mapped to $\neg X_2 \wedge X_1$,
X/d_3 is mapped to $X_2 \wedge \neg X_1$ and
X/d_4 is mapped to $X_2 \wedge X_1$.

To see what happens when the domain size is not a power of two, reconsider X to have the domain $\{d_1, d_2, d_3\}$. If we map X/d_1, X/d_2 and X/d_3 as above then there is a problem in that the Boolean assignment that satisfies $X_2 \wedge X_1$ does not correspond to an assignment of a domain value to X. One solution to this would be to add an ALO formula,

$$(\neg X_2 \wedge \neg X_1) \vee (\neg X_2 \wedge \neg X_1) \vee (X_2 \wedge X_1),$$

which ensures that the *extraneous* binary combination $X_2 \wedge X_1$ cannot be satisfied in any solution. Alternatively, one could make the logically-equivalent statement that the extraneous binary combination must be false: $\neg(X_2 \wedge X_1)$. The latter of these two has the advantage that it can be put into CNF without any blowup, and is the method adopted by Hoos (1998, page 180).

Frisch and Peugniez (2001) introduced a version of the binary transform in which no extraneous combinations are produced and therefore no ALO formula is required. We call this the *enhanced binary transform*, and the version with extraneous combinations the *basic binary transform*. We use the term *binary transform* to refer generically to any version of the transform.

In the example considered above the extraneous combination is eliminated if

X/d_1 is mapped to $\neg X_2$,
X/d_2 is mapped to $X_2 \wedge \neg X_1$ and
X/d_3 is mapped to $X_2 \wedge X_1$.

Here, the transform of X/d_1 covers two binary combinations: $(\neg X_2 \wedge X_1)$ and $(\neg X_2 \wedge \neg X_1)$.

To see what happens in general, let X be a variable with domain $\{d_1,\ldots, d_n\}$ and let k be $2^{\lceil \lg n \rceil} - n$. Then $X/d_1,\ldots, X/d_k$ are each mapped to cover two binary combinations, and $X/d_{k+1},\ldots, X/d_n$ are each mapped to cover a single binary combination.

Notice that this transform generates no extraneous binary combinations. Also notice that, as a special case, if n is a power of two, then each X/d_i $(1 \leq i \leq n)$ is

---

[*] The ceiling of a real value x, written $\lceil x \rceil$, is the smallest integer that is greater than or equal to x.

mapped to cover a single binary combination and thus is identical to the basic binary transform. Finally, to confirm that the extended binary transform requires no AMO formula and no ALO formula, observe that every Boolean assignment must satisfy the extended binary transform of exactly one of $X/d_1, \ldots, X/d_n$.

Since the enhanced binary transform replaces each nb-atom with a conjunction of at least $\lfloor \lg D \rfloor$ b-atoms and at most $\lceil \lg D \rceil$ b-atoms, it produces a formula whose size is $\lfloor \lg D \rfloor$ to $\lceil \lg D \rceil$ times that of the original formula.[*]

Notice that the enhanced binary transformation of a CNF formula is not necessarily in CNF. However, the enhanced binary transformation of a negative CNF formula is *almost* in CNF; it is a conjunction of disjunctions of negated conjunctions of literals. For example, using variables X and Y, both with the domain $\{d_1, d_2, d_3\}$, the enhanced binary transform of the clause $\neg X/d_1 \lor \neg Y/d_2$ is $\neg(\neg X_2) \lor \neg(Y_2 \land \neg Y_1)$. By using De Morgan's law, the negations can be moved inside of the innermost conjunctions, resulting in a CNF formula of the same size. Thus, our example formula becomes the clause $X_2 \lor \neg Y_2 \lor Y_1$. At the other extreme, the enhanced binary transformation of a positive CNF formula is a conjunction of disjunctions of conjunctions of literals. One way of transforming this to CNF is to distribute the disjunctions over the conjunctions. Unfortunately, applying this distribution to a disjunction of n conjunctions, each with m literals, produces a CNF formula with n^m conjuncts, each with m literals. Thus, if an nb-clause has J literals, its enhanced binary transformation consists of between $\lfloor \lg D \rfloor^J$ and $\lceil \lg D \rceil^J$ clauses, each with J literals. Thus, if a positive nb-formula consists of L/J clauses each with J literals, then the size of its enhanced binary transform is between $L \lfloor \lg D \rfloor^J$ and $L \lceil \lg D \rceil^J$.

It is possible to avoid this exponential expansion by introducing new variables into the formula and, indeed, this is what is generated by the unary/binary transform to which we now turn our attention.

4.3. THE UNARY/BINARY TRANSFORM

The unary/binary transform, originally introduced by Frisch and Peugniez (2001), produces the same kernel as the unary/unary transform. The ALO and AMO formulas it produces achieve their effect by introducing the enhanced binary encodings of nb-atoms and adding formulas linking the two encodings together. Following the practice of the constraint programming community, we call these linking formulas "channeling" formulas. Since the enhanced binary encoding requires no ALO or AMO formulas, the unary/binary encoding requires no ALO or AMO formulas beyond the channeling formulas.

The channeling formulas that act as AMO formulas state that the unary encoding of each nb-atom implies its enhanced binary encoding. So, for ex-

---

[*] The floor of a real value x, written $\lfloor x \rfloor$, is the largest integer that is less than or equal to x.

ample, if the nb-variable X has domain $\{d_1, d_2, d_3\}$, then the AMO formula for X is

$$(X{:}d_1 \rightarrow \neg X_2) \wedge$$
$$(X{:}d_2 \rightarrow (X_2 \wedge \neg X_1)) \wedge$$
$$(X{:}d_3 \rightarrow (X_2 \wedge X_1))$$

which is logically equivalent to the CNF formula

$$(\neg X{:}d_1 \vee \neg X_2) \wedge$$
$$(\neg X{:}d_2 \vee X_2) \wedge (\neg X{:}d_2 \vee \neg X_1) \wedge$$
$$(\neg X{:}d_3 \vee X_2) \wedge (\neg X{:}d_3 \vee X_1).$$

The entire AMO formula is a conjunction of such channeling formulas, one for each of nb-variable.

It is easy to see that the CNF of the channeling formula for each variable consists of between $D \lfloor \lg D \rfloor$ and $D \lceil \lg D \rceil$ clauses of two literals. Since the entire AMO formula consists of a conjunction of channeling formulas for each of V variables, its total size is between $2VD\lfloor \lg D \rfloor$ and $2VD\lceil \lg D \rceil$.

The channeling formulas that act as ALO formulas state that for each nb-atom, its unary encoding is implied by its enhanced binary encoding. So, for example, if the nb-variable X has domain $\{d_1, d_2, d_3\}$, then the ALO formula for X is

$$(\neg X_2 \rightarrow X{:}d_1) \wedge$$
$$((X_2 \wedge \neg X_1) \rightarrow X{:}d_2) \wedge$$
$$((X_2 \wedge X_1) \rightarrow X{:}d_3)$$

which is logically equivalent to the CNF formula

$$(X_2 \vee X/d_1) \wedge$$
$$(\neg X_2 \vee X_1 \vee X{:}d_2) \wedge$$
$$(\neg X_2 \vee \neg X_1 \vee X{:}d_3).$$

The entire ALO formula is a conjunction of channeling formulas, one linking formula for each nb-variable. The ALO formula for each nb-variable is a conjunction of D clauses each of size $\lfloor \lg D \rfloor + 1$ or $\lceil \lg D \rceil + 1$; thus the entire ALO formula is a conjunction of DV clauses and has as a total size of between $DV(\lfloor \lg D \rfloor + 1)$ and $DV(\lceil \lg D \rceil + 1)$.

4.4. WHEN ARE ALO AND AMO FORMULAS NEEDED?

It has been known for some time that certain unary SAT-encodings do not require ALO clauses and certain others do not require AMO clauses. For example, Jonsson and Ginsberg (1993) argue that AMO clauses are not needed in graph coloring. It has also been observed that when it is possible to omit either the AMO or ALO clauses, doing so improves the performance of local search algorithms. Prestwich (2004) hypothesizes that this improvement is partly a result of increasing the solution density of the search space. The important open question is when can ALO and AMO clauses be omitted?

This section shows that the need for such clauses is *not* a property of the problem, but rather a property of the non-Boolean encoding of the problem. This section identifies, and proves correct, a sufficient syntactic condition for excluding ALO clauses and another for excluding AMO clauses. In fact, we shall state this on a variable-by-variable basis; some variables may require ALO and/or AMO clauses while others may not.

The following definition applies to all formulas, both Boolean and non-Boolean.

DEFINITION 1 (Positive and Negative Formulas). A formula occurs positively within itself. If α occurs positively (negatively) within γ, then α occurs positively (negatively) within $\gamma \wedge \beta$, $\beta \wedge \gamma$, $\beta \vee \gamma$, $\gamma \vee \beta$, $\beta \rightarrow \gamma$, $\gamma \leftrightarrow \beta$ and $\beta \leftrightarrow \gamma$. If α occurs positively (negatively) within γ, then α occurs negatively (positively) within $\neg\gamma$, $\gamma \rightarrow \beta$, $\gamma \leftrightarrow \beta$ and $\beta \leftrightarrow \gamma$. A formula is said to be negative (positive) with respect to an atom if that atom does not occur positively (negatively) in the formula. A formula is said to be positive (negative) if it is positive (negative) with respect to all atoms.

Notice that this generalizes our previous definition that a CNF formula is negative if it contains no positive literals and it is positive if it contains no negative literals.

We can partially order the Boolean assignments by the atoms that they satisfy. If A is an atom then we write $\alpha \geq_A \beta$ to mean that α and β are identical with the possible exception that α satisfies A but β does not.

LEMMA 1 (Monotonicity). *Let ϕ be a formula, let A be an atom, and let α and β be two Boolean assignments such that $\alpha \geq_A \beta$. If ϕ is formula that is positive with respect to A and is satisfied by β, then it is satisfied by α. If ϕ as negative with respect to A and is satisfied by α, then it is satisfied by β.*

Proof. Both statements can be proved simultaneously by a straightforward induction on the structure of ϕ.   □

We now turn our attention to the main theorem, which identifies conditions under which AMO and ALO formulas can be omitted without affecting satisfiability. The correctness of the theorem depends on the semantics, not the syntax, of the ALO and AMO formulas. In particular, all that matters is that an ALO (AMO) formula for $X{:}d_1,\ldots, X{:}d_n$, is satisfied by an assignment if and only if at least (most) one of $X{:}d_1,\ldots, X{:}d_n$, is satisfied by that assignment.

THEOREM 1 (Satisfiability without ALO or AMO). *Let K be an arbitrary Boolean formula, L be a conjunction of ALO formulas, and M be a conjunction of AMO formulas. Let AMO(X) and ALO(X) be AMO and ALO formulas, respectively, for $X:d_1,\dots, X:d_n$. (1) If K is negative with respect to each of $X:d_1,\dots, X:d_n$ and $K \wedge L \wedge M$ is satisfiable, then so is $K \wedge L \wedge M \wedge AMO(X)$. (2) If K is positive with respect to each of $X:d_1,\dots, X:d_n$ and $K \wedge L \wedge M$ is satisfiable, then so is $K \wedge L \wedge M \wedge ALO(X)$.*

Proof. Parts (1) and (2) are proved separately.

(1) The proof proceeds by assuming the antecedent and proving the consequent. Let α be an assignment that satisfies $K \wedge L \wedge M$. We now prove that $K \wedge L \wedge M \wedge AMO(X)$ is satisfiable by induction on m, the number of atoms in $X:d_1,\dots, X:d_n$, that are satisfied by α.

Base case, m is 0 or 1: In this case α itself satisfies $K \wedge L \wedge M \wedge AMO(X)$.

Inductive case, $m \geq 2$: The inductive hypothesis is that if K is negative with respect to each of $X:d_1,\dots, X:d_n$, and $K \wedge L \wedge M$ is satisfied by an assignment that satisfies $m-1$ of $X:d_1,\dots, X:d_n$, then $K \wedge L \wedge M \wedge AMO(X)$ is satisfiable. Let $X:d_i$ be any one of the m atoms of $X:d_1,\dots, X:d_n$, that are satisfied by α. Let α' be an assignment that is identical to α except that it falsifies $X:d_i$. We now show, in turn, that α' satisfies K, L and M. Since K is negative with respect to $X:d_i$ and α satisfies K, by the Monotonicity Lemma α' also satisfies K. Second, L must be satisfied by α'; the truth of an ALO formula for a variable other than X is unaffected by the change of $X:d_i$ and we have constructed α' so that it satisfies $m-1 \geq 1$ of $X:d_1,\dots, X:d_n$. Finally, α' satisfies M since α satisfies M and α' satisfies fewer atoms than α. Since α' satisfies $K \wedge L \wedge M$ and $m-1$ of $X:d_1,\dots, X:d_n$ then, by the inductive hypothesis, $K \wedge L \wedge M \wedge AMO(X)$ is satisfiable.

(2) We assume the antecedent and prove the consequent. Let α be an assignment that satisfies $K \wedge L \wedge M$. If α also satisfies $ALO(X)$, then the consequent trivially holds. Otherwise, α doesn't satisfy $ALO(X)$; rather it falsifies each of $X:d_1,\dots, X:d_n$. Let $X:d_i$ be any one of $X:d_1,\dots, X:d_n$, and let α' be an assignment that is identical to α except that it satisfies $X:d_i$. Clearly α' satisfies $ALO(X)$ so it remains to show that α' satisfies K, L and M, which we do in turn. Since K is positive with respect to $X:d_i$ and α satisfies K, by the Monotonicity Lemma α' also satisfies K. Second, α' satisfies L since α satisfies L and α' satisfies more atoms than α. Finally, M must be satisfied by α'; the truth of an AMO formula for a variable other than X is unaffected by the change of $X:d_i$ and we have constructed α' so that it satisfies exactly one of $X:d_1,\dots, X:d_n$. $\square$

COROLLARY 1 (Unary Transform without ALO or AMO). *The unary translation of a negative NB-formula is satisfiable if and only if it is satisjiable when the AMO clauses are omitted. The unary translation of a positive NB-formula is satisfiable if and only if it is satisfiable when the ALO clauses are omitted.*

Proof. We prove the first statement; the second is analogous. Let α be the unary translation of an arbitrary negative NB-formula from which n AMO formulas have been omitted. The "only-if" part is obvious. The "if" part is proved by induction on n. For the base case, if $n = 0$ then the corollary is obvious. The inductive case follows from Theorem 1 by taking K to be the kernel of α, L and M to be the ALO formulas and AMO formulas of α, and $AMO(X)$ to be one of the AMO formulas omitted from α. If α is satisfiable then, by the theorem, it remains satisfiable if we conjoin it with $AMO(X)$.   □

To see that the need for AMO and ALO clauses is solely a property of the encoding, not the problem being encoded, consider the problem of coloring a graph of two connected nodes with the colors red, blue, and green. We can encode this in NB-SAT by using two variables, X and Y, for the nodes and $\{red, blue, green\}$ as the domain of each. There are (at least) two ways to encode the constraint that both nodes cannot be red.

$$\neg X/red \ \lor \ \neg Y/red \tag{2}$$

$$X/blue \lor X/green \lor Y/blue \lor Y/green \tag{3}$$

According to Corollary 1, AMO clauses are not needed with (2), and ALO clauses are not needed with (3).

4.5. MIXED TRANSFORMATIONS

In presenting the three transformations it was assumed that the same transformation is applied to all nb-variables. However, there is no reason why different transformations couldn't be applied to different variables. Nor is there any reason why the AMO formula for a variable couldn't use one encoding (say, binary) while its ALO formula uses another encoding (say, unary).

This flexibility extends to the issue of whether ALO and AMO formulas are required in a unary transformation. Observe that Theorem 1 applies to the translation of a single nb-variable, X. Thus the need for ALO and AMO formulas can be considered on a variable-by-variable basis.

5. Comparison of Search Spaces

This section considers the search spaces confronted by the four solution methods: the direct non-Boolean method and the three transformation methods based on the transforms of the previous section. For each method, the states in the search space are all assignments to the variables of the formula – Boolean or non-Boolean – and the state transitions are made by flipping a single literal.

Consider an nb-formula F containing V variables, each with a domain of size D. The search space consists of D^V states with $V(D-1)$ transitions from each.

The unary/unary transformation of F contains DV b-variables and hence has 2^{DV} states with DV transitions from each. An nb-variable X with the domain $\{d_1,\ldots, d_n\}$ is represented in the unary/unary transformation by the b-atoms $X{:}d_1,\ldots, X{:}d_n$. A non-Boolean assignment that maps X to d_i corresponds to a Boolean assignment that maps $X{:}d_j$ to $TRUE$ if $j = i$ and $FALSE$ if $j \neq i$. In a Boolean assignment such as this, where exactly one $X{:}d_j$ is mapped to $TRUE$, we say that X is *singularly* assigned. *Nonsingular* assignments of X are either *empty*, mapping every $X{:}d_j$ to $FALSE$, or *multiple*, mapping more than one $X{:}d_j$ to $TRUE$. We also use the term "singular" to describe an entire assignment in which every nb-variable is singularly assigned.

Though nonsingular assignments occur in the unary/unary search space, they cannot be solutions if all AMO and ALO clauses are included in the encoding. As domain sizes grow the unary/unary search space becomes dominated by non-singular assignments. A variable with domain size D has D singular assignments compared with $2^D - D$ nonsingular assignments. In a problem with V nb-variables the ratio of nonsingular to singular assignments is raised to the power of V.

Consider a transition from state S to state S' in in the search space of F. This transition changes the value assigned to some variable, X, from value d to a different value d'. Both S and S' correspond to singular states in the search space of the unary/unary transform of F. However, the latter search space contains no transition between these two states. The shortest paths between these two states contain two moves: flipping $X{:}d$ from $FALSE$ to $TRUE$ and flipping $X{:}d'$ from $TRUE$ to $FALSE$ in either order. A local search procedure operating on the unary/unary transformation must inevitably move through some nonsingular states because there are no transitions between two singular states.

Much work on SLS has noted that solution density (the ratio of number of solutions to number of states in the search space) is one factor influencing the effectiveness of SLS. An nb-encoding has the same number of solutions as its unary/unary transform if all ALO and AMO clauses are included. As the unary/unary encoding generally has many more states, it generally has a lower solution density. Removing ALO or AMO clauses from a unary/unary encoding potentially increases the number of solutions without changing the number of states.

The binary transformation of F contains $\lceil \lg D \rceil V$ variables, and hence has $2^{\lceil \lg D \rceil V}$ states; from each there are $\lceil \lg D \rceil V$ transitions. If D is a power of 2, then the non-Boolean states and binary states are in a one-to-one correspondence and, hence, contain the same number of solutions, same number of states, and same solution density. However, the $\lceil \lg D \rceil V$ transitions from each binary state are a subset of the $(D-1)V$ transitions in the corresponding nb-state. If D is not a power of two, then the binary search space has more states than the nb-search space. The basic binary encoding has the same number of solutions as the nb-encoding, but the extended binary encoding potentially has more solutions.

Notice that if all variables in F have a domain size of 2, then the binary transform of F is essentially the same as F, and the non-Boolean and binary search spaces are isomorphic. NB-Walksat operating on F behaves identically to Walksat operating on the binary transform of F. This equivalence was exploited in testing the correctness of the NB-Walksat implementation.

The unary/binary transformation of F contains both the variables produced by the unary/unary transform and those produced by the binary transform, a total of $DV + \lceil \lg D \rceil V$ variables. Its search space is a cross product of the other two search spaces. More precisely, if we let S_U be the states of the unary/unary space and S_B be the states of the binary space, then the states of the unary/binary space are the cross product of S_U and S_B. If u and u' are elements of S_U and b and b' are elements of S_B, then there is a transition from $\langle u, b \rangle$ to $\langle u', b' \rangle$ in the unary/binary space if and only if either (1) $b = b'$ and there is a transition from u to u' in the unary/unary space, or (2) $u = u'$ and there is a transition from b to b' in the binary space.

This discussion raises two questions: Are nonsingular states helpful to the search, perhaps by providing useful paths to a solution or out of local minima, or is better performance achieved by restricting search to a smaller space containing only singular assignments? Does the reduction of transitions that results from using the binary representation help or hinder the search process?

6. Performance Evaluation

Using four problem domains, this section presents experiments that compare the performance of the four methods, which we shall refer to as NB (non-Boolean encoding), UU (unary/unary encoding), EB (enhanced binary encoding), and UB (unary/binary encoding). In all experiments, Walksat version 35 was used to solve the Boolean encodings. The non-Boolean encodings, even in cases where the domain size is 2, were solved with NB-Walksat; version 4 was used for the graph coloring problems in Section 6.1 and version 6 was used in all other experiments. Both Walksat and NB-Walksat provide the user the option of either compiling the program with fixed-size data structures or allocating the data structures when the formula is input at runtime; the latter option was used in all experiments. The random formulas (Section 6.2) and round-robin tournament problems (Section 6.3) were run on a 700 MHz Athlon with 256 MB of memory. The quasigroup problems (Section 6.4) were run on an Athlon XP 2400 + 2 GHz with 512 MB of memory.

Considerable care must be taken in setting the P_{noise} parameter for the experiments. Much work in this area has been reported without giving the value used for P_{noise}, and thus is irreproducible. Setting the parameter to any fixed value over all formulas is not acceptable; we have observed that a parameter setting that is optimal for one formula can, in another formula, yield performance that is several orders of magnitude below optimal. The best option is to report performance at the optimal setting for P_{noise}, which – in the absence of any known method to determine this *a priori* – we have determined experimentally. This is also the route followed by Hoos (1998) in his extremely careful work.

In using SLS procedures it is common practice to restart the search at a new, randomly selected assignment if the procedure has not found a solution after a prescribed number of flips. Since the runtime distribution using a restart strategy is a function of the runtime distribution without restarts, this study need be concerned only with the performance without restarts.

6.1. GRAPH COLORING

Frisch and Peugniez (2001) report experiments with six instances of the graph coloring problem. Each problem instance was encoded as a CNF nb-formula. For each node in the graph the formula uses a distinct variable whose domain is the set of colors. The formula itself is a conjunction of all clauses of the form $\neg X/c \lor \neg Y/c$, such that X and Y are a pair of nodes connected by an arc and c is a color. For each instance the domain size of the variables is the number of colors, which for these six instances is 5, 5, 15, 17, 18, and 25.

Three SAT-encodings of each problem instance were produced by applying the unary/unary, enhanced binary and unary/binary transforms. Since the nb-encodings are negative, AMO clauses were omitted from the UU and UB encodings, as justified by Corollary 1. Also note that because the nb-encodings are negative, the enhanced binary transform maps each nb-clause to a single b-clause (as discussed at the end of Section 4.2).

Frisch and Peugniez's experiments reveal that NB and UU are effective on all six instances and have roughly comparable solution times (within a factor of 2 to 3). On the two problem instances with domain size five, the three transformation methods equaled or outperformed the direct method. However, on each of the other four instances (domain size 15 to 25), the direct method equaled or bettered each of the transformation methods. Of these same four instances, UB was ineffective on three and EB was ineffective on two.

Overall, their graph-coloring experiments show that with increasing domain size, NB scales much better than both UB and EB and slightly better than UU.

6.2. RANDOM NON-BOOLEAN CNF FORMULAS

Since we can control certain parameters in the generation of random CNF nb-formulas, they provide a good testbed. In particular, since this paper is a study of solving problems with domain sizes greater than two, we would like to know how problem-solving performance varies with domain size. To measure this we need to select problem instances that have different domain sizes but are otherwise similar. Formulating a notion of "otherwise similar" has been one of the most stubborn problems faced by this research.

We have developed a program that generates random, positive CNF nb-formulas using five parameters: N, D, C, V, and L. Each generated formula consists of exactly C clauses. Using a fixed set of N variables each with a domain size of D, each clause is generated by randomly (with uniform distribution) chasing V distinct variables and then, for each, randomly (with uniform distribution) choosing L values from its domain. Each of the chosen variables is coupled with each of its L chosen values to form $L \cdot V$ positive literals, which are disjoined together to form a clause.

The simplest conjecture on how to study varying domain size is to fix the values of N, C, V, and L and then to systematically vary D. One can see that performance on this task would exhibit typical phase-transition behavior (Mitchell et al., 1992): small values of D would produce under-constrained instances, which would become critically-constrained and then over-constrained as D increases. The problem instances generated by this method would not be similar in terms of their location relative the solubility phase transition.

Our solution to this shortcoming is to vary D and to adjust the other four parameters so as to put the problem class at the solubility phase transition – that is, at the point where half the instances in the class are satisfiable. But for any given value of D many combinations of values for N, C, V, and L put the problem class at the phase transition.

Our first attempt to solve this was based on the idea of keeping the problem size constant. With each formula consisting of 1,000 clauses, each with three literals, we experimentally determined the appropriate value of N to put the problem class at the phase transition. As we later discovered, this approach is faulty, a consequence of the somewhat counterintuitive observation that the appropriate value of N grows fairly rapidly with D. A problem instance with 1,000 clauses of three literals is at the phase transition if it has 1,031 variables with domain size 64. Such a problem instance contains only 3,000 literal occurrences drawn out of the possible 65,984 atoms (1031×64). That is, only about one in 21 of the possible atoms occur in the formula; so, on the average, each variable occurs with only about three of its 64 possible values. Since the problem instance has all positive literals, each variable has, in effect, a domain size of approximately 3. Even for a problem with domain size 8, about half of the possible atoms do not occur in a random problem instance.

The solution we have adopted is to keep D^N, the size of the search space, at a fixed value for all problem instances and then requiring all clauses to have the same "constrainedness," as measured by $(L/D)^V$. Mimicking Boolean 3CNF, we set V to three and aim to keep $(L/D)^V$ at 1/8, which is achieved by setting L to

Problem	Method	P_{noise} Setting	Formula Size	Flip Rate (flips/s)	Median Flips	Median Time (ms)
Domain size 2	NB	.53	783	272,000	506	1.9
60 vars	UU	.44	903	684,000	3,450	5.0
261 clauses	UB	.39	1,023	792,000	9,560	12.1
	EB	.53	783	443,000	502	1.1
Domain size 4	NB	.42	1,680	179,000	803	4.5
30 vars	UU	.17	2,040	414,000	8,770	21.2
280 clauses	UB	.16	2,160	608,000	44,600	73.4
	EB		319,448			
Domain size 8	NB	.31	3,528	101,000	1,130	11.2
20 vars	UU	.05	4,648	251,000	20,400	81.0
294 clauses	UB	.05	4,488	513,000	519,000	1,010
Domain size 16	NB	.24	7,248	55,400	2,250	40.6
15 vars	UU	.018	10,848	145,000	86,0000	592
302 clauses	UB		9,168			
Domain size 32	NB	.18	14,736	27,900	4,770	171
12 vars	UU	.01	26,640	77,000	515,000	6,690
307 clauses	UB		18,576			

Figure 3. Results, to no more than three significant figures, for a suite of 101 satisfiable non-Boolean CNF formulas chosen at random. The values recorded in the flips and time column are the flips and time required to solve a single formula, not the entire suite. On those rows missing entries, the median number of flips to solution of 101 runs at noise levels 0.01, 0.02, and 0.03 all exceeded 5,000,000.

$D/2$. This follows the constant length model advocated by Mitchell et al. (1992). Finally C is set to whatever value puts the problem class at the solubility phase transition. Thus, while varying D, the parameters that we are holding constant are search space size, the number of variables constrained by each clause and the amount of constraint placed on each, and the proportion of instances with that parameter setting that are solvable.

Our experiments were conducted on domain sizes of 2, 4, 8, 16, and 32. Following the model above we kept D^N at a constant value; 2^{60} was chosen since $2^{60} = 2^{N_2} = 4^{N_4} = 8^{N_8} = 16^{N_{16}} = 32^{N_{32}}$ if $N_2 = 60$, $N_4 = 30$, $N_8 = 20$, $N_{16} = 15$ and $N_{32} = 12$. Then for each domain size, we used NB-Satz* (Stock, 2000) to experimentally locate the point of the phase transition The leftmost column of Figure 3 shows the value of C (number of clauses) at which these experiments located the phase transitions.

With the parameters of the random formulas determined, at each domain size we generated a series of random formulas according to the above method and kept the first 101 satisfiable ones as identified by NB-Satz. At each domain size, 1,001 attempts were made to solve the suite of 101 formulas with the NB, UU, and UB methods. By Corollary 1 positive CNF nb-formula can be transformed to a b-formula without the ALO formulas. Since our randomly generated formulas are

---

* Satz (Li and Anbulagan, 1997) is an implementation of the DPLL algorithm (Davis et al., 1962) for deciding Boolean satisfiability. NB-Satz generalizes Satz to handle non-Boolean formulas. Satz and other Boolean decision procedures are incapable of solving these random instances with large domain size.

positive, the unary/unary and unary/binary encodings that are used here contain only kernels and AMO formulas.

The results of these experiments,[*] as shown in Figure 3, consistently follow a clear pattern. At all domain sizes, in terms of both time and number of flips, NB outperforms UU, which in turn outperforms UB. All the methods show a decline in performance as domain size grows. The decline is so sharp for the transformation methods that UB is ineffective on domain size 16, and UU is two orders of magnitude slower than NB on domain size 32. On these random formulas, as on the graph coloring problems, the flip rates of all methods decline with increasing domain size.

Results on the EB method are reported only for domain size 2 since at larger domain sizes the enhanced binary transformation produces unreasonably large formulas. As discussed at the end of Section 4.2, if the enhanced binary transform is used to produce a CNF b-formula from a positive CNF nb-formula, the size of the resulting b-formula is exponential in the clause length of the original nb-formula-which in this case is $\frac{3}{2}D$. With a domain size of 4 the transformation produces a b-formula with 319,488 atoms (which Walksat cannot solve even with hours of CPU time) and with a domain size of 8, the b-formula has over $5 \cdot 10^9$ atoms. Finally, recall (from Section 4.2) that applying the binary transform to an nb-formula of domain size 2 results in an essentially identical Boolean formula. Hence at domain size 2, the only difference between the NB and EB methods are that NB uses NB-Walksat and EB uses Walksat. The results in the table show that for these random formulas NB-Walksat's flip rate is 61% of Walksat's flip rate; this slow down is the overhead incurred by the generality of NB-Walksat. It should be noted that the amount of overhead could be quite different on problems with other characteristics.

6.3. ROUND-ROBIN TOURNAMENT SCHEDULING

The round robin tournament scheduling problem appears as problem 26 in CSPLib (Gent and Walsh,), where it is specified as follows:

The problem is to schedule a tournament of n teams over $n-1$ weeks, with each week divided into $n/2$ periods, and each period divided into two slots. The first team in each slot plays at home, whilst the second plays the first team

---

[*] The experiments reported here improve upon similar ones reported by Frisch and Peugniez (2001). Here we correct a faulty P_{noise} setting (that for UU at domain size 4), use larger test suites (101 instances each, instead of 25), and use more sample more runs (1,001 instead of 101). The median flips to solution is generally higher in these experiments than in the previous ones. We believe that this is a consequence of using larger test suites. Since the P_{noise} parameter is set to optimize performance over the entire suite, it more closely fits the optimal settings of the instances in a small suite than those in a large suite. To see this, just consider a one-instance suite and a two-instance suite.

away. A tournament must satisfy the following three constraints: (1) every team plays once a week; (2) every team plays at most twice in the same period over the tournament; (3) every team plays every other team.

An example schedule for eight teams is as follows:

	Week 1	Week 2	Week 3	Week 4	Week 5	Week 6	Week 7
Period 1	8 vs. 1	8 vs. 2	4 vs. 7	3 vs. 6	3 vs. 7	1 vs. 5	2 vs. 4
Period 2	2 vs. 3	1 vs. 7	8 vs. 3	5 vs. 7	1 vs. 4	8 vs. 6	5 vs. 6
Period 3	4 vs. 5	3 vs. 5	1 vs. 6	8 vs. 4	2 vs. 6	2 vs. 7	8 vs. 7
Period 4	6 vs. 7	4 vs. 6	2 vs. 5	1 vs. 2	8 vs. 5	3 vs. 4	1 vs. 3

Before proceeding it is worth observing a constraint that is implied by the given ones. Since a team plays exactly $n-1$ times and at most twice in each of the $n/2$ periods, it follows that a given team plays twice in all but one period and in the remaining period it plays once.

We use two general approaches to encoding this problem in NB-SAT. In the *singleton approach* the domains of the variables are the teams, so each match is represented by a pair of variables. In the *pairwise approach* the domains of the variables are unordered pairs of teams, so each match is represented by a single variable.

To aid conceptualization, we define three macros for producing sets of NB-formulas. Let *Vars* be a set of nb-variables and *Atoms* be a set of m nb-atoms. Then ALLDIFF(*Vars*) is true if and only if every variable in *Vars* is assigned a different value; AM2(*Atoms*) is true if and only if at most two of the atoms in *Atoms* is true; and AL2(*Atoms*) is true if and only if at least two of the atoms in *Atoms* is true. The AL2 macro works by asserting that for every $m-1$ atoms chosen from *Atoms* at least one of the $m-1$ is true.

$$\text{ALLDIFF}(Vars) \stackrel{def}{=}$$
$$\{\neg v_1/d \vee \neg v_2/d | \{v_1, v_2\} \subseteq Vars, d \in dom(v_1) \cap dom(v_2)\}^{\star}$$
$$\text{AM2}(Atoms) \stackrel{def}{=} \{\neg a_1 \vee \neg a_2 \vee \neg a_3 | \{a_1, a_2, a_3\} \subseteq Atoms\}$$
$$\text{AL2}(Atoms) \stackrel{def}{=} \{a_1 \vee a_2 \vee \cdots \vee a_{m-1} | \{a_1, \ldots, a_{m-1}\} \subseteq Atoms\}$$

ALLDIFF(*Vars*) comprises $\sum_{\{v_1,v_2\} \subseteq Vars} |dom(v_1) \cap dom(v_2)|$ clauses, each containing two literals. AM2(*Atoms*) comprises $m(m-1)$ $(m-2)/6$ clauses, each containing three literals, and AL2(*Atoms*) comprises m clauses, each containing $m-1$ literals.

$\star$ The notation $\{v_1, v_2\} \subseteq Vars$ means that a two-element subset is selected from *Vars* and, without loss of generality, the two elements are arbitrarily named v_1 and v_2.

6.3.1. *Singleton Approach*

For each period p and each week w we use a pair of variables, $\langle X_{p,w}, Y_{p,w} \rangle$ to represent the pair of teams that play against each other in period p during week w. We consider the n teams to be denoted by the integers 1 to n, hence the domain of every variable is $\{1,\ldots, n\}$. By symmetry and the fact that a team cannot play itself, we can limit our search to solutions in which $X_{p,w}$ takes a value that is strictly less than that of $Y_{p,w}$. Hence, the domain of each $X_{p,w}$ is $\{1,\ldots, n-1\}$ and the domain of each $Y_{p,w}$ is $\{2,\ldots, n\}$. Furthermore, our encoding of the problem includes a symmetry-breaking constraint, which asserts that the value of $X_{p,w}$ is strictly less than that of $Y_{p,w}$. As we shall see, the inclusion of the symmetry-breaking constraints allows one of the other constraints to be stated much more compactly with the overall effect of producing a more compact encoding of the entire problem.

Hence to represent the four team problem we use 12 variables as follows:

	Week 1	Week 2	Week 3
Period 1	$X_{1,1}$ vs. $Y_{1,1}$	$X_{1,2}$ vs. $Y_{1,2}$	$X_{1,3}$ vs. $Y_{1,3}$
Period 2	$X_{2,1}$ vs. $Y_{2,1}$	$X_{2,2}$ vs. $Y_{2,2}$	$X_{2,3}$ vs. $Y_{2,3}$

where each $X_{p,w}$ has domain $\{1, 2, 3\}$ and each $Y_{p,w}$ has domain $\{2, 3, 4\}$.

There are many ways to encode in NB-SAT the three constraints of the original problem statement and the symmetry-breaking constraint. Here we present one way of handling each of the problem constraints and two ways of handling the symmetry-breaking constraint.

(1) Every team plays once a week. Since there are n slots each week and there are n teams, it suffices to stipulate that each team plays at most once in each week. For each week w, we use the formula

$$\text{ALLDIFF}\left(\{X_{p,w}|p \in periods\} \cup \{Y_{p,w}|p \in periods\}\right) \qquad (s1)$$

Each instance of ALLDIFF generates $\Omega(n^3)$ clauses of size two. Overall, $\Omega(n^4)$ clauses are generated.

(2) Every team plays at most twice in the same period over the tournament. For any team t, for every period p we have the clauses

$$\text{AM2}\left(\{X_{p,w}/t|w \in weeks, t \neq n\} \cup \{Y_{p,w}/t|w \in weeks, t \neq 1\}\right) \qquad (s2)$$

The restrictions $t \neq n$ and $t \neq 1$ prevent the set comprehensions from generating the atoms $X_{p,w} / n$ and $Y_{p,w} / 1$, respectively, both of which are ill-formed because the specified value is not in the domain of the specified variable. Each instance of AM2 generates $\Omega(n^3)$ clauses of size three. Overall, $\Omega(n^5)$ clauses are generated.

(3) Every team plays every other team. This constraint can be obtained by stipulating that no two teams play each other twice. For any two distinct weeks, w and w', and any teams t and t' such that $t < t'$ and any periods p and p' we have the formula

$$\neg X_{p,w}/t \;\vee\; \neg X_{p',w'}/t \;\vee\; \neg Y_{p,w}/t' \;\vee\; \neg Y_{p',w'}/t' \tag{s3}$$

We need to consider only teams t and t' such that $t < t'$ because the symmetry-breaking constraint ensures that in every solution $X_{p,w}$ has a strictly smaller value than does $Y_{p,w}$. Furthermore, because of the symmetry-breaking constraint, we need enforce only $\langle X_{p,w}, Y_{p,w} \rangle \neq \langle X_{p',w'}, Y_{p',w'} \rangle$, and not $\langle X_{p,w}, Y_{p,w} \rangle \neq \langle X_{p',w'}, Y_{p',w'} \rangle$. Each of these considerations halves the number of clauses needed to impose this constraint. Attention can be restricted to distinct weeks since no team plays more than once in the same week. This encoding produces $\Omega(n^6)$ clauses, each with four literals. As we will see, the symmetry-breaking constraint is encoded far more compactly than the present constraint, so using the symmetry-breaking constraint enables a smaller encoding of the entire problem.

Symmetry breaking. The symmetry-breaking constraint requires that for each period p and each week w the value of $X_{p,w}$ is strictly less than that of $Y_{p,w}$. Notice that this also enforces the constraint that no team ever plays itself. We consider two ways to encode this constraint.

The first encoding, called *lopsided*, states that if $X_{p,w}$ has value t then $Y_{p,w}$ has a value strictly greater than t. The value of $X_{p,w}$ implies a restriction on the value of $Y_{p,w}$. For every team t such that $2 \leq t \leq n-1$ and every period p and every week w we have the clause

$$\neg X_{p,w}/t \;\vee\; Y_{p,w}/t+1 \;\vee\; Y_{p,w}/t+2 \;\vee\; \cdots \;\vee\; Y_{p,w}/n. \tag{lopsided}$$

This encoding generates $\Omega(n^3)$ clauses ranging in size from 2 to $n-1$ literals.

The second encoding, called *negated*, states that $X_{p,w}$ and $Y_{p,w}$ cannot take on any pair of values that results in $Y_{p,w}$ being less than or equal to $X_{p,w}$. For every two teams t and t' such that $2 \leq t \leq t' \leq n-1$ and every period p and week w we have the clause

$$\neg X_{p,w}/t' \;\vee\; \neg Y_{p,w}/t \tag{negated}$$

This encoding produces $\Omega(n^4)$ clauses, each containing two literals.

Béjar and Manyá have experimented with two singleton encodings. In one paper (Béjar and Manyà, 1999b) they use the constraints s1, s2, s3, and lopsided. In another paper (Béjar and Manyà, 2000) they use a UU encoding of the constraints s1, s2, s3, and negated. In this UU enoding they added ALO clauses but no AMO clauses.

We experimented with two nb-encodings of the problem. The first encoding uses s1, s2, s3, and negated. The unary/unary transformation was applied to

Instance	Method	P_{noise} Setting	Clauses	Formula Size
6 teams	NB	0.310	2,790	9,300
DS=5	UU	0.250	2,820	9,450
8 teams	NB	0.130	18,088	61,992
DS=7	UU	0.090	18,144	62,384
10 teams	NB	0.051	72,900	254,520
DS=9	UU	0.033	72,990	255,330

Instance	Method	Flip Rate (flips/s)	Median Flips	Median Time (s)	Mean Flips	S.D. Flips
6 teams	NB	49,528	333	0.0067	476	461
DS=5	UU	246,867	1,485	0.0060	2,019	1,853
8 teams	NB	20,658	1,718	0.0832	2,408	2,221
DS=7	UU	126,675	7,386	0.0583	10,778	9,423
10 teams	NB	12,730	15,786	1.2401	23,990	24,577
DS=9	UU	73,369	73,079	0.9961	100,838	99,678

Figure 4. Round robin formulated with s1, s2, s3, negated and ALO. The domain size (*DS*) is one less than the number of teams. Sample size is 1,000.

produce a Boolean encoding. As the original nb-formula is negative, ALO clauses are included in the UU encoding, but AMO clauses are omitted. Figure 4 shows the results of 1,000 runs each on the UU and NB encodings for 6, 8, and 10 teams.

The second encoding uses s1, s2, s3, and lopsided. The unary/unary transformation was applied to produce a Boolean encoding. As the original nb-formula is neither negative nor positive, both ALO and AMO clauses are included in the UU encoding. Figure 5 shows the results of 1,000 runs each on the UU and NB encodings for 6, 8 and 10 teams.

Instance	Method	P_{noise} Setting	Clauses	Formula Size
6 teams	NB	0.270	2,700	9,165
DS=5	UU	0.180	3,030	9,915
8 teams	NB	0.100	17,668	61,432
DS=7	UU	0.090	18,900	64,176
10 teams	NB	0.052	71,640	252,945
DS=9	UU	0.028	72,970	260,235

Instance	Method	Flip Rate (flips/s)	Median Flips	Median Time (s)	Mean Flips	S.D. Flips
6 teams	NB	50,258	304	0.0060	467	475
DS=5	UU	227,018	1,683	0.0074	2,372	2,249
8 teams	NB	22,762	1,957	0.0860	2,714	2,604
DS=7	UU	120,935	12,997	0.1075	19,540	19,380
10 teams	NB	12,899	16,672	1.2925	22,260	20,857
DS=9	UU	69,153	313,134	4.5281	445,906	449,436

Figure 5. Round robin formulated with s1, s2, s3, lopsided, ALO and AMO. The domain size (*DS*) is one less than the number of teams. Sample size is 1,000.

The two tables exhibit similar patterns. NB requires fewer flips to solve the problem instances, and its advantage over UU grows as the domain size increases, markedly so for the lopsided encodings. Both figures show that UU has a significantly higher flip rate; consequently UU has a slightly faster solution time in the negated encodings. However, since UU scales so poorly with the lopsided encodings, NB has a time advantage here and its advantage grows as the domain size grows. No results are given for UB or EB as there are ineffective on these instances.

6.3.2. *Pairwise Approach*

The pairwise approach uses a single variable $XY_{p,w}$ for each period p and week w. The domain of each variable is the set of all unordered pairs of distinct teams. We shall refer to this set of values as *matches* and note that it has $n(n-1)/2$ elements. We shall also write *matches(t)* to denote those pairs in *matches* that contain team t and note that for all t this set contains $n-1$ elements. Hence to represent the four-team problem we use six variables as follows:

	Week 1	Week 2	Week 3
Period 1	$XY_{1,1}$	$XY_{1,2}$	$XY_{1,3}$
Period 2	$XY_{2,1}$	$XY_{2,2}$	$XY_{2,3}$

where each $XY_{p,w}$ has the domain:

$$matches = \{\{1,2\},\{1,3\},\{1,4\},\{2,3\},\{2,4\},\{3,4\}\}$$

Also, to illustrate the notation, matches(2) = $\{\{1, 2\}, \{2, 3\}\{2, 4\}\}$.

We now present a single encoding of each of the three problem constraints.

(1) Every team plays once a week. Unlike the singleton approach, we impose this constraint by saying that each team plays at least once each week. For every week w, for each team t we have the following clause:

$$\bigvee_{p \in periods, \, m \in matches(t)} XY_{p,w}/m \tag{p1}$$

This encoding produces $\Omega(n^2)$ clauses, each of length $\Omega(n^2)$.

(2) Every team plays at most twice in the same period over the tournament. To impose this constraint we add an "imaginary" extra week and write *weeks*[+] to denote the expanded set of weeks. It follows that over the course of n *weeks*[+] a team plays at most twice in the same period if and only if it plays at least twice in the same period. For each period p for each team t we have the following formula:

$$\text{AL2}\left(\{XY_{p,w}/m \mid m \in matches(t), w \in weeks^+\}\right) \tag{p2}$$

Each instance of AL2 produces $\Omega(n^2)$ clauses each with $\Omega(n^2)$ literals. Overall, this produces $\Omega(n^4)$ clauses.

(3) Every team plays every other team. In the pairwise approach it is straightforward to stipulate that every pair of teams at least once. This can be done with one clause for each m in *matches*:

$$\bigvee_{p \in periods,\, w \in weeks} XY_{p,w}/m \tag{p3}$$

This yields $\Omega(n)$ clauses, each containing $\Omega(n^2)$ literals.

We experimented with the NB encoding of p1, p2, and p3, and the UU transform of this. As the NB encoding is neither positive nor negative, the UU encoding contains both ALO and AMO clauses. Figure 6 shows the results of 1000 runs each on the NB encodings for 6, 8, 10, and 12 teams, and the UU encoding for six teams. Beyond six teams, the UU encoding is ineffective and the UB and EB encodings are ineffective even for six teams. Indeed, the Boolean encodings rapidly become prohibitively large as the number of teams increase. However, the NB method is highly effective and easily the best of all the solution methods considered in this section. Here we see that with large domain sizes, NB can be the only effective solution method.

Instance	Method	P_{noise} Setting	Clauses	Formula Size
6 teams	NB	0.120	159	3,465
DS=15	UU	0.010	2,049	7,245
8 teams	NB	0.020	348	15,120
DS=28				
10 teams	NB	0.012	645	47,025
DS=45				
12 teams	NB	0.008	1,074	118,404
DS=66				
14 teams	NB	0.002	1,659	257,985
DS=91				

Instance	Method	Flip Rate (flips/s)	Median Flips	Median Time (s)	Mean Flips	S.D. Flips
6 teams	NB	86,067	294	0.0034	404	364
DS=15	UU	240,768	7,787	0.0323	11,523	11,198
8 teams	NB	45,136	973	0.0216	1,373	1,260
DS=28						
10 teams	NB	24,333	6,026	0.2476	8,619	7,846
DS=45						
12 teams	NB	13,809	28,290	2.0487	41,010	40,375
DS=66						
14 teams	NB	8,308	21,8574	26.3087	318,896	319,472
DS=91						

Figure 6. Round robin formulated with p1, p2 and p3. The domain size (*DS*) is $n(n-1)/2$, where n is the number of teams. The sample size is 1,000.

6.4. THE QUASI-GROUP COMPLETION PROBLEM

A quasi-group (also called a Latin square[*]) of order n is an $n \times n$ table of symbols. There are n symbols and each symbol occurs exactly once in each row and column of the table. Therefore each row and each column are permutations of the symbols.

Generating a quasi-group of order n is trivial and can be done in $O(n^2)$ time. However, completing a quasi-group that is partially filled is an NP-complete problem (Colbourn, 1983). This is known as the quasi-group completion problem (QCP). For a fixed n, as the number of unfilled slots (or holes, h) increases, QCP exhibits both a phase transition from unsatisfiable to satisfiable and an easy-hard-easy pattern of solvability (Gomes and Selman, 1997).

In order to evaluate local search procedures with QCP, the instances must be filtered with a systematic search procedure so that the only satisfiable ones remain. Achlioptas et al. (2000) found generating QCP instances and filtering with a complete search procedure too compute-intensive. They suggest generating complete quasi-groups then emptying some of the slots to create h holes. Problems generated this way are clearly guaranteed to be satisfiable, so they do not have traditional phase-transition behavior. However, they do retain the easy-hard-easy pattern with increasing h. This method of generating QCP instances is referred to as quasi-group with holes (QWH). QWH does include all satisfiable QCP instances; however Kautz et al. (2001) observe that it is biased away from the uniform distribution of satisfiable instances because QWH can generate the same QCP instance from a variable number of complete quasi-groups. Empirically, the most difficult QWH instances are found where $h = 1.6n^{1.55}$ (Achlioptas et al., 2000). This result follows from observation of the performance of Walksat on the unary/unary transform with ALO clauses.

6.4.1. Generating QWH Instances

For each order size $n \in \{4, 8, 12, 16, 20\}$, we generated a suite of 25 QWH instances. We used the lsencode v1.0 software (Gomes et al., 2001) to systematically generate a complete quasi-group instance and then shuffle it 10,000 times. This gives a uniform distribution over all complete quasi-groups of order n. Using lsencode, $1.6n^{1.55}$ holes were then poked in the quasi-group by the random method.

6.4.2. The Non-Boolean Encoding

We used our own program, PLS-NB, to encode each of the generated QWH instances as an NB-formula. We initially encoded each instance with n^2

---

[*] A quasi-group is a group whose multiplication table is a Latin square. However, in the AI community the table is commonly referred to as the quasi-group.

variables, one for each entry in the quasi-group table. For each row and column, the variables must be assigned a permutation of the values. For a row or column containing variables, it is sufficient to assert that each value appears at least once in *variables*, since this entails that each value appears exactly once. For each row or column containing *variables*, and each symbol s we have the clause

$$\bigvee_{A \in variables} A/s \tag{4}$$

For each variable A that corresponds to a filled entry in the table (i.e., not a hole), we add the unit clause A/s, where s is the symbol that fills the entry. This gives us a CNF NB-formula that encodes the QWH instance.

This NB representation is then simplified by performing unit propagation. To propagate the unit clause A/s, all other clauses containing the variable A are processed with one of two rules:

- *Unit subsumption* applies to a clause C containing A/s. The unit clause logically subsumes C, so C is removed from the formula.
- *Unit resolution* applies to a clause C containing A/t, where $t \neq s$. The literal A/t is removed from C because $(A/t \vee \phi) \wedge (A/s)$ *entails* ϕ.

Unit propagation is performed to closure, after which all unit clauses are deleted from the NB formula.

The variables remaining in the formula correspond to the holes in the QWH instance. The domains of these variables typically contain fewer than n values and can vary from variable to variable. For each suite Figure 7 shows the mean domain size (MDS) of the NB encodings for each suite of QWH instances.

It is possible to simplify QWH instances much more than the unit propagation that we have done. For example, before encoding an instance into NB-SAT, one could consider the instance as a clique of disequalities for each row and column and perform arc-consistency. Or even stronger, one could consider an instance as an alldifferent constraint for each row and column and perform generalized arc-consistency (Kautz et al., 2001; Shaw et al., 1998). Unfortunately, both of these simplifications reduce the domains of the variables so effectively, that all reasonably sized problems have small domains. For example, consider simplifying the instances with arc-consistency (as explained above) and then with unit propagation (as we have done). Then our suite of 25 instances for order 4 has a mean domain size of 2.84; for order 16 it is 3.85; and for order 20 it is 4.09. As such it is impossible to investigate the effect of increasing domain size because the problem instances become too hard for large n. Since we are interested in producing a useful testbed, not with solving the problem as fast as possible, we preprocess by unit propagation only.

Problem	Method	P_{noise} Setting	Mean Variables	Mean Clauses	Mean Formula Size
Order 4	NB	.22	13.0	26.0	88.3
13 holes	UU	.16	51.1	101	238
3.93 MDS	UB	.41	77.1	127	290
	EB	.50	26.0	293	1,074
Order 8	NB	.20	40.0	79.9	424
40 holes	UU	.029	279	936	2,136
7.01 MDS	UB	.16	399	890	2,024
	EB	.45*	119	51,720	345,085
Order 12	NB	15	75.0	150	998
75 holes	UU	.035	709	3,215	7,129
9.46 MDS	UB	.10*	992	2,504	5,707
Order 16	NB	.12	117	234	1826
117 holes	UU	.020	1,354	7,558	1,6473
11.57 MDS					
Order 20	NB	.108	166	332	2,953
166 holes	UU	.015	2,244	14,711	31,711
13.52 MDS					

Problem	Method	Mean Flip Rate (flips/ms)	Median Flips	Mean Flips	Median Time (ms)	Mean Time (ms)
Order 4	NB		27.2	27.5		
	UU		154	161		
	UB		568	590		
	EB		56.0	57.9		
Order 8	NB	1,228	702	721	0.62	0.64
	UU	1,375	4,982	5,383	3.63	3.91
	UB	1,472	57,279	60,377	38.8	41.0
	EB	7.26			> 16,000	> 16,000
Order 12	NB	954	7,819	8,122	7.97	8.33
	UU	1,116	56,458	58,966	50.5	52.7
	UB	1,422			> 16,000	> 16,000
Order 16	NB	780	59,865	61,673	56.0	58.0
	UU	1,002	354,759	374,878	351	369
Order 20	NB	736	167,738	183,396	228	249
	UU	779	1,412,583	1,422,320	1,810	1,830

Figure 7. Performance on quasigroup with holes.

6.4.3. *The Boolean Encodings*

In addition to the NB-encoding, three Boolean transforms of the non-Boolean formula are considered: UU, UB and EB. As the NB encodings are all positive, no ALO clauses are included in the UU or UB encodings.

Kautz et al. (2001) use two other Boolean encodings, which we (but not they) now describe as Boolean transforms of non-Boolean encodings. In both encodings they preprocess the instance by performing generalized arc-consistency as described above. In the encoding they call "2D" they do not use (4), but instead impose ALLDIFF(*variables*) on each row and column. Finally they apply the unary/unary transform, including ALO clauses, but not AMO clauses. In their "3D" encoding they impose both (4) and ALLDIFF(*variables*) on all rows and columns. Finally, they apply the unary/unary transform, including both ALO and AMO clauses.

6.4.4. *Results*

Once again, we treat the process of solving an entire suite as a single sample execution. For each solution method, for each test suite, the optimal P_{noise} setting eas experimentally determined. These are shown in Figure 7. However, using a cutoff of 400 seconds (for the suite), EB could not solve the suites with $n \geq 8$ and UB could not solve those with $n \geq 12$.

In particular, EB made nine attempts to solve the order 8 suite at each of the P_{noise} settings 0.4, 0.45, 0.5, 0.55 and 0.6. None of the attempts completed the suite in 400 seconds; the most successful was $P_{noise} = 0.45$, which completed the first 12 instances on one of its runs. Thus, a P_{noise} setting of 0.45 is recorded in Figure 7, with an asterisk to indicate that this is a special situation.

UB made nine attempts to solve the order 12 suite at each of the P_{noise} settings 0.05, 0.1, 0.15, 0.2, and 0.25. The most successful was $P_{noise} = 0.1$, though not all of its runs completed within the cutoff of 400 seconds. Thus a P_{noise} setting of 0.10 is recorded in Figure 7, with an asterisk to indicate that this is a special situation.

For all the other methods and suites, 101 runs were performed and all completed within the 400 seconds limit. The results are shown in Figure 7, where the flips and time measurements are reported per instance (i.e., the measurements for the suite are divided by 25). The order 4 suite was solved so fast that a reliable measure of CPU time could not be obtained; thus no flip rates or times are given.

The results reported in Figure 7 show that the performances of EB and UB scale poorly as domain size increases. EB is competitive for order 4 instances (MDS = 3.93), but not for order 8 (MDS = 7.01). UB is effective, though substantially inferior to NB and UU for instances of order 4 and 8; it is ineffective for order 12 instances (MDS = 9.46).

The results also show that both UU and NB remain effective for instances of order 20 (MDS = 13.52), though NB is superior to UU, and its superiority grows as domain size increases.

7. Related Work

This section considers related work, first work on solving problems without encoding, then work on the direct approach and finally work on the transformational approach.

7.1. SOLVING PROBLEMS WITHOUT ENCODING

A substantial body of work takes a purely direct approach by applying local search directly to a problem, for example, to vehicle routing (Shaw, 1998). This typically involves the overhead of building a domain-specific solver from scratch, but allows the development of problem-specific neighborhoods and heuristics. Brafman and Hoos (1999) show that for planning problems this approach can result in a solver that is more efficient than encoding and solving with SAT. Recent work on the development of the COMET system (Van Hentenryck and Michel, 2003) shows that generic facilities, such as incremental data structures, can be provided to ease the development of domain-specific local search systems.

The advantage of encoding a problem into SAT or NB-SAT is that developing an effective encoding is likely to be less difficult than implementing a problem-specific local search procedure. This is demonstrated by the continuing increase in the number of problems that can be solved effectively by applying both systematic and SLS solvers to encodings of the problems.

7.2. OTHER WORK ON THE DIRECT APPROACH

As far as we know, only one other group has worked on a direct approach to solving non-Boolean satisfiability problems with stochastic local search. Bejar and his colleagues (Béjar, 2000; Béjar and Manyà, 1999a; Béjar and Manyà, 2000; Béjar et al., 2001) have generalized GSAT, Walksat, and some of their variants to operate directly on regular formulas of finitely valued logic. In regular formulas all variables have the same finite, totally ordered domain, which for the sake of presentation is usually taken to be $\{1, \ldots, n\}$.[*] A regular literal is of the form $\uparrow i{:}X$ or $\downarrow i{:}X$ where i its a domain element and X is a variable. Assignments in regular SAT are the same as those in NB-SAT. An assignment satisfies $\uparrow i{:}X$ if the value assigned to X is at least i; it satisfies $\downarrow i{:}X$ if the value assigned to X is at most i. A regular CNF formula is a conjunction of disjunctions of regular literals. Negation is not used in regular CNF; nor is it needed as the negation of $\uparrow i{:}X$ (resp. $\downarrow i{:}X$) is logically equal to $\downarrow(i-1){:}X$ (resp. $\uparrow(i+1){:}X$).

The NB-Walksat and Regular–Walksat algorithms can be seen as having only two differences. The first is that instead of step (g) (see Figure 1), Regular–Walksat uses

(g′) From among the variables that appear in L select one at random. Call it X. Let D be the set of values such that flipping X to that value would satisfy the clause. Randomly select a member of D and call it d.

The second difference is that the published descriptions of Regular–Walksat do not specify distributions for the random selections made in steps (d) or $(g′)$. Assuming that all selections are made with uniform distribution, in certain situations (g) and (g′) can choose among flips with different distributions. To see

---

[*] Here we stick with the terminology of this paper. Their presentation uses the terminology of multivalued logic.

this, consider two variables, X and Y, each with domains $\{1, 2, 3\}$. Then the nb-clause $X/2 \lor X/3 \lor Y/3$ is logically equivalent to the regular clause $\uparrow 2{:}X \lor \uparrow 3{:}Y$. If these clauses are false, then each could be "repaired" by one of three flips: X to 2, X to 3 or Y to 3. In a noisy move, NB-Walksat would chose each flip with probability 1/3, whereas Regular–Walksat would choose between X and Y with probability 1/2 and, if X were chosen it would chose between 2 and 3 with probability 1/2. Hence, Regular Walksat would choose among the three flips with probability 1/4, 1/4 and 1/2, respectively. This situation could arise only if a problem has a clause in which different variables participate in a different number of repairing flips. Of all the formulations considered in Section 6, this situation arises only in the lopsided and pairwise formulations of the round-robin problem.

If we ignore the issue of distributions, NB-Walksat and Regular–Walksat are functionally equivalent in the following sense. Let $C_{\text{reg}} = C_1, \ldots, C_n$ be a set of regular clauses and $C_{\text{NB}} = C'_1, \ldots, C'_n$ be a set of NB-clauses. If C_i and C'_i are logically equivalent for $1 \leq i \leq n$, then the set of runs available to Regular–Walksat running on C_{reg} is the same as those available to NB-Walksat running on C_{NB}.

How do the NB and regular languages compare in terms of their ability to represent problems and solve them with NB-Walksat and Regular–Walksat? Considering the equivalence between the algorithms, this issue hinges on the relative expressiveness of NB-clauses and regular clauses.

Regular clauses can be transformed easily to NB-clauses by replacing each occurrence of $\uparrow i{:}X$ (resp. $\downarrow i{:}X$) with $\lor_{j > i} X/j$ (resp. $\lor_{j < i} X/j$). Going the other way, negative NB-clauses can be transformed easily to regular clauses by replacing each occurrence of $\neg X/i$ with $\uparrow (i + 1){:}X \lor \downarrow (i-1){:}X$. However, non-negative NB-clauses are not, in general, equivalent to any regular clause. The unit clause X/i is equivalent to $\uparrow i{:}X \land \downarrow i{:}X$, but it is not equivalent to any regular clause. Consequently, NB-Walsksat is capable of all the behaviors that Regular–Walksat is, but not vice versa. To be clear, the issue is not that Regular–Walksat lacks capabilities; rather, it is that regular-CNF is not sufficiently expressive.

Of course, every nonnegative NB-formula ϕ_{NB} in CNF is logically equivalent to some regular formula ϕ_{reg} (by the correspondences mentioned in the last paragraph) and ϕ_{reg} can be transformed to a CNF formula ϕ'_{reg} by distributing disjunctions over conjunctions. ϕ_{NB} and ϕ'_{reg} will be logically equivalent, though generally they will not correspond clause by clause. Indeed, ϕ'_{reg} may be unreasonably large. For this reason, Regular–Walksat is typically ineffective on encodings that correspond to negative NB-formulas in CNF. The two problems used in the Regular–Walksat experiments of Béjar and Manyà (2000) use negative encodings: graph coloring using the encoding of Section 6.1 and round-robin tournament scheduling using clauses s1, s2, s3, and lopsided of Section 6.3.1. The most effective round-robin encoding, the pairwise one, uses both negative and positive clauses and is therefore ill-suited for Regular–Walksat. Again, the shortcoming is not with the Regular–Walksat algorithm; it is that this nonnegative encoding cannot be expressed in regular CNF.

An obvious difference between NB-SAT and regular SAT is that regular SAT uses a totally ordered domain. One consequence is that in representing inequalities, regular CNF can be more compact. For example, the lopsided symmetry-breaking constraint of Section 6.3.1 can be represented by the regular formula

$$\uparrow(t+1){:}X_{p,w} \vee \downarrow(t-1){:}X_{p,w} \vee \uparrow(t+1){:}Y_{p,w}$$

A second consequence is that Regular–Walksat is able to exploit this compactness in its internal data structures. This, in effect, is a benefit that accrues from the limited expressiveness of regular clauses.

7.3. OTHER WORK ON THE TRANSFORMATIONAL APPROACH

Let us now turn our attention to related work on using the transformation approach to solving problems with SLS on Boolean SAT. Among the numerous problems attacked with this approach are the nqueens problem (Selman et al., 1992), graph coloring (Selman et al., 1992; Hoos, 1998), the quasi-group completion problem (or quasi-group with holes) (Kautz et al., 2001; Achlioptas et al., 2000; Béjar et al., 2001), the all-interval-series problem (Hoos, 1998; Béjar et al., 2001), the Hamiltonian circuit problem (Hoos, 1998; Hoos, 1999), random instances of the finite-domain constraint satisfaction problem (Hoos, 1998; Hoos, 1999; Gent, 2002), the round-robin tournament problem (Béjar and Manyà, 2000), and planning (Kautz and Selman, 1992; Kautz and Selman, 1996; Kautz et al., 1996; Ernst et al., 1997; Hoos, 1998; Brafman and Hoos, 1999). Despite this widespread use we know only three studies, other than our own, that have compared the performance of SLS on different SAT encodings of non-Boolean variables; we discuss these below. Other than these three comparative studies, all work cited above uses the unary/unary encoding. As far as we know, our work is the first to use or mention the unary/binary encoding.

We preface our discussion of the three studies by noting that no work we know of considers the SAT-encoding process as two mappings, one from the problem to NB-SAT and then a second from NB-SAT to SAT.[★] Researchers who take the single-stage viewpoint often overlook some encodings. For example, from our viewpoint, we might see that a study considers three ways of mapping a problem to NB-SAT, and produces four SAT encodings by applying the unary/unary transform to all three but the binary transform to only one. A similar oversight sometimes occurs in considering the inclusion/exclusion

---

[★] The nearest exception is that Hoos (1998, 1999) maps the Hamiltonian Cycle Problem to SAT by mapping it first to the constraint satisfaction problem and then mapping this to SAT.

of ALO and AMO clauses. To aid presentation, we shall adopt the two-stage viewpoint in the following discussion.

Hoos (1998; 1999) compares the performance of Walksat using the basic binary and unary/unary encodings of random instances of the Hamiltonian cycle problem (HCP) and of the finite-domain constraint satisfaction problem (CSP). The CSP instances are mapped to NBSAT using the well-known "direct encoding." The HCP instances are first mapped to CSP, and then treated the same as the CSP instances. In both test sets, the NB-SAT encoding is negative; nonetheless, all the unary/unary encodings include both ALO and AMO clauses. The experiments show that the unary/unary encodings can be solved with fewer flips than the basic binary encodings; about seven times fewer in CSP and 1.5 times fewer in the HCP.

Ernst et al. (1997) systematically study eight Boolean encodings for the STRIPS-style planning problem. Over an unidentified suite of 23 instances of the planning problem, they compare the size of each encoding and the average time that Walksat takes to solve each encoding. The eight encodings they explore are systematically generated by selecting one of two frame axioms (called classical and explanatory) and one of four action representations (called regular, simple splitting, overloaded splitting and bitwise). The regular, simple splitting, and overloaded splitting encodings are three ways of representing the choice of actions and all three employ a unary/unary encoding. The bitwise action representation is not truly a different action representation; it is a binary encoding of the regular action representation. Thus, in terms of encoding non-Boolean variables, their study makes two relevant comparisons: between the classical/regular and the classical/bitwise encodings and between the explanatory/regular and explanatory/bitwise encodings. Ernst, Millstein, and Weld are keenly aware that the unary/unary encoding does not always need ALO and AMO formulas, and they pay particular attention to creating and identifying opportunities for omitting them. Though their binary encoding is not specified, their claim that it has no extraneous values means that it is the enhanced version or something similar. On the whole, it appears that each unary/unary encoding generally outperforms the corresponding binary encoding, but, as Ernst, Millstein, and Weld note, the "timing data is hard to interpret."

Prestwich (2004) considers seven SAT-encodings of the graph coloring problem. From our point of view these use four ways of mapping coloring to NB-SAT. Three of these are mapped to SAT using solely the unary/unary transform. The fourth, which is based on conflict clauses, is the one of interest here as it is mapped to SAT in four ways: (UULM) unary/unary with ALO and AMO, (UUL) unary/unary with ALO, (BB) basic binary, and (EB) enhanced binary. On a suite of 30 coloring instances with between 4 and 49 colors, each encoded in seven ways, he tests the performance of Walksat with the best heuristic. He observes that in no instance does EB require more flips on average than BB. And in almost all instances UUL requires fewer flips on average than

UULM. Since EB and UUL encodings admit more solutions than the BB and UULM encodings, respectively, these results are consistent with the hypothesis that higher solution density (solutions divided by number of possible assignments) tends to yield better performance for SLS. A surprising result of the experiments is that the EB and BB encodings performed much better than one would have expected from the previous work of us and others. The puzzling pattern presented by the literature on the whole is that EB and BB sometimes perform quite well and other times very poorly. Our conjecture is that these two encodings do not perform well on intrinsically hard instances. Prestwich's instances are mostly much easier than the ones we used for coloring and other problems. On the hardest instances of his, EB and BB perform poorly. On three of the four easiest graph coloring instances tested by Frisch and Peugniez (2001) EB performed competitively, but it was totally ineffective on the two hardest instances.

8. Conclusion

Boolean variables are merely a special case of non-Boolean variables, and, intuitively, the difference between the non-Boolean and Boolean variables grows as the domain size of the nb-variable increases. Consequently, one would expect that in a comparison of encodings for non-Boolean problems that domain size would be the most important parameter to consider and that one would find that any difference in performance between the encodings would increase when domain size is increased. Nonetheless, this issue has been overlooked. All problem instances that Hoos considers have a domain size of 10. The planning instances used by Ernst, Millstein and Weld are not identified and domain sizes are not reported. The coloring instances used by Prestwich do vary considerably in domain size, but his experiments are not designed to control this parameter. In contrast to all other studies, ours considers the effect of varying domain size and hence is able to confirm the expectation that domain size is generally a critical parameter. Our study is also the first to explicitly consider the role of a formulation's polarity (being positive or negative). By considering polarity and domain size we are able to make some observations not revealed by other studies.

- Of all the methods considered here, NB scales best with increasing domain size.
- Many researchers have remarked that solving a problem by mapping it to SAT (inevitably with the unary/unary encoding) and using an SLS SAT solver can compete with using a custom-made SLS solver directly on the problem. Though our results show the UU method to be quite robust, it can run into difficulties with very large domain sizes. This is particularly true for nonnegative formulations, since excessively many AMO clauses must be included.

- The UB method is rarely effective, and it is never effective on problems with moderate or large domain sizes.
- On nonnegative formulations, the EB method is ineffective since the encoding becomes prohibitively large with modest domain sizes.
- On negative formulations the EB method is sometimes effective but often ineffective. It always requires more flips than NB. It sometimes requires somewhat fewer flips than UU (as shown in Prestwich's results), but sometimes requires vastly more. We know of no good explanation for this puzzling pattern with respect to UU, but we can offer a conjecture. The EB encoding generates a difficult search space for SLS (a point argued well by Hoos), so a problem that is inherently difficult becomes practically unsolvable by EB. On the other hand, the EB search space is much smaller than than that of UU, especially with large domain sizes. We thus hypothesize that EB will be more effective than UU on problem instances that have very large domain sizes but are very easy. Note the we, and almost everyone else, have focussed on hard problem instances, often deliberately selecting ones at the phase transition. The one exception is the set of coloring instances used by Prestwich, and he has observed the most success with BB and EB.

Many questions remain to be addressed by future work. A wide range of problems and encodings have yet to be explored. Stamm-Wilbrandt (1993) shows how more than two dozen problems – most of which are NP-complete – can be transformed to SAT. The present paper shows that there is great flexibility in combining the different transforms. For example, it is possible to use a binary AMO formula with a unary ALO formula, and it is possible to use different transforms on each variable. From this we see that of all the possible ways of encoding non-Boolean problems in Boolean formulas, very few have ever been tried. Even within the small sphere of well-studied problems and well-studied encodings, there are untried combinations.

The biggest challenge facing the study of problem encodings – including all encoding issues, not just the handling of non-Boolean variables – is the quest for generality. What can we say about about encoding issues that can guide us in producing effective encodings of new problems? This challenge must be decomposed if progress is to be made. This paper's biggest contribution toward this end is separating out the issue of non-Boolean variables and identifying domain size and polarity as the critical parameters.

In addition to developing new problem encodings, we claim that the applicability of SLS technology can also be extended by enriching the language on which the SLS can operate. This claim is supported by recent results on pseudo-Boolean constraints (Walser, 1997) and integer optimization (Walser, 1999), nonclausal formulas (Sebastiani, 1994); and efficient handling of variable dependencies (Kautz et al., 1997). Our success with NB-Walksat adds further weight to the claim.

Acknowledgements

We thank Henry Kautz and Bram Cohen for providing their Walksat code so that we could develop NB-Walksat from it; Carla Gomes for allowing us to use their quasigroup problem generator; Peter Stock for providing his NB-Satz program and for using it to filter out the unsatisfiable instances from our suite of random formulas; and Toby Walsh, Ian Gent, Steve Minton, Bart Selman and the anonymous referees for useful suggestions.

References

Achlioptas, D., Gomes, C. P., Kautz, H. A. and Selman, B. (2000) Generating satisfiable problem instances, in *Proc. of the Seventeenth National Conf. on Artificial Intelligence*, pp. 256–261.

Béjar, R. (2000) Systematic and Regular Search Algorithms for Regular-SAT. Ph.D. thesis, Universitat Autònoma de Barcelona.

Béjar, R. and Manyà, F. (1999a) A comparison of systematic and local search algorithms for regular CNF formulas, in A. Hunter and S. Parsons (eds.), *Proc. Fifth European Conference on Symbolic and Quantitative Approaches to Reasoning with Uncertainty, ECSQARU'99, London, UK*, Vol. 1638 of *Lecture Notes in Artificial Intelligence*, pp. 22–31.

Béjar, R. and Manyà, F. (1999b) Solving combinatorial problems with regular local search algorithm, in H. Ganzinger and D. McAllester (eds.), *Proc. 6th Int. Conference on Logic for Programming and Automated Reasoning, LPAR, Tbilisi, Georgia*, Vol. 1705 of *Lecture Notes in Artificial Intelligence*, pp. 33–43.

Béjar, R. and Manyà, F. (2000) Solving the round robin problem using propositional logic, in *Proc. of the Seventeenth National Conf. on Artificial Intelligence*, pp. 261–266.

Béjar, R., Cabicol, A., Fernàndez, C., Manyá, F. and Gomes, C. P. (2001) Capturing structure with satisfiability, in T. Walsh (ed.), *Principles and Practice of Constraint Programming – CP 2001*, pp. 135–149.

Brafman, R. I. and Hoos, H. H. (1999) To encode or not to encode – I: linear planning, in *Proc. of the Sixteenth Int. Joint Conf. on Artificial Intelligence*, pp. 988–993.

Colbourn, C. J. (1983) Embedding partial steiner triple systems is NP-complete, *J. Comb. Theory* **35**.

Davis, M., Logemann, G. and Loveland, D. (1962) A machine program for theorem proving, *Commun. ACM* **5**(7).

Ernst, M. D., Millstein, T. D. and Weld, D. S. (1997) Automatic SAT-compilation of planning problems, in *Proc. of the Fifteenth Int. Joint Conf. on Artificial Intelligence*, pp. 1169–1176.

Frisch, A. M. and Peugniez, T. J. (1998) Solving non-Boolean satisfiability problems with local search, in *Fifth Workshop on Automated Reasoning: Bridging the Gap between Theory and Practice*, St. Andrews, Scotland.

Frisch, A. M. and Peugniez, T. J. (2001) Solving non-Boolean satisfiability problems with stochastic local search, in *Proc. of the Seventeenth Int. Joint Conf. on Artificial Intelligence*, Seattle, Washington, pp. 282–288.

Gent, I. P. (2002) Arc consistency in SAT, in *Proc. of the Fifteenth European Conf. on Artificial Intelligence*, pp. 121–125.

Gent, I. P. and Walsh, T. (eds.), *CSPLib: A Problem Library for Constraints*. http://www.csplib.org.

Gomes, C. P. and Selman, B. (1997) Problem structure in the presence of perturbations, in *Proc. of the Fourteenth National Conf. on Artificial Intelligence*, pp. 221–226.

Gomes, C. P., Kautz, H. A. and Ruan, Y. (2001) lsencode: A Generator of Quasigroup with Holes and Quasigroup Completion Problems.

Hoos, H. H. (1998) Stochastic Local Search–Methods, Models, Applications. Ph.D. thesis, Technical University of Darmstadt.

Hoos, H. H. (1999) SAT-encodings, search space structure, and local search performance, in *Proc. of the Sixteenth Int. Joint Conf. on Artificial Intelligence*, pp. 296–302.

Jonsson, A. K. and Ginsberg, M. L. (1993) Experimenting with new systematic and nonsystematic search techniques, in *Working Notes of the 1993 AAAI Spring Symposium on AI and NP-Hard Problems*, Stanford University in Palo Alto, California.

Kautz, H. A. and Selman, B. (1992) Planning as satisfiability, in B. Neumann (ed.), *Proc. of the Tenth European Conf. on Artificial Intelligence*, Vienna, Austria, pp. 359–363.

Kautz, H. A. and Selman, B. (1996) Pushing the envelope: planning, propositional logic, and stochastic search, in *Proc. of the Thirteenth National Conf. on Artificial Intelligence*, Portland, Oregon, USA, pp. 1202–1207.

Kautz, H. A., McAllester, D. and Selman, B. (1996) Encoding plans in propositional logic, in L. C. Aiello, J. Doyle, and S. Shapiro (eds.), *Principles of Knowledge Representation and Reasoning: Proc. of the Fifth Int. Conf. San Francisco*, pp. 374–385.

Kautz, H. A., McAllester, D. and Selman, B. (1997) Exploiting variable dependency in local search (Abstract), in *Poster Session Abstracts of IJCAI-97*, p. 57.

Kautz, H. A., Ruan, Y., Achioptas, D., Gomes, C., Selman, B. and Stickel, M. (2001) Balance and filtering in structured satisfiable problems, in *Proc. of the Seventeenth Int. Joint Conf. on Artificial Intelligence*, Seattle, Washington, pp. 351–358.

Li, C. M. and Anbulagan (1997) Heuristics based on unit propagation for satisfiability problems, in *Proc. of the Fifteenth Int. Joint Conf. on Artificial Intelligence*, pp. 366–371.

Mitchell, D., Selman, B. and Levesque, H. J. (1992) Hard and easy distributions of SAT problems, in *Proc. of the Tenth National Conf. on Artificial Intelligence*, San Jose, CA, pp. 459–465.

Peugniez, T. J. (1998) *Solving Non-Boolean Satisfiability Problems with Local Search*. BSc dissertation, Department of Computer Science, University of York.

Prestwich, S. (2004) Local search on SAT-encoded colouring problems, in *Theory and Applications of Satisfiability Testing: 6th Int. Conf.*, pp. 105–119.

Sebastiani, R. (1994) Applying GSAT to non-clausal formulas, *J. Artif. Intell. Res.* **1**, 309–314.

Selman, B., Levesque, H. J. and Mitchell, D. (1992) A new method for solving hard satisfiability problems in *Proc. of the Tenth National Conf. on Artificial Intelligence*, pp. 440–446.

Selman, B., Kautz, H. A. and Cohen, B. (1994) Noise strategies for improving local search, in *Proc. of the Twelfth National Conf. on Artificial Intelligence*, Menlo Park, CA, USA, pp. 337–343.

Shaw, P. (1998) Using constraint programming and local search methods to solve vehicle routing problems, in *Principles and Practice of Constraint Programming – CP 1998*, pp. 417–431.

Shaw, P., Stergiou, K. and Walsh, T. (1998) Arc consistency and quasigroup completion, in *Proceedings of ECAI98 Workshop on Non-binary Constraints*.

Stamm-Wilbrandt, H. (1993) Programming in Propositional Logic, or Reductions: Back to the Roots (Satisfiability), Technical report, Institut für Informatik III, Universität Bonn.

Stock, P. G. (2000) *Solving Non-Boolean Satisfiability with the Davis-Putnam Method*, BSc dissertation, Dept. of Computer Science, Univ. of York.

Van Hentenryck, P. and Michel, L. (2003) Control abstractions for local search, in *Principles and Practice of Constraint Programming – CP 2003*, pp. 65–80.

Walser, J. P. (1997) Solving linear pseudo-boolean constraint problems with local search, in *Proc. of the Fourteenth National Conf. on Artificial Intelligence*, pp. 269–274.

Walser, J. P. (1999) *Integer Optimization by Local Search: A Domain-Independent Approach*, Springer, Berlin Heidelberg New York.

Journal of Automated Reasoning (2005) 35: 181–200
DOI: 10.1007/s10817-005-9012-z

© Springer 2006

Regular Random k-SAT: Properties of Balanced Formulas

YACINE BOUFKHAD[1], OLIVIER DUBOIS[2], YANNET INTERIAN[3]
and BART SELMAN[4]

[1]LIAFA, CNRS-Université Denis Diderot- Case 7014, 2, place Jussieu, 75251 Paris Cedex 05,
France. e-mail: boufkhad@liafa.jussieu.fr
[2]LIP6, Box 169, CNRS-Université Paris 6, 4 place Jussieu, 75252, Paris Cedex 05, France.
e-mail: Olivier.Dubois@lip6.fr
[3]Center for Applied Mathematics, Cornell University, Ithaca, NY 14853, USA.
e-mail: interian@cam.cornell.edu
[4]Depatiment of Computer Science, Cornell University, Ithaca, NY 14853, USA.
e-mail: selman@cs.cornell.edu

Abstract. We consider a model for generating random k-SAT formulas, in which each literal occurs approximately the same number of times in the formula clauses (regular random and k-SAT). Our experimental results show that such regular random k-SAT instances are much harder than the usual uniform random k-SAT problems. This is in agreement with other results that show that more balanced instances of random combinatorial problems are often much more difficult to solve than uniformly random instances, even at phase transition boundaries. There are almost no formal results known for such problem distributions. The balancing constraints add a dependency between variables that complicates a standard analysis. Regular random 3-SAT exhibits a phase transition as a function of the ratio α of clauses to variables. The transition takes place at approximately $\alpha = 3.5$. We show that for $\alpha > 3.78$ with high probability (w.h.p.) random regular 3-SAT formulas are unsatisfiable. Specifically, the events $\mathcal{E}_n$ hold with high probability if $\mathbf{Pr}(\mathcal{E}_n) \to 1$ when $n \to \infty$. We also show that the analysis of a greedy algorithm proposed by Kaporis et al. for the uniform 3-SAT model can be adapted for regular random 3-SAT. In particular, we show that for formulas with ratio $\alpha < 2.46$, a greedy algorithm finds a satisfying assignment with positive probability.

Key words: satisfiability, phase transition, k-SAT, regular, Boolean formulae.

1. Introduction

The introduction of new methods for generating random hard instances is an important factor in the development of new search algorithms for satisfiability testing (SAT) (Le Berre and Simon, 2004). In addition, randomly generated SAT problems provide important insights into typical case complexity.

The most popular model for generating random SAT problems is the uniform k-SAT model, formed by selecting uniformly and independently m clauses from the set of all $2^k \binom{n}{k}$ k-clauses on a given set of n variables. Such randomly generated instances exhibit a "phase transition" as a function of the ratio α of clauses to variables (Mitchell et al., 1992). Uniform k-SAT problems with a small α value typically have one or more satisfying assignments, whereas problems with a large α value have too many constraints and become unsatisfiable.

Experimental results showing the phase transition phenomenon motivated theoretical interest in understanding uniform k-SAT. The main open question for uniform k-SAT concerns the existence of a sharp threshold as the ratio of clauses to variables increases. More precisely, the question is whether there exist constants α_k such that a random formula with $\alpha < \alpha_k$ is satisfiable w.h.p., whereas a random formula with $\alpha > \alpha_k$ is unsatisfiable w.h.p. For $k = 2$, Chvatal and Reed (1992), Goerdt (1996), and Fernandez de la Vega (1992) independently proved the existence of the sharp threshold at $\alpha_2 = 1$. For $k \geq 3$, much less is known. Friedgut (1999) proved the existence of a sharp threshold around a critical sequence of values. In particular, he showed that there exists a function $\alpha_k(n)$ such that when the number of clauses is around $\alpha_k(n)n$ the satisfiability of the formula drops abruptly from near 1 to near 0. However, these results do not provide information about the value of $\alpha_k(n)$ and its dependence on n.

For uniform 3-SAT there has been a number of results on bounds for the threshold α_3 (see (Achlioptas, 2001) for a survey); the best known result for the lower bound proves that a random uniform instance for 3-SAT is satisfiable w.h.p. if $\alpha < 3.52$ (Kaporis et al., 2003; Hajiaghayi and Sorkin, 2004). The best known result for upper bounds states that for $\alpha > 4.506$, random uniform 3-SAT formulas are unsatisfiable w.h.p. (Dubois et al., 2000) (for a survey of upper bounds see (Dubois, 2001)). For general k-SAT, the best known bounds are in (Achlioptas and Peres, 2004; Achlioptas and Moore, 2002) for lower bounds and in (Dubios and Boufkhad, 1997) and with a slightly less precise method in (Kirousis et al., 1998) for upper bounds.

In this paper we give experimental and theoretical results for a different model for random satisfiability, which we call regular k-SAT (Reg k-SAT). In this model, each literal has nearly the same number of occurrences in the formula. More specifically, given α, the expected ratio of clauses to variables, and n, the number of variables, let $r = \frac{k\alpha}{2}$ be the expected number of occurrences of each literal in the formula. We will generate instances such that each literal appears $\lfloor r \rfloor$ or $\lfloor r \rfloor + 1$ times in the formula.

In Figure 1(a), we first consider the computational properties of the Reg k-SAT model. We plot the complexity of experimentally solving uniform 3-SAT and Reg 3-SAT as a function of the ratio α, using the *kcnfs* solver (Dubois and Dequen, 2001). The hardest problems with 300 variables for uniform 3-SAT require less than 4000 branches (median cost) while for the same number of variables Reg 3-SAT requires around $5e + 05$ branches – more than two orders of magnitude difference. The same hardness is observed with another complete SAT solver satz (Li, http://www.laria.u-picardie.fr/cli/EnglishPage.html) and with incomplete solver WalkSAT. Bayardo and Schrag (1996) reported

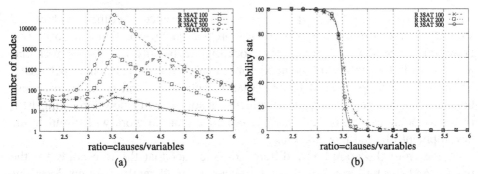

Figure 1. (a) Median of the number of branches needed to solve Reg 3-SAT versus 3-SAT as a function of the ratio α. We consider problems with 100, 200 and 300 variables for Reg 3-SAT and 300 variables for 3-SAT (*triangle* data points). The plot is in log scale. (b) Phase transition in Reg 3-SAT. Probability that a Reg 3-Sat problem has at least one satisfying assignment as a function of the ratio.

comparable results on a model similar to the one we present here. (In the Bayardo and Schrag (1996) model each literal has at least $\lfloor r \rfloor$ but in general could have more than $\lfloor r \rfloor + 1$ occurrences.) Reg 3-SAT also exhibits a phase transition similar to that of uniform 3-SAT. However, the transition is at a quite different ratio: around $\alpha = 3.5$, Reg 3-SAT instances change from satisfiable to unsatisfiable (see Figure 1(b)). As one might expect, the figures show that the complexity peak and the phase transition coincide.

Achlioptas et al. (2000) introduced a generator of satisfiability formulas based on Latin squares that creates only satisfiable instances. More recently, that model was modified to obtain a more "balanced" version (Kautz et al., 2001), thereby significantly increasing the difficulty of the instances. As in the comparison of uniform 3-SAT versus Reg 3-SAT, in these generators the effect of balancing dramatically increases the hardness of the problem. Another example of this phenomenon appears in coloring random graphs. When considering the Erdős – Rényi model $G\left(n, p = \frac{r}{n}\right)$ versus the regular graphs $G(n, r)$ with the same average degree r, regular graphs are much harder to color than graphs in $G(n, p)$.

It is interesting to consider for a moment why solvers have so much more trouble with regular or balanced problem instances. The key issue appears to be that in the standard uniform random formula and graph models, solvers can exploit variations between variable occurrences (or node degrees). In particular, most solvers will first focus on variables that occur relatively frequently or nodes with relatively high degree. In the uniform k-SAT model, literal occurrences range from 0 to $log(n)$, in n variable instances. This is a rather significant range, and heuristics for variable selection exploit these differences quite successfully. In the Reg k-SAT model, on the other hand, each literal occurs either r times or $r + 1$ times for some small constant r (independent of n). So, one cannot exploit obvious differences in the frequency of literal occurrences. Setting variables and simplifying the formula may disturb the precise balance of literal occurrences. However, since the maximum literal occurrence is only $r + 1$, the formulas remain nearly balanced with the maximum range of literal occurrences between 0 and $r + 1$. Because of the lack of variation between literal occurrences, these balanced models require the development of solvers with new branching heuristics to tackle them more effectively. We hope that our work will stimulate the development of such new solvers.

Aside from the complexity differences, the fact that the thresholds for the regular and the uniform k-SAT model occur at significantly different locations also suggests that there are interesting differences between the two models. In terms of the bounds on the threshold phenomena in the regular SAT model, we will see how one can exploit the properties of the limited degree variation to obtain bounds that are tighter than the bounds obtained for the uniform random formula model. A deeper understanding as to why these bounds in the regular SAT model are better may also lead us to new insights into the analysis of the uniform SAT model.

An interesting direction for future research is to consider what happens when one pushes the uniform random k-SAT model in the other direction: instead of making them more balanced, make the literal occurrences even less balanced. In particular, one could consider power-law distributions in terms of literal occurrences. This would be analogous to the work on random graphs, where one has found that power-law distributed node degrees are most prevalent in real-world networks (e.g., the World Wide Web). Real-world SAT instances, such as derived from bounded model-checking, also exhibit large variations in literal occurrences. So, a random formula model with power-law literal occurrence distribution would provide an interesting complement to our results for regular SAT.

We begin the next section with a precise definition of our model. We use the results of Cooper et al. (2002) to derive the sharp threshold for Reg 2-SAT. The threshold for regular 2-SAT is at the same ratio of $\alpha = 1$ as for the uniform random 2-SAT model. So, only for $k > 2$ do the properties of the models diverge in an interesting way. In Section 3, we use the first moment method combined with a subtle argument based on literal occurrences to prove that for $\alpha > 3.78$ a Reg 3-SAT formula is unsatisfiable w.h.p. In Section 4, we analyze a greedy algorithm on Reg 3-SAT formulas to prove that for $\alpha < 2.46$ the algorithm finds a satisfying assignment with positive probability.

2. The Model

A k-SAT formula is a finite set of clauses, each clause being a disjunction of k literals over the set of Boolean variables.

We are interested in generating random k-SAT formulas where each literal appears in approximately the same number of clauses. For the case $k = 2$, this problem is very similar to the problem of generating a regular random graph. A generalization of the usual procedure to generate random regular graphs is used here to generate random regular k-SAT formulas. For simplicity, suppose we want to generate a random 3-SAT formula in which each literal appears exactly four times. We take a box in which we place four copies of each literal. If n is the number of variables, we have $4 \times 2n$ literals in the box. To form a clause, we take 3 literals from the box without replacement. We continue until we have $m = 8n/3$ clauses. The problem with this procedure is that we may obtain "illegal" clauses, that is, clauses in which a variable appears more than once. If that happens, we start the process again. In practice, instead of restarting, we can also just erase the illegal clauses.

With the algorithm described above one can obtain formulas in which all literals appear exactly r times, for nonnegative integers r. Therefore, we get just some values of the ratio $\alpha = 2r/3$. We generalize this procedure to obtain formulas with average ratio α for every real α. In essence, to obtain a balanced SAT formula with a ratio α that lies in between $2r/3$ and $2(r + 1)/3$, for some value of r, we will create a random balanced formula where each literal has either r occurrences or $r + 1$ occurrences. The ratio of the number of literals with r occurrences to the number with $r + 1$ occurrences will be chosen carefully to obtain the desired value of α. Our model is inspired by the way random graphs with prescribed literal degrees have been defined.

We first introduce the notion of the literal degree sequence of a formula. Let n be the number of variables, $m = \lfloor \alpha n \rfloor$, $\alpha > 0$, the number of clauses in a k-CNF formula F. We say that a literal x has degree l if x appears l times in the formula. Let $r = k\alpha/2$ be the average literal degree. The degree sequence associated with a formula F is the sequence $\{d_1, d_{-1} \ldots d_n, d_{-n}\}$, where d_x is the number of clauses in which the literal x occurs. So, the degree sequence simply tells us how often each literal occurs in the formula.

The actual formula generation process consists of two steps. First, we randomly generate a desired degree sequence for our formula. Then, to obtain our balanced formula, we randomly generate a set of clauses that satisfies this degree sequence.

Let $\{p_l\}_{l \geq 0}$ with $\sum_{l \geq 0} p_l = 1$ be a sequence of nonnegative real numbers, where p_l is the probability of a literal having degree l. In our regular SAT model, this sequence of probabilities is very simple: $p_{\lfloor r \rfloor} = p$ and $p_{\lfloor r \rfloor + 1} = 1 - p$, where p is defined so that the expected number of clauses is $m = \alpha n$, that is, $p = \lfloor r \rfloor + 1 - r$, and all the other values for p_l are zero. Given these probabilities for each degree, we can generate a sequence of actual literals of degrees $\{d_1, d_{-1} \ldots d_n, d_{-n}\}$ drawn independently from that distribution and conditioned on the event that the sum of all degrees is a multiple of k. Note that in our regular SAT model, each literal will have either degree $\lfloor r \rfloor$ or degree $\lfloor r \rfloor + 1$ in this degree sequence.

After having obtained a literal degree sequence for our random formula, we generate a random formula with this degree sequence. To do so, we generalize the example discussed at the beginning of this section. Let W_d be the set of literals associated with a degree sequence d where literal l appears d_l times, i.e., $\mathcal{D} = |W_d| = \sum_l d_l$. A *configuration* F is a partition of W_d into $\mathcal{D}/k$ groups of k literals. For each configuration we obtain a formula with the desired degree sequence by assigning literals in one group to literals in a clause. The problem with that mapping is that some of these clauses may not be "legal". A legal clause is one in which there are no repeated or complementary literals. Call a *configuration formula* a formula that is not necessarily legal as opposed to a *simple formula*, one with legal clauses. In the context of regular graphs, this procedure is known as the *configuration model* (Janson et al., 2000).

For the analysis of Section 4, we need a slightly more general configuration model. For simplicity consider the case in which we have a 3-SAT formula. After we set some variables, and remove unit clauses by unit propagation, the formula will consist of a mixture of 2- and 3-clauses and a certain degree sequence. Let W_d be the set of literals associated with a degree sequence d. To obtain a configuration formula with degree sequence d, C_2 2-clauses, and C_3 3-clauses such that $\mathcal{D} = |W_d| = \sum_l d_l = 2C_2 + 3C_3$, we partition W_d randomly in C_2 groups of two and C_3 groups of three literals and associate each group with a clause.

The next lemmas will help us to extend properties of the configuration formulas to properties of simple formulas. Let **Pr**(*SIMPLE*) be the probability that a configuration formula is simple.

LEMMA 1. *Let* $m_2 = an$, $m_3 = bn$, $a \geq 0$, $b \geq 0$, $a + b > 0$, *and let* $d = \{d_1, d_{-1} \ldots d_n, d_{-n}\}$, *a bounded degree sequence* $d_i + d_{-i} < \Delta$, *for some constant* Δ. *Let* F *be a configuration formula with* n *variables*, m_i *i-clauses* $i = 1, 2$, *and degree sequence* d *(where* $\sum_i d_i + d_{-1} = 2an + 3bn$*). Then there exists a constant* $\delta > 0$ *such that*

$$\textbf{Pr}(F \text{ is SIMPLE}) \rightarrow \delta > 0 \text{ as } n \rightarrow \infty$$

Applying previous result for $a = 0$ we get the following corollary.

COROLLARY 1. *If* F *is a 3-Reg formula, there exist* $\delta > 0$ *such that*

$$\textbf{Pr}(F \text{ is SIMPLE}) \rightarrow \delta > 0 \text{ as } n \rightarrow \infty$$

LEMMA 2. *Let* F *be as in the hypothesis of Lemma 1 and let* y *be a fixed variable, the probability that we have a clause with 2 occurrences of the variable* y *bounded by* C/n.

The proofs of these lemmas are in the Appendix.

REG 2-SAT

Let $d = \{d_1, d_{-1} \ldots d_n, d_{-n}\}$, a degree sequence corresponding to a 2-SAT formula. In the following theorem, we limit the maximum degree in the degree sequence. To do so, we say that d is Δ-proper if $d_i < \Delta$ $\{1, -1, \ldots, n, -n\}$, where Δ is a constant depending on n.

The location of the threshold for the Reg 2-SAT model can be derived by using the following theorem.

THEOREM 1 (Cooper et al., 2002). *Let $0 < \epsilon < 1$ and $n \to \infty$. Let d be any Δ-proper degree sequence over n variables, with $\Delta = n^{1/11}$, and let F be a uniform random simple formula with degree sequence d. Then*

If $D < (1 - \epsilon)m$, then $P(F$ is satisfiable$) \to 1$

If $D > (1 + \epsilon)m$, then $P(F$ is satisfiable$) \to 0$

where m is the number of clauses and $D = \sum_{i=1}^{n} d_i d_{-1}$.

COROLLARY 2. *The Reg 2-SAT formulas have a threshold at $\alpha = 1$.*

Proof. We prove that w.h.p. degree sequences generated with our Reg 2-SAT model have the property that $\frac{D}{m} \to \alpha$. Using Theorem 1, we can conclude that $\alpha = 1$ is the value of the threshold.

Let $D = \sum_{i=1}^{n} d_i d_{-i}$ a random variable. Note that the expected value $E(D)$ of D is $\alpha^2 n$ and $E(m) = \alpha n$. Note that $2m = \sum_{i=1}^{n} d_i + d_{-i}$; the variables d_i, $i \in \{1, -1, \ldots, n, -n\}$ are independent identically distributed random variables. The variance of the variables D and m are easy to compute, and there exist constants c, c' such that $Var(D) = cn$ and $Var(m) = c'n$.

Using Chebyshev's inequality, we get that $P(|D - \alpha^2 n| \geq n^{1/2+\delta}) \to 0$ as n goes to infinity for any $\delta > 0$. A similar property follows for the variable m, $P(|m - \alpha n| \geq n^{1/2+\delta}) \to 0$ as n goes to infinity. Therefore the property follows and then the claim. □

3. Upper Bound on the Threshold

In order to estimate the probability that a random formula is satisfiable, we bound that probability by the expected number of solutions:

$$\mathbf{Pr}(F \text{ is sat}) \leq \mathbf{E}(\# \text{ solutions } F) = 2^n \mathbf{Pr}(x \text{ is a solution}) \tag{1}$$

The last equality follows from the fact that the occurrences of each literal has the same distribution. All assignments $x \in \{0, 1\}^n$ have the same probability of being a solution. The use of the first inequality in (1) is known as the first moment method.

For a clauses to variables ratio α, let $q = \lfloor 3\alpha n/2 \rfloor - \lfloor 3\alpha/2 \rfloor n$. In a configuration formula, a subset of q among n variables chosen uniformly at random will have $\lfloor 3\alpha/2 \rfloor + 1$ positive copies and $\lfloor 3\alpha/2 \rfloor + 1$ negative copies. The remaining $n - q$ variables will have $\lfloor 3\alpha/2 \rfloor$ copies for each sign. (If $3\alpha n$ is odd, then a literal chosen randomly will have a positive or negative copy more than the copies of opposite sign but this has a negligible effect on the calculation of the expectation). For the following we define, $\mu = q/n$.

Thanks to Lemma 1, it is sufficient to compute a bound on configuration formulas. Let $\mathbf{Pr}(SIMPLE)$ be the probability that a configuration formula is simple.

Let $\mathbf{Pr}(SAT)$ be the probability that a configuration formula is satisfiable and $\mathbf{Pr}_0(SAT)$ the probability that a simple formula is satisfiable. We have

$$1 - \frac{1 - \mathbf{Pr}(SAT)}{\mathbf{Pr}(SIMPLE)} \leq \mathbf{Pr}_0(SAT) \leq \frac{\mathbf{Pr}(SAT)}{\mathbf{Pr}(SIMPLE)}$$

Thanks to Lemma 1 and the preceding inequalities, the threshold for simple formulas has the same location as the threshold for configuration formulas, if it exists.

We consider a truth assignment T and compute the number of Reg-3-SAT formulas satisfied by T. A clause is said to be of type i if it contains i true literals with respect to T. Denote by δ_i the fraction of clauses of type i in a formula.

In the uniform 3-SAT model, formulas are typically satisfied by some fixed truth assignment in such a way that the proportion of each clause type concentrates around its mean, namely, $\delta_1 = 3/7$, $\delta_2 = 3/7$, and $\delta_3 = 1/7$. This follows from the following observation. A random uniform 3-SAT formula F is obtained by taking uniformly at random $m = \alpha n$ clauses out of the $8\binom{n}{3}$ possible clauses. A formula that satisfied a certain assignment T is formed by taking $m = \alpha n$ clauses from the $7\binom{n}{3}$ possible clauses that satisfy T. From these $7\binom{n}{3}$ clauses $3\binom{n}{3}$ are of type 1, $3\binom{n}{3}$ are of type 2 and $\binom{n}{3}$ are of type 3.

Thus, the number of true literals is $\delta_1 \alpha_n + 2\delta_2 \alpha n + 3\delta_3 \alpha n = \frac{12}{7}\alpha n$, and the number of false literals is $2\delta_1 \alpha n + \delta_2 \alpha n = \frac{9}{7}\alpha n$. So in the uniform model the typical formulas are satisfied by truth assignments that skew true and false literals in favor of true ones. Clearly, the random regular formulas are not among these typical formulas because whatever truth assignment one considers, the number of true and false literals is equal to $3\alpha n/2$ (simply because each variable and its negation occur equally often in the formula). Thus, by restricting the δ_i to take only values that satisfy the balance between signs, one can expect to get a better bound than 5.19. Indeed, we establish the following:

THEOREM 2. *Let* $\beta = \frac{9-3\sqrt{5}}{4}$ *and* $\alpha^* = \frac{\log(2)}{3\log(2)+\beta\log(\frac{2}{3})+(\frac{3}{2}-2\beta)\log(\frac{1}{2}-\frac{2}{3}\beta)+(\beta-\frac{1}{2})\log(\beta-\frac{1}{2})}$
$\simeq 3.7822$ *If* $\alpha > \alpha^*$ *then w.h.p. every formula is unsatisfiable.*

Proof. In the following, a configuration formula is viewed as $3\alpha n$ ordered cells such that cells numbered 1, 2, and 3 form the first clause, 4, 5 and 6 the second clause and so on. A formula is then built by assigning a literal to each cell. Then the total number of formulas is

$$\binom{n}{\mu n} \frac{(3\alpha n)!}{(\lfloor 3\alpha/2 \rfloor + 1)!^{2\mu n} \lfloor 3\alpha/2 \rfloor!^{2(1-\mu)n}}$$

Now, we count the number of Reg 3-SAT1 formulas satisfied by T. There are

$$\frac{(\alpha n)!}{(\delta_1 \alpha n)!(\delta_2 \alpha n)!(\delta_3 \alpha n)!} 3^{\delta_1 \alpha n} 3^{\delta_2 \alpha n}$$

ways to choose clauses of each type and to choose the cells for the i true liter and in clauses of type i with the δ_i subject to the following constraints:

$$\delta_1 + \delta_2 + \delta_3 = 1 \tag{2}$$

and

$$\delta_1 + 2\delta_2 + 3\delta_3 = 3/2 \tag{3}$$

At this point, the cells that will be filled with true and false literals are fixed. It remains to fill them with literals. There are

$$\binom{n}{\mu n} \left(\frac{\lfloor 3\alpha n/2 \rfloor!}{(\lfloor 3\alpha/2 \rfloor + 1)!^{\mu n} \lfloor 3\alpha/2 \rfloor!^{(1-\mu)n}} \right)^2$$

ways to fill correctly these cells with literals.

To sum up the probability that T satisfies a random Reg-3-SAT formula is

$$\mathbf{Pr}(T \text{ satisfies } F) = \left(\frac{\lfloor 3\alpha n/2 \rfloor!}{(\lfloor 3\alpha/2 \rfloor + 1)!^{\mu n} \lfloor 3\alpha/2 \rfloor!^{(1-\mu)n}} \right)^2$$

$$\frac{(\lfloor 3\alpha/2 \rfloor + 1)!^{2\mu n} \lfloor 3\alpha/2 \rfloor!^{2(1-\mu)n}}{(3\alpha n)!} \sum_{(\delta_1,\delta_2,\delta_3) \in A} \frac{3^{\delta_1 \alpha n} 3^{\delta_2 \alpha n} (\alpha n)!}{(\delta_1 \alpha n)!(\delta_2 \alpha n)!(\delta_3 \alpha n)!}$$

where

$$A = \left\{ (\delta_1, \delta_2, \delta_3) / \text{ for some integers } \Delta_1, \Delta_2, \Delta_3 \right.$$

$$\left. \delta_1 = \frac{\Delta_1}{n}, \delta_2 = \frac{\Delta_2}{n} \text{ and } \delta_3 = \frac{\Delta_3}{n} \text{ subject to constraints (2) and (3)} \right\}$$

After simplification:

$$\mathbf{Pr}(T \text{ satisfies } F) = \frac{(\lfloor 3\alpha n/2 \rfloor!)^2}{(3\alpha n)!} \sum_{(\delta_1, \delta_2, \delta_3) \in A} \frac{3^{\delta_1 \alpha n} 3^{\delta_2 \alpha n} (\alpha n)!}{(\delta_1 \alpha n)!(\delta_2 \alpha n)!(\delta_3 \alpha n)!}$$

We use the fact that $|A| = O(n^3)$ (i.e., the number of terms of the sum is bounded by a polynome) and the following inequality:

$$\left(\frac{p}{e}\right)^p \sqrt{2\pi p} \le p! \le \left(\frac{p}{e}\right)^p \sqrt{2\pi p} \left(1 + \frac{1}{12p - 1}\right)$$

We get the exponential order of expectation of the number of solutions:

$$\mathbf{E}(\# \text{ solutions of } F) = 2^n \mathbf{Pr}(T \text{ satisfies } F)$$

$$\asymp \max_{(\delta_1, \delta_2, \delta_3) \in A} \left(2^{-3\alpha} 2 \left(\frac{3}{\delta_1}\right)^{\delta_1 \alpha} \left(\frac{3}{\delta_2}\right)^{\delta_2 \alpha} \left(\frac{1}{\delta_3}\right)^{\delta_3 \alpha}\right)^n$$

Let $f_\alpha(\delta_1, \delta_2, \delta_3) = 2^{-3\alpha} 2 \left(\frac{3}{\delta_1}\right)^{\delta_1 \alpha} \left(\frac{3}{\delta_2}\right)^{\delta_2 \alpha} \left(\frac{1}{\delta_3}\right)^{\delta_3 \alpha}$. The problem amounts to maximize $f_\alpha(\delta_1, \delta_2, \delta_3)$ subject to constraints[*] (2) and (3). (The calculation for general Reg k-SAT gives an analogous function $f_\alpha(\delta_1, \delta_2, \ldots, \delta_k) = 2^{-k\alpha} 2 \prod_{i=1..k} \left(\frac{\binom{k}{i}}{\delta_1}\right)^{\delta_1 \alpha}$; the maximization is subject to analogous constraints and can be solved using standard Lagrange maximization method.)

From (2) and (3), we have $\delta_2 = 3/2 - 2\delta_i$ and $\delta_3 = \delta_1 - 1/2$. f_α can then be expressed in terms of δ_1 alone. By applying *log*, we have to maximize the following function of δ_1

$$g_\alpha(\delta_1) = (1 - 3\alpha) \log(2) + \alpha(3/2 - \delta_1) \log(3) - \alpha\delta_1 \log(\delta_1)$$

$$- \alpha(3/2 - 2\delta_1) \log(3/2 - 2\delta_1) - \alpha(\delta_1 - 1/2) \log(\delta_1 - 1/2)$$

which attains its maximum at $\delta_1^* = \frac{9 - 3\sqrt{5}}{4}$.

The upper bound is obtained by solving w.r.t. α the equation $g_\alpha(\delta_1^*) = 0$. □

4. Lower Bound on the Threshold

In this section, we analyze a greedy algorithm and prove that it finds a satisfying assignment with positive probability for formulas with $\alpha < 2.46$. This result by itself does not give a lower bound on the threshold. To prove a lower bound, we

---

[*]   By ignoring the constraint of balancing between signs $\delta_1 + 2\delta_2 + 3\delta_3 = 3/2$, the maximum is at $\delta_1 = 3/7$, $\delta_2 = 3/7$, $\delta_3 = 1/7$ and the bound is 5.19 as for the uniform 3-SAT model. Surprising, the fact that all variables have almost the same number of occurrences disappears in the expectation. There remains only the constraint that each variable have the same number of positive and negative occurrences.

need that property to hold w.h.p. In previous work on lower bounds for uniform 3-SAT, this problem was solved by using the result in (Friedgut, 1999) that implies that if such property holds with positive probability it also holds w.h.p. That result is not known for our model.

We first prove that configuration formulas with $\alpha < 2.46$ are satisfiable with positive probability. At the end of the section we discuss how to modify the proof to get the same result for simple formulas.

To achieve our claim, it is enough to prove that with positive probability the algorithm does not generate empty clauses. The algorithm we analyze makes *n* iterations, setting one variable at each iteration. Keeping track of the number of 2-clauses at each iteration, of the algorithm and checking that for ($\alpha < 2.46$ the density of 2-clauses is bounded below 1 is sufficient to obtain the results.

The method of differential equations proposed in (Wormald, 1995) is used in this analysis to keep track of the number of 2-clauses at each time. In particular, our analysis follows closely the one done by Kaporis et al. (2002) for random uniform S-SAT formulas. This is a well-known approach that has been used in most of the lower bounds for the threshold of random uniform 3-SAT (e.g., see (Achlioptas, 2001; Kaporis et al., 2002; Kaporis et al., 2003; Hajiaghayi and Sorkin, 2004)).

For a fixed ratio a and the corresponding $r = 3\alpha/2$, let *h* be the smallest integer greater than *r*. Let $\mathcal{X}_j$ for $j = 0, \ldots, h$ be the current collection of literals of degree *j*. We consider an algorithm that at each time sets a literal with the higher occurrence in the formula and sets unit clauses anytime they appear. Let's call a *round* the first while loop of the following algorithm. In a round we assign a random literal and unit clauses that may appear.

Greedy algorithm
begin
    let $j = h$
    while unset literals exists
        while $\mathcal{X}_j \neq \emptyset$
            set an arbitrary literal from $\mathcal{X}_j$ to TRUE
            and its negation to FALSE and Del&Shrink
            while unit clauses exits
                set an arbitrary unit clause to True
                its negation to FALSE and Del&Shrink
            end
        end
        $j = j - 1$
    end
end

Note that in the process of choosing the literal to be assigned to true at the beginning of each round, the greedy algorithm does not use any information about the negation of that literal. Therefore the negated literal is random; in particular its degree has the same distribution as any other literal in the formula.

As we already mentioned, the analysis of the algorithm relies on the method of differential equations described in (Wormald, 1995). The idea is as follows: suppose $Y^t = (Y^t_1, \ldots, Y^t_s)$ are stochastic parameters related to a formula. In our case, these parameters are the number of variables (literals), the number of 2-clauses and S-clauses, and the number of liter and of degree i, $0 \le i \le h$, in the formula at time t. We want to estimate the trajectory of Y^t through the duration of our algorithm. In a restricted version, the theorem states that if

(a) $\mathbf{Pr}(\left| Y^{t+1} - Y^t \right| > n^{1/5}) = o(n^{-3})$
(b) $\mathbf{E}(Y^{t+1} - Y^t \mid Y^t) = f(t/n, Y^t/n) + o(1)$
(c) the function f is continuous and satisfies a Lipschitz condition on some set D, then

$$Y^t = ny(t/n) + o(n) \tag{4}$$

where $y(x)$ is the solution of the system of differential equations

$$\frac{dy}{dn} = f(x, y) \quad y(0) = \frac{Y^0}{n} \tag{5}$$

The precise statement of the theorem is given in the Appendix.

In order to make use of the previous theorem to analyze an algorithm one needs to choose the algorithm, the set of parameters Y^t, and the random model, to satisfy the following property: after each round the resulting formula is random, given the values of the parameters in Y^t. Precisely, let $Y^t = (L(t), C_3(t), C_2(t), X_1(t), \ldots, X_h(t))$, where $L(t)$ is the number of unset literals and at time t, $C_3(t)$ and $C_2(t)$ is respectively the number of 3-clauses and 2-clauses, and X_i is the number of literals with degree i, $0 \le i \le h$. That is, we need the following lemma.

LEMMA 3 (Kaporis et al., 2002). *During the evolution of the algorithm, the formula remains random conditional on the current value of the parameters Y^t.*

Using Lemma 3, we are able to compute the expression in (b). In the Appendix we give the expression for the function f in our case. Equation (4) allows us to use the solution of the differential Equation (5) to trace our parameter Y_t. In particular we use the values of $C_2(t)$ to prove that with positive probability the algorithm does not generate empty clauses.

If the density of 2-clauses $\frac{2C_2(t)}{L(t)}$ is bounded below 1, that property holds. A proof for that result can be found in (Kaporis et al., 2002). The argument goes as follows: The number of unit clauses generated in one of the while loops in the algorithm can be approximated by a branching process. Suppose we start by satisfying a unit clause. That assignment can produce some new unit clauses that can be seen as the offspring of the first unit clause. The process continues until all unit clauses are satisfied. The expected number of unit clauses produced by one assignment has mean $\frac{2C_2(t)}{L(t)}$. If $\mu = \frac{2C_2(t)}{L(t)}$ for some constant ρ and for all t, the process is subcritical, and its expected size is $1/(1 - \mu)$. The probability of the appearance of a literal b and its complement $\bar{b}$ in a single round can be proved to be less than C/n for some constant $C > 0$ independent of t, and therefore the probability of not having an empty clause is bounded by $(1 - O(1/n))^n$, which is greater than $e^{-C'}$ for some constant C'.

Equation (4) holds for values of t such that the scaled number of literals $l(t) = L(t)/n > \epsilon$ for any fixed $\epsilon > 0$. Using the previous argument, we are able to prove that for $t < t^*$ our main claim holds with positive probability. To finish the proof we use Theorem 1 from Section 2 to prove that the remaining formula is satisfiable w.h.p. We choose t^* such that the degree sequence at time t^* satisfies the conditions of Theorem 1. Note that if we delete one literal from the every 3-clause, we get a 2-SAT formula satisfiable w.h.p., and so the original formula is also satisfiable.

We solve the differential equations (see Appendix B.1), associated with the Equation (5), numerically using the *ode45* function of matlab. The results are in agreement with simulation of the algorithm on randomly generated formulas. We find that for $\alpha = 2.46$, $\frac{2c_2(x)}{l(x)}$ is bounded below 1 for $x < x^*$. We can conclude the following result.

THEOREM 3. *Let F be a configuration formula with ratio $\alpha < 2.46$. The greedy algorithm finds a satisfying assignment for F with positive probability.*

To extend Theorem 3 for simple formulas, we just have to introduce some minor changes in the proof. By exposing a variable x we mean disclosing the information pertaining to this variable (e.g., the number of occurrences of x and $\bar{x}$ in i-clauses). At each step we expose the variable we want to assign, some of the information we expose is whether two literals from the same variable are in a single clause. Let us call such event a *bad* event. Also the appearance of an empty clause is considered a bad event. We are going to prove that the probability of a bad event in a round t is bounded by C/n for some constant $C > 0$ independent of t.

Claim: at any round the probability of having a bad event is less that C/n, for some $C > 0$.

If T is the number of steps in a round, at that round we expose the information about T variables. By Lemma 2, after exposing one variable the probability of getting a cycle is bounded by C'/n, where C' is independent of the round. The probability that we get a cycle in the round conditioned on the number of steps in a round being T, is bounded by TC/n. The unconditional probability is less than $E(T)C/n$ ($E(T)$ can also be bounded independently of the round). These facts, together with the fact that the probability of getting an empty clause is bounded by C''/n independently of the round, complete the claim.

To finish we have to argue that the final subformula is simple and satisfiable with positive probability. Prom our previous discussion we know it is satisfiable. It is simple with positive probability by Lemma 1. We conclude the following result.

THEOREM 4. *Let F be a Reg 3-SAT formula with ratio $\alpha < 2.46$. The greedy algorithm finds a satisfying assignment for F with positive probability.*

5. Conclusions

We proposed a new model for random k-SAT, in which every literal appears in approximately the same number of clauses. Experimental results show that the new model leads to formulas that are substantially more difficult to solve than the well-known uniform k-SAT model. Experiments also show that the model exhibits a phase transition as a function of α, the ratio of clauses to variables. The hardest instances are concentrated around the value $\alpha = 3.5$, where the probability that a formula is satisfiable falls from 1 to 0. We provide the first rigorous bounds for this model. In particular, we obtain an upper bound of 3.78 for the location of the phase transition. This bound was obtained by exploiting the special balanced nature of the formulas. Our analysis of a greedy algorithm shows that we can find satisfying assignments for formulas with $\alpha < 2.46$ with positive probability.

The underlying theme of this research is to develop interesting alternatives to the uniform random k-SAT model. In this paper, we have changed the almost Poisson degree distribution of the uniform random and k-SAT to an almost constant degree distribution of the regular random and k-SAT model. As we discussed in the introduction, given the limited variance in degrees, solvers have much more difficulty identifying good variables to branch on. It will require new ideas for branching heuristics or different techniques altogether to make progress on these formulas. (We did some preliminary experiments with WalkSAT and survey propagation. Again, these formulas appear much harder than uniform random k-SAT instances.) Eventually, we hope to develop other analyzable models that that are closer to real-world instances. One interesting possibility in this regard is to consider random formulas with power law distributed literal degree distributions.

There are still other results to pursue for regular SAT. To get a proper lower bound using our result for the greedy algorithm, one has to extend the proof of Friedgut (1999) of the existence of a sharp threshold around some critical sequence of values. Another interesting problem is to extend the results of Chvatal and Szemeredi (1988). Chvatal and Szemeredi proved that for the uniform and k-SAT model for $k \geq 3$, unsatisfiable formulas need an exponential refutation proof. Their proof extends to our model. But, more interesting, by exploiting the additional balanced structure in our model as we did for the upper bound result, we may be able to obtain sharper results.

Appendix

A. Proof of Lemmas 1 and 2

In this section we prove that the probability that a configuration formula F, with parameter as in Lemma 1, is simple goes to a constant as the number of variables goes to infinity.

Denote $D_i = d_i + d_{-i}$, the number of occurrences of the variable i in the formula F. Let $\lambda = \sum_{i=1}^{n} D_i(D_i - 1)/n$. Note that if x_l is the fraction of variables with degree (number of occurrences) l, then $\lambda = \sum_{l=2}^{\Delta} l(l-1)x_l$. To be able to take the limit, we are assuming that when n goes to infinity, the densities x_l $0 \le l \le \Delta$ are fixed. We prove the following result:

$$\mathbf{Pr}(F \text{ is SIMPLE}) \to e^{-\Lambda} > 0 \text{ as } n \to \infty \tag{6}$$

where $\Lambda = 2\lambda \frac{a+b}{(2a+3b)^2}\left(1 + \frac{3}{2a+3b}\right)$.

Let us call a *cycle* a nonlegal clause in F. Let Z be the number cycles in F. A configuration formula F is simple if and only if $Z = 0$.

Our proof follows a standard procedure (see (Janson et al., 2000) chapter 9, (Bollobas, 2001) chapter 2). We are going to prove that the distribution of 2 converges to a Poisson distribution with mean Λ. Then Equation (6) follows, because the right-hand side is just the probability of the event $Z = 0$.

To prove that Z converges in distribution to a Poisson, we use the method of moments (see Theorem 6.10 in (Janson et al., 2000)). Let $(Z)_k$ be the number of ordered k disjoint cycles in F. We are going to prove that for every $k \ge 1$

$$\mathbf{E}(Z)_k \to \Lambda^k \text{ as } n \to \infty$$

to conclude that the distribution of Z approaches the distribution of a Poisson random variable with mean Λ.

Let $\beta(m_2, m_3)$ be the number of configurations with m_2 2-clauses and m_3 3-clauses. Note that $\beta(m_2, m_3) = \frac{(2m_2+3m_3)!}{2^{m_2}6^{m_3}(m_2+m_3)!}$. The probability $q_{1,0}$ that a particular 2-clause is present in a configuration is $q_{1,0} = \frac{\beta(m_2-1,m_3)}{\beta(m_2,m_3)}$. Moreover, the probability $q_{k,j}$ that any disjoint k 2-clause and j 3-clauses are present in a configuration is $q_{k,j} = \frac{\beta(m_2-k,m_3-j)}{\beta(m_2,m_3)}$. For fixed, k and j one can check that[*]

$$q_{k,j} \sim \frac{2^k 6^j}{n^{k+2j}(2a+3b)^{2k+3j}}(a+b)^{k+j}$$

---

[*] We say that $a(n) \sim b(n)$ when $n \to \infty$ if $\lim_{n\to\infty}\frac{a(n)}{b(n)} = 1$.

To compute $E(Z)$, note that we can divide cycles into two groups: the ones coming from clauses with two different variables (for example $x \vee \bar{x} \vee y, x \vee x \vee y, x \vee x$), or the ones involving one variable ($x \vee \bar{x} \vee x$). We prove that the last ones have a very small probability and they do not contribute to our calculation. Let $Z = Y' + Y''$, where Y' are the number of cycles in the first group and Y'' the ones in the second.

Now we have to count how many clauses form cycles. Consider the first case. Here we have the 2-clause cycles and 3-clause cycles. The number of cycles coming from 2-clauses is

$$a_{1,0} = \sum_{i=1}^{n} D_i(D_i - 1) = \lambda n$$

The one coming from 3-clauses is

$$a_{1,0} = \sum_{i=1}^{n} D_i(D_i - 1)(n - D_i) \sim \lambda n^2$$

Therefore $E(Y') = a_{1,0}q_{1,2} + a_{0,1}q_{0,1} \sim \Lambda$. Note now that if we count how many edges give us cycles of the second type, there are just $\sum_{i=1}^{n} D_i(D_i - 1)(D_i - 2) < \Delta^3 n$, as $q_{0,1}n$ goes to 0 then $E(Y'') \to 0$ as $n \to \infty$.

Next, we compute $E((Z)_s)$. Recall the $(Z)_s$ is the number of ordered s disjoint cycles. This time divide $(Z)_s$ into two sets: cycles in Y' not only are cycles on the first kind described before but also each cycle corresponds to different variable, cycles in Y'' have either a cycle of the second type or two or more cycles correspond to the same variable. Similar to what we have done before, one can prove that $E(Y'') \to 0$ as $n \to \infty$.

We can write

$$E(Y') = \sum_{k+j=s} q_{k,j}a_{k,j}$$

where $a_{k,j}$ is the number of s disjoint cycles with k 2-clause cycles and j 3-clause cycles.

Note that $a_{k,j}$ has the following expression (if we approximate as before $n - D_i$ by n)

$$a_{k,j} = \binom{k+j}{j} n^j \sum_{i_1, i_2, \ldots, i_{k+j}} D_{i_1}(D_{i_1} - 1) \cdots D_{i_{k+j}}(D_{i_{k+j}} - 1) \qquad (7)$$

where the sum over $\{i_1, i_2, \ldots, i_{k+j}\}$ is over the set of disjoint indexes.

Claim: $a_{k,j} = \binom{k+j}{j} n^{2j+k}$.

Note that the difference between the above expression and (7) are the terms in which the same index is repeated but those terms are going to 0 when we divide by n^{k+j}.

Now note that

$$q_{k,j} a_{k,j} \sim \left(\frac{2\lambda(a+b)}{(2a+3b)^2} \right)^{k+j} \left(\frac{3}{2a+3b} \right)^j \binom{k+j}{j}$$

So we get $E(Y') \sim \Lambda^k$. This completes the proof.

Proof of Lemma 2. The proof uses some of the ideas explained before. Let D be the number of occurrences of variable y in F and Z be the number of clauses with two occurrences of the variable y. As is the previous proof,

$$\mathbf{E}(Z) = D(D-1)q_{1,0} + D(D-1)(n-D)q_{0,1}$$

$$\leq \frac{D^2}{n} \frac{2(a+b)}{(2a+3b)^2} \left[1 + \frac{3}{2a+3b} \right].$$

$P(Z > 1) \leq \mathbf{E}(Z) \leq C/n$, and the lemma follows, where C is given in the expression above.

REMARK. The constant C can be bound uniformly for all the configuration formulas consider though the analysis. Note that we set variables until time t^* as explained in the prove of the Section 4, the remaining clauses at that time is of order order n so $2a + 3b = c > 0$ for some constant c. Therefore we have that at any state of the algorithm $D^2 \frac{2(a+b)}{(2a+3b)^2} \left[1 + \frac{3}{2a+3b} \right] < \Delta^2 \frac{\alpha}{c^2}(1 + 3/c)$.

B. Differential Equations

In this section we discuss the main theorem used in Section 4 to analyze the random process.

We consider here a sequence of random process $Y_t = Y_t(n)$, $n = 1, 2, \ldots$, For simplicity the dependence on n is dropped from the notation. Let $\mathcal{F}_t$ be the σ-field generated by the process up to time t, i.e., $\mathcal{F}_t = \sigma(Y_0, Y_1, \ldots, Y_t)$. Our process $Y_t = (Y_t^{(1)}, \ldots, Y_t^{(j)})$ is a vector of dimension j. Let $\|Y\| = \max(|Y^{(1)}|, \ldots, |Y^{(j)}|)$. Suppose that $Y_0 = z_0 n$ the value of the process at time 0.

We say that $X = o(f(n))$ *always* if $\max\{x: \mathbf{Pr}(X = x) \neq 0\} = o(f(n))$. The term *uniformly* means that the convergence implicit in the o( ) is uniform on t.

THEOREM 5 (Wormald, 1995). *Let* $f: \mathfrak{R}^{j+1} \to \mathfrak{R}^j$. *Suppose there exists a constant* C *such that the process* Y_t *is bounded by* Cn, *i.e.,* $\|Yt\| < Cn$. *Suppose also that for some function* $m = m(n)$:

(i) *for all* $t < m$ *and all* 1

$$\mathbf{Pr}\left(\|Y_{t+1} - Y_t\| > n^{1/5} | \mathcal{F}_t \right) = o\left(n^{-3} \right)$$

always;

(ii) *for all l and uniformly over all $t < m$,*

$$\mathbf{E}(Y_{t+1} - Y_t | \mathcal{F}_t) = f(t/n, Y_t/n) + o(1)$$

always;

(iii) *The function f is continuous and satisfies a Lipschitz condition on D, where D is some bounded open set containing $(0, z_0^{(1)}, \ldots, z_0^{(j)})$.*

Then:

(a) *The system of differential equations*

$$\frac{dz}{ds} = f(s, z)$$

has a unique solution in D for $z : \mathfrak{R} \rightarrow \mathfrak{R}^j$ with initial conditions $z(0) = z_0$ and which extends to points arbitrarily closed to the boundary of D.

(b)

$$Y_t = nz(t/n) + o(n) \ w.h.p.$$

uniformly for $0 \leq t \leq \min\{\sigma n, m\}$, where σ is the supremum of those s to which the solution can be extended.

B.1. DIFFERENTIAL EQUATIONS FOR THE LOWER BOUND

Let l be the scaled number of current unset literals, c_3, c_2 the scaled number of 3-clauses and 2-clauses, respectively, and x_s the scaled number of literals of degree s, $s = 1, \ldots, 4$. The equations for round j are

$$\frac{dl}{dt} = -2 - 4\frac{c_2}{l - 2c_2}$$

$$\frac{dc_3}{dt} = -\frac{3jc_3}{p} - \frac{3c_3}{l} + \left(-\frac{3jc_3}{p} - \frac{3c_3}{l}\right)\frac{2c_2}{l - 2c_2}$$

$$\frac{dc_2}{dt} = \frac{3c_3 - 2c_2}{l} - \frac{2jc_2}{p} + \left(\frac{3c_3 - 2c_2}{l} - \frac{2jc_2}{p}\right)\frac{2c_2}{l - 2c_2}$$

$$\frac{dx_4}{dt} = -(6c_3 + 2c_2)\frac{4x_4}{p^2}j - \frac{x_4}{l} - \delta_{4,j}$$

$$- \left((6c_3 + 2c_2)\frac{4x_4}{p^2}j + \frac{x_4}{l} + \frac{4x_4}{p}\right)\frac{2c_2}{l - 2c_2}$$

$$\frac{dx_s}{dt} = (6c_3 + 2c_2)\frac{(s+1)x_{s+1} - (s)x_s}{p^2}d^j - \frac{x_s}{l} - \delta_{s,j}$$

$$\left((6c_3 + 2c_2)\frac{(s+1)x_{s+1} - (s)x_s}{p^2}d^j - \frac{x_s}{l} - \frac{sx_s}{p}\right)\frac{2c_2}{l - 2c_2} \text{ for } s = 1, 2, 3$$

with initial conditions $l = 2$, $c_3 = c$, $c_2 = 0$, $x_4 = 2p$, $x_3 = 2(1 - p)$, $x_2 = 0$, $x_1 = 0$.

References

Achlioptas, D. (2001) Lower bounds for random 3-SAT via differential equations, *Theor. Comp. Sci.* **265**, pp. 159–185.

Achlioptas, D. and Moore, C. (2002) The asymptotic order of the random k-SAT threshold, in *43th Annual Symposium on Foundations of Computer Science*, Vancouver, pp. 779–788.

Achlioptas, D. and Peres, Y. (2004) The threshold for random k-SAT is $2^k ln2 - O(k)$, *J. Amer. Math. Soc.* **17**, 947–973.

Achlioptas, D., Gomes, C. P., Kautz, H. A., and Selman, B. (2000) Generating satisfiable problems instances, in *Proceedings of 17th National Conference on Artificial Intelligence*, pp. 256–261.

Bayardo, R. J. and Schrag, R. (1996) Using CSP look-back techniques to solve exceptionally hard SAT instances, in *Proceedings of the Second Int. Conf. on Principles and Practice of Constraint Programming*, pp. 46–60.

Bollobas, B. (2001) *Random Graphs Second Edition,* Cambridge University Press, United Kingdom.

Chvatal, V. and Reed, B. (1992) Mick gets some (the odds are on his side). *Proceedings of 33rd FOCS*, pp. 620–627.

Chvatal, V. and Szemeredi, E. (1988) Many hard examples for resolution, *J. Assoc. Comput. Mach.* **35** 759–768.

Cooper, C., Frieze, A. and Sorkin, G. B. (2002) A note on random 2-SAT with prescribed literal degrees. *Proceedings of the 13th Annual ACM-SIAM Symposium on Discrete Algorithms.*

Dubois, O. (2001) Upper bounds on the satisfiability threshold, *Theor. Comput. Sci. Vol.* **265**, 187–197.

Dubois, O. and Boufkhad, Y. (1997) A general upper bound for the satisfiability threshold of random r-SAT formulae, *J. Algorithms* **24**(2), 395–420.

Dubois, O. and Dequen, G. (2001) A backbone search heuristic for efficient solving of hard 3-SAT formulae, in *Proceedings of 17th International Joint Conference on Artificial Intelligence*, Seattle, pp. 248–253.

Dubois, O., Boufkhad, Y. and Mandler, J. (2000) Typical random 3-SAT formulae and the satisfiability threshold, in *SODA*, pp. 126–127. Full version in Electronic Colloquium on Computational Complexity (ECCC 2003).

Fernandez de la Vega, W. (1992) On random 2-SAT. *Manuscript.*

Friedgut, E. (1999) Sharp thresholds for graph properties and the k-sat problem, *J. Amer. Math. Soc.* **12**, 1017–1054.

Goerdt, A. (1996) A threshold for unsatisfiability, *J. Comput. Syst. Sci.* **53**(3), 469–486.

Hajiaghayi, M. and Sorkin, G. (2004) The satisfiability threshold of random 3-SAT is at least 3.52. www.math.mit.edu/hajiagha/3satRCl.ps.

Janson, S., Luczak, T. and Rucinski, A. (2002) *Random Graphs*, Wiley, New York.

Kaporis, A. C., Kirousis, L. M. and Lalas, E. G. (2002) The probabilistic analysis of a greedy satisfiability algorithm, in *10th Annual European Symposium on Algorithms.*

Kaporis, A. C., Kirousis, L. M. and Lalas, E. (2003) Selecting complementary pairs of literals. *Electron. Notes Discrete Mathem.* **16**.

Kautz, H., Ruan, Y., Achlioptas, D., Gomes, C. P., Selman, B. and Stickel, M. (2001) Balance and filtering in structured satisfiable problems, in *Proceedings of the Seventeenth International Joint Conference on Artificial Intelligence.*

Kirousis, L. M., Kranakis, E., Krizanc, D. and Stamatiou, Y. C. (1998) Approximating the unsatisfiability threshold of random formulas, *Random Struct. Algorithms* **12**(3), 253–269.

Le Berre, D. and Simon, L. (2004) 2004 SAT competitions. http://www.lri.fr/simon/contest/results/

Li, C.-M. SATZ. http://www.laria.u-picardie.fr/cli/EnglishPage.html.

Mitchell, D., Selman, B. and Levesque, H. (1992) Hard and easy distributions of SAT problems, in *Proceedings of the 10th National Conf. on Artificial Intelligence*, pp. 459–465.

Wormald, N. C. (1995) Differential equations for random processes and random graphs, *Ann. Appl. Probab.* **5**(4), 1217–1235.

Journal of Automated Reasoning (2005) 35: 201–235
DOI: 10.1007/s10817-005-9003-0

© Springer 2006

Applying SAT Solving in Classification of Finite Algebras

ANDREAS MEIER[1] and VOLKER SORGE[2]
[1]*DFKI GmbH, Saarbrucken, Germany. e-mail: ameier72@web.de*
[2]*School of Computer Science, University of Birmingham, Birmingham, UK.*
e-mail: v.sorge@cs.bham.ac.uk

Abstract. The classification of mathematical structures plays an important role for research in pure mathematics. It is, however, a meticulous task that can be aided by using automated techniques. Many automated methods concentrate on the quantitative side of classification, like counting isomorphism classes for certain structures with given cardinality. In contrast, we have devised a bootstrapping algorithm that performs qualitative classification by producing classification theorems that describe unique distinguishing properties for isomorphism classes. In order to fully verify the classification it is essential to prove a range of problems, which can become quite challenging for classical automated theorem provers even in the case of relatively small algebraic structures. But since the problems are in a finite domain, employing Boolean satisfiability solving is possible. In this paper we present the application of satisfiability solvers to generate fully verified classification theorems in finite algebra. We explore diverse methods to efficiently encode the arising problems both for Boolean SAT solvers as well as for solvers with built-in equational theory. We give experimental evidence for their effectiveness, which leads to an improvement of the overall bootstrapping algorithm.

Key words: application of SAT, finite algebra, mathematics.

1. Introduction

The classification of finite algebraic structures is an important task in research in pure mathematics. Often, the first step toward full classification is to determine how many structures exist up to isomorphism for each cardinality. In particular, in domains where many structures have to be considered, this is an laborious task, which can be supported by automated techniques. For instance, isomorphism-free enumeration techniques can be applied to count isomorphism classes for quasigroups and loops up to order 11 [14, 15]. While quantitative results of this type already give some insight into the size and complexity of an algebraic domains, classification theorems of a more qualitative nature are often more interesting. Their information can sometimes allow one to use properties of relatively small structures to help classify larger structures.

Automated techniques such as constraint solving and the Davis-Putnam method have been used extensively to determine the number of algebras of a given type and size, and this has answered many open questions. For instance, [6, 12, 20, 27] report on the use of model generation techniques and satisfiability (SAT) solvers to tackle quasigroup existence problems. J. Zhang was the first to use a general reasoning program to solve an open quasigroup existence problems. Later, Fujita, Slaney, Stickel, McCune, and H. Zhang used their systems to solve several open cases and reported very competitive results. More recently, completing partial quasigroups has been proposed as a structured benchmark domain for the study of constraint satisfaction methods [9]. In addition to classifying structures within an algebraic axiomatization, automated theorem proving has been used to find new axiomatizations for algebras, thus enabling better intraclassification of algebras. In particular, new representations of groups have been found [10, 11].

In [5], we have presented a bootstrapping algorithm that enables the fully verified qualitative classification of algebras up to isomorphism. The algorithm starts with only the basic axioms of a particular algebraic structure, successively computes properties to separate nonisomorphic structures, and returns a set of unique distinguishing properties for all isomorphism classes. As a simple example, given the axioms of group theory and the cardinality 6, our algorithm returns the following (paraphrased) result: "All groups of size 6 belong to either of two isomorphism classes where one contains all Abelian and the other all non-Abelian groups." The algorithm itself incorporates diverse reasoning techniques by employing state of the art systems; in particular it uses model generation, machine learning, computer algebra, and automated theorem proving to obtain its results. For instance, it incorporates the first-order prover Spass [24] to verify the results of the classification. One of the problems that needs to be proved is to show that a particular set of properties uniquely defines an isomorphism class for particular algebraic structures of a given cardinality. When conducting experiments with the algorithm, the theorem-proving part turned out to be the main bottleneck. Although Spass was the only first-order prover that solved a significant number of problems for our domain, its application is still very limited. For instance, Spass failed to solve all necessary problems for the verification of the classification of relatively small structures such as quasigroups of cardinality 5. Since our classification is concerned with finite algebras, we considered SAT solvers as substitute proof engines. In this article we present a variety of approaches to an efficient encoding of quasigroup classification problems for several types of SAT solvers and their experimental comparison. The main contribution of our work is an extension of work presented in [26] on the encoding of quasigroup problems in propositional logic and the development of three alternative approaches to encode isomorphisms between quasigroups.

In detail, Section 2 presents an overview of our bootstrapping algorithm, which has already been described in [5], concentrating mainly on the aspects that are important for this article.

In Section 3 we present a formalization of our problems in propositional logic that builds on aspects of the work done by Zhang in [26]. In particular, we use Zhang's techniques for eliminating universal quantifications over finite domains and for encoding simple equations and inequations as propositional variables. We extend his work by two approaches to deal with existential quantifications as well as by equations that contain nested operator applications. We furthermore adapt the clause normalization procedure of Nonnengart and Weidenbach [17] to produce small clausal normal forms that are suitable both for pure SAT and for solvers with built-in equational theories.

When constructing classification theorems for quasiqroups the most challenging problems are concerned with showing that all structures with certain properties are isomorphic. In Section 4 we present three encodings for isomorphisms inside satisfiability problems we have developed: a naïve way of enumerating all isomorphisms, and two more refined approaches that take advantage of computer algebra computations to reduce the number of isomorphisms by considering generating systems for the structures involved. These two approaches are particularly well suited for the domain of quasigroups.

We have tested our approaches by experimenting with three different SAT solvers: (1) zChaff [16], a Boolean SAT solver combining the Davis-Putnam procedure with Boolean constraint propagation; (2) CVClite [3], a validity checker that accepts full first-order formulas with equality as input but that reasons on propositional problems with an efficient internal SAT solver; (3) DPLLT [7], a satisfiability solver with built-in procedures and equational theory that accepts ground clauses with equations.[★] The results of these experiments – given in detail in Section 5 – show not only that employing satisfiability checking instead of theorem proving can greatly improve the power of our classification algorithm but also that the more elaborate isomorphism encodings significantly increase the solvability horizon of the single solvers.

2. Problem Domain

The problem domain for classification in finite algebra has been introduced in detail in [5]. Here we only briefly present the problem of generating classification theorems in finite algebra and illustrate it with a concrete example, to which we shall refer throughout this article. We then sketch the bootstrapping algorithm that we have designed to solve the problem and focus, in particular, on the proof problems that occur during the bootstrapping procedure.

[★] Note that the DPLLT system we use in our experiments is just one instance of the general DPLLT engine based on the very first implementation of this principle.

2.1. CLASSIFICATION PROBLEMS IN FINITE ALGEBRA

General classification problems in algebra can be defined with respect to any equivalence relation given on a class of algebras. In this article we restrict ourselves to the isomorphism relation on algebras. We define the classification problem as follows. Let $\mathfrak{A}$ be a finite collection of algebraic structures, and let $\cong$ be the isomorphic equivalence relation on $\mathfrak{A}$. Then $\cong$ induces a partition into equivalence classes $[A_1]_\cong$, $[A_2]_\cong$, ..., $[A_n]_\cong$, where $A_i \in \mathfrak{A}$ for $i = 1, ..., n$. We call the $[A_i]_\cong$ *isomorphism classes* and A_i a *representant* for the isomorphism class $[A_i]_\cong$. Thus an isomorphism class is a collection of algebras that are all isomorphic to each other.

Let P be a property that is invariant under isomorphism. Then P acts as a *discriminant* for any two structures A and B in $\mathfrak{A}$, in the sense that if $P(A)$ and $\neg P(B)$, then $A \ncong B$. If, in addition, P holds for every element of an isomorphism class $[A_i]_\cong$, but does not hold for any element in $\mathfrak{A} \backslash [A_i]_\cong$, then we call P a *classifying property* for $[A_i]_\cong$. A full set of classifying properties – with one property for each isomorphism class – comprises a classifying theorem stating that each element of $\mathfrak{A}$ exhibits exactly one of the classifying properties. The classification problem is therefore to find a full set of classifying properties.

Although our approach to solve the classification problem is general, in this article we restrict the class of algebras to quasigroups and loops. We call a non-empty set Q together with a closed binary operation $\circ : Q \times Q \rightarrow Q$ a quasigroup if, for each $(a, b) \in Q \times Q$, there is a unique $(x, y) \in Q \times Q$, so that $a \circ x = y \circ a = b$. In other words, for each pair of elements in Q there exist uniquely determined left and right divisors and therefore the property is sometimes also called *unique solvability* [18]. Moreover, for finite structures, the property guarantees that in the multiplication table of Q each element occurs exactly once in each row and each column. This property is also known as the *Latin square property*. We call a quasigroup L a loop if it contains a unit element, that is, there exists a *unit* $\in L$ such that for each $x \in L$ we have $x \circ unit = unit \circ x = x$. Note that in the general case neither quasigroups nor loops are associative. If they are associative they are groups.

An example of quasigroups of order 3 is given in Figure 1 in terms of multiplication tables for the respective operations $\circ$. In fact the five quasigroups Q_1 to Q_5 are representants of the five isomorphism classes for quasigroups of order 3. The classification problem is then to find five properties, one for each Q_1 to Q_5, that uniquely characterize each isomorphism class and moreover to show that these five quasigroups indeed represent all possible isomorphism classes.

Q_1	a b c	Q_2	a b c	Q_3	a b c	Q_4	a b c	Q_5	a b c
a	b a c	a	a c b	a	a b c	a	a b c	a	a c b
b	a c b	b	c b a	b	b c a	b	c a b	b	b a c
c	c b a	c	b a c	c	c a b	c	b c a	c	c b a

Figure 1. Isomorphism class representants of quasigroups of order 3.

2.2. BOOTSTRAPPING ALGORITHM

The bootstrapping algorithm to generate classification theorems takes a set of properties $\mathcal{P}$ and a cardinality n as input. It returns a decision tree that contains the classification theorem for the algebraic structures of order n that satisfy $\mathcal{P}$, as well as a set of representants for each isomorphism class.

The algorithm itself works as follows: Given a set of properties $\mathcal{P}$ and a cardinality n it initializes a decision tree with the root node $\mathcal{N}$ labeled with the properties $\mathcal{P}$. We denote the properties a node is labeled with by $\mathcal{P}_{\mathcal{N}}$. The algorithm then constructs an example of an algebraic structure of order n satisfying $\mathcal{P}_{\mathcal{N}}$. If no example can be produced, the algorithm will show that indeed no structure of size n with properties $\mathcal{P}_{\mathcal{N}}$ can exist. If an example exists, the algorithm does either of the following two things: (1) It shows that the node represents an isomorphism class; that is, it proves that all structures of order n that satisfy the properties $\mathcal{P}_{\mathcal{N}}$ are isomorphic to each other, or, (2) it constructs another algebraic structure satisfying $\mathcal{P}_{\mathcal{N}}$ that is not isomorphic to the first one.

In case (2) the algorithm computes discriminating properties for the two structures. Either it computes one discriminating property P such that P holds for one structure and $\neg P$ holds for the other structure, or it computes two discriminating properties P_1 and P_2, one for each structure. These properties are then used to further expand the decision tree: For one property P two new nodes $\mathcal{N}'$ and $\mathcal{N}''$ are added, with labels $\mathcal{P}_{\mathcal{N}'} = \mathcal{P}_{\mathcal{N}} \cup \{P\}$ and $\mathcal{P}_{\mathcal{N}''} = \mathcal{P}_{\mathcal{N}} \cup \{\neg P\}$, respectively. For two properties, P_1 and P_2, four new nodes have to be created: one for each of the possible combinations of discriminants, namely, $P_1 \wedge P_2$, $\neg P_1 \wedge P_2$, $P_1 \wedge \neg P_2$, and $\neg P_1 \wedge \neg P_2$.

After new nodes have been created for each of these nodes, the above steps are carried out again. The algorithm terminates once no more expansions can be applied. The leaf nodes then either represent isomorphism classes or are empty, that is, no structure exists with the properties given in the node. We generally call the former *isoclass* nodes and the latter *dead-end* nodes, and we refer to all nonleaf nodes as *branching* nodes. The final classification theorem corresponds then to the disjunction of the properties given as labels of the isoclass nodes.

An example of a fully constructed decision tree is given in Figure 2. The three represents the classification theorem for quasigroups of order 3. The leaves 2, 4, 6, 7, and 8 are isoclass nodes, whereas leaf 9 is a dead-end node. The representants of the isoclass nodes correspond, from left to right, to the quasigroups given in Figure 1 (i.e., Q_1 is the representant of node 2, and so on). To preserve space, the properties have been denoted at the edges rather than at the vertices in the tree. Thus, the properties of a node correspond to the conjunction of the properties given on a path from the vertex to the root. In addition, the basic properties of quasigroups have been omitted.

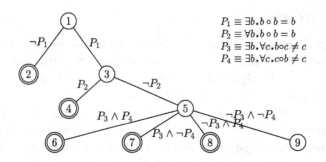

$P_1 \equiv \exists b.b \circ b = b$
$P_2 \equiv \forall b.b \circ b = b$
$P_3 \equiv \exists b.\forall c.b \circ c \neq c$
$P_4 \equiv \exists b.\forall c.c \circ b \neq c$

Figure 2. Decision tree for the classification problem of order 3 quasigroups.

The bootstrapping algorithm itself coordinates only the construction of the decision tree, while the occurring challenging deductive problems are outsourced to specialized systems:

- model generators (Finder [19], Sem [29], and Mace [13]) to generate example structures in each node,
- the machine learning program HR [4] to find discriminants, and
- automated theorem proving to solve the occurring proof problems.

2.3. PROOF PROBLEMS

The decision tree constructed by the bootstrapping algorithm represents a classification theorem and is thus the mathematical result of the classification process. For instance, the tree in Figure 2 represents the classification theorem that there are five isomorphism classes of quasigroups of order 3, which can be uniquely described by the properties associated with the isoclass nodes. The proof of the overall classification theorem is done stepwise by showing the correctness of the decision tree in each step of its construction. The proof problems resulting from these correctness checks are therefore essentially artefacts of our bootstrapping approach. In this article we concern ourselves mainly with these proof problems and describe them in more detail in the remainder of this section. The two subsequent sections discuss their encoding in propositional logic.

The proof problems can be roughly divided into two categories:

1. Checking the correctness of computations in branching nodes.
2. Establishing properties of the final classification theorem.

Problems of type 1 are mainly concerned with verifying computations from systems external to the bootstrapping algorithm, that is, model generation and machine learning. They are not strictly necessary for the construction of the decision tree but are required if we want to generate a fully verified classification theorem.

Let A, A_1, A_2 be algebraic structures, let P, P_1, P_2 be properties, and let $\mathcal{P}$ be the algebraic properties given as input to the bootstrapping algorithm. Then we can formulate the following theorems that need to be proved during the decision tree construction:

1. **Representant Theorem:** A satisfies the properties P and $\mathcal{P}$: we write formally $P(A) \wedge \mathcal{P}(A)$.
2. **Nonisomorphic Theorem:** A_1 and A_2, both satisfying P and $\mathcal{P}$, are not isomorphic $A_1 \not\cong A_2$.
3. **Discriminant Theorem:** P is a discriminant, i.e., if P holds for one algebra but does not hold for another algebra, then the two algebras are not isomorphic: $\forall A_1, A_2 . P(A_1) \wedge \neg P(A_2) \rightarrow A_1 \not\cong A_2$.
4. **Isomorphism-Class Theorem:** All algebras of cardinality n that satisfy P and $\mathcal{P}$ are isomorphic: $\forall A_1, A_2 . [\mathcal{P}(A_1) \wedge \mathcal{P}(A_2) \wedge P(A_1) \wedge P(A_2)] \rightarrow A_1 \cong A_2$.
5. **Dead-end Theorem:** No algebra of cardinality n satisfies P and $\mathcal{P}$: $\neg \exists A . \mathcal{P}(A) \wedge P(A)$.

Theorems 1–3 belong to the first of the above categories, while Theorems 4 and 5 belong to the second. In detail, the representant and nonisomorphic theorems verify the model generation: the former checks that a constructed model has indeed the desired properties. The latter verifies that the two models are indeed nonisomorphic and thus guarantees against the construction of too many isomorphism classes. Theorem 3 verifies that the constructed property is indeed a valid discriminant.

Finally, the Isomorphism-Class and the Dead-End Theorem are used to establish that the algorithm has reached a leaf of the decision tree. The Isomorphism-Class Theorem verifies that all algebras satisfying the property given by the node's label form an isomorphism class. The Dead-End Theorem, on the other hand, establishes that a leaf node is indeed empty. Both theorems can also be regarded as a verification of failed model generation attempts, either to generate a nonisomorphic model or to construct a model at all.

As an example we examine the theorems proved in the first steps of the construction of the decision tree for quasigroups of order 3 given in Figure 2. In node 1 the only property to consider is the unique solvability property for quasigroups. Q_1 from Figure 1 is generated as representant that satisfies this property. This leads to the Representant Theorem:

$$[\forall a, b \in Q_1 . \exists x, y \in Q_1 . a \circ x = b \wedge y \circ a = b]. \tag{1}$$

Then Q_2 is generated as a second model, not isomorphic to Q_1, which is shown with the Nonisomorphic Theorem

$$Q_1 \not\cong Q_2. \tag{2}$$

Given Q_1 and Q_2 the algorithm constructs the discriminant P_1, which is verified with the Discriminant Theorem and leads to the construction to two child nodes 2 and 3:

$$\forall A_1, A_2.[\exists b \in A_1. b \circ b = b] \wedge [\neg \exists b \in A_2. b \circ b = b] \rightarrow A_1 \ncong A_2. \tag{3}$$

In node 2 no further nonisomorphic model can be constructed, but instead we can show that all structures with the properties P and $\neg P_1$ are isomorphic to each other. Since with Q_1 we already have a representant of the isomorphism class, for which we have shown that the properties holds, it suffices to prove that all structures satisfying these properties are isomorphic to Q_1:

$$\forall A. \ [[\forall a, b \in A. \exists x, y \in A. a \circ x = b \wedge y \circ a = b]$$
$$\wedge [\neg \exists b \in A. b \circ b = b]] \quad \rightarrow Q_1 \cong A. \tag{4}$$

Finally, in order to give also an example of a Dead-End Theorem we have to shift our attention to node 9 in the decision tree for quasigroups of order 3. The assertion to prove is the following lengthy theorem:

$$\neg \exists A. \ \ [\forall a, b \in A. \exists x, y \in A. a \circ x = b \wedge y \circ a = b]$$
$$\wedge [\exists b \in A. b \circ b = b] \wedge [\neg \forall b \in A. b \circ b = b]$$
$$\wedge [\neg \exists b \in A. \forall c \in A. b \circ c \neq c] \wedge [\neg \exists b \in A. \forall c \in A. c \circ b \neq c]. \tag{5}$$

Although the formulation of some of the above theorems is second order, all theorems can be formulated in propositional logic and passed to a SAT solver, since we work in a finite domain. We omit a transformation to propositional logic for Discriminant Theorems, since these theorems hold in general and not only for algebras of a certain size. Indeed in our experiments in [5] the first-order theorem prover Spass proved those theorems generally without problems.

The Representant and Nonisomorphic Theorems are relatively simple to prove, even for structures of large cardinality, since they make statements about concrete structures (e.g., Q_1 and Q_2 in our example). Spass was also successful on these theorems in the experiments described in [5] but struggled and quite often failed to show Isomorphism-Class Theorems and Dead-End Theorems for quasigroups of order greater than 4 and loops of order greater than 5.[*] We shall therefore concentrate on Theorems 4 and 5 in the remainder of this article.

---

[*] In fact, Spass was the only prover that managed to show any of the Isomorphism-Class and Dead-End Theorems for structures of order greater than 4, which is documented by the results of the 2004 CASC system competition [21], where these theorems were given as new entries for the TPTP [22].

3. Specifying Theorems in Propositional Logic

In this section, we present an encoding of the theorems given in the previous section in propositional logic. While basic ideas for the encoding are taken from Zhang's article on the specification of Latin square existence problems in propositional logic [26], we extended his work in order to deal with more general and complex properties. We first discuss Zhang's approach and then generalize it for our domain. Finally, we explain the generation of different input formats for the different SAT solvers under consideration.

3.1. AN ENCODING OF LATIN SQUARE PROBLEMS

In [26], Zhang describes the encoding of Latin square existence problems in propositional logic. That is, his problems are concerned with the question of whether a Latin square A of a certain cardinality n exists that satisfies particular properties $P_1, \ldots, P_l$, where the properties P_i are of the form

$$\forall x_1, \ldots, x_n \in A.x_{1_1} \circ x_{1_2} = x_{1_3} \land \ldots \land x_{l_1} \circ x_{l_2} = x_{l_3} \rightarrow x_{r_1} \circ x_{r_2} = x_{r_3}$$

or

$$\forall x_1, \ldots, x_n \in A.x_{1_1} \circ x_{1_2} = x_{1_3} \land \ldots \land x_{l_1} \circ x_{l_2} = x_{l_3} \rightarrow x_{r_1} = x_{r_2}$$

with $x_{i_1}, x_{i_2}, x_{i_3} \in \{x_1, \ldots, x_n\}$ for $i = 1, \ldots, l, r$. Thus, the properties are restricted to the use of universal quantifiers only. They consist of simple equations without nested application of the operation $\circ$ and always have only a simple element on the right-hand side of the equations. In addition, Zhang expresses the Latin square property in this form by

$$\forall x, y, u, w \in A \cdot x \circ u = y \land x \circ w = y \rightarrow u = w$$

$$\forall x, y, u, w \in A \cdot u \circ x = y \land w \circ x = y \rightarrow u = w.$$

This formulation is equivalent to our mathematical formalization of the quasigroup property for finite cardinalities.

To specify a Latin square existence problem of the above type in propositional logic, Zhang uses the following transformation steps:

1. The second-order quantifier over a structure A is replaced by using an arbitrary structure of cardinality n, $A = \{e_1, \ldots, e_n\}$ together with a binary operation $\circ$, where the e_i are new constants. In order to make sure that the structure is indeed of order n, the n elements are explicitly stated to be distinct by adding the assumption

$$e_1 \neq e_2 \land e_1 \neq e_3 \land \ldots \land e_{n-1} \neq e_n.$$

Moreover, for each constant an instance of the reflexivity axiom is added:
$e_1 = e_1 \wedge \ldots \wedge en = en$.

2. To the list of required properties $P_1, \ldots, P_l$ which include the formalization of the Latin square property, the following properties are explicitly added:

$$\forall x, y, u, w \in A . x \circ y = u \wedge x \circ y = w \rightarrow u = w$$
$$\forall x, y \in A . x \circ y = e_1 \vee \ldots \vee x \circ y = e_n.$$

The former property is called the unique image property, whereas the latter is called the closure property. Note that these additional properties also have only universal quantifiers and consist of simple equations without nested $\circ$ operations.

3. All ground instances of the properties $P_1, \ldots, P_l$ and the additional properties with the constants $e_1, \ldots, e_n$ of the instantiation of the algebra A are constructed.

This creates clauses with ground equality, which can already be passed to a satisfiability solver with a built-in equational theory. In order to obtain a purely propositional logic formula, the following additional step is necessary:

4. Replace each ground equation $e_i \circ e_j = e_k$ by a Boolean variable p_{ijk} with $i, j, k = 1 \ldots n$ and replace each occurrence of $e_i = e_k$ by a Boolean variable q_{ij} with $i, j = 1 \ldots n$.

This results in a Boolean satisfiability problem containing altogether $n^3 + n^2$ Boolean variables.

In contrast to the properties and formulas considered by Zhang, the properties constructed during our classification procedure can be of a more complex nature. In particular, they can contain

- (nested) universal and existential quantifiers,
- terms containing nested $\circ$ operations,
- complex terms, containing applications of $\circ$, on the right-hand sides of equations, and
- further interpreted symbols such as a special unit element *unit*.

While we can directly adopt the first two steps of Zhang's transformations for our properties, we need to extend steps three and four in order to cope with the above complications. Moreover, as opposed to the properties considered by Zhang, our properties do not necessarily result immediately in clausal normal form after transformation to propositional logic. Hence, we must also explicitly consider efficient methods of clause normalization.

3.2. ELIMINATION OF QUANTIFIERS

In our properties, the first-order quantifiers ranging over elements of the instantiated algebra $A = \{e_1, \ldots, e_n\}$ can be both universal and existential. Moreover, the quantifiers can be arbitrarily nested. In order to eliminate the quantifiers to obtain ground instances, we have the choice between two different procedures, which differ wrt. the handling of the existential quantifiers.

The first approach replaces existentially quantified formulas by disjunctions over the finite set of elements. Universally quantified formulas are replaced by conjunctions over the finite set of elements. That is, for a given property all quantified subformulas in P are processed recursively: An existentially quantified formula $\exists x \in A.F[x]$ results in a disjunction of the instantiations, $F[e_1] \vee \ldots \vee F[e_n]$, whereas a universally quantified formula $\forall x \in A.F[x]$ results in a conjuction of the instantiations, $F[e_1] \wedge \ldots \wedge F[e_n]$.

We illustrate the extended quantifier elimination procedure by its application to property $P_3 = \exists b \in A.\forall c \in A.b \circ c \neq c$ from the decision tree in Figure 2, where $A = \{e_1, e_2, e_3\}$. The procedure first tackles the outside existential quantifier of P_3, which results in the disjunction

$$\forall c \in A.e_1 \circ c \neq c \vee \forall c \in A.e_2 \circ c \neq c \vee \forall c \in A.e_3 \circ c \neq c.$$

Afterwards, the three resulting universal quantifiers are tackled, yielding the following fully grounded formula:

$$(e_1 \circ e_1 \neq e_1 \wedge e_1 \circ e_2 \neq e_2 \wedge e_1 \circ e_3 \neq e_3)$$
$$\vee (e_2 \circ e_1 \neq e_1 \wedge e_2 \circ e_2 \neq e_2 \wedge e_2 \circ e_3 \neq e_3)$$
$$\vee (e_3 \circ e_1 \neq e_1 \wedge e_3 \circ e_2 \neq e_2 \wedge e_3 \circ e_3 \neq e_3).$$

An alternative approach to deal with existential quantifiers is Skolemization. The Skolemization transformation consists of three steps: (1) push all negations to the literals, (2) replace existential quantifiers by Skolem-functions, and (3) add formulas expressing the closure of the introduced Skolem-functions. The result is a formula, which contains only universal quantifiers, which can be replaced by conjunctions as described above.[*]

In the example of property P_3, Skolemization yields

$$[\forall c \in A.sk_b \circ c \neq c] \wedge [sk_b = e_1 \vee sk_b = e_2 \vee sk_b = e_3]$$

---

[*] The described procedure introduces Skolem-functions whose arity depends on the number of universal quantifiers in whose range the original existential quantifier was. An alternative is the recursive intertwined elimination of universal quantifiers and Skolemization such that only Skolem-constants, that is, 0-arity functions, have to be introduced.

where sk_b is the Skolem-function introduced for the variable b. The elimination of the universal quantifier then yields

$$[sk_b \circ e_1 \neq e_1 \wedge sk_b \circ e_2 \neq e_2 \wedge sk_b \circ e_3 \neq e_3]$$
$$\wedge [sk_b = e_1 \vee sk_b = e_2 \vee sk_b = e_3].$$

The use of Skolemization instead of a disjunctive treatment of existential quantifiers generally results in formulas with fewer and less-nested disjunctions and conjunctions. This is beneficial for the clause normalization described in Section 3.5 and is indeed helpful for SAT solvers with equational theory such as CVClite (see results of our experiments in Section 5). However, Skolemization is counterproductive for purely Boolean satisfiability solvers such as zChaff for reasons we will explain in Section 3.4.

3.3. FLATTENING

Equations containing terms with nested applications of the operation $\circ$ as well as occurrences of $\circ$ operations on right-hand sides of equations can be simplified by a process, which we call *flattening*. The idea of flattening is to recursively replace subexpressions like $x \circ y$ by new existentially quantified variables r with $x \circ y = r$ until all occurring equations are of the form $x \circ y = z$.

We demonstrate the flattening procedure with the property of associativity $\forall a,b,c \in A.(a \circ (b \circ c)) = ((a \circ b) \circ c)$. The following stepwise transformation fully flattens the occurring equations:

$$\forall a,b,c \in A.(a \circ (b \circ c)) = ((a \circ b) \circ c)$$
$$\hookrightarrow \forall a,b,c \in A.\exists z_1 \in A.(b \circ c = z_1) \wedge (a \circ z_1) = ((a \circ b) \circ c)$$
$$\hookrightarrow \forall a,b,c \in A.\exists z_1,z_2 \in A.(b \circ c = z_1) \wedge (a \circ b = z_2) \wedge (a \circ z_1) = (z_2 \circ c)$$
$$\hookrightarrow \forall a,b,c \in A.\exists z_1,z_2,z_3 \in A.(b \circ c = z_1) \wedge (a \circ b = z_2)$$
$$\wedge (z_2 \circ c = z_3) \wedge (a \circ z_1 = z_3)$$

Quantifiers introduced by flattening can then be eliminated as described in Section 3.2.

3.4. AXIOMATIZATION OF EQUATIONAL THEORY

For systems such as zChaff that provide no built-in equational theory, the necessary equational theory has to be stated explicitly. Zhang's approach already contains the encoding of a basic equational theory: step 1 adds the reflexibility of the new constants e_i as well as the condition that they are pairwise distinct. Step 2 introduces the unique image property. These axioms suffice in the general case, which deals only with fully quantified formulas without interpreted symbols. In the case of interpreted symbols, however, we have to enrich the formalization by axioms explicitly specifying further properties of equality with respect to the given symbol.

For instance, if we are dealing with loops we have to axiomatize equality for the unit element *unit* explicitly, by adding the following axioms to our problem formalization:

$$\forall x, y, z \in A. (x \circ y = z) \wedge z = unit \rightarrow (x \circ y = unit) \text{ (Substitution 1)}$$

$$\forall x, y, z \in A. (x \circ y = z) \wedge y = unit \rightarrow (x \circ unit = z) \text{ (Substitution 2)}$$

$$\forall x, y, z \in A. (x \circ y = z) \wedge x = unit \rightarrow (unit \circ y = z) \text{ (Substitution 3)}$$

$$\forall x, y, z \in A. (x \circ y = unit) \wedge z = unit \rightarrow (x \circ y = z) \text{ (Substitution 4)}$$

$$\forall x, y, z \in A. (x \circ unit = z) \wedge y = unit \rightarrow (x \circ y = z) \text{ (Substitution 5)}$$

$$\forall x, y, z \in A. (unit \circ y = z) \wedge x = unit \rightarrow (x \circ y = z) \text{ (Substitution 6)}$$

$$unit = unit \qquad\qquad\qquad\qquad\qquad\qquad\text{(Reflexibility)}$$

$$\forall x \in A. unit = x \Leftrightarrow x = unit \qquad\qquad\qquad\text{(Symmetry)}$$

$$\forall x, y \in A. unit = x \wedge unit = y \rightarrow x = y \qquad\quad\text{(Transitivity)}$$

With the introduction of the *unit* symbol, ground equations of the form $e_i \circ e_j = unit$, $e_i \circ unit = e_j$, $unit \circ e_i = e_j$ for $i, j = 1 \ldots n$ and $unit = e_i$ and $e_i = unit$ for $i = 1 \ldots n$ and $unit = unit$ can be created. Hence, to replace the equations by Boolean variables additional corresponding variables are necessary. Altogether these are $3n^2 + 2n + 1$ additional Boolean variables.

In consequence, introducing interpreted symbols adds considerably to the complexity of the theorem. This increase in complexity is the reason why the Skolemization approach described in Section 3.2 is not feasible to construct Boolean satisfiability problems since each new Skolem-function would have to be fully axiomatized as above. On the other hand, since introduced interpreted symbols can be used to construct discriminants, they can improve the bootstrapping algorithm by allowing for further discriminants (see Section 5 for an example of a discriminant with *unit*). However, since the discriminants computed in the bootstrapping algorithm never introduce new interpreted symbols, we restrict the algorithm to the symbols explicity given in the domain theory, which in our case is only *unit*.

3.5. CONSTRUCTING CLAUSAL NORMAL FORMS

The properties we are dealing with can contain an arbitrary composition of logical connectives and quantifiers. This means that the quantifier elimination of nested universal and existential quantifiers can result in lengthy and nested disjunctions and conjunctions of equational literals. In other words, our formulas –

contrary to the restricted properties considered in [26] – are generally not in clausal normal form after quantifier elimination. Hence, when working with systems that require normal form as input, such as zChaff or DPLLT, we have to explicitly perform clause normalization. Because of the nested disjunctions and conjuctions of equational literals, a naïve clause normalization approach would suffer from a combinatorial explosion of the number and the length of the resulting clauses. For our implementation, we adopted clause normalization techniques from [17] that aim to create *small clausal normal forms*. The basic technique is the introduction of additional Boolean variables to suitably *break formulas*. This avoids combinatorial explosion but extends the theorem formalization by additional propositional variables.

For instance, consider the formula $F_1 \vee F_2$. A naïve clause normalization would compute the clause set C_1 for F_1 and the clause set C_2 for F_2. The clause set of $F_1 \vee F_2$ is then the Cartesian product $C_1 \times C_2$. The following introduction of the new Boolean variable p, $(F_1 \vee p) \wedge (\neg p \vee F_2)$, is satisfiability preserving but results in a different set of clauses: If C_1' and C_2' are the clause sets of $F_1 \vee p$ and $\neg p \vee F_2$, respectively, then the clause set of $(F_1 \vee p) \wedge (\neg p \vee F_2)$ is the union $C_1' \cup C_2'$.

We can further simplify clause normalization by using Skolemization as discussed in Section 3.2, which reduces the complexity of the formulas resulting from the quantifier elimination. However, as discussed in the previous subsection, Skolemization is inappropriate for use with purely Boolean satisfiability solvers.

3.6. GENERATING DIFFERENT INPUT FORMATS

Since the aim of our formalization is to produce input for different types of SAT solvers, we conclude the section with a brief description of the transformations required to produce the different input formats we need. The three systems we are concerned with – CVClite, DPLLT, and zChaff – accept ground first-order formulas with equality, ground first-order clauses with equality, and purely Boolean formulas in clausal normal form, respectively. Therefore, all three systems require the transformation step 1 from Section 3.1, which replaces the quantifiers over algebras A by arbitrary instances of the required cardinality. All three systems also require the explicit statement of the cardinality of A, that is, that all elements of the instance of A are distinct, which corresponds to the first part of step 2 in Section 3.1. From there on, however, CVClite and DPLLT strongly differ from zChaff with respect to which further transformations are necessary.

Both CVClite and DPLLT have built-in equational theory and accept ground first-order terms as input. Thus they do not require flattening or axiomatization of the equational theory or the replacement of ground equations by Boolean variables. They require only quantifier elimination applied to the properties. For the elimination of existentially quantified variables, both treatments are possible since the equational theory for Skolem-functions does not have to be explicity axiomatized. While DPLLT needs its input in clausal form, and we therefore have to perform clause normalization, this step can be omitted for CVClite, as it accepts full formulas as input.

zChaff accepts as input Boolean satisfiability problems in the DIMACS format, which requires clauses. Hence, to create input for zChaff, the full set of transformations has to be applied in the following order: flattening, axiomatization of equational theory for additional symbols, quantifier elimination (without the option of Skolemization), replacement of ground equations by Boolean variables, and clause normalization.

4. Dealing with Isomorphisms

The formalization discussed so far can essentially deal with all properties on quasigroups that are potentially constructed during the classification process. However, it is not yet sufficient to fully deal with the most challenging problems of our domain, the Isomorphism-Class Theorems. As an example of such a problem, consider again the theorem for node 2 in the decision tree in Figure 2 already given in formula (4):

$$\forall A. [[\forall a, b \in A. \exists x, y \in A. a \circ x = b \land y \circ a = b] \land [\neg \exists b \in A. b \circ b = b]]$$
$$\rightarrow Q_1 \cong A$$

The theorem states that all structures of order 3 satisfying the quasi-group property and the property $\neg P_1$ given in Figure 2 are isomorphic to the structure Q_1 (see Figure 1).

Following the transformations introduced in the preceding section we can start rewriting the theorem by eliminating the universal quantifier on A with an arbitrary set $A = \{e_1, e_2, e_3\}$ and adding an explicit encoding of the representant structure Q_1 as additional assumption. This results in the assumptions

$$e_1 \neq e_2 \land e_1 \neq e_2 \land e_2 \neq e_3 \qquad \text{(Cardinality of } A) \qquad \}$$

$$\forall a, b \in A. \exists x, y \in A. a \circ x = b \land y \circ a = b \qquad \text{(Quasigroup property)}$$

$$\neg \exists b \in A. b \circ b = b \qquad \text{(Classifying property } \neg P_1)$$

$$e_1' \circ e_1' = e_2' \land e_1' \circ e_2' = e_1' \land e_1' \circ e_3' = e_3'$$
$$\land e_2' \circ e_1' = e_1' \land e_2' \circ e_2' = e_3' \land e_2' \circ e_3' = e_2' \qquad \text{(Representant } Q_1)$$
$$\land e_3' \circ e_1' = e_3' \land e_3' \circ e_2' = e_2' \land e_3' \circ e_3' = e_1'$$

and a conclusion of the form

$$\exists h \in \{Q_1 \mapsto A\}.\text{bijective}(h) \land \text{homomorphism}(h).$$

Observe that, unlike in Figure 2, we have denoted the elements of Q_1 as $\{e'_1, e'_2, e'_3\}$ to avoid confusion with the elements introduced for A. In a similar manner, $\mathbin{\mathrm{d}}$ denotes the operation on Q_1, in order to distinguish it from $\circ$, the operation on A. Note also that the conclusion now states explicitly that there has to exist a mapping h from the represent Q_1 to A that is a bijective homomorphism.

While we can transform all the assumptions into propositional logic using the techniques discussed in Section 3, translating the conclusion is not that straightforward. We have developed three encodings for isomorphisms inside satisfiability problems that we describe in this section. We first present the naïve approach of enumerating all possible isomorphisms, followed by two more refined approaches that take advantage of computer algebra computations to reduce the number of isomorphisms.

4.1. NAÏVE APPROACH

The conclusion of the Isomorphism-Class Theorem existentially quantifies over a mapping h from Q_1 to A. Since the structures involved are finite, we can eliminate the quantifier by considering all possible mappings between the two structures. In the general case of structures with cardinality n, there are n^n possible mappings. We can, however, reduce this number immediately by taking into account that we only have to consider bijective mappings in the first place, which leaves $n!$ possible mappings. For our example theorem there are six possible bijections $h_1, \ldots, h_6$ from Q_1 to A:

$$h_1(e'_1) = e_1, h_1(e'_2) = e_2, h_1(e'_3) = e_3 \quad h_2(e'_1) = e_1, h_2(e'_2) = e_3, h_2(e'_3) = e_2$$

$$h_3(e'_1) = e_2, h_3(e'_2) = e_1, h_3(e'_3) = e_3 \quad h_4(e'_1) = e_2, h_4(e'_2) = e_3, h_4(e'_3) = e_1$$

$$h_5(e'_1) = e_3, h_5(e'_2) = e_1, h_5(e'_3) = e_2 \quad h_6(e'_1) = e_3, h_6(e'_2) = e_2, h_6(e'_3) = e_1.$$

Given these six functions the original conclusion can be replaced by

$$\text{homomorphism}(h_1) \lor \text{homomorphism}(h_2) \lor \text{homomorphism}(h_3)$$

$$\lor \text{homomorphism}(h_4) \lor \text{homomorphism}(h_5) \lor \text{homomorphism}(h_6).$$

Here homomorphism (h_i) for $i = 1, \ldots, 6$ is an abbreviation for the homomorphism property $\forall x, y \in Q_1.h_i(x \mathbin{\mathrm{d}} y) = h_i(x) \circ h_i(y)$. Note that we can omit the bijective property for each h_i, since they are bijective by construction. The quantified variables x and y ranging over Q_1 can be eliminated as explained in Section 3.2, which results in the following conjunction of equations:

$$h_i(e_1' \circ' e_1') = h_i(e_1') \circ h_i(e_1') \wedge h_i(e_1' \circ' e_2') = h_i(e_1') \circ h_i(e_2') \wedge h_i(e_1' \circ' e_3') = h_i(e_1') \circ h_i(e_3')$$

$$\wedge h_i(e_2' \circ' e_1') = h_i(e_2') \circ h_i(e_1') \wedge h_i(e_2' \circ' e_2') = h_i(e_2') \circ h_i(e_2') \wedge h_i(e_2' \circ' e_3') = h_i(e_2') \circ h_i(e_3')$$

$$\wedge h_i(e_3' \circ' e_1') = h_i(e_3') \circ h_i(e_1') \wedge h_i(e_3' \circ' e_2') = h_i(e_3') \circ h_i(e_2') \wedge h_i(e_3' \circ' e_3') = h_i(e_3') \circ h_i(e_3').$$

Since the results of expressions such as $e_j' \circ' e_k'$ are given by the multiplication table of Q_1 we can simplify the left hand sides of the above equations to

$$h_i(e_2') = h_i(e_1') \circ h_i(e_1') \wedge h_i(e_1') = h_i(e_1') \circ h_i(e_2') \wedge h_i(e_3') = h_i(e_1') \circ h_i(e_3')$$

$$\wedge h_i(e_1') = h_i(e_2') \circ h_i(e_1') \wedge h_i(e_3') = h_i(e_2') \circ h_i(e_2') \wedge h_i(e_2') = h_i(e_2') \circ h_i(e_3')$$

$$\wedge h_i(e_3') = h_i(e_3') \circ h_i(e_1') \wedge h_i(e_2') = h_i(e_3') \circ h_i(e_2') \wedge h_i(e_1') = h_i(e_3') \circ h_i(e_3').$$

Finally, for each h_i the expression $h_i(e_j')$ can be replace by its image. For instance, in the case of h_1 this yields

$$e_2 = e_1 \circ e_1 \wedge e_1 = e_1 \circ e_2 \wedge e_3 = e_1 \circ e_3$$

$$\wedge e_1 = e_2 \circ e_1 \wedge e_3 = e_2 \circ e_2 \wedge e_2 = e_2 \circ e_3$$

$$\wedge e_3 = e_3 \circ e_1 \wedge e_2 = e_3 \circ e_2 \wedge e_1 = e_3 \circ e_3.$$

Note that in the above formula there is no reference to the homomorphisms h_i anymore. And indeed the h_i were intermediate concepts only, and the final conclusion no longer contains them anymore. Similarly, while the final conclusion describes the structures that are isomorphic to Q_1, there is no mention of the actual elements of Q_1 anymore. We can therefore also remove the encoding for the representant Q_1 from the assumptions.

Since the resulting formula contains only flat equations, it can be directly translated into a Boolean satisfiability problem. Thus the naïve approach is suitable for all the input formats we are interested in generating. It suffers, however, from combinatorial explosion. For structures of cardinality n there are $n!$ possible bijective mappings, and each mapping finally results in a conjunction of n^2 equations $e_i \circ e_j = e_k$ with $i, j, k = 1 \ldots n$. Hence, altogether the conclusion results in $n! n^2$ equation literals.

4.2. REPRESENTANT GENERATING SYSTEMS

In order to reduce the complexity of the conclusion for the Isomorphism-Class Theorems we have developed two encodings that generally result in smaller encodings. Both are based on the computation of sets of generators and factorisations to decrease the number of potential isomorphism mappings. A structure A with binary operation $\circ$ is said to be *generated* by as set of elements $\{a_1, \ldots, a_m\} \subseteq A$ if every element of A can be expressed as a combination – usually called a factorisation or word – of the a_i under the operation $\circ$. For example, Q_1 in Figure 1, can be generated by element $e_1' \in Q_1$, as both $e_2' = e_1' \circ' e_1'$ and $e_3' = (e_1' \circ' e_1') \circ' (e_1' \circ' e_1')$ can be expressed as factorisations in e_1'. We call a set of generators together with the corresponding factorisations a *generating system*.

Given a generating system, we can exploit the fact that each isomorphism is uniquely determined by the images of the generators in order to reduce the total number of isomorphisms we need to consider. If we again consider our example theorem and the generating system for Q_1 we have only three potential mappings for the generator e_1' to the elements of $A = \{e_1, e_2, e_3\}$, namely, $h_1(e_1') = e_1$, $h_2(e_1') = e_2$, $h_3(e_1') = e_3$. Taking the factorizations for e_2' and e_3' together with the homomorphism property, one can complete the mappings as follows:

$$h_1 : h_1(e_2') = h_1(e_1' \circ' e_1') = h_1(e_1') \circ h_1(e_1') = e_1 \circ e_1$$

$$h_1(e_3') = h_1((e_1' \circ' e_1') \circ' (e_1' \circ' e_1')) = (h_1(e_1') \circ h_1(e_1')) \circ (h_1(e_1') \circ h_1(e_1'))$$

$$= (e_1 \circ e_1) \circ (e_1 \circ e_1).$$

For h_2 and h_3 we get the analogous result, where e_1 is replaced by e_2 and e_3, respectively. Taking these three potential mappings, one can replace the original conclusion of the Isomorphism-Class Theorem by the disjunction

$$(\text{homomorphism}(h_1) \wedge \text{bijectives}(h_1))$$

$$\vee\ (\text{homomorphism}(h_2) \wedge \text{bijectives}(h_2))$$

$$\vee\ (\text{homomorphism}(h_3) \wedge \text{bijectives}(h_3)).$$

Here it is necessary to show bijectivity for each mapping, since it is no longer guaranteed by the construction. Naturally, it suffices to prove injectivity as the mapping is between finite structures. In other words we have to add that $h_i(e_j') \neq h_i(e_k')$ for all $j \neq k$, or in the concrete case of h_1 we add: $h_1(e_1') \neq h_1(e_2') \wedge h_1(e_1') \neq h_1(e_3') \wedge h_1(e_2') \neq h_1(e_3')$. These inequalities together with the grounded homomorphism properties can then be simplified analogously to the naïve approach in Section 3.2; that is, we simplify the left-hand sides of the equations and replace all occurrences of $h_1(e_j')$ by their respective images. This approach eventually

yields the following lenghty conjunction for h_1, which has already been simplified by removing redundant conjuncts:

$$e_1 = e_1 \circ (e_1 \circ e_1) \wedge (e_1 \circ e_1) \circ (e_1 \circ e_1) = e_1 \circ ((e_1 \circ e_1) \circ (e_1 \circ e_1))$$

$$\wedge\, e_1 = (e_1 \circ e_1) \circ e_1 \wedge (e_1 \circ e_1) = (e_1 \circ e_1) \circ e_1((e_1 \circ e_1) \circ (e_1 \circ e_1))$$

$$\wedge\, (e_1 \circ e_1) \circ (e_1 \circ e_1) = ((e_1 \circ e_1) \circ (e_1 \circ e_1)) \circ e_1$$

$$\wedge\, e_1 = ((e_1 \circ e_1) \circ (e_1 \circ e_1)) \circ ((e_1 \circ e_1) \circ (e_1 \circ e_1))$$

$$\wedge\, e_1 \neq (e_1 \circ e_1) \wedge e_1 \neq (e_1 \circ e_1) \circ (e_1 \circ e_1) \wedge (e_1 \circ e_1) \neq (e_1 \circ e_1) \circ (e_1 \circ e_1).$$

We have implemented an algorithm to compute a minimal generating system
for a given structure in the computer algebra system Gap [8] (see [5] for more
details on the algorithm). Calls to the algorithm are integrated into the overall
bootstrapping algorithm, which employs it to compute generating systems for
the representants of potential isomorphism classes. Once a generating system is
computed, the bootstrapping algorithm verifies its correctness by showing an
additional theorem that simply checks that the representant in question actually
complies with the generating system. We call this theorem *Representant Gensys-
Verification Theorem*, but since it is fairly easy to check, we will not go into
details here.

Employing the verified generating system of the representant can reduce the
number of mappings that are candidates for isomorphisms. If n is the cardinality
of the structures and m is the number of generators, then, instead of $n!$, there are
only $\frac{n!}{(n-m)!}$ possible mappings, since only the m generators have to be mapped
explicitly. However, this reduction is only effective when we produce input for
solvers such as CVClite and DPLLT that can deal with the complex terms on
both sides of the ground equations. For the generation of a purely Boolean
encoding for a SAT solver like zChaff, flattening of the equations (see Section
3.3) is required. This, however, introduces new quantifiers, which have to be
eliminated again later. For instance, to flatten the conjunct above, we need two
additional quantified variables x_1 and x_2 that replace $x_1 = e_1 \circ e_1$ and $x_2 = x_1 \circ$
$x_1 = (e_1 \circ e_1) \circ (e_1 \circ e_1)$ and whose scope is the complete conjunct. Their
subsequent elimination would result in a disjunction with nine parts, which are
the different instantiations of the variables x_1 and x_2 in the conjunct. Indeed, we
found that the factor by which the encoding is enlarged is related to the number
m of generators in the computed generating system. When there are m generators,
then there are $n - m$ factorized elements. These $n - m$ factorized elements result
in $n - m$ different terms in the ground equations, which require $n - m$ variables
for flattening. The elimination of these $n - m$ variables leads to a disjunction with
$(n - m)^n$ parts, that is, flattening and quantifier elimination enlarges the encoding
by a factor of $(n - m)^n$. This factor clearly outweighs the benefits of the reduction
of isomorphisms, and indeed experiments confirmed that zChaff's performance

was worse for this encoding as opposed to the naïve approach. Thus, employing representant generating systems is not suitable when creating Boolean satisfiability problems.

The use of generating systems is particularly suitable for structures like quasigroups. In our experiments the algorithm could generally come up with generating systems of at most two generators, even for quasigroup structures of cardinality 7. This subsequently led to at most $n(n - 1)$ possible mappings as opposed to the $n!$ mappings created by the naïve approach. For algebraic structures that tend to have large generating systems, this approach might be counterproductive. As an example, consider a semi-group A whose operation maps every pair of inputs x, y to one element c only. Its only generating system is $A-\{c\}$, which does not decrease the number of possible mappings to consider, but introduces the additional burden of proving the *Representant Gensys-Verification Theorem*. Thus, in theory the computation and usage of generating systems is generally applicable; however, its practical impact is limited depending on the type of structures considered.

4.3. GENERAL GENERATING SYSTEMS

We will now generalize our notion of generating systems to further simplify Isomorphism-Class Theorems. The idea is based on the observation that generating systems are invariants under isomorphism. That is, isomorphic structures have similar generating systems.

We can exploit this fact in our context as follows. To verify that a node in the classification tree represents an isomorphism class, we first show that every structure satisfying the properties of the node also has a generating system similar to the one for the representant of the node.[*] We call this the *General Gensys-Verification Theorem*, and, having successfully proved it, we can express the Isomorphism-Class Theorem using the general generating system.

Let's consider again our representant Q_1 together with its generating system consisting of e_1' as generator and factorizations $e_2' = e_1' \circ' e_1'$ and $e_3' = (e_1' \circ' e_1') \circ (e_1' \circ' e_1')$. From the proof of the General Gensys-Verification Theorem we know that all structures of the form $A = \{e_1, e_2, e_3\}$ with operation $\circ$ that exhibit the properties given by the node 2 in the decision tree contain a similar generating system. Without loss of generality we can fix it as follows. Let e_1 be the generator and let $e_2 = e_1 \circ e_1$ and $e_3 = (e_1 \circ e_1) \circ (e_1 \circ e_1)$. Since an isomorphism is determined by its actions on the generators, we only have to consider the 3 possible mappings of the single generator. However, as opposed to the two

---

[*] Clearly, if the node does not represent an isomorphism class, this does not have to be the case

preceding approaches, this time we consider the possible mappings from A to the representant Q_1:

$$h_1(e_1) = e_1' \quad h_1(e_2) = e_1' \circ' e_1' \quad h_1(e_3) = (e_1' \circ' e_1') \circ' (e'_1 \circ' e_1')$$
$$h_2(e_1) = e_2' \quad h_2(e_2) = e_2' \circ' e_2' \quad h_2(e_3) = (e_2' \circ' e'_2) \circ' (e_2' \circ' e_2')$$
$$h_3(e_1) = e_3' \quad h_3(e_2) = e_3' \circ' e_3' \quad h_3(e_3) = (e'_3 \circ' e_3') \circ' (e_3' \circ' e_3').$$

We can now replace the right-hand sides of the equations by the values determined by the multiplication table for Q_1, resulting in

$$h_1(e_1) = e_1' \quad h_1(e_2) = e_2' \quad h_1(e_3) = e_3'$$
$$h_2(e_1) = e_2' \quad h_2(e_2) = e_3' \quad h_2(e_3) = e_1'$$
$$h_3(e_1) = e_3' \quad h_3(e_2) = e_1' \quad h_3(e_3) = e_2'.$$

We then remove all mappings that are not bijective. While in our example all mappings are bijective, when dealing with structures of larger cardinality this step often reduces the number of mappings considerably. For the remaining mappings it suffices to show that one of them is a homomorphism to assure that there is indeed an isomorphism between A and Q_1. In other words the Isomorphism-Class Theorem is replaced by the disjunction

$$\text{homomorphism}(h_1) \lor \text{homomorphism}(h_2) \lor \text{homomorphism}(h_3)$$

As in the previous two approaches we now replace each occurrence of homomorphism(h_i) for $i = 1, \ldots, 3$ with the actual homomorphism property, eliminate the quantifiers and simplify as far as possible. In the case of the mapping h_1 this yields the following conjunction of equations:

$$h_1(e_1 \circ e_1) = e_2' \land h_1(e_1 \circ e_2) = e_1' \land h_1(e_1 \circ e_3) = e_3'$$
$$\land\, h_1(e_2 \circ e_1) = e_1' \land h_1(e_2 \circ e_2) = e_3' \land h_1(e_2 \circ e_3) = e_2'$$
$$\land\, h_1(e_3 \circ e_1) = e_3' \land h_1(e_3 \circ e_2) = e_2' \land h_1(e_3 \circ e_3) = e_1'.$$

Since the resulting equations are of the form $h_1(e_i \circ e_j) = e_k'$, the left-hand sides $e_i \circ e_j$ cannot be simplified. However, we can exploit the fact that h_1 is bijective and that the pre-image for each e_k' is uniquely determined by $h_1(e_l) = e_k'$. Hence, we can replace the right-hand sides of the equations and then drop the function application of h_1:

$$e_1 \circ e_1 = e_2 \land e_1 \circ e_2 = e_1 \land e_1 \circ e_3 = e_3$$
$$\land\, e_2 \circ e_1 = e_1 \land e_2 \circ e_2 = e_3 \land e_2 \circ e_3 = e_2$$
$$\land\, e_3 \circ e_1 = e_3 \land e_3 \circ e_2 = e_2 \land e_3 \circ e_3 = e_1.$$

This final formalization of the isomorphism contains only expressions of the form $e_i \circ e_j = e_k$, which are *a priori* flat and are therefore suitable for the translation into Boolean SAT problems as well. And, as there are at most $\frac{n!}{(n-m)!}$ – in most cases even fewer – possible mappings to consider, where m is the number of generators, the complexity is generally better than in either of the previous approaches. However, some of the complexity of general generating systems is actually hidden in the proof of the General Gensys-Verification Theorem, which we have ignored so far.

In the case of our example the theorem states that any structure A satisfying the quasigroup property and $\neg P_1$ has the same generating system as the representant Q_1. The conclusion of the theorem is therefore

$$\exists x_1, x_2, x_3 \in A. (x_1 \neq x_2 \wedge x_1 \neq x_3 \wedge x_2 \neq x_3) \wedge (x_2 = x_1 \circ x_1)$$

$$\wedge (x_3 = (x_1 \circ x_1) \circ (x_1 \circ x_1)).$$

We can now rearrange and shrink the equations by using the fact that $x_2 = x_1 \circ x_1$ holds, and therefore $(x_1 \circ x_1)$ can be replaced by x_2 in the equation for x_3. The formula then has the form

$$\exists x_1, x_2, x_3 \in A. (x_1 \neq x_2 \wedge x_1 \neq x_3 \wedge x_2 \neq x_3)$$

$$\wedge (x_1 \circ x_1 = x_2 \wedge x_2 \circ x_2 = x_3).$$

For the expansion of the quantifiers we can exploit the information from the inequalities to immediately eliminate inconsistent instantiations, which gives us the following six cases.

$$[e_1 \circ e_1 = e_2 \wedge e_2 \circ e_2 = e_3] \vee [e_1 \circ e_1 = e_3 \wedge e_3 \circ e_3 = e_2]$$

$$\vee [e_2 \circ e_2 = e_1 \wedge e_1 \circ e_1 = e_3] \vee [e_2 \circ e_2 = e_1 \wedge e_1 \circ e_1 = e_3]$$

$$\vee [e_3 \circ e_3 = e_1 \wedge e_1 \circ e_1 = e_2] \vee [e_3 \circ e_3 = e_2 \wedge e_2 \circ e_2 = e_1].$$

Our computer algebra algorithm always returns generating systems that can be shrunk such that we always have a fully flat formalization. This makes formalization of the General Gensys-Verification Theorem well suited for purely Boolean SAT solvers. Both formalization of the General Gensys-Verification Theorem and the naïve isoclass transformation consist of $n!$ cases. However, the complexity of the former is generally better since a case consists of a conjunction of $n - m$ equations of the form $e_i \circ e_j = e_k$, where $n - m$ is the number of factorizations. On the contrary, the cases for the naïve transformation consist of n^2 equations of that form. While this means that, when using general generating systems, the General Gensys-Verification Theorem is the bottleneck, in practice the approach still behaves better than the naïve approach, as described in the next section.

5. Experiments and Results

In order to test the usefulness of the different encodings, we have developed, we have conducted a number of experiments. We were particularly interested in the following three main question:

How do the different systems compare? We are interested in comparing the performance of CVClite, DPLLT, and zChaff in order to see whether the additional effort to transform our theorems from full formulas to clausal normal form and further to Boolean satisfiability problems is justified. And since our original motivation to develop encodings for SAT solvers was the limitation of first-order automated theorem provers in our domain, we are also interested in comparing the performance of the SAT approach to the first-order theorem prover Spass.

How do the different encodings compare? Here we want to test how useful the elaborate encodings for Isomorphism-Class Theorems including the computation of generating systems as opposed to the naïve encoding are. Moreover, we want to test whether the Skolemization of existential variables has an advantage over the disjunctive existential quantifier elimination for the systems CVClite and DPLLT.

How does our approach scale up? This question can be investigated along two dimensions: On the one hand, the problem size increases with increasing cardinality of the structures. On the other hand, within the same domain, problems become increasingly difficult as more and more properties are added during the classification.

In the remainder of this section we describe the general experimental setup and then discuss the results. The tables containing the actual results are given in the Appendix.

5.1. EXPERIMENTAL SETUP

In our experiments we used the solvers DPLLT, CVClite, and zChaff. The input was prepared in the format of the respective systems as described in full in Section 3.6. For a comparison with our experiments in [5] we also used Spass, where Spass received the same specification as input as CVClite.

We applied the systems to satisfiability problems from the following classification trees:

1. Quasigroups of order 5 (abbreviated as Q5) containing 1,283 isoclass nodes, 66 dead-end nodes and 1,327 branching nodes.

2. Loops of order 6 (Loops6): 109 isoclass nodes, 18 dead-end nodes, and 106 branching nodes.
3. Quasigroups of order 6 (Q6+) with additional property $\exists x.\forall y.(y \circ x) \circ (x \circ y) = x$: 13 isoclass nodes, 2 dead-end nodes and 17 branching nodes. [*]
4. Quasigroups of order 7 (Q7-qg9) with the additional property QG9 $\forall x.$ $\forall y.(((y \circ x) \circ x) \circ x) = y$: 7 isoclass and 55 branching nodes.

Except for Loops6, the above classification trees are intermediate decision trees, since the classifications were still running when we started the experiments with the SAT solvers. Hence, the number of isomorphism classes used in the experiments in this article is smaller than the actual number. Meanwhile, we have completed the classification of Q5 and Q6+. While we have also completed other classifications, for instance, the QG3–QG8 quasigroups of order 6 and 7; the resulting decision trees were too small to conduct meaningful experiments. The classifications above, on the other hand, provide a large number of challenging problems.

To answer our three main questions, we conducted a number of experiments with different settings. The experiments can roughly be divided into (1) *main experiments* applying the systems to the problems of all four classification trees wrt. a common encoding and (2) *additional experiments* applying the systems wrt. alternative encodings to problems from selected classification trees.

(1) In the main experiments we applied zChaff, DPPLT, and CVClite to all problems of the four classification trees and Spass to the Loops6 and Q6+ problems. As common encoding we took one that is suitable for all systems, namely the non-Skolemized version of the Isomorphism-Class Theorem formalization with general generating systems from Section 4.3. The results of these experiments are given in the Tables III–V in the Appendix.

For the nodes in the classification trees, we generated and checked the following problems: for dead-end nodes the Dead-end Theorems (abbreviated by Deadend-Th in the result tables), for isoclass nodes the general Gensys-Verification Theorems (Gensys-Th) and the Isomorphism-Class Theorems (Iso-Th). For branching nodes either the General Gensys-Verification Theorem or the Isomorphism-Class Theorem does not hold. Hence, there are both General Gensys-Verification Theorems (BrGsys-Th) and nontheorems (BrGsys-Nth) as well as Isomorphism-Class Theorems (BrIso-Th) and nontheorems (BrIso-NTh).

(2) For the comparison of different encodings we applied DPLLT and CVClite to the Skolemized problems from Q6+ and Q7-qg9. The results are given in Tables VI and VII. Moreover, we also applied DPLLT, zChaff, and

---

[*] The property is a generalised form of the QG3 property $\forall x.; \forall y.(y \circ x) \circ (x \circ y) = x$.

CVClite to problems from Q6+ and Q7-qg9 using different formalizations for the Isomorphism-Class Theorems; these results are given in the Tables VIII–X. In these experiments, DPLLT and CVClite were applied to both the formalization using no generating system, that is, using the naïve isomorphism encoding described in Section 4.1 (indicated by Withoutgensys in the result tables) and the formalization with representant generating system as introduced on Section 4.2 (Withrepgensys). zChaff was applied to the Withoutgensys problems only. For DPLLT and CVClite we also compared the Skolemized and non-Skolemized versions of these problems.

All experiments were conducted on a cluster of 140 identical Pentium IV machines, each with 1 GB of main memory, using SUN GridEngine to distribute the experiments. We ran the systems in a mode that would not record proof objects or traces in a file. For each single problem in each problem suite the systems got a time limit of 5 days pure CPU time and a 512 MB memory limit. While this seems to make for a very long overall time for the experiments considering the large number of problems and the relatively high failure rate in the experiments, this can be relativized by the fact that the majority of failed runs were when experimenting with CVClite, which generally failed because of reaching the memory limit after just a few hours.

The Tables III–X in the Appendix detail the results of the experiments. They are structured as follows: The first three columns state the problem domain and the name and number of theorems or non-theorems considered. The subsequent four columns give timing information in seconds; the minimum and maximum time needed to successfully solve a problem for the considered problem suite, the average run time taken only over successful runs in the problem suite, and the median run time over all runs in the problem suite, including the failed funs that received the full five day runtime (i.e., 432,000 s) as penalty. The last column gives the number of problems a system failed to solve for the considered problem set.

5.2. RESULTS

5.2.1. *Comparison of Systems*

When comparing the systems' performances in the main experiments (Tables III–V) we can observe that zChaff was, on average, the fastest system. DPLLT occasionally outperformed zChaff in minimum run-time (i.e., the fastest solution to a problem of a given category) but was slower overall. Finally CVClite and Spass clearly performed worse, in particular considering that they failed to solve a substantial number of problems. Thus, the results indicate that zChaff shows the best performance in our domain, followed, with some distance, by DPLLT. Hence, the encoding of Boolean satisfiability problems for zChaff pays off to push the solvability horizon in our domain. Moreover, the

Table I. Characteristic number for Gensys-Th problems in zChaff input.

Problem Class	Cardinality	Depth of Node	# Variables	# Clauses	Time
Q5	5	1	150	2055	<1
Q5	5	23	352	4531	132
Q6+	6	1	257	5925	286
Q6+	6	7	405	6975	4877
Q7-qg9	7	1	2401	20,594	<1
Q7-qg9	7	8	4044	24,907	6345

SAT solver zChaff and DPLLT clearly outperform the first-order theorem prover Spass.

5.2.2. *Comparison of Encodings*

When looking at different formalizations of the Isomorphism-Class Theorems we have to first consider which theorems we have to compare. For the formalization with general generating systems we are required to prove the Isomorphism-Class Theorems as well as the corresponding general Gensys-Verification Theorems, where the latter are clearly more difficult. However, for the other two formalizations, the naïve and the representant generating system formalization, the Isomorphism-Class Theorem is shown independently and essentially contains the complexity of the problem. Hence we have to compare the performance of the systems on the Iso-Th problems for these two formalizations with the Gensys-Th problems of the main experiments.

For the naïve formalization, DPLLT and CVClite performed worse than for the other two formalizations: they failed for more problems and for the problems they solved they needed considerably more time. This result is only partially true for zChaff. For the Q6+ problems zChaff's performance was on average exactly as good for the naïve formalization as for the formalization with general generating systems. For the Q7-qg9 problems it performs on average worse for the naïve formalization. This indicates that the disadvantages of the naïve formalization will have more impact for higher cardinalities.

For DPLLT the formalization with representant generating systems clearly outperforms the formalization with general generating systems wrt. to runtime. However, for Q7-qg9, DPLLT failed for more Iso-Th problems of this formalization. Since CVClite fails for almost all Iso-Th and Gensys-Th problems of Q6+ and Q7-qg9, a substantiated analysis of its performance is not possible.

Overall these results indicate that the elaborate Isomorphism-Class Theorem formalizations based on the computation of generating systems outperform the naïve formalization. A comparison of the formalization with representant generating systems as opposed to the formalization with general generating systems, which is possible for DPLLT and CVClite only, shows no clear result.

In order to test the impact of Skolemization, CVClite and DPLLT were applied to Skolemized problems of Q6+ and Q7-qg9. The results are quite different for the two systems, see Tables VI and VII. On the one hand, CVClite can solve considerably more problems with Skolemization than without and is also faster. On the other hand, DPLLT fails on more Skolemized problems and it needs more time for the problems it solves. The same behavior can also be observed for Skolemized and non-Skolemized versions of different Isomorphism-Class Theorem formalizations. Hence, there is no clear result for the impact of Skolemization for the employed SAT solvers in our domain.

5.2.3. *Scalability*

The tables in the Appendix do not give a clear scalability result wrt. to run-times and solved problems such as "the higher the cardinality of the classification tree the more difficult the problems, i.e., the longer the SAT solvers take and the less problems can be solved." Indeed, none of the three SAT solvers shows a definite increase in maximal, average, and median run-times or in the number or percentage of failed attempts with increasing cardinality of the tackled problems.

Instead we can observe a generally very high variance within the set of problems of a classification tree. For instance, consider the minimal run-time of less than one second as opposed to the maximal run-time of 266,359 seconds for DPLLT on Q7-qg9 gensys-Th problems (see Table III). There are essentially two reasons for this large variance:

- Some properties introduced during the classification are particularly well suited for the search procedures of the systems, for instance, the idempotency property $\forall x.x \circ x = x$. This effect can also be observed by a comparison of the average results of Loops6 and Q6+. Although both classifications are concerned with quasigroups of order 6, the performance of the systems on the problems of these two classes varies considerably. Whereas the unit property prunes the search rather well, the special property of Q6+ turned out to be particularly difficult.
- The deeper a node is in the classification tree, the more properties it is associated with. For instance, in the Q5 tree there are isoclass nodes at depth 5 associated with five additional properties and at depth 23 with 23 additional properties. And indeed showing theorems for the latter takes considerably longer than for the former. Moreover, the properties can become more complex than in our example classification

in Figure 2, adding to the complexity of the resulting problems. As examples consider the following properties from the Q5 and Loops6 trees:

$$\exists b. \exists c. (c \circ c = b) \wedge (b \circ b = c) \wedge (b \circ c = unit) \wedge (c \circ b = unit) \wedge b \neq unit$$

$$\exists b. \exists c. \exists d. (b \circ c = b) \wedge (b \circ b \neq c) \wedge (d \circ d = b)$$

$$\forall b. \exists c. \exists e. (c \circ b = e \circ e) \wedge (c \circ (e \circ e) = b)$$

To illustrate the impact of the properties on the complexity of the resulting satisfiability problems, consider the figures characterizing Gensys-Th problems in zChaff input in Table I. Both the number of Boolean variables and the number of clauses of the satisfiability problems increase for larger cardinalities *and* for nodes deeper in the decision tree. With the increase in complexity the time necessary to solve the problems also increases. However, we can again observe that there is not necessarily an increase in time needed wrt. to the cardinality of the structures involved.

6. Conclusion

We have presented the application of satisfiability solving in the challenging problem of classification in finite algebra. We have extended existing approaches to encode quasigroup existence problems for SAT solvers in order to deal with the more complex properties of our domain. Our developed techniques are not restricted to our problem domain but are applicable in the general case of transforming equality problems over finite domains to Boolean satisfiability problems.

The most challenging problem for our particular domain was to efficiently encode isomorphism problems by reducing the number of possible isomorphisms that have to be considered. We solved this by developing two formalizations employing the concept of generating systems that significantly improve over a naïve encoding and that are particularly effective in our domain of quasigroups. This enables us to substitute the first-order theorem provers so far used in our bootstrapping algorithm for constructing classification theorems by SAT solvers. The developed encodings are not geared toward only one particular type of solver but can be used to produce several input formats, which enables us to employ and experiment with diverse systems, such as zChaff, DPLLT, and CVClite.

The results of our experiments lead us to three conclusions. (1) SAT solvers can successfully extend the solvability horizon of our bootstrapping algorithm; that is, they clearly outperformed the first-order theorem prover Spass. Indeed, employing SAT solvers instead of Spass has led to new mathematical classification results such as a full classification theorem for quasigroups of order 5. (2) Moreover, the developed elaborate formalizations of isomorphism problems also help to push the solvability horizon of the bootsrapping algorithm even further, since for the classification of quasigroups the SAT solvers clearly perform better for the elaborate formalizations than for a naïve formalization. (3) Overall, the results indicate that zChaff shows the best performance, followed, with some distance, by DPLLT. Hence, the encoding in the less intuitive input format of zChaff pays off in our domain. Another advantage of zChaff as opposed to DPLLT is that it creates a proof trace output for unsatisfiable problems, which can be checked as a resolution proof by independent proof checkers. This is an important issue considering that we are interested in fully verifiable classification theorems.

Future work could include investigating the use of further solvers, for instance one with integrated computations for specialized mathematical domains [2]. Besides classification wrt. isomorphism it is also worthwhile to consider other equivalence relations. For instance, in terms of quantitative classifications for quasigroups and loops representatives for every isomorphism and isotopy class have been generated up to order 10 [14]. Investigating isotopism classes is even more interesting from a mathematical viewpoint than isomorphism classes; however, it might present an even greater challenge from the automated reasoning side; firstly, because finding appropriate properties strong enough to discriminate structures with respect to isotopy presents a hard problem for HR, and second, an easy transfer of our techniques to reduce the number of mappings between structures to the case of showing isotopy class theorems is not obvious.

Acknowledgements

We would like to thank Simon Colton and Roy McCasland for their cooperation on the classification of quasigroups, and Albert Oliveras Llunell, Zhaohui Fu, Clark Barrett, and Thomas Hillenbrand for their support in using the systems DPLLT, zChaff, CVClite, and Spass, respectively. We also wish to thank the anonymous reviewers for their detailed and extremely helpful comments.

Appendix

Table II. Main experiments Spass.

Domain	Problem	#	Min	Max	Avg.	Median	Fall
Q6+	BrGsys-Nth	14	14	135,450	20,515	14,251	0
	BrGsys-Th	3	–	–	–	432,000	3
	BrIso-NTh	13	8	814	319	359	0
	BrIso-Th	4	534	22,960	6732	1717	0
	Deadend-Th	2	–	–	–	432,000	2
	Gensys-Th	13	96,436	96,436	96,436	432,000	12
	Iso-Th	13	22	190,746	20,315	475	1
Loops6	BrGsys-NTh	81	<1	271,606	3692	1	2
	BrGsys-Th	25	3	63,898	10,129	432,000	17
	BrIso-NTh	77	<1	186,248	3732	2	6
	BrIso-Th	29	<1	166,906	10,426	5	6
	Deadend-th	18	27	94,713	10,058	5500	6
	Gensys-Th	109	<1	100,611	5904	432,000	56
	Iso-th	109	<1	363,181	26,907	699	27

Table III. Main experiments DPLLT.

Domain	Problem	#	Min	Max	Avg.	Median	Fail
Q5	BrGsys-NTh	1079	<1	45	1	<1	0
	BrGsys-Th	248	<1	310	29	15	0
	BrIso-NTh	872	<1	<1	<1	<1	0
	BrIso-Th	455	<1	<1	<1	<1	0
	Deadend-Th	66	<1	216	25	14	0
	Gensys-Th	1283	<1	1692	32	17	0
	Iso-Th	1283	<1	1	<1	<1	0
Q6+	BrGsys-NTh	14	1	176	27	15	0
	BrGsys-Th	3	520	3924	2319	2515	0
	BrIso-NTh	13	<1	3	1	<1	0
	BrIso-Th	4	<1	1	<1	<1	0
	Deadend-Th	2	578	1736	1157	1157	0
	Gensys-Th	13	219	5738	3345	3542	0
	Iso-Th	13	<1	3	1	<1	0
Loops6	BrGsys-NTh	81	<1	21	1	<1	0
	BrGsys-Th	25	<1	27	7	5	0
	BrIso-NTh	79	<1	1	<1	<1	0
	BrIso-Th	27	<1	1	<1	<1	0
	Deadend-Th	18	<1	14	3	1	0
	Gensys-Th	109	<1	25	5	3	0
	Iso-Th	109	<1	10	<1	<1	0
Q7-qg9	BrGsys-NTh	55	<1	83	4	1	0
	BrIso-NTh	26	<1	1	<1	<1	0
	BrIso-Th	29	<1	2	<1	<1	0
	Gensys-Th	7	<1	266,359	44,519	170	1
	Iso-Th	7	<1	<1	<1	<1	0

Table IV. Main experiments CVClite.

Domain	Problem	#	Min	Max	Avg.	Median	Fail
Q5	BrGsys-NTh	1079	<1	20,184	261	169	98
	BrGsys-Th	248	6	17,634	1788	432,000	128
	BrIso-NTh	872	<1	393	11	4	2
	BrIso-Th	455	<1	211	18	8	2
	Deadend-Th	66	<1	392,345	13,907	34,560	27
	Gensys-Th	1283	<1	20,462	670	432,000	777
	Iso-Th	1283	<1	806	20	8	0
Q6+	BrGsys-NTh	14	951	951	951	432,000	13
	BrGsys-Th	3	–	–	–	432,000	3
	BrIso-NTh	13	114	6136	2178	3712	4
	BrIso-Th	4	3256	3256	3256	432,000	3
	Deadend-Th	2	–	–	–	432,000	2
	Gensys-Th	13	–	–	–	432,000	13
	Iso-Th	13	266	3464	1082	432,000	7
Loops6	BrGsys-NTh	81	1	5131	378	604	29
	BrGsys-Th	25	15	13,866	1974	432,000	13
	BrIso-NTh	79	1	31,156	701	102	4
	BrIso-Th	27	2	1711	330	127	0
	Deadend-Th	18	10	87,957	21,221	432,000	10
	Gensys-Th	109	<1	20,776	1671	4022	45
	Iso-Th	109	8	3515	333	812	29
Q7-qg9	BrGsys-NTh	55	30	7831	785	913	19
	BrIso-NTh	26	12	22,263	1412	58	0
	BrIso-Th	29	3	3292	216	107	6
	Gensys-Th	7	12	2485	1026	432,000	4
	Iso-Th	7	2	64	23	16	0

Table V. Main experiments zChaff.

Domain	Problem	#	Min	Max	Avg.	Median	Fail
Q5	BrGsys-NTh	1079	<1	4	<1	<1	0
	BrGsys-Th	248	<1	97	12	6	0
	BrIso-NTh	872	<1	<1	<1	<1	0
	BrIso-Th	455	<1	<1	<1	<1	0
	Deadend-Th	66	<1	75	11	5	0
	Gensys-Th	1283	<1	132	13	7	0
	Iso-Th	1283	<1	<1	<1	<1	0
Q6+	BrGsys-NTh	14	<1	7	2	2	0
	BrGsys-Th	3	1590	2966	2392	2619	0
	BrIso-NTh	13	<1	5	2	2	0
	BrIso-Th	4	3	6	4	4	0
	Deadend-Th	2	1685	2182	1933	1933	0
	Gensys-Th	13	286	4877	2350	2387	0
	Iso-Th	13	<1	12	5	5	0
Loops6	BrGsys-NTh	81	<1	1	<1	<1	0
	BrGsys-Th	25	<1	13	3	3	0
	BrIso-NTh	77	<1	<1	<1	<1	0
	BrIso-Th	29	<1	<1	<1	<1	0
	Deadend-Th	18	<1	8	1	1	0
	Gensys-Th	109	<1	11	2	2	0
	Iso-Th	109	<1	<1	<1	<1	0
Q7-qg9	BrGsys-NTh	55	<1	1029	300	255	0
	BrIso-NTh	26	<1	<1	<1	<1	0
	BrIso-Th	29	<1	2	<1	<1	0
	Gensys-Th	7	<1	6345	2846	2604	0
	Iso-Th	7	<1	<1	<1	<1	0

Table VI. Skolemization experiments DPLLT.

Domain	Problem	#	Min	Max	Avg.	Median	Fail
Q6+ Skolem	BrGsys-NTh	14	<1	109	17	5	0
	BrGsys-Th	3	46,692	82,812	68,019	74,554	0
	BrIso-NTh	13	<1	<1	<1	<1	0
	BrIso-Th	4	<1	<1	<1	<1	0
	Deadend-Th	2	716	716	716	216,358	1
	Gensys-Th	13	273	185,391	94,458	166,908	4
	Iso-Th	13	<1	4	1	<1	0
Q7-qg9 Skolem	BrGsys-NTh	55	<1	230	18	2	0
	BrIso-NTh	26	<1	<1	<1	<1	0
	BrIso-Th	29	<1	3	<1	<1	0
	Gensys-Th	7	<1	33,254	11,129	432,000	4
	Iso-Th	7	<1	<1	<1	<1	0

Table VII. Skolemization experiments CVClite.

Domain	Problem	#	Min	Max	Avg.	Median	Fail
Q6+ Skolem	BrGsys-NTh	14	9	414	104	62	0
	BrGsys-Th	3	–	–	–	432,000	3
	BrIso-NTh	13	9	110	34	23	0
	BrIso-Th	4	21	51	31	26	0
	Deadend-Th	2	–	–	–	432,000	2
	Gensys-Th	13	2828	5981	3764	5981	6
	Iso-Th	13	22	111	57	61	0
Q7-qg9 Skolem	BrGsys-NTh	55	49	4227	500	265	1
	BrIso-NTh	26	11	83	40	34	0
	BrIso-Th	29	19	1116	156	58	0
	Gensys-Th	7	13	624	318	432,000	5
	Iso-Th	7	<1	94	32	29	0

Table VIII. Different isomorphism formalization experiments DPLLT.

Domain	Special	Problem	#	Min	Max	Avg.	Median	Fail
Q6+	Withoutgensys	BrIso-NTh	17	<1	155	29	7	0
		Iso-Th	13	259	10,712	3526	3412	1
	Withoutgensys+	BrIso-NTh	17	<1	135	16	4	0
	Skolem	Iso-Th	13	457	142,264	89,217	114,334	3
	Withoutgensys	BrIso-NTh	17	1	386	145	139	0
		Iso-Th	13	1	308	103	2448	0
	Withoutgensys+	BrIso-NTh	17	1	308	174	143	1
	Skolem	Iso-Th	13	131	82,404	27,069	19,256	2
Q7-qg9	Withoutgensys	BrIso-NTh	20	–	–	–	432,000	20
		Iso-Th	7	<1	<1	<1	432,000	5
	Withoutgensys+	BrIso-NTh	20	–	–	–	432,000	20
	Skolem	Iso-Th	7	–	–	–	432,000	7
	Withoutgensys	BrIso-NTh	55	<1	318	28	6	0
		Iso-Th	7	33	663	313	663	3
	Withoutgensys+	BrIso-NTh	55	<1	204	32	9	0
	Skolem	Iso-Th	7	183	211,297	105,740	432,000	5

Table IX. Different isomorphism formalization experiments CVClite.

Domain	Special	Problem	#	Min	Max	Avg.	Median	Fail
Q6+	Withoutgensys	BrIso-NTh	17	526	526	526	432,000	16
		Iso-Th	13	–	–	–	432,000	13
	Withoutgensys+	BrIso-NTh	17	13	506	87	42	0
	Skolem	Iso-Th	13	2798	7172	3988	432,000	8
	Withoutgensys	BrIso-NTh	17	767	767	767	432,000	16
		Iso-Th	13	–	–	–	432,000	13
	Withoutgensys+	BrIso-NTh	17	8	105	33	27	0
	Skolem	Iso-Th	13	1639	6374	3883	432,000	8
Q7-qg9	Withoutgensys	BrIso-NTh	20	58	805	232	291	6
		Iso-Th	7	17	1307	455	432,000	4
	Withoutgensys+	BrIso-NTh	20	56	2700	437	187	0
	Skolem	Iso-Th	7	45	610	327	432,000	5
	Withoutgensys	BrIso-NTh	55	14	5726	623	471	20
		Iso-Th	7	42	2749	1395	432,000	5
	Withoutgensys+	BrIso-NTh	55	21	2373	374	163	0
	Skolem	Iso-Th	7	317	8900	3582	432,000	4

Table X. Different isomorphism formalization experiments zChaff.

Domain	Problem	#	Min	Max	Avg.	Median	Fail
Q6+ Withoutgensys	BrIso-NTh	17	<1	4	1	<1	0
	Iso-Th	13	476	3068	2092	2105	0
Q7-qg9 Withoutgensys	BrIso-NTh	55	<1	14	2	1	0
	Iso-Th	7	341	44,092	11,264	6194	2

References

1. Alur, R. and Peled, D. (eds.): Proc. of Computer Aided Verification, *16th International Conference, CAV 2004*, Vol. 3114 of *LNCS*, Springer, 2004.
2. Audemard, G., Bertoli, P., Cimatti, A., Korniłowicz, A. and Sebastiani, R.: Integrating Boolean and mathematical solving: foundations, basic algorithms and requirements, in *Proc. of CALCULEMUS-2002, Vol. 2385 of LNAI*, 2002.
3. Barrett, C. and Berezin, S.: CVC Lite: A New Implementation of the Cooperating Validity Checker, in [1], 2004, pp. 515–518.
4. Colton, S.: The HR program for theorem generation, in [23], 2002.
5. Colton, S., Meier, A., Sorge, V. and McCasland, R.: Automatic generation of classification theorems for finite algebras, in *Proc. of IJCAR 2004*, Vol. 3097 of *LNAI*, 2004, pp. 400–414. Springer.

6. Fujita, M., Slaney, J. and Bennett, F.: Automatic generation of some results in finite algebra, in *Proc. IJCAI-13*, 1993, pp. 52–57.

7. Ganzinger, H., Hagen, G., Nieuwenhuis, R., Oliveras, A. and Tinelli, C.: DPLL(T): Fast Decision Procedures, in [1], 2004, pp. 175–188.

8. Gap: GAP Reference Manual, The GAP Group, School of Mathematical and Computational Sciences, University of St. Andrews, 2000.

9. Gomes, C. P., Selman, B., Crato, N. and Kautz, H.: Heavy-tailed phenomena in satisfiability and constraint satisfaction problems, *J. Autom. Reason.* **24** (2000), 67–100.

10. Kunen, K: Single axioms for groups, *J. Autom. Reason.* **9**(3) (1992), 291–308.

11. McCune, W.: Single axioms for groups and Abelian groups with various operations, *J. Autom. Reason.* **10**(1) (1993), 1–3.

12. McCune, W.: A Davis-Putnam program and its application to finite first order model search: quasigroup existence problems. Technical report ANL/MCS-TM-194, Argonne National Laboratory, Division of MSC, 1994.

13. McCune, W.: Mace4 Reference Manual and Guide, Argonne National Laboratory. ANL/MCS-TM-264, 2003.

14. Mckay, B. D., Meinart, A. and Myrvold, W.: Counting small Latin squares, in *European Women in Mathematics Int. Workshop on Groups and Graphs*, 2002, pp. 67–72.

15. McKay, B. D. and Wanless, I. M.: The number of Latin squares of order eleven. Submitted for publication. Available at http://cs.anu.edu.au/~bdm/papers/1s11.pdf.

16. Moskewicz, M., Madigan, C., Zhao, Y., Zhang, L. and Malik, S.: Chaff: engineering an efficient SAT solver, in *Proc. of the Design Automation Conference*, 2001, pp. 530–535.

17. Nonnengart, A. and Weidenbach, C.: Computing small clause normal forms, in *Handbook of Automated Reasoning*, Elsevier, 2001.

18. Pflugfelder, H. O.: *Quasigroups and Loops: Introduction*, Vol. 7 of *Sigma Series in Pure Mathematics*, Helderman Verlag, 1990.

19. Slaney, J.: FINDER, Notes and Guide, Center for Information Science Research Australian National University, 1995.

20. Slaney, J., Fujita, M. and Stickel, M. E.: Automated reasoning and exhaustive search: quasigroup existense problems, *Comput. Math. Appl.* **29** (1995), 115–132.

21. Sutcliffe, G.: The IJCAR-2004 Automated Theorem Proving Competition, *AI Communications* **18**(1) (2005), 33–40.

22. Sutcliffe, G. and Suttner, C.: The TPTP problem library: CNF release v1.2.1, *J. Aut. Reason.* **21**(2) (1998), 177–203.

23. Voronkov, A. (ed.): *Proc. of the 18th International Conference on Automated Deduction (CADE-18)*, Vol. 2392 of *LNAI*, Springer, 2002.

24. Weidenbach, C., Brahm, U., Hillenbrand, T., Keen, E., Theobald, C. and Topic, D.: SPASS Version 2.0. in [23], pp. 275–279.

25. Zhang, H.: SATO: an efficient propositional prover, in *Proc. of CADE-14*, vol. 1249 of *LNAI*, 1997, pp. 272–275.

26. Zhang, H.: Specifying Latin squares in propositional logic, in *Automated Reasoning and Its Applications, Essays in honor of Larry Wos*, MIT Press, 1997.

27. Zhang, H., Bonacina, M. P. and Hsiang, J.: PSATO: a distributed propositional prover and its application to quasigroup problems, *J. Symb. Comput.* **21** (1996), 543–560.

28. Zhang, H. and Hsiang, J.: Solving open quasigroup problems by propositional reasoning, in *Proc. of Int. Computer Symposium*, Hsinchu, Taiwan, 1994.

29. Zhang, J. and Zhang, H.: SEM User's Guide, Department of Computer Science, University of Iowa, 2001.

Journal of Automated Reasoning (2005) 35: 237–263
DOI: 10.1007/s10817-005-9002-1

© Springer 2005

The SAT-based Approach to Separation Logic

ALESSANDRO ARMANDO, CLAUDIO CASTELLINI,
ENRICO GIUNCHIGLIA and MARCO MARATEA
DIST, University of Geneva, Viale F. Causa, 13-16145 Geneva, Italy.
e-mail: {armando, drwho, enrico, marco}@dist.unige.it

Abstract. The SAT-based approach to the decision problem for expressive, decidable, quantifier-free first-order theories has been investigated with remarkable results at least since 1993. One such theory, successfully employed in the formal verification of complex, infinite state systems, is Separation Logic (SL), which combines Boolean logic with arithmetic constraints of the form $x - y \bowtie c$, where $\bowtie$ is $\leq, <, >, \geq, =$, or $\neq$. The SAT-based approach to SL was first proposed and implemented in 1999: the results in terms of performance were good, and since then a number of other systems for SL have appeared. In this paper we focus on the problem of building efficient SAT-based decision procedures for SL. We present the basic procedure and four optimizations that improve dramatically its effectiveness in most cases: (a) IS_2 preprocessing, (b) early pruning, (c) model reduction, and (d) best reason detection. For each technique we give an example of how it might improve the performance. Furthermore, for the first three techniques, we give a pseudo-code representation and formally state the soundness and completeness of the resulting optimized procedure. We also show how it is possible to check the satisfiability of valuations involving constraints of the form $x - y < c$ using the Bellman–Ford algorithm. Lastly, we present an extensive comparative experimental analysis, showing that our solver TSAT++, built along the lines described in this paper, is currently the state of the art on various classes of problems, including randomly generated, hand-made, and real-world instances.

Key words: SAT-based decision procedures, separation logic.

1. Introduction

The SAT-based approach to satisfiability problems beyond propositional logic dates back to at least the early 1990s (Armando and Giunchiglia, 1993), when it was noted that, under some suitable conditions, the problem of determining the satisfiability of any decidable, quantifier-free first-order theory can be reduced to Boolean search coupled with a satisfiability procedure (i.e., procedure capable of deciding whether any given set of literals in satisfiable or not w.r.t. the given theory). In more detail, the SAT-based approach to the satisfiability problem of a formula ϕ in a theory T amounts to using:

- a SAT solver to *generate* a valuation μ entailing ϕ in propositional logic, and
- a satisfiability procedure to *test* whether μ is satisfiable in the theory T,

till a satisfiable μ is found (in which case also ϕ is satisfiable), or a set of valuations whose disjunction is logically equivalent to ϕ has been generated and tested (in which case ϕ is unsatisfiable). Over the years, the SAT-based approach has been applied to more theories and even to different problems, such as propositional modal logics (Giunchiglia and Sebastiani, 1996; Giunchiglia et al., 2002), conformant planning (Castellini et al., 2003), and combination of expressive theories (Stump et al., 2002), with remarkable results. As the research proceeded, it became clear that the approach could harvest the technological improvements achieved in propositional satisfiability. See (Armando et al., 2005b) for a unifying perspective on the SAT-based approach.

Many verification and scheduling problems involve arithmetic constraints of the form $x - y \bowtie c$, where x and y are variables ranging over the reals or the integers and $\bowtie$ is $\leq, <, >, \geq, =$, or $\neq$. These constraints are called *separation terms* by Pratt (Pratt, 1977), and *Separation Logic* (from now on, SL) is the name now used to denote the logic allowing for arbitrary Boolean combination of separation terms.[*] SL is also called "difference logic" by some authors (see, e.g., Cotton et al., (2004)) and can be seen as a generalization of a well-known framework for temporal reasoning, the Temporal Constraint Network, introduced by Decther, Meiri and Pearl (Dechter et al., 1989). SL is the logic we focus on in this paper.

The first application of the SAT-based approach to a significant fragment of SL was given in Armando et al. (1999). In this case, as well as with modal logics and conformant planning, excellent results were obtained. Since then, a number of other systems for SL have appeared (see, e.g., Oddi and Cesta, 2000; Audemard et al., 2002; Strichman et al., 2002; Armando et al., 2005a; Cotton et al., 2004).

In this paper we focus on the problem of building efficient SAT-based decision procedures for SL. To this end, we present the basic procedure and four optimizations that improve dramatically its effectiveness in most cases: (a) IS_2 preprocessing, (b) early pruning, (c) model reduction, and (d) best reason detection. Optimizations (a) and (b) were first proposed in Armando et al. (1999), whereas (c) and (d) have been presented for the first time in Armando et al. (2005a). For each technique we give an example of how it might improve performance. Furthermore, for the first three techniques, we give a pseudo-code representation and formally state the soundness and completeness of the corresponding procedure. We also show how it is possible to check the satisfiability of valuations involving constraints of the form $x - y < c$ using the well-known Bellman–Ford algorithm (from now on, BF).

We then present an extensive comparative experimental analysis, showing that our solver TSAT++, built along the theoretical lines of the approach, is

---

[*] Unfortunately, the name *Separation Logic* is also used to denote an extension of Hoare logic. Strichman et al. (2002) is the first reference we are aware of where the name is resumed from Pratt's paper.

currently the state of the art on various classes of problems, including randomly generated, hand-made, and real-world instances.

The paper is structured as follows. Section 2 is about SL and presents its syntax, semantics, and some other formal properties of SL; Section 3 introduces the basic SAT-based procedure for SL, while the optimizations are presented in Section 4; in Section 5 we present a satisfiability algorithm for valuations based on BF; in Section 6 we describe the actual implementation of our system and present a thorough experimental evaluation; in Section 7 we outline the related work; lastly, in Section 8 we have the conclusions.

2. Theoretical Background

In this section we give some theoretical background and fix the terminology that will be used throughout the paper.

2.1. SEPARATION LOGIC

2.1.1. *Syntax*

Let V and P be two disjoint sets of symbols, called *variables* and *propositional letters*, respectively. A *constraint* is an expression of the form $x - y \bowtie c$, where $x, y \in V$, $\bowtie \in \{\leq, <, >, \geq, =, \neq\}$ and c is a numeric constant. The notations $\underline{x} \bowtie y + c$ and $x - c \bowtie y$ will also be freely used in place of $x - y \bowtie c$. An *atom* is either a constraint or a propositional letter. A *formula* is a combination of atoms via the unary connective "$\neg$" for negation and the n-ary connectives "$\wedge$" and "$\vee$" ($n \geq 0$) for conjunction and disjunction, respectively. We will write $\top$ and $\bot$ for the empty conjunction and the empty disjunction, respectively. A *literal* is either an atom or its negation. If a is an atom, then $\bar{a}$ abbreviates $\neg a$ and $\overline{\neg a}$ stands for a.

EXAMPLE 1. In Bryant et al. (2002), the case-study is introduced of a bounded model checking problem for the memory unit of the Motorola Elf microprocessor. The unit is initially modeled as 20 K lines of VERILOG, with 80 integer-valued variables and 70 propositional letters. After some translation stages, the problem is reduced to checking satisfiability of a formula in SL, a fragment of which, call it ϕ_{Elf}, looks like this:

$$
\begin{array}{ll}
(p_1 \vee \neg(VPred = I_{RR})) & \wedge \\
(\neg p_1 \vee VPred = I_{RR}) & \wedge \\
(\neg p_2 \vee VPred < I_{RR} + 1) & \wedge \\
(p_2 \vee \neg(VPred < I_{RR} + 1)) & \wedge \\
(p_3 \vee p_4) & \wedge \\
(p_3 \vee \neg p_4 \vee \neg VenI' = VenI) & \wedge \\
(p_5 \vee \neg(VenI' + 2 = VenI)) & \wedge \\
(\neg p_5 \vee VenI' + 2 = VenI)
\end{array}
$$

In the above formula, $VPred$, I_{RR}, $VenI$, $VenI'$ are variables and p_1, p_2, p_3, p_4, p_5 are propositional letters. $VPred < I_{RR} + 1$ is a constraint, and $p5$ and $\neg(VenI' + 2 = VenI)$ are literals.

2.1.2. Semantics

Let the set $\mathbb{D}$ (*domain of interpretation*) be either the set of the real numbers $\mathbb{R}$ or the set of integers $\mathbb{Z}$. An *assignment* is a total function mapping variables to $\mathbb{D}$ and propositional letters to the truth values *false* and *true*, standing for falsehood and truth respectively.

Let σ be an assignment and ϕ be a formula. Then $\sigma \vDash \phi$ (σ satisfies *a formula* ϕ) is defined as follows.

$\sigma \vDash x - y \bowtie c$ if and only if $\sigma(x) - \sigma(y) \bowtie c$,
$\sigma \vDash p$ with $p \in \mathcal{P}$ if and only if $\sigma(p) = true$,
$\sigma \vDash \neg\phi$ if and only if it is not the case that $\sigma \vDash \phi$,
$\sigma \vDash (\bigwedge_{i=1}^{n} \phi_i)$ if and only if for each $i \in [1, n]$, $\sigma \vDash \phi_i$, and
$\sigma \vDash (\bigvee_{i=1}^{n} \phi_i)$ if and only if for some $i \in [1, n]$, $\sigma \vDash \phi_i$.

If $\sigma \vDash \phi$, then σ will also be called a *model* of ϕ. We also say that

- a formula ϕ is *satisfiable* if and only if there exists an assignment satisfying it;
- a formula ϕ is *valid* if and only if every assignment satisfies it;
- two formulas ϕ and ψ are *logically equivalent* if and only if the formula $(\neg\phi \vee \psi) \wedge (\phi \vee \neg\psi)$ is valid.

Here we consider the problem of deciding whether a formula is satisfiable or not in the given domain of interpretation $\mathbb{D}$. Notice that satisfiability of a formula depends on $\mathbb{D}$, e.g., $x - y > 0 \wedge x - y < 1$ is clearly satisfiable if $\mathbb{D}$ is $\mathbb{R}$ but unsatisfiable if $\mathbb{D}$ is $\mathbb{Z}$. However, the problems of checking satisfiability in $\mathbb{Z}$ and $\mathbb{R}$ are closely related and will be treated uniformly almost always. Therefore, from now on, we will drop the distinction, and we will reintroduce it only when needed.

EXAMPLE 2. Consider Example 1. ϕ_{Elf} is satisfiable, and a model is $\sigma = \{p_1 \mapsto true, VPred \mapsto 12, I_{RR} \mapsto 12, p_2 \mapsto true, p_3 \mapsto true, p_4 \mapsto true, p_5 \mapsto true, VenI \mapsto 10, VenI' \mapsto 8\}$.

2.2. VALUATIONS

A *valuation* is a finite set μ of literals such that for each atom a, if $a \in \mu$ then $\neg a \notin \mu$. In the following if μ is a valuation, then by μ we also denote the formula $\bigwedge_{l\in\mu}l$. Context will make clear what is intended. Moreover, we say that

1. a valuation μ *propositionally entails* a formula ϕ if $(\neg\mu \wedge \phi)$ can be proved in propositional logic;
2. two formulas are *propositionallly logically equivalent* if one formula propositionally entails the other, and *vice versa*.

The following result shows the importance of valuations.

THEOREM 3. *A formula ϕ is satisfiable if and only if there exists a valuation μ such that*

1. *μ is satisfiable,*
2. *all atoms in μ occur in ϕ, and*
3. *μ propositionally entails ϕ.*

Proof. The right-to-left direction is trivial. For the left-to-right direction, first notice that it is always possible to convert ϕ to a logically equivalent formula in the same atoms and in disjunctive normal form (DNF). Let S be the set of disjuncts in the DNF. Then by the semantics of $\wedge$ it follows that ϕ is satisfiable if and only if there is $\mu \in S$ such that μ is satisfiable. Furthermore, for such μ, also the second and third properties hold. $\square$

Given the above result, in order to check the satisfiability of a formula ϕ, the issue becomes that of efficiently building a set S of valuations that is *propositionally complete for* ϕ, that is, such that the disjunction of the valuations in S is propositionally logically equivalent to ϕ. Given such a set, we can then separately check the satisfiability of its elements.

3. The SAT-based Approach to Separation Logic

Theorem 3 lays the foundation of a simple method for determining the satisfiability of a formula ϕ:

1. *generate* a set S of valuations that is propositionally complete for ϕ, and then
2. *test* whether at least one of the valuations in S is satisfiable: if this is the case, then ϕ is satisfiable; otherwise ϕ is unsatisfiable.

Further, if one valuation μ in S is satisfiable, then the models of μ are also models of ϕ. Thus, in the above schema, the problem of finding a model of an arbitrary formula has been reduced to the problem of finding a model of a valuation. Notice that the ability to return a model if the formula is satisfiable is highly desirable in many applications. For example, if the formula represents an instance of a bounded model-checking problem, then from any model of the formula it is usually possible to extract a trace witnessing the violation of the desired property.

The reason why this method has become quite popular is that state-of-the-art SAT solvers can be employed to efficiently generate valuations on-the-fly. In fact, valuations propositionally entailing the formula can be generated one by one, and each can then be checked for satisfiability before generating the next one, until a positive answer is returned, or there are no more valuations left. This way the need to generate all (potentially exponentially many) satisfying valuations beforehand is avoided. This is the foundation of the SAT-based approach, first envisioned in Armando and Giunchiglia (1993) and first applied to SL in Armando et al. (1999).

The reasons of its success are at least three:

1. more than 40 years of research on propositional satisfiability have made SAT solvers reliable, efficient and, in some cases, reusable;
2. the two phases, namely, enumeration and satisfiability checking, can be effectively decoupled, nevertheless allowing for a great deal of search guiding information to flow between the modules that take care of each phase;
3. the range of theories this approach can tackle is quite wide and interesting.

In the rest of this section we give a precise characterization of the SAT-based approach and prove its fundamental properties.

Without loss of generality, in the following we assume that all formulas are in conjunctive normal form (CNF) and do not contain any constraint of the form $x - y - c$ or $x - y \neq c$. Constraints of the form $x - y = c$ and $x - y \neq c$ can be always replaced by the logically equivalent formulas $(x - y \leq c) \wedge (x - y \geq c)$ and $(x - y > c) \vee (x - y < c)$ respectively. Further, by using the structure-preserving clause form transformation described in, for example, Tseitin, 1970; Plaisted and Greenbaum, 1986, translation in CNF can be done efficiently. Given the CNF assumption, a formula is represented as a conjunctively intended set of clauses, each *clause* being a disjunctively intended set of literals.

3.1. BASIC PROCEDURE

A pseudo-code description of a procedure that can be used to carry out the propositional analysis phase is given in Figure 1. It is essentially the Davis, Logemann and Loveland algorithm (from now on, DLL) (Davis et al., 1962) for propositional satisfiability extended in such a way to support the enumeration of all the valuations propositionally entailing the input formula.

```
function DLL_ENUM(φ,μ)
 1  if {} ∈ φ then return FALSE
 2  if φ = ∅ then Print(μ); return FALSE
 3  if {l} ∈ φ then return DLL_ENUM(Simplify(l,φ),μ ∧ l)
 4  l := ChooseLiteral(φ)
 5  return DLL_ENUM(Simplify(l,φ),μ ∧ l) or
           DLL_ENUM(Simplify(l̄,φ),μ ∧ l̄)
```

Figure 1. DLL algorithm as enumerator.

In the procedure:

1. Simplify (l, ϕ) simplifies the formula ϕ under the assumption that the literal l is true. This is done by removing from ϕ all clauses in which l appears and by moving $\bar{l}$ from all clauses in which $\bar{l}$ appears;
2. ChooseLiteral(ϕ) picks a literal l in ϕ according to some heuristic function.

Notice that if $\phi = \emptyset$, then the current valuation, μ, is printed and FALSE is returned so as to force backtracking.

There is strong empirical evidence in the literature (see, e.g., Le Berre and Simon (2003)) that DLL is the current best among the complete algorithms for solving the SAT problem. A number of improvements to DLL have been proposed, especially on the heuristic function used in ChooseLiteral(ϕ), on the data structures employed, on the way unit propagation and backtracking are performed, but the basic algorithm still stands unchanged.

LEMMA 4 (DLL as an enumerator). *Let ϕ be a propositional formula. DLL_ENUM(ϕ, ⊤) prints a set of valuations that is propositionally complete for ϕ.*
   Proof. The statement is proved in Giunchiglia et al. (2002).   □

DLL_ENUM(ϕ,μ) can be readily turned into a decision procedure for SL as shown in Figure 2. The modifications are limited to the case in which $\phi = \emptyset$ Instead of printing μ and unconditionally returning FALSE, we now return the result of invoking SatCheck(μ), where SatCheck(μ) is a satisfiability procedure for valuations, that is, it returns TRUE if μ is satisfiable, and FALSE otherwise. This procedure clearly depends on the decidable theory under consideration. As we will see in Section 5, a satisfiability procedure for SL valuations can be readily built by using BF, which runs in polynomial time (see, e.g., Cormen et al. (2001)).

THEOREM 5 (Soundess and completeness of TSAT). *Let ϕ be a formula. Then TSAT $(\phi, ⊤)$ returns TRUE if ϕ is satisfiable, and FALSE otherwise.*
   Proof. It readily follows from Theorem 3, from the soundness and completeness of the DLL algorithm, and from Lemma 4.   □

```
function TSAT(φ,μ)
  1  if {} ∈ φ then return FALSE
  2  if φ = ∅ then return SatCheck(μ)
  3  if {l} ∈ φ then return TSAT(Simplify(l,φ),μ ∧ l)
  4  l := ChooseLiteral(φ)
  5  return TSAT(Simplify(l,φ),μ ∧ l) or
            TSAT(Simplify(l̄,φ),μ ∧ l̄)
```

Figure 2. Basic SAT-based decision procedure based on DLL.

EXAMPLE 6. Once again, let us consider Example 1. Assume, moreover, that ChooseLiteral simply returns the first atom in lexicographical order. Then here is how TSAT (ϕ_{Elf}, T) works:

1. since there are no unit clauses, p_1 is chosen and $\mu = \{p_1\}$;
2. after Simplify (p_1, ϕ_{Elf}) is executed, the second clause has become unit since $\neg p_1$ has been removed from it; therefore $VPred = I_{RR}$ is detected as appearing in a unit clause and added to μ;
3. same as Items 1 and 2, but with p_2 and $VPred < I_{RR} + 1$; now $\mu = \{p_1, VPred = I_{RR,p2}, VPRED < I_{RR} + 1\}$;
4. again, there are no unit clauses, and therefore p_3 is chosen and added to μ;
5. after Simplify (p_3, ϕ_{Elf}) is executed, no unit clauses are left, so p_5 is chosen and added to μ;
6. lastly, $VenI' + 2 = VenI$ is detected in a unit clauses and added to μ where now $\{p_1, VPred = I_{RR,p2}, VPred < I_{RR} +1, p_3, p_5, VenI' + 2 = VenI\}$;
7. ϕ_{Elf} has now become empty; SatCheck is called and a model of μ, which also is a model of ϕ_{Elf}, is found, for instance, the model in Example 2.

4. Optimizations

The clear separation between the enumeration of valuations propositionally entailing ϕ and the check of their satisfiability is the key feature of the SAT-based approach to building decision procedure. However, the naïve application of this idea may suffer from the generation of exponentially many unsatisfiable valuations. The reason for this inefficiency is that the SAT solver is not aware of the properties of the background theory, in our case SL. To illustrate this point, let us again consider the problem of Example 1. If $VPred = I_{RR}$ is assigned to true then it is pointless to assign false to $VPred < I_{RR} + 1$ as this valuation (or any extension thereof) will be later found to be unsatisfiable and hence rejected by SatCheck.

As a matter of fact most optimizations to the basic procedure that have been proposed in the literature aim at preventing the generation of unsatisfiable (and hence useless) valuation. In this section we described four optimization that – as shown in Section 6 – make TSAT++ the current fastest decision procedure for SL on a wide range of benchmark problems.

4.1. IS_n PREPROCESSING

To reduce the enumeration of unfruitful valuations at a reasonable price, Armando et al., 1999 introduced the so-called IS_n preprocessing. The name stands for *inconsistent subsets* and the subscript number represents the size of the subsets sought for. Naively put, if P is the set of constraint literals occurring positively in the input formula, IS_n checks the satisfiability of all the valuations P' subset of P such that $|P'| \le n$: for each unsatisfiable subset P', the clause $\bigvee_{l \in P'} \bar{l}$ is added to the imput formula before calling TSAT.

Although IS_n can be exponential in general, for each fixed n polynomially many subsets of cardinality n exists, and if satisfiability checking is done in polynomial time, the resulting procedure runs in polynomial time.

For a given value of n, it also makes sense to generalize the idea in order to check the satisfiability of set P, with $|P| \le n$, of literals whose atom occurs in the input formula. To ease the presentation, we restrict to the case in which $n = 2$. The generalization of IS_2 works as follows: for each unordered pair $\{c_i, c_j\}$ of distinct SL-constraints appearing in ϕ and involving the same variables, all possible pairs of literals built out of them are checked for satisfiability.

The resulting optimized version of TSAT is given in Figure 3.

THEOREM 7   (Soundness and completeness of TSAT_IS_2). *Let ϕ be a formula. Then* TSAT_IS_2 (ϕ) *returns* TRUE *if ϕ satisfiable, and* FALSE *otherwise.*

   Proof. By Theorem 5, since ϕ_0 is logically valid and therefore ϕ and $\phi_0 \wedge \phi$ are logically equivalent.   □

EXAMPLE 8.   Consider Example 1 once more. After the preprocessing step of TSAT_$IS_2(\phi_{Elf})$, the clauses

$$\neg(VPred = I_{RR}) \vee VPred < I_{RR} + 1$$

and

$$\neg(VenI' = VenI) \vee \neg(VenI' + 2 = VenI)$$

are added to ϕ_{Elf}. These added clauses allow for more pruning while descending the search tree.

```
function TSAT_IS₂(φ)
1    let φ₀ := ⊤
2    foreach unordered pair of SL-constraints {cᵢ, cⱼ} in φ
3              involving the same variables,
4        if SatCheck(cᵢ ∧ cⱼ)=FALSE then    φ₀ := φ₀ ∧ (¬cᵢ ∨ ¬cⱼ)
5        else if SatCheck(¬cᵢ ∧ cⱼ)=FALSE then    φ₀ := φ₀ ∧ (cᵢ ∨ ¬cⱼ)
6        else if SatCheck(cᵢ ∧ ¬cⱼ)=FALSE then    φ₀ := φ₀ ∧ (¬cᵢ ∨ cⱼ)
7        else if SatCheck(¬cᵢ ∧ ¬cⱼ)=FALSE then    φ₀ := φ₀ ∧ (cᵢ ∨ cⱼ)
8    return TSAT((φ₀ ∧ φ),⊤)
```

Figure 3. IS_2 preprocessing.

Consider Example 6. In TSAT_$IS_2(\phi_{Elf})$, choosing p_1 forces $VPred = I_{RR}$ by unit propagation; but now, thanks to the clause added by IS_2, this also forces $VPred < I_{RR} + 1$, which in turn forces p_2. TSAT (ϕ_{Elf}, $\top$) on the other hand, had to branch on p_2.

IS_2 is a simple way of guiding the generation phase by taking into account the structure of the constraints in the input formula. IS_2 has been proved to speed the search, especially on randomly generated problems such as the binary disjunctive temporal problems (DPTs), which are made of binary clauses containing constraints only (see Section 6.1). In that case, the effectiveness of the technique is dramatic, since adding more binary clauses, which is what IS_2 does, paves the way to detect and propagate more unit clauses once a literal has been selected by ChooseLiteral.

4.2. EARLY PRUNING

An alternative approach that aims at limiting the generation of unsatisfiable valuations is based on the idea of checking the valuations while they are generated by TSAT. This technique is called *early pruning* (EP) and relies on the fact that no unsatisfiable valuation can be extended into a satisfiable one by adding more constraints. EP can be readily incorporated in TAST, as shown in Figure 4.

THEOREM 9 (Soundness and completeness of TSAT_EP). *Let ϕ be a formula.* TSAT_EP (ϕ, $\top$) *returns true if ϕ is satisfiable, and* FALSE *otherwise.*

Proof. By Theorem 5 we know that TSAT is sound and complete. Now, first notice that TSAT_EP differs from TSAT only in that one more recursion base case, possibly returning FALSE, has been introduced at line 4. This fact ensures soundness of the function: if TSAT finds no model of ϕ, neither will TSAT_EP.

As far as completeness is concerned, assume by contradiction that a satisfiable valuation μ is found by TSAT, which is not found by TSAT_EP. By the above consideration, this means that a subset of μ, call it μ', must have been reached by

```
function TSAT_EP(φ,μ)
   1   if {} ∈ φ then return FALSE
   2   if φ = ∅ then return SatCheck(μ)
   3   if {l} ∈ φ then return TSAT_EP(Simplify(l,φ),μ ∧ l)
   4   if SatCheck(μ)=FALSE then return FALSE
   5   l := ChooseLiteral(φ)
   6   return TSAT_EP(Simplify(l,φ),μ ∧ l) or
              TSAT_EP(Simplify(l̄,φ),μ ∧ l̄)
```

Figure 4. TSAT with early pruning.

TSAT_EP and rejected. This means that μ' is unsatisfiable and μ, a superset of it, is satisfiable, which is contradictory. □

EXAMPLE 10. Consider Example 1, TSAT_EP as in the figure, and assume ChooseLiteral returns the first literal that appears in the formula. Then, TSAT_EP $(\phi_{Elf}, \top)$ picks and add to μ, in turn, p_1, $VPred = I_{RR}$ and $\neg p_2$. The last choice force $\neg(VPred < I_{RR} + 1)$ into μ by unit propagation, but clearly the valuation is now unsatisfiable. Therefore backtracking happens, and both $\neg(VPred < I_{RR} + 1)$ and $\neg p_2$ are removed from μ. ChooseLiteral then switches to p_2, and the algorithm goes on as in Example 6.

Notice that in this case TSAT, with the same ChooseLiteral, would have explored a totally useless portion of the search space, namely, checking all models prefixed with the unsatisfiable μ detected above by EP.

4.3. MODEL REDUCTION

A further optimization, called *model reduction*, is based on the observation that a valuation μ generated by TSAT can be *redundant*; that is, there might exist a valuation $\mu' \subset \mu$ that propositional entails the input formula. When this is the case, we can check the satisfiability of μ' instead μ. This has the following advantages:

1. if μ and μ' are either both satisfiable or both unsatisfiable, then the value returned by SatCheck is the same. However, checking the satisfiability of μ' can be easier if we use, for example, BF.
2. if μ is unsatisfiable, it may nevertheless be the case that μ' is satisfiable: in this case SatCheck(μ') returns TRUE, thereby pruning any further search.

Model reduction can be easily incorporated in TSAT as shown in Figure 5. The main difference with respect to TSAT is that the reduced valuation μ', rather than μ, is checked for satisfiability. It is assumed that ReduceModel(μ) returns a valuation $\mu' \subseteq \mu$ propositionally entailing the initial input formula.

THEOREM 11 (Soundness and completeness of TSAT_MR). *Let ϕ be a formula.* TSAT_MR $(\phi, \top)$ *returns* TRUE *if ϕ is satisfiable, and* FALSE *otherwise.*

Proof. It suffices to note that, since $\mu' \subseteq \mu$, there are three possible cases: both μ' and μ are satisfiable; both are unsatisfiable; or μ' is satisfiable, but μ is not. In the first two cases, SatCheck(ReduceModel(μ)) coincides with SatCheck(μ); in the third case, a satisfiable valuation propositionally entailing the input formula has been found, and the algorithm terminates. □

Here again it is important to check that, on average, the time spent in reducing the valuation does not overwhelm the advantage gained by reduc-

```
function TSAT_MR(φ,μ)
  1  if {} ∈ φ then return FALSE
  2  if φ = ∅ then return SatCheck(ReduceModel(μ))
  3  if {l} ∈ φ then return TSAT_MR(Simplify(l,φ),μ ∧ l)
  4  l := ChooseLiteral(φ)
  5  return TSAT_MR(Simplify(l,φ),μ ∧ l) or
           TSAT_MR(Simplify(l̄,φ),μ ∧ l̄)
```

Figure 5. TSAT with model reduction.

ing it. So far, we have been experimenting with two techniques for reducing valuations:

Triggering: if μ contains a literal l that does not belong to any clause in the input formula ϕ, then μ propositionally entails ϕ if and only if $\mu\backslash\{l\}$ does; therefore l can be safely removed from μ. This technique, introduced in Wolfman and Weld (1999), is called *triggering*. Triggering has a linear cost in $|\mu|$ if realized, for example, via a simple table of the occurrences of literals in ϕ.

Minimization: a better idea is to remove as many redundant constraint literal l as possible. This can be done by recursively eliminating from μ one constraint literal l at a time such that for each clause C containing l, there exists another literal l' in $\mu \cup C$. Minimization can be done in linear time in the size of the input formula ϕ provided that a data structure associating to each literal l the clauses of ϕ whom l belongs to is available.

EXAMPLE 12. Consider again ϕ_{Elf}; in this case, a possible valuation found by TSAT_MR is $\mu = \{p_1, VPred = I_{RR}, p_2, VPred < I_{RR} + 1, VenI' = VenI, p_4, p_3, p_5, VenI' + 2 = VenI\}$. A reduced version of it, according to minimization, is $\mu' = \{p_1, VPred = I_{RR}, p_2\ VPred < I_{RR} + 1, p_3, p_4, p_5, VenI' + 2 = VenI\}$, obtained from μ by removing the constraint literal $VenI' = VenI$. Further, while μ is unsatisfiable, μ' is not.

Given a valuation μ it is important to notice that model reduction that is, ReducedModel(μ) in Figure 5, does not consider the set *IS* of clauses possibly added by IS_n to the input formula ϕ: these clauses are valid and thus do not need to be taken into account. Considering them would slow ReduceModel(μ) and, even worse, may partly shadow its effects. In fact if μ' and μ'' are the valuations returned by ReduceModel(μ) when considering ϕ and $\phi \cup IS$ respectively, we have that $\mu' \subseteq \mu''$. Furthermore, ReducedModel(μ) is not performed when the valuation μ does not propositionally entail the input formula ϕ, that is, when we are checking the satisfiability of a valuation because of early pruning. Indeed, with early pruning we hope to detect the unsatisfiability of μ in order to cut the search. On the other hand, it may be the case that $\mu' =$ ReducedModel(μ) in satisfiable while μ is not: in this case, considering μ' instead of μ would make vain early pruning.

4.4. BEST REASON DETECTION

So far, we have discussed how to extend an SAT solver in order to obtain a decider for SL, focusing in particular on SAT solvers based on DLL. Our motivation for this has been that most of the state-of-the-art complete SAT solvers are based on DLL. However, such solvers extend the basic DLL procedure in different ways in order to be more effective on different classes of problems. Broadly speaking, we can divide such solvers in two categories, following the distinction that is usually made in the SAT competition (Le Berre and Simon, 2003):

- those designed for real-world problems, e.g., zchaff (Moskewicz et al., 2001), the winner of the last SAT competition in this category. The features of these solvers are that they have a fast-to-compute heuristics, a simple but efficient pruning mechanism based on unit propagation, and a sophisticated backtracking mechanism based on back-jumping and learning (see Moskewicz et al., 2001).
- those designed for solving difficult either randomly generated or hand-made problems, for example, kcnfs (Dequen and Dubois, 2004) and March_eq (Heule and Maaren, 2005) the winners of the last SAT competition in these categories. These solvers have a complex-to-compute heuristics, sophisticated pruning mechanisms significantly extending unit-propagation, and a simple but efficient back-tracking mechanism without learning.

The modification needed in order to obtain a SAT-based solver for SL can be done along the lines so far outlined if we start from a solver without back-jumping and/or learning. Still, in case we want to use a backtracking schema based on learning, whenever FALSE is returned, a "reason" for the failure has to be computed. Intuitively, whenever we are backtracking from a valuation μ, a reason is a subset μ' of μ such that any valuation extending μ' will fail. While backtracking, these reasons μ' are used in order to back-jump over the literals which are not in μ'. Further, if the solver uses learning, the clause $\vee_{l \in \mu'} \bar{l}$ is (temporarily) added to the input set of clauses in order to avoid future explorations of valuations extending μ'.

Thus, in order to use SAT solvers with learning, it is not enough for SatCheck(μ) to return FALSE when μ is not satisfiable. Indeed, SatCheck(μ) must also compute a reason for such a failure, that is, an unsatisfiable subset μ' of μ. One such set is obviously μ itself. However, in order to try to maximize the advantages of learning, it is important that μ' be as "small" as possible with respect to some ordering relation on valuations. Let μ be an unsatisfiable valuation. We found it useful to consider the following forms of minimality:

- **Minimal reasons with respect to set inclusion.** An unsatisfiable valuation $\mu' \subseteq \mu$ is a *minimal reason for μ with respect to set inclusion* if and only if for all unsatisfiable valuations μ'' such that $\mu'' \subseteq \mu'$ we have that $\mu'' = \mu'$.

- **Reasons of minimal cardinality.** An unsatisfiable valuation $\mu' \subseteq \mu$ is a *reason for μ of minimal cardinality* if and only if for all unsatisfiable valuation $\mu'' \subseteq \mu$, we have that $|\mu'| \leq |\mu''|$.
- **Shallowest reasons.** Let $l_1, l_2, \ldots l_n$ ($n \geq 0$) be the literals in μ, listed according to the total order with which they have been assigned. Such a sequence induces a total order on the subsets of μ defined as follows: if μ' and μ'' are subsets of μ, then $\mu' \preceq \mu''$ if and only if for all literals $l_i \in \mu' \backslash \mu''$ there exists a literal $l_j \in \mu'' \backslash \mu'$ such that $i \leq j$. An unsatisfiable valuation $\mu' \subseteq \mu$ is the *shallowest reason for μ* if and only if unsatisfiable valuation $\mu'' \subseteq \mu$, we have that $\mu' \preceq \mu''$.

Intuitively, there is no point in returning a reason that is not minimal under set inclusion: if we unnecessarily include a literal l in the reason, this may lead to branch on $\bar{l}$, and such a branch is bound to fail. Among the reasons that are minimal under set inclusion, those with minimal cardinality have the further advantage that, once added to the input formula because of learning, they prune a larger portion of the search space. Finally, while backtracking from a valuation μ, and even returning a reason μ' with minimal cardinality, it may still be the case that the next branch being explored is deemed to fail. In fact, μ may still contain a shallowest reason.

EXAMPLE 13. Consider Example 1 once again and assume that the heuristics is such that it first sets p_1 (forcing also $VPred = I_{RR}$ by unit propagation), then $\neg p_2$ (forcing $\neg(VPred < I_{RR} + 1)$), and then $VenI' = VenI$, p_3 and p_5 (this last one forcing also $VenI' + 2 = VenI$). The corresponding valuation $\{p_1, VPred = I_{RR}, \neg p_2, \neg(VPred < I_{RR} + 1), VenI' = VenI, p_3, p_5, VenI' + 2 = VenI\}$ propositionally entails ϕ_{Elf} but is unsatisfiable. The standard procedure detects that μ is unsatisfiable, but it backtracks only up to the choice of p_5, which is not involved in the unsatisfiability of μ; then a whole search branch is explored, which is totally useless, since the assignment still contains both $VPred = I_{RR}$ and $\neg(VPred < I_{RR} + 1)$, which are responsible of the contradiction. The same, even worse, goes for the choice of p_3.

On the other hand, if reason detection is enabled, upon detection of the unsatisfiability of μ, a reason is found, backtracking starts up to a point where the contradiction corresponding to the reason is solved. In our example, there are two minimal reasons, namely, $\xi = \{VPred = I_{RR}, \neg(Vpred < I_{RR} + 1)\}$ and $\xi' = \{VenI' = VenI, VenI' + 2 = VenI\}$. Both ξ and ξ' are minimal under set inclusion and of minimal cardinality. However, ξ is the shallowest. Indeed, if the reason is set to ξ, backtracking will stop at the choice point where $\neg p_2$ was chosen. Also notice that, assuming the reason being returned is ξ', backtracking will stop at the choice $VenI' = VenI$: however, the following search is bound to fail given that the valuation will still contain ξ.

The above example and discussion seems to point out that a reason of minimal size is better than a reason minimal under set inclusion, and that the shallowest reason is better than a reason of minimal size. Indeed, the shallowest reason tries to remove as soon as possible the unsatisfiability from the valuation built so far. However, despite the "smartness" of the reason being returned, there is no guarantee whatsoever that the tree being explored with a "smart" reason mechanism will be smaller than the tree explored with another reason mechanism. As Prosser (1993) pointed out, it may be the case that the *a priori* known fruitless exploration of a branch will lead to a failure and the discovery of a reason causing a long jump to the top of the search stack. To this end, a simple implementation of SatCheck(μ) returning, μ as reason whenever, μ is not satisfiable, can turn out to be more effective than other implementations, at least in some cases. However, trivially, a solver with back-jumping and/or learning can never explore more nodes than a solver with backtracking, assuming, for example, a static branching heuristics.

The first SAT-based solver for SL using a backtracking schema with learning has been proposed in Audemard et al. (2002). However, in that paper, there is no indication about how the reason is computed when SatCheck(μ) fails.

5. Satisfiability Checking

It is a well-known fact that BF can be used to check the satisfiability of a finite set Q of constraints of the form $x - y \leq c$; see, for example, Cormen et al. (2001). This is done by first building a *constraint graph for* Q, that is, a weighted directed graph whose nodes are the variables occurring in Q and having an *edge* from y to x of weight c for each constraint $x - y \leq c$ in Q. An extra node, the *source*, is also included and is linked to all the other nodes with edges of weight 0. BF is then used to solve the "single source shortest-paths" problem. The set of constraints Q is satisfiable if and only if the constraint graph for Q contains no *negative cycles*, that is, cycles with cumulative negative weight.

Here we show that satisfiability checking of a generic valuation μ can be done efficiently with BF. As a preliminary step, we turn μ into an equisatisfiable set $\mu^{\leq,<}$ whose literals are of the form $x - y \leq c$ or $x - y < c$. This can be done by deleting all the literals of the form p and $\neg p$ where p is a propositional letter and by replacing constraint literals

- $y - x \geq -c$, $\neg(y - x < -c)$, $\neg(x - y > c)$ with the logically equivalent constraint $x - y \leq c$, and
- $y - x > -c$, $\neg(y - x \leq -c)$, $\neg(x - y \geq c)$ with the logically equivalent constraint $x - y < c$.

A further step is needed to transform the valuation $\mu^{\leq,<}$ into an equisatisfiable set of constraints of the form $x - y \leq c$ whose satisfiability can be checked with

BF. If the domain of interpretation is $\mathbb{Z}$, this can be done by replacing in $\mu^{\leq,<}$ every constraint of the form $x - y < c$ with $x - y \leq c'$, where c' is the maximum integer strictly smaller than c. It is easy to see that the resulting set of constraint is satisfiable if and only if $\mu^{\leq,<}$ is. If the domain of interpretation is R, then we rely on the following result.

LEMMA 14. *Let Q and Q' be two finite sets of constraints of the form $x - y \leq c$ and $x - y < c$, respectively. Let n be the number of variables in Q'. Let p be the maximum number of digits appearing to the right of the decimal point in any numeric constant in $Q \cup Q'$. If C is $x - y < c$, let $C_{\leq}$ be $x - y \leq c - \frac{1}{10^p(n+1)}$. Finally, let $Q'_{\leq} = \{C_{\leq} : C \in Q'\}$.*

$Q \cup Q'$ is satisfiable in R if and only if $Q \cup Q'_{\leq}$ is satisfiable in $\mathbb{R}$.

Proof. The right-to-left direction is trivial, and therefore here we focus on the left to right direction. In the following, if $Q'' \subseteq Q \cup Q'$ is a set of constraints, by $Q''_{\leq}$ we mean the set obtained from Q'' by replacing each constraint C of the form $x - y < c$ with $C_{\leq}$. Further, ϵ is $\frac{1}{10^p(n+1)}$.

We proceed by contradiction and assume that $Q \cup Q'$ is satisfiable while $Q \cup Q'_{\leq}$ is not. In this case, there exists a subset Q'' of $Q \cup Q'$ such that

- Q'' is satisfiable and $Q''_{\leq}$ is not,
- $Q''_{\leq}$ has the form $\{x_1 - x_2 \leq c_1 - e_1, x_2 - x_3 \leq c_2 - e_2, \ldots, x_m - x_i \leq c_m - e_m\}$, where each e_i is either 0 or ϵ, and
- in $Q''_{\leq}$ there are at least one and at most n constraints for which $e_i = \epsilon$, that is, $1 \leq |Q'' \cap Q'| \leq n$.

Q'' is satisfiable and $Q''_{\leq}$ unsatisfiable imply $\sum_{i=1}^{m} c_i > 0$ and $\sum_{i=1}^{m}(c_i - e_i) < 0$ respectively (notice that it cannot be the case that $\sum_{i=1}^{m} c_i = 0$ because $Q'' \cap Q' \neq \emptyset$ and Q'' has to be satisfiable by hypothesis). Since $\sum_{i=1}^{m} c_i > 0$, then $\sum_{i=1}^{m} c_i \geq \frac{1}{10^p}$. But then we have a contradiction, because

$$
\begin{aligned}
\sum_{i=1}^{m}(c_i - e_i) &= \\
\sum_{i=1}^{m} c_i - \sum_{i=1}^{m} e_i &\geq \\
\sum_{i=1}^{m} c_i - n\epsilon &= \\
\sum_{i=1}^{m} c_i - \frac{1}{10^p}\frac{n}{n+1} &\geq \\
\frac{1}{10^p} - \frac{1}{10^p}\frac{n}{n+1} &> 0
\end{aligned}
$$

$\square$

Notice that the application of the above result requires, if the domain of interpretation is $\mathbb{R}$, to determine the values of n and p, which in turn depend on μ. The next result shows that the values for n and p can be computed beforehand and once and for all, on the basis of the input formula ϕ.

THEOREM 15. *Let ϕ be a formula with n variables. Let p be the maximum number of digits appearing to the right of the decimal point in any numeric constant in ϕ. Let μ be a valuation whose atoms occur in ϕ. The valuation μ is* *satisfiable in $\mathbb{R}$ if and only ij the valuation obtained from $\mu^{\leq,<}$ by replacing each constraint $x - y \leq c - \frac{1}{10^p(n+1)}$ is satisfiable in $\mathbb{R}$.*

Proof. Clearly, μ is satisfiable in $\mathbb{R}$ if and only if $\mu^{\leq,<}$ is satisfiable in $\mathbb{R}$. The thesis trivially follows from Lemma 14 once we observe that, given that the atoms in μ occur in ϕ,

- the number of variables in $\mu^{\leq,<}$ is less than or equal to n and
- the maximum number of digits appearing to the right of the decimal point in any of the numeric constants in $\mu^{\leq,<}$ is less than or equal to the maximum number of digits appearing to the right of the decimal point in any of the numeric constants in ϕ.   □

The above results allow us to use BF in order to check the satisfiability of any valuation. Given a valuation μ with n variables, BF runs in time $O(n \times |\mu|)$, and is the current best known method for this task (see Cormen et al., 2001). Further BF has the following advantages, in the case the valuation μ is unsatisfiable:

- each negative cycle in the constraint graph G corresponds to a minimal (with respect to set inclusion) unsatisfiable subset of μ, and
- assuming there is more than one negative cycle in G and that R is the corresponding set of reasons, it is easy to modify BF so to make it return a reason that is of minimal cardinality or the shallowest *among those in R* without modifying its overall complexity $O(n \times |\mu|)$.

6. Implementation and Experimental Analysis

We have implemented the techniques described in Sections 3–5 in a system called TSAT++. The system is based on a C++ implementation of an iterative version of the algorithm of Figure 2 featuring all optimizations presented in Section 4.

TSAT++ uses two distinct modules for the enumeration of valuations, μ propositionally entailing the input formula ϕ and for checking the satisfiability of μ. A detailed analysis of the architecture of TSAT++ is beyond the scope of this paper; the interested reader may refer to Armando et al. (2004).

In the current version, enumeration is done by a modified version of SIMO (Giunchiglia et al., 2003). SIMO features a number of SAT optimization techniques inspired by Chaff, among which are 1-UIP learning, VSIDS heuristics, and two-literal watching (Moskewicz et al., 2001).

In order to assess the effectiveness of the optimizations described in Section 4, we have carried out a thorough experimental analysis using TSAT++ and TSAT++ plain, on a wide variety of publicly available random, hand-made, and real-world SL-formulas.[*] TSAT++ plain is the same as TSAT++ except that IS_2, early pruning, and model reduction are disabled while best reason detection is set so to return a reason minimal with respect to set inclusion. Further, in order to evaluate the effectiveness of our system, we have compared TSAT++ with a number of rival, publicly available, and state-of-the-art systems specifically designed for (a significant fragment of) SL or with a specialized satisfiability procedure for SL valuations.[**] We have thus considered the system presented in Stergiou and Koubarakis (1998), which we will call SK; Tsat (Armando et al., 1999), the predecessor of TSAT++; CSPi (Oddi and Cesta, 2000); and Epilitis (Tsamardinos and Pollack, 2003). All these systems are restricted to DTPs (see Section 6.1). Moreover, we have considered SEP (Strichman et al., 2002) and MathSAT (Audemard et al., 2002). TSAT++ is as expressive as SEP and not comparable to MathSAT: while MathSAT allows for arbitrary linear constraints as atoms, it does not allow to consider the integers as domain of interpretation. After a first run, we have discarded SK, because it is clearly noncompetitive with respect to the others.

Each solver has been run on all the benchmarks it can deal with, not only on the benchmarks the solver was analyzed on by the authors. In particular, Epilitis can handle only DTPs with integer-valued variables; CSPi and TSAT can handle only DTPs with real-valued variables; Math-SAT can handle arbitrary SL-formulas with real-valued variables; SEP and TSAT++ can handle arbitrary SL-formulas with real- or integer-valued variables. Each solver has been run by using the settings or the version of the solver suggested by the authors for the *specific* class of problems. All the experiments have been run on a Linux box equipped with a Pentium IV 2.4 GHz processor and 1 GB of RAM. CPU time is measured in seconds; timeout has been set to 1,000 s.

6.1. DISJUNCTIVE TEMPORAL PROBLEMS

We start our analysis considering randomly generated DTPs as introduced in Stergiou and Koubarakis (1998) and since then used as a benchmark in (Armando et al., 1999; Oddi and Cesta, 2000: Audemard et al., 2002; Tsamardinos and Pollack, 2003). DTPs are randomly generated by fixing the number k of disjuncts per clause, the number n of arithmetic variables, and a

---

[*] The classification of the benchmarks in "tandem," "handmade," and "real-world" problems is borrowed from the SAT competition (Le Berre and Simon, 2003).

[**] Notice that there exist other systems capable of handling SL, e.g., ICS (de Moura et al., 2004), CVC (Stump et al., 2002), CVC-Lite (Barrett and Berezin, 2004), Verifun (Flanagan et al., 2003). We did not include these solvers in our analysis since they are not tailored for SL. MathSAT has been included since it has a specialized satisfiability checker for SL based on BF.

positive integer L such that all the constants are taken in $[-L, L]$. Then, (1) the number of clauses m is increased in order to range from satisfiable to unsatisfiable instances, (2) for each tuple of values of the parameters, 100 instances are generated and then fed to the solvers, and (3) the median of the CPU time is plotted against the m/n ratio. The results for $k = 2, L = 100$, and $n = 35$ are given in Figure 6: plots (a) and (b) show the performance when the variables are real- and integer-valued respectively.

When $m/n \geq 6$, TSAT++ clearly outperforms the other systems, including TSAT++plain: in the peak region, the solver that is closer to TSAT++ in this domain, namely Epilitis, is a factor of 6 slower on 35 variables (Plot (b)). This is a very positive result, taking into account that Epilitis works only on DTP with $k = 2$, and it has been thoroughly tested and optimized on this type of problems (see Tsamardinos and Pollack (2003)). All the other systems are about two orders of magnitude slower than TSAT++ in the peak region. Even more important is the fact that the gap in performance between TSAT++ and the other systems increases with the number of variables (we have experimented with problems up to 50 variables). For this class of problems TSAT++ has been run with early pruning and preprocessing enabled, with the best reason detection optimization set to return shortest reason, and with model reduction disabled. The role of the optimizations is fundamental for the performance on this test set: TSAT++ is more than one order of magnitude faster than TSAT++plain in the peak region.

6.2. REAL-WORLD PROBLEMS

We have also carried out experiments on

1. the 40 post-office benchmarks introduced in Audemard et al. (2002), coming in four series (consisting of 7, 9, 11, and 13 instances, respectively) of increasing difficult. In these problems the domain of the interpretation is the set of real numbers.
2. the 16 hardware verification problems from Strichman et al. (2002), nine (resp. 7) of which are with real- (resp. integer-) valued variables.

The post-office benchmarks are bounded model checking problems for timed automata; the hardware verification suite includes scheduling, cache coherence protocol, load-store unit, and out-of-order execution problems. Considering the results of MathSAT, SEP, and TSAT++ on the post-office problems, our first observation is that SEP is not competitive on these problems: on 13 of the hardest instances, SEP had a segmentation fault in 11 cases, and on the other two hardest instances SEP is outperformed by different orders of magnitude by TSAT++ and MathSAT. Our second observation is that TSAT++ (with IS_2 pre-better than MathSAT up to a factor of 6 on *each single instance*: this is particularly remarkable given that the authors have customized a version of

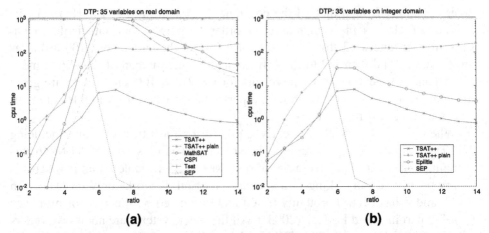

Figure 6. Performance on (a) randomly generated DTPs with 35 real valued variables and on (b) randomly generated DTPs with 35 integer-valued variables. The *dotted plot* indicates satisfiability percentage both in (a) and in (b).

MathSAT explicitly for this kind of problems.[★] Considering the hardware verification problems, all of them are easy to solve (i.e., in less than 3 s each) for all the three solvers, except for SEP that timeouts on one instance. Of the nine (resp. 16) runs of MathSAT (resp. SEP and TSAT++), only three take more than 0.1 s. These observations are confirmed by Figure 7, which gives the overall picture of the results for MathSAT, SEP, and TSAT++ on the 49 instances with real valued variables: the x-axis is the number of instances solved by each solver within the CPU time specified on the y-axis. The plot also shows that TSAT++ plain can be faster than TSAT++ on the easy instances, that is, those requiring less than 1 s to be solved. For such problems, the overhead of the optimizations (and in particular of the preprocessing) outweighs the benefits.

6.3. HAND-MADE PROBLEMS

Finally, we have considered the "hand-made" diamond problems from Strichman et al. (2002). A diamond problem is a formula ϕ that depends on a parameter $K > 0$ and such that there exists a number of unsatisfiable valuations propositionally entailing ϕ that is exponential in K. Moreover, hard instances having a single satisfiable valuation propositionally entailing them can be generated. A second parameter T is also used and it affects the number of variables and the size of the problem. Variables range over the reals.

[★] As indicated by the authors, we have used this customized version of MathSAT on this class of problems.

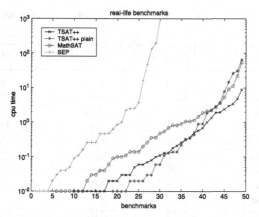

Figure 7. Performance on real-problems.

Table I shows comparative results on the diamond problems for various settings of K and T. In particular, we considered all the settings corresponding to nontrivially solvable instances reported in (Strichman et al., 2002). The third column denotes whether the problem has a unique valuation propositionally entailing it; the remaining columns show CPU times for TSAT++, TSAT++ plain, MathSAT, and SEP. For this class of problems TSAT++ has been run with best-reason detection set to shortest reason, and with model reduction. The experimental results clearly show that TSAT++ performs best, often by orders of magnitude. Instances with a unique solution are more difficult than nonunique ones, as expected, except for SEP.[*]

For this test set, it is of fundamental importance the model reduction optimization: without it, TSAT++ performance is significantly worse, up to the point that problems that are solved in 1 s by TSAT++ are not solved without model reduction within the time limit.

7. Related Work

Several systems tailored for SL, employing different approaches and techniques, have been built and tested over the years. We now give an overview of them, highlighting the pros and cons of each one and chronologically reviewing the techniques introduced by each one. SK (Stergiou and Koubarakis, 1998); Stergiou

---

[*] Following a suggestion by Offer Strichman, we have also tried SEP with an option that disables the use of a specialized data structure called "conjunction matrix" (Strichman et al., 2002). This can have a dramatic impact on SEP: some problems that are solved with conjunction matrix within the time limit are not solved without, and vice versa.

Table I. Diamond problems: "TIME" indicates that the solver does not solve the instance within the time limit.

K	T	Unique	TSAT++	TSAT++ plain	MathSAT	SEP
50	4	NO	0.00	0.02	0.05	0.12
50	4	YES	0.01	0.14	TIME	0.07
100	5	NO	0.01	0.11	0.61	1.18
100	5	YES	0.04	7.57	TIME	0.17
250	5	NO	0.08	0.76	5.40	52.20
250	5	YES	0.21	194.99	TIME	0.77
500	5	NO	0.29	4.46	21.22	742.99
500	5	YES	1.05	TIME	TIME	4.85
1000	5	NO	1.07	22.3	–	TIME
1000	5	YES	6.45	TIME	–	22.53
2000	5	NO	3.76	94.23	–	–
2000	5	YES	29.90	TIME	–	–

and Koubarakis, 2000). The procedure SK has been the first dealing with a significant fragment of SL. Its main features are the combined usage of *forward-checking*, back-jumping, and the minimum remaining value heuristic (MRV). Forward-checking works by checking whether the valuation built so far entails either a literal or its negation, form each literal not yet in the valuation. This actually reduces the search space, at the price of performing a potentially large number of useless satisfiability. SK is also able to detect conflict sets and to improve on backtracking via a technique similar to back-jumping. MRV is used to choose literals that appear in disjunctions with the smallest number of unassigned disjuncts: if there is a unit clause, the literal in it will be selected by MRV and then propagated, thus mimicking unit propagation.

The main difference between SK and SAT-based procedures lies in the way valuations propositionally entailing the input formula are searched. In fact, SK is based on *syntatic branching*: given a disjunction $l \vee l'$, first l is added to the current valuation, and, upon failure, l' is considered. As explained below, this type of search may lead to the exploration of search space already explored.

Tsat (Armando et al., 1999). Tsat was the first application of the SAT-based approach to SL. The system employs a branching schema now known as *semantic branching*. Unlike syntactic branching, semantic branching selects a not yet assigned literal l, and considers in turn the case in which l is true and the case in which l is false. Notice that in the second case, the conjunction of $\bar{l}$ with $(l \vee l')$ forces the assignment of l' by unit propagation: as already observed in D'Agostino (1992), syntactic branching may lead to redundant exploration of parts of the search space, which semantic branching avoids. The following example, adapted from Armando et al. (1999), clearly illustrates this issue.

EXAMPLE 16. Let ϕ be a formula including the following clauses:

$$x_1 - x_2 \leq 3 \vee x_7 - x_8 \leq 20$$
$$x_1 - x_3 \leq 4 \vee x_4 - x_3 \leq -2$$
$$x_2 - x_4 \leq 2 \vee x_3 - x_2 \leq 1$$
$$\vdots$$

Let $\phi(i, j)$ denote the jth disjunct of the ith disjunction displayed in ϕ; for example, $\phi(1, 2)$ is $x_7 - x_8 \leq 20$. Assume that the dots stand for further (possibly many) unspecified clauses such that no satisfiable extension of the valuation $\{\phi(1, 1), \phi(2, 1)\}$ exists.

Consider the behavior of syntactic *versus* semantic branching when $\{\phi(1, 1), \phi(2, 1)\}$ is the valuation built so far. Since no satisfiable extension of it exists, after some search, failure is necessarily detected; both procedures backtrack and remove $\phi(2, 1)$ from the current valuation.

Now syntactic branching goes on with the valuation $\{\phi(1, 1), \phi(2, 2)\}$, whereas semantic branching proceeds with $\{\phi(1, 1), \neg\phi(2, 1)\}$, which leads immediately, via unit propagation, to $\{\phi(1, 1), \neg\phi(2, 1), \phi(2, 2)\}$.

Working with the latter valuation rather than with the former may lead to considerable savings: assume that both procedures extend the valuation with $\phi(3, 1)$; since $\{\phi(1, 1), \neg\phi(2, 1), \phi(2, 2)\ \phi(3, 1)\}$ is unsatisfiable, semantic branching immediately backtracks and considers $\phi(3, 2)$, whereas syntactic branching may waste a big amount of resources in the vain attempt of finding a satisfiable extension of $\{\phi(1, 1), \phi(2, 2), \phi(3, 1)\}$.

Semantic branching was shown in Armando et al. (1999) to dramatically improve the performance with respect to SK, up to one order of magnitude on randomly generated binary DTPs.

In Tsat, also IS_2 was introduced, gaining to the system another order of magnitude in performance—this despite the fact that, to enumerate valuations, Tsat adapted a rather simple SAT solver, due to Böhm (Böhm and Speckenmeyer 1996), which did not employ any modern optimization such as back-jumping and learning. Satisfiability checking used *lp_solve* v2.2 (Berkelaar, 1997), which provided a free implementation of the Simplex method.

CSPi (Oddi and Cesta, 2000). CSPi features an essentially CSP-based solution schema, implementing an efficient incremental procedure for forward-checking. Semantic branching is used, showing results that are better than Tsat on small instances, and comparable on bigger ones. Notice that performance, up to (Oddi and Cesta, 2000), was measured in terms of how many calls to the satisfiability check function were done, rather than CPU time.

MathSAT (Audemard et al., 2002). MathSAT uses SIM (Giunchiglia et al. 2001) as enumerator and a hierarchical satisfiability checker employing – in this order – equality reasoning, BF for SL-constraints, the Simplex method for full linear arithmetic, and inequalities reasoning. The simplest solver is chosen on-the-fly, thereby obtaining both expressivity and efficiency at the same time. MathSAT also introduces a number of optimizations, among which are prepro-cessing based upon syntactic equivalence, enhanced early pruning, that is, early pruning conditioned upon a heuristic function, and back-jumping/learning based upon reason detection. Also, a form of model reduction is used, based upon triggering. On randomly generated binary DTPs, MathSAT improves the per-formance over Tsat in terms of CPU time. However, the gap between the two solvers decreases as the number of variables increases.

Epilitis (Tsamardinos and Pollack, 2003). Epilitis is, so far, the last CSP-based system. Epilitis is restricted to binary DTPs. It uses semantic branching, incremental forward checking, a MRV heuristics, and *size-bounded learning* of size n (Bayardo and Miranker, 1996). This means that conflict clauses are re-trieved and stored only if they contain less than n literals (in practice, $n = 10$ is used). Once stored, a clause is never forgotten. On randomly generated binary DTPs, Epilitis shows significantly better performance than Tsat in terms of CPU time, of up to one order of magnitude.

SEP (Strichman et al., 2002). SEP is a back-end to the UCLID verification tool (Lahiri et al., 2002), employing the so-called eager variant of the SAT-based approach. Given a formula ϕ, rather than enumerating valuations and checking them for satisfiability, SEP builds a propositional formula ϕ' whose satisfying valuations are ensured to correspond to satisfiable valuations of ϕ. The current version of SEP uses Chaff to find valuations satisfying ϕ'. To the best of our knowledge, SEP is so far the only solver using the eager SAT-based approach to SL. SEP suffers from the fact that the size of ϕ' can be exponential in the size of ϕ. On the other hand, as reported in Strichman et al. (2002), if SEP can get past the encoding phase, the problem is easy to solve for Chaff.

8. Conclusions

In this paper we have focused on the problem of building efficient SAT-based decision procedures for SL. We have presented the basic procedure from Armando et al. (1999) along with some key optimizations. We have also shown how it is possible to check the satisfiability of valuations involving constraints of the form $x - y < c$ using BF. An extensive comparative experimental analysis shows that our solver TSAT++, built along the lines described in this paper, is currently the state of the art on various classes of problems, including randomly generated, hand-made, and real-world instances. We believe that the techniques described in this paper can be fruitfully extended to other (more expressive) logics than SL.

The benchmark problems used for the experiments presented in this paper and the executable of TSAT++ are publicly available at the URL http://www.ai.dist. unige.it/Tsat.

Acknowledgements

We acknowledge Massimo Idini's work on the satisfiability checking module. Mauro Di Manzo is thanked for the many fruitful discussions on the subject of this paper. Moreover, the authors of the solvers we have compared have helped us a lot: Gilles Audemard, Angelo Oddi, Ofer Strichman, Ioannis Tsamardinos. Sergey Berezin and Leonardo De Moura are thanked for discussions related to the topic of this paper. Sanjit Seshia and the UCLID group provided us with a lot of interesting problems. We are partially supported by MIUR.

References

Armando, A. and Giunchiglia, E. (1993) Embedding complex decision procedures inside an interactive theorem prover, *Ann. Math. Artif. Intell.* **8**(3–4), 475–502.

Armando, A., Castellini, C. and Giunchiglia, E. (1999) SAT-based procedures for temporal reasoning, in S. Biundo and M. Fox (eds.), *Proceedings of the 5th European Conferevace on Planning (Durham, UK)*, Vol. 1809 of *Lecture Notes in Computer Science*, Springer, pp. 97–108.

Armando, A., Castellini, C., Giunchiglia, E., Idini, M. and Maratea, M. (2004) TSAT++: an open platform for satisfiability modulo theories, in *Proceedings of PDPAR, Pragmatics of Decision Procedures in Automated Reasoning, Cork (Ireland)*, Vol. 125, Issue 3 of *ENTCS*, Elsevier, pp. 25–36.

Armando, A., Castellini, C., Giunchiglia, E. and Maratea, M. (2005a) A SAT-based decision procedure for the boolean combination of difference constraints, in *Proceedings of SAT, International Conference on Theory and Applications of Satisfiability Testing, Vancouver (Canada)*, Vol. 3542 of *LNCS*, Springer, pp. 16–29.

Armando, A., Castellini, C., Giunchiglia, E., Giunchiglia, F. and Tacchella, A. (2005b) SAT-based decision procedures for automated reasoning: a unifying perspective, in *Mechanizing Mathematical Reasoning: Essays in Honor of Jrg H. Siekmann on the Occasion of His 60th Birthday*, Vol. 2605 of *Lecture Notes in Computer Science*, Springer.

Audemard, G., Bertoli, P., Cimatti, A., Kornilowicz, A. and Sebastiani, R. (2002) A SAT based approach for solving formulas over Boolean and linear mathematical propositions, in A. Voronkov (ed.), *Automated Deduction – CADE-18*, Vol. 2392 of *Lecture Notes in Computer Science*, Springer, pp. 195–210.

Barrett, C. W. and Berezin, S. (2004) CVC Lite: a new implementation of the cooperating validity checker category B, in *16th International Conference on Computer Aided Verification (CAV'04)*, Vol. 3114, Springer, pp. 515–518.

Bayardo, Jr., R. J. and Miranker, D. P. (1996) A complexity analysis of space-bounded learning algorithms for the constraint satisfaction problem, in *Proceedings of the Thirteenth National Conference on Artificial Intelligence and the Eighth Innovative Applications of Artificial Intelligence Conference*, Menlo Park, AAAI/MIT, pp. 298–304.

Berkelaar, M. (1997) The *lp_solve* Solver for Mixed Integer-Linear Programming. Version 2.2. Available at http://www.cs.sunysb.edu/~algorith/implement/lpsolve/implement.shtml.

Böhm, M. and Speckenmeyer, E. (1996) A fast parallel SAT-solver – efficient workload balancing, *Ann. Math. Artif. Intell.* **17**, 381–400.

Bryant, R. E., Lahiri, S. K. and Seshia, S. A. (2002) Deciding CLU logic formulas via Boolean and pseudo-Boolean encodings, in *Proceedings of International Workshop on Constraints in Formal Verification*. Associated with International Conference on Principles and Practice of Constraint Programming, Ithaca, New York (USA).

Castellini, C., Giunchiglia, E. and Tacchella, A. (2003) SAT-based planning in complex domains: concurrency, constraints and nondeterminism, *Artif. Intell.* **147**, 85–117.

Cormen, T. H., Leiserson, C. E., Rivest, R. L. and Stein, C. (2001) *Introduction to Algorithms*, MIT.

Cotton, S., Asarin, E., Maler, O. and Niebert, P. (2004) Some progress in satisfiability checking for difference logic, in *Joint International Conferences on Formal Modelling and Analysis of Timed Systems (FORMATS) and Formal Techniques in Real-Time and Fault-Tolerant Systems (FTRTFT)*, Vol. 3253 of *Lecture Notes in Computer Science*, Springer, pp. 263–276.

D'Agostino, M. (1992) Are tableaux an improvement on truth-tables? *J. Logic, Lang. Inf.* **1**, 235–252.

Davis, M., Logemann, G. and Loveland, D. (1962) A machine program for theorem proving, *Journal of the ACM* **5**(7).

de Moura, L., Ruess, H., Shankar, N. and Rushby, J. (2004) The ICS decision procedures for embedded deduction, in *Proceedings of IJCAR, International Joint Conference on Automated Reasoning*, Cork, Ireland.

Dechter, R., Meiri, I. and Pearl, J. (1989) Temporal constraint networks, in H. J. L. R. J. Brachman and R. Reiter (eds.), *Proceedings of the 1st International Conference on Principles of Knowledge Representation and Reasoning*, Toronto, Canada, Morgan Kaufmann, pp. 83–93.

Dequen, G. and Dubois, O. (2004) kcnfs: an efficient solver for random K-Sat formulae, in E. Giunchiglia and A. Taicchella (eds.), *6th International Conference on Theory an Applications of Satisfiability Testing. Selected Revised Papers*, Vol. 2919 of *Lecture Notes in Computer Science*, Springer, pp. 486–501.

Flanagan, C., Joshi, R., Ou, X. and Saxe, J. B. (2003) Theorem proving using lazy proof explication, in *15th International Conference on Computer Aided Verification (CAV'03)*, Vol. 2725, Springer, pp. 355–367.

Gent, I., Maaren, H. V. and Walsh, T. (eds.) (2000) *SAT2000. Highlights of Satisfiability Research in the Year 2000*, IOS.

Giunchiglia, F. and Sebastiani, R. (1996) Building decision procedures for modal logics from propositional decision procedures – the case study of modal K, in *Proc. CADE-96*, New Brunswick, New Jersey, USA, Springer.

Giunchiglia, E., Maratea, M., Tacchella, A. and Zambonin, D. (2001) Evaluating search heuristics and optimization techniques in propositional satisfiability, in *Automated Reasoning, First International Joint Conference (IJCAR)*, Vol. 2083 of *Lecture Notes an Computer Science*, Springer, pp. 347–363.

Giunchiglia, E., Giunchiglia, F. and Tacchella, A. (2002) SAT-based decision procedures for classical modal logics, *J. Autom. Reason.* **28**, 143–171. Reprinted in (Gent et al., 2000).

Giunchiglia, E., Maratea, M. and Tacchella, A. (2003) (In)Effectiveness of look-ahead techniques in a modern SAT solver, in *Principles and Practice of Constraint Programming (CP)*, Vol. 2833 of *Lecture Notes in Computer Science*, Springer, pp. 842–846.

Heule, M. and Maaren, H. V. (2005) March_eq: implementing additional reasoning into an efficient look-ahead SAT solver, in *8th International Conference on Theory an Applications of Satisfiability Testing*, Vol. 3542 of *LNCS*, Springer, pp. 345–353.

Lahiri, S. K., Seshia, S. A. and Bryant, B. (2002) Modeling and verification of out-of-order microprocessors in UCLID, *Lect. Notes Comput. Sci.* **2517**, 142–155.

Le Berre, D. and Simon, L. (2003) The essentials of the SAT'03 competition, in *Proceedings of the 6th International Conference on the Theory and Applications of Satisfiability Testing (SAT'03). Selected revised papers*, Vol. 2919 of *LNCS*.

Moskewicz, M. W., Madigan, C. F., Zhao, Y., Zhang, L. and Malik, S. (2001) Chaff: engineering an efficient SAT solver, in *Proceedings of the 38th Design Automation Conference (DAC'01)*.

Oddi, A. and Cesta, A. (2000) Incremental forward checking for the disjunctive temporal problem, in *Proceedings of the 14th European Conference on Artificial Intelligence (ECAI-2000)*, Berlin, pp. 108–112.

Plaisted, D. and Greenbaum, S. (1986) A structure-preserving clause form translation, *J. Symb. Comput.* **2**, 293–304.

Pratt, V. R. (1977) Two easy theories whose combination is hard, Technical report, Massachusetts Institute of Technology.

Prosser, P. (1993) Domain filtering can degrade intelligent backjumping search, in *Proc. IJCAI*, pp. 262–267.

Siekmann, J. and Wrightson, G. (eds.) (1983) *Automation of Reasoning: Classical Papers in Computational Logic 1967–1970*, Vol. 1–2, Springer.

Stergiou, K. and Koubarakis, M. (1998) Backtracking algorithms for disjunctions of temporal constraints, in *Proceedings of AAAI/IAAI, Madison, WI (USA)*, pp. 248–253.

Stergiou, K. and Koubarakis, M. (2000) Backtracking algorithms for disjunctions of temporal constraints, *Artif. Intell.* **120**(1), 81–117.

Strichman, O., Seshia, S. A. and Bryant, R. E. (2002) Deciding separation formulas with SAT, *Lect. Notes Comput. Sci.* **2404**, 209–222.

Stump, A., Barrett, C. W. and Dill, D. L. (2002) CVC: a cooperating validity checker, in J. C. Godskesen (ed.), *Proceedings of the International Conference on Computer-Aided Verification.*

Tsamardinos, I. and Pollack, M. (2003) Efficient solution techniques for disjunctive temporal reasoning problems, *Artif. Intell.* **151**, 43–89.

Tseitin, G. (1970) On the complexity of proofs in propositional logics, *Semin. Mat.* **8**. Reprinted in (Siekmann and Wrightson, 1983).

Wolfman, S. and Weld, D. (1999) The LPSAT-engine and its application to resource planning, in *Proceedings IJCAI-99.*

Journal of Automated Reasoning (2005) 35: 265–293
DOI: 10.1007/s10817-005-9004-z

© Springer 2005

MATHSAT: Tight Integration of SAT and Mathematical Decision Procedures[*]

MARCO BOZZANO[1], ROBERTO BRUTTOMESSO[1],
ALESSANDRO CIMATTI[1], TOMMI JUNTTILA[2],
PETER VAN ROSSUM[1], STEPHAN SCHULZ[3],
and ROBERTO SEBASTIANI[4]

[1]*ITC-IRST, via Sommarive 18, 38050, Povo, Trento, Italy.*
e-mail: {bozzano, bruttomesso, cimatti, vanrossum}@itc.it
[2]*Helsinki University of Technology, P.O. Box 5400, FIN-02015 TKK, Helsinki, Finland.*
e-mail: tommi.junttila@tkk.fi
[3]*Università di Verona, Strada le Grazie 15, 37134, Verona, Italy. e-mail: schulz@eprover.org*
[4]*DIT, Università di Trento, via Sommarive 14, 38050, Povo, Trento, Italy.*
e-mail: roberto.sebastiani@dit.unitn.it

Abstract. Recent improvements in propositional satisfiability techniques (SAT) made it possible to tackle successfully some hard real-world problems (e.g., model-checking, circuit testing, propositional planning) by encoding into SAT. However, a purely Boolean representation is not expressive enough for many other real-world applications, including the verification of timed and hybrid systems, of proof obligations in software, and of circuit design at RTL level. These problems can be naturally modeled as satisfiability in linear arithmetic logic (LAL), that is, the Boolean combination of propositional variables and linear constraints over numerical variables. In this paper we present MATHSAT, a new, SAT-based decision procedure for LAL, based on the (known approach) of integrating a state-of-the-art SAT solver with a dedicated mathematical solver for LAL. We improve MATHSAT in two different directions. First, the top-level line procedure is enhanced and now features a tighter integration between the Boolean search and the mathematical solver. In particular, we allow for theory-driven backjumping and learning, and theory-driven deduction; we use static learning in order to reduce the number of Boolean models that are mathematically inconsistent; we exploit problem clustering in order to partition mathematical reasoning; and we define a stack-based interface that allows us to implement mathematical reasoning in an incremental and backtrackable way. Second, the mathematical solver is based on layering; that is, the consistency of (partial) assignments is checked in theories of increasing strength (equality and uninterpreted functions, linear arithmetic over the reals, linear arithmetic over the integers). For each of these layers, a dedicated (sub)solver is used. Cheaper solvers are called first, and detection of inconsistency makes call of the subsequent solvers superfluous. We provide a through experimental evaluation of our approach, by taking into account a large set of previously proposed benchmarks. We first investigate the relative benefits and drawbacks of each proposed technique by

★ This work has been partly supported by ISAAC, a European-sponsored project, contract no. AST3-CT-2003-501848; by ORCHID, a project sponsored by Provincia Autonoma di Trento; and by a grant from Intel Corporation. The work of T. Junttila has also been supported by the Academy of Finland, project 53695. S. Schulz has also been supported by a grant of the Italian Ministero dell'Istruzione, dell'Università e della Ricerca and the University of Verona.

comparison with respect to a reference option setting. We then demonstrate the global effectiveness of our approach by a comparison with several state-of-the-art decision procedures. We show that the behavior of MATHSAT is often superior to its competitors, both on LAL and in the subclass of difference logic.

Key words: satisfiability module theory, integrated decision procedures, linear arithmetic logic, propositional satisfiability.

1. Motivations and Goals

Many practical domains of reasoning require a degree of expressiveness beyond propositonal logic. For instance, timed and hybrid systems have a discrete component as well as a dynamic evolution of real variables; proof obligations arising in software verification are often Boolean combinations of constraints over integer variables; circuits described at the register transfer level, even though expressible via Booleanization, might be easier to analyze at a higher level of abstraction (see e.g., [12]). The verification problems arising in such domains can often be modeled as satisfiability in Linear Arithmetic Logic (LAL), that is, the Boolean combination of propositional variables and linear constraints over numerical variables. Because of its practical relevance, LAL has attracted a lot of interest, and several decision procedures (e.g., SVC [15], ICS [18, 23], CVCLite [7, 15], UCLID [35, 43], HDPLL [31]) are able to deal with it.

In this paper, we propose a new decision procedure for the satisfiability of LAL, both for the real-valued and for the integer-valued case. We start from a well-known approach, previously applied in MathSAT [3, 27] and in several other systems [2, 7, 15, 18, 20, 23, 42]: a propositional SAT procedure, modified to enumerate propositional assignments for the propositional abstraction of the problem, is integrated with dedicated theory deciders, used to check consistency of propositional assignments with respects to the theory. We extend this approach by improving (1) the top-level procedure, and (2) the mathematical reasoner.

The *top-level procedure* features a tighter integration between the Boolean search and the mathematical solver. First, we allow for theory conflict-driven backjumping (i.e., sets of inconsistent constraints identified in the mathematical solver are used to drive backjumping and learning at the Boolean level) and theory deduction (i.e., when possible, assignments for unassigned theory atoms are automatically inferred from the current partial assignment). Both theory conflicts and theory deductions are learned as clauses codifying the relationships between mathematical atoms at the Boolean level; subsequent search will thus avoid the generation of Boolean assignments that are not mathematically consistent. Second, we suggest a systematic use of *static learning*, that is, the *a priori* encoding of some basic mathematical facts at the Boolean level before the Boolean search. This will stop many inconsistent assignments from ever being enumerated. A moderate increase in the size of the problem is often compensated by significant speedups in performance. In this way MathSAT settles in the middle ground between the "eager" approach, where mathematical facts are discovered during the search, and the "lazy approaches" approach (e.g., [39, 43]), where a very large number of facts may be required in order to lift mathematical reasoning to Boolean reasoning. Third, we define a *stack-based interface* between the Boolean level and the mathematical level, which enables the top level to add constraints, set points of backtracking, and backjump, in order to exploit the fact that increasingly larger sets of constraints are analyzed while extending a Boolean model. As a result, the mathematical reasoner can be incremental and backtrackable and can exploit previously derived information rather than restarting from scratch at each call. Finally, we consider that mathematical reasoning is, in many practical cases, performed on the disjoint union of several subtheories (or *clusters*). Therefore, rather than solving the problem with a single, monolithic mathematical solver, we use a separate instance of the mathematical solver for each independent cluster.

The main idea underlying the *mathematical solver* for linear arithmetic is that it is *layered*, that is, implemented as a hierarchy of solvers for theories of increasing strength. The consistency of (partial) assignments is checked first in the logic of equality and uninterpreted function (EUF), then in difference logics, then in linear arithmetic over the reals, and then in linear arithmetic over the integers (if needed by the problem). The rationale is that cheaper, more abstract solvers are called first. If unsatisfiability at a more abstract level is detected, this is sufficient to prune the search.

We provide a thorough experimental evaluation of our approach, based on a large set of benchmarks previously proposed in the literature. We first show the respective merits of each of the proposed optimizations, comparing different configurations of MATHSAT with respect to a "golden setting", and we show to which extent each of the improvements impacts performance. Then we compare MATHSAT against the state-of-the-art systems (ICS, CVCLITE, and UCLID) on general LAL problems. We show that our approach is able to deal efficiently with a wide class of problems, with performance comparable with and often superior to the other systems. We also compare MATHSAT against the specialized decision procedures DLSAT and TSAT++ on the subclass of difference logics.

This paper is structured as follows. In Section 2 we define linear arithmetic logic. In Section 3 we describe the basic MATHSAT approach, and in Section 4 we present the enhanced algorithm. In Section 5 we describe the ideas underlying the mathematical solver. In Section 6 we described the implementation of the MATHSAT system. In Section 7 we present the result of the experimental evaluation. In Section 8 we discuss some related work; and in Section 9 we draw some conclusions and outline the directions for future work.

This paper updates and extends the content and results presented in a much shorter conference paper [11].

2. Background: Linear Arithmetic Logic

Let $\mathbb{B} := \{\perp, \top\}$ be the domain of Boolean values. Let $\mathbb{R}$ and $\mathbb{Z}$ be the domains of real and integer numbers, respectively, and let $\mathcal{D}$ denote either of them. By *math-terms* over $\mathcal{D}$ we denote the linear mathematical expressions built on constants, variables, and arithmetical operators over $\mathcal{D}$. Examples of math-terms are constants $c_i \in \mathcal{D}$, variables v_i over $\mathcal{D}$, possibly with coefficients (i.e., $c_i v_j$), and applications of the arithmetic operators $+$ and $-$ to math-terms. *Boolean atoms* are proposition A_i, from $\mathbb{B}$. *Mathematical atoms* are formed by the application of the arithmetic relations $=, \neq, >, <, \geq, \leq$ to math-terms. Unspecified *atoms* can be either Boolean or mathematical. By *math-formulas* we denote atoms and their combinations through the standard Boolean connectives $\wedge, \neg, \vee, \rightarrow, \leftrightarrow$. For instance, $A_1 \wedge ((v_1 + 5) \leq 2v_3)$ is a math-formula on either $\mathbb{R}$ or $\mathbb{Z}$. A *literal* is either an atom (a *positive* literal) or its negation (a *negative* literal). Examples of literals are $A_1, \neg A_2, (v_1 + 5v_2 \leq 2v_3 - 2), \neg(2v_1 - v_2 = 5)$. If l is a negative literal $\neg \psi$, then by "$\neg l$" we denote ψ rather than $\neg \neg \psi$. We denote the set of all atoms in ϕ by $Atoms(\phi)$, and the subset of mathematical atoms by $MathAtoms(\phi)$.

An *interpretation* in $\mathcal{D}$ is a mapping I which assigns values in $\mathcal{D}$ to variables and truth values in $\mathbb{B}$ to Boolean atoms. Given an interpretation, math-terms and math-formulas are given values $\mathcal{D}$ and in $\mathbb{B}$, respectively, by interpreting constants, arithmetical operators and Boolean connectives according to their standard (arithmetical or logical) semantics. We write $I(\phi)$ for the truth value of ϕ under the interpretation I, and similarly $I(t)$ for the domain value of the math-term t. We say that I *satisfies* a math-formula ϕ, written $I \models \phi$, iff $I(\phi) = \top$. For example, the math-formula $\varphi := (A_1 \rightarrow (v_1 - 2v_2 \geq 4)) \wedge (\neg A_1 \rightarrow (v_1 = v_2 + 3))$ is satisfied by an interpretation I in $\mathbb{Z}$ s.t. $I(A_1) = \top$, $I(v_1) = 8$, and $I(v_2) = 1$.

We say that a math-formula φ is satisfiable in $\mathcal{D}$ if there exists an interpretation in $\mathcal{D}$ which satisfies φ. The problem of checking the satisfiability of math-formulas is NP-hard, since standard Boolean formulas are a strict subcase

```
function MATHSAT (Math-formula φ, interpretation & I)
    return MATHDPLL (M2B(φ), {}, I);

function MATHDPLL (Boolean-formula φ, assignment & μ,
                   interpretation & I)
    if (φ == ⊤)                                    /* base      */
        then return MATHSOLVE (B2M(μ), I) ;
    if (φ == ⊥)                                    /* backtrack */
        then return Unsat;
    if {l occurs in φ as a unit clause}            /* unit prop. */
        then return MATHDPLL (assign(l, φ), μ ∪ {l}, I);
    if (MATHSOLVE (B2M(μ), I) == Unsat)            /* early pruning */
        then return Unsat;
    l := choose-literal(φ);                        /* split     */
    if ( MATHDPLL (assign(l, φ), μ ∪ {l}, I) == Sat )
        then return Sat;
        else return MATHDPLL (assign(¬l, φ), μ ∪ {¬l}, I);
```

Figure 1. High level view of the MATHSAT algorithm.

of math-formulas (this means theoretically "at least as hard" as standard Boolean satisfiability, but in practice it turns out to be much harder).

A total (resp., partial) *truth assignment* for a math-formula ϕ is a function μ from all (resp., a subset of) the atoms of ϕ to truth values. We represent a truth assignment as a set of literals, with the intended meaning that positive and negative literals represent atoms assigned to true and to false, respectively. We use the notation $\mu = \{\alpha_1, \ldots, \alpha_N, \neg\beta_1, \ldots, \neg\beta_M, A_1, \ldots, A_R, \neg A_{R+1}, \ldots, \neg A_S\}$, where $\alpha_1, \ldots, \alpha_N, \beta_1, \ldots, \beta_M$ are mathematical atoms and $A_1, \ldots, A_S$ are Boolean atoms. We say that μ *propositionally satisfies* ϕ, written $\mu \models_p \phi$, iff it makes ϕ evaluate to true. We say that an interpretation I satisfies a truth assignment μ iff I satisfies all the elements of μ; if there exists an (resp., no) interpretation that satisfies an assignment μ, then μ is said LAL-satisfiable (resp., LAL-unsatisfiable). The truth assignment $\{A_1, (v_1 - 2v_2 \geq 4), \neg(v_1 = v_2 + 3)\}$ propositionally satisfies $(A_1 \to (v_1 - 2v_2 \geq 4)) \wedge (\neg A_1 \to (v_1 = v_2 + 3))$, and it is satisfied by I s.t. $I(A_1) = \top$, $I(v_1) = 8$, and $I(v_2) = 1$.

EXAMPLE 2.1   Consider the following math-formula φ:

$$\left\{\underline{\neg(2v_2 - v_3 > 2)} \vee A_1\right\} \wedge \left\{\underline{\neg A_2} \vee (2v_1 - 4v_5 > 3)\right\}$$
$$\wedge\left\{\underline{(3v_1 - 2v_2 \leq 3)} \vee A_2\right\} \wedge \left\{\neg(2v_3 + v_4 \geq 5) \vee \underline{\neg(3v_1 - v_3 \leq 6)} \vee \neg A_1\right\}$$
$$\wedge\left\{A_1 \vee \underline{(3v_1 - 2v_2 \leq 3)}\right\} \wedge \left\{\underline{(v_1 - v_5 \leq 1)} \vee (v_5 = 5 - 3v_4) \vee \neg A_1\right\}$$
$$\wedge\left\{A_1 \vee \underline{(v_3 = 3v_5 + 4)} \vee A_2\right\}.$$

The truth assignment μ corresponding to the underlined literals is

$$\{\neg(2v_2 - v_3 > 2), \neg A_2, (3v_1 - 2v_2 \leq 3), \neg(3v_1 - v_3 \leq 6), (v_1 - v_5 \leq 1),$$
$$(v_3 = 3v_5 + 4)\}.$$

(Notice that μ is a partial assignment, because it assigns truth values only to a subset of the atoms of φ.) μ propositionally satisfies φ as it sets to true one literal of every disjunction in φ. Notice that μ is not LAL-satisfiable – in fact, neither of the following subassignments of μ has a satisfying interpretation:

$$\{\neg(2v_2 - v_3 > 2), (3v_1 - 2v_2 \leq 3), \neg(3v_1 - v_3 \leq 6)\} \tag{1}$$

$$\{\neg(3v_1 - v_3 \leq 6), (v_1 - v_5 \leq 1), (v_3 = 3v_5 + 4)\}. \tag{2}$$

Given a LAL-unsatisfiable assignment μ, we call a *conflict set* any LAL-unsatisfiable subassignment $\mu' \subseteq \mu$; we say that μ' is a *minimal* conflict set if all subsets of μ' are LAL-consistent. For example, both (1) and (2) are minimal conflict sets of μ.

3. The MathSAT Algorithm: Basics

A much simplified, recursive representation of the basic MathSAT procedure is outlined in Figure 1. MathSAT takes as input a math-formula ϕ, and (by reference) any empty interpretation I. Without loss of generality, ϕ is assumed to be in conjunctive normal form (CNF). MathSAT returns $\top$ if ϕ is LAL-satisfiable (with I containing a satisfying interpretation), and $\bot$ otherwise. MathSAT invokes MathDpll passing as arguments the Boolean formula $\varphi := \mathcal{M}2\mathcal{B}(\phi)$ and (by reference) an empty assignment for φ and the empty interpretation I.

We introduce a bijective function $\mathcal{M}2\mathcal{B}$ (for "Math-to-Boolean"), also called *boolean abstraction* function, that maps Boolean atoms into themselves, math-atoms into fresh Boolean atoms – so that two atom instances in φ are mapped into the same Boolean atom iff they are syntactically identical and distributes over sets and Boolean connectives. Its inverse function $\mathcal{B}2\mathcal{M}(\mu)$ (for "Boolean-to-Math") is called *refinement*, respectively. Both functions can be implemented efficiently, so that they require a small constant time for mapping one atom.

MathDpll tries to build an assignment μ satisfying φ, such that its refinement is satisfiable in LAL, and the interpretation I satisfies $\mathcal{B}2\mathcal{M}(\mu)$ (and ϕ). This is done recursively, with a variant of DPLL modified to enumerate assignments, and trying to refine them according to LAL. In particular:

Base. If $\varphi == \top$, then μ propositionally satisfies $\mathcal{M}2\mathcal{B}(\phi)$. In order to check whether μ is LAL-satisfiable, which shows that φ is LAL-satisfiable, MathDpll invokes the linear mathematical solver MathSolve on the refinement $\mathcal{B}2\mathcal{M}(\mu)$, and returns a *Sat* or *Unsat* value accordingly.

Backtrack. If $\varphi == \bot$, then μ has led to a propositional contradiction. Therefore MathDpll returns *Unsat* and backtracks.

Unit. If a literal l occurs in φ as a unit clauses, then l must be assigned a true value. Thus MathDpll is invoked recursively with the formula returned by *assign* (l, φ) and the assignment obtained by adding l to μ as arguments. *assign* (l, φ) substitutes every occurrence of l in φ with $\top$ and propositionally simplifies the result.

Early pruning. MathSolve is invoked on (the refinement of) the current assignment μ. If this is found unsatisfiable, then there is no need to proceed, and the procedure backtracks.

Split. If none of the above situations occurs, then *choose-literal* (φ) returns an unassigned l according to some heuristic criterion. Then MATHDPLL is first invoked recursively with arguments *assign*(l, φ) and $\mu \cup \{l\}$. If the result is *Unsat*, then MATHDPLL is invoked with argument *assign* ($\neg l$, φ) and $\mu \cup \{\neg l\}$.

4. The MATHSAT Algorithm: Enhancements

The algorithm presented in the previous section is oversimplified for explanatory purposes. It can be easily adapted to deal with advanced SAT solving techniques such as splitting heuristics, two-literals watching, and restarts (see [44] for an overview). This section describes several enhancement that have been made to the interplay between the Boolean and mathematical solvers.

4.1. THEORY-DRIVEN BACKJUMPING AND LEARNING

When MATHSOLVE finds the assignment μ to be LAL-unsatisfiable, it also returns a conflict set η causing the unsatisfiability. This enables MATHDPLL to backjump in its search to the most recent branching point in which at least one literal $l \in \eta$ is not assigned a truth value, pruning the search space below. We call this technique *theory-driven backjumping*. Clearly, its effectiveness strongly depends on the quality of the conflict sets generated.

EXAMPLE 4.1. Consider the formula φ and the assignment μ of Example 2.1. Suppose that MATHDPLL generates μ following the order to occurrence within φ, and that MATHSOLVE(μ) returns the conflict set (1). Thus MATHDPLL can jump back directly to the branching point $\neg(3v_1 - v_3 \leq 6)$ without exploring the right branches of ($v_3 = 3v_5 + 4$) and ($v_1 - v_5 \leq 1$). If instead MATHSOLVE(μ) returns the conflict set (2), then MATHSAT backtracks to ($v_3 = 3v_5 + 4$). Thus, (2) causes no reduction in search.

When MATHSOLVE returns a conflict set η, the clause $\neg \eta$ can be added in conjunction to φ: this will prevent MATHDPLL from generating again any branch containing η. We call this technique *theory-driven learning*.

EXAMPLE 4.2. As in Example 4.1, suppose MATHSOLVE(μ) returns the conflict set (1). Then the clause $(2v_2 - v_3 > 2) \vee \neg(3v_1 - 2v_2 \leq 3) \vee (3v_1 - v_3 \leq 6)$ is added in conjunction to ϕ. Thus, whenever a branch contaits two elements of (1), MATHDPLL will assign the third to false by unit propagation.

As in the Boolean case, learning must be used with some care, since it may cause an explosion in the size of φ. Therefore, some techniques can be used to discard learned clauses when necessary [8]. Notice however the difference with standard Boolean backjumping and learning [8]: in the latter case, the conflict set propositionally falsifies the formula, while in our case it is inconsistent from the mathematically viewpoint.

4.2. THEORY-DRIVEN DEDUCTION

With early pruning, MATHSOLVE is used to check whether μ is LAL-satisfiable and thus to possibly prune whole branches of the search. It is also possible to use MATHSOLVE to reduce the remaining Boolean search: the mathematical analysis of μ performed by MATHSOLVE can discover that the value of some mathematical atom $\psi \notin \mu$ is already determined, based on some subset $\mu' \in \mu$ of the current assignment. For instance, consider the case where the literals $(v_1 = v_2)$ and $(v_2 - v_3 = 4)$ are in the current (partial) assignment μ, while $(v_1 - v_3 = 4)$ is currently unassigned. Since $\{(v_1 = v_2), (v_2 - v_3 = 4)\} \models (v_1 - v_3 = 4)$, atom $(v_1 - v_3 = 4)$ must be assigned to $\top$, because assigning it to $\bot$ would make μ LAL-inconsistent.

MATHSOLVE is therefore used to detect and suggest to the Boolean search which unassigned literals have forced values. This kind of deduction is often very useful because it can trigger new Boolean constraint propagation: the search is deepened without the need to split. Moreover, the implication clauses describing the deduction (e.g., $\neg(v_1 = v_2) \vee \neg(v_2 - v_3 = 4) \vee (v_1 - v_3 = 4)$) can be learned at the Boolean level, and added to the main formula: this constrains the remaining Boolean search even after backtracking.

4.3. A STACK-BASED INTERFACE TO MATHSOLVE

Since the search is driven by the 'stack-based' Boolean procedure, we define a stack-based interface to call the math solver. In this way, MATHSOLVE can significantly exploit previous computations. Consider the following trace (left column first, then right):

MATHSOLVE (μ_1)	$\Rightarrow Sat$	Undo μ_2		
MATHSOLVE $(\mu_1 \cup \mu_2)$	$\Rightarrow Sat$	MATHSOLVE $(\mu_1 \cup \mu_2')$	$\Rightarrow Sat$	
MATHSOLVE $(\mu_1 \cup \mu_2 \cup \mu_3)$	$\Rightarrow Sat$	MATHSOLVE $(\mu_1 \cup \mu_2' \cup \mu_3')$	$\Rightarrow Sat$	
MATHSOLVE $(\mu_1 \cup \mu_2 \cup \mu_3 \cup \mu_4)$	$\Rightarrow Unsat$	MATHSOLVE $(\mu_1 \cup \mu_2' \cup \mu_3' \cup \mu_4')$	$\Rightarrow Sat$	

On the left, an assignment is repeatedly extended until a conflict is found. We notice that MATHSOLVE is invoked (during early pruning calls) on *incremental* assignments. When a conflict is found, the search backtracks to a previous point (on the right), and MATHSOLVE is then restarted from a previously visited state. Based on these considerations, our MATHSOLVE is not a function call: it has a persistent state and is *incremental* and *backtrackable*. Incremental means that it avoids restarting the computation from scratch whenever it is given in input an assignment μ' such that $\mu' \supset \mu$ and μ has already proved satisfiable. Backtrackable means that it is possible to return to a previous state on the stack in a relatively efficient manner. Therefore MATHSOLVE has primitives to *add* constraints to the current state, to *set backtrack points*, and to *jump back* to a previously set backtrack point.

4.4. FILTERING

Another way of speeding MATHSOLVE is to give it smaller but in some sense sufficient sets of constraints.

4.4.1. *Pure Literal Filtering*

Assume that a math-atom ψ occurs only positively in the formula ϕ, that is, there is no clause in ϕ having the literal $\neg\psi$. That is, ψ is a *pure literal*. Now if ψ is assigned to false in the current truth assignment μ, that is, $\neg\psi \in \mu$, we don't have to pass $\neg\psi$ to MATHSOLVE. The reason is that if an extension μ' of μ propositionally satisfies ϕ, so will $\mu'\setminus\{\neg\psi\}$ as ψ is a pure literal. Similar analysis applies to the case in which ψ occurs only negatively in ϕ.

Notice that if a pure literal ψ is assigned to true in μ, then it *has to* be passed to MATHSOLVE. Furthermore, one may *not* fix ψ to true before the MATHDPLL search as in the purely Boolean case.

4.4.2. *Theory-Deduced Literal Filtering*

Another way of reducing the number of math-atoms given to MATHSOLVE is to exploit theory-deduced clauses, i.e., those clauses resulting from theory-driven learning (Section 4.1), theory-driven deduction (Section 4.2), and static learning (Section 4.6). For each theory-deduced clause $C = l_1 \vee \ldots \vee l_n$, each l_i being a math-atom or its negation, the truth assignment $\{\neg l_1, \ldots, \neg l_n\}$ is LAL-unsatisfiable. That is, all interpretations that satisfy all $\neg l_1, \ldots, \neg l_{n-1}$ must satisfy the literal l_n. Therefore, if the current truth assignment μ contains the literals $\neg l_1, \ldots, \neg l_{n-1}$, and the literal l_n is forced to true by unit propagation on the clause C, there is no need to pass l_n to MATHSOLVE as μ is LAL-satisfiable iff $\mu \cup \{l_n\}$ is. In order to detect these cases, the theory-deduced clauses can be marked with a flag.

Combining the filtering methods requires some care. The literals $\neg l_1, \ldots, \neg l_{n-1}$ in the current truth assignment must have been passed to MATHSOLVE (i.e., not filtered) in order to apply theory-deduced literal filtering to l_n.

4.5. WEAKENED EARLY PRUNING

Early pruning calls are used only to prune the search; if the current (partial) assignment μ is found to be unsatisfiable, the search backtracks, but if it is found to be satisfiable, the search goes deeper and the assignment will be extended.

Therefore, during early pruning calls MathSolve does not have to detect *all* inconsistencies; as long as calls to MathSolve at the end of a search branch faithfully detect inconsistency, correctness and completeness are guaranteed.

We exploit this fact by using a faster, but less powerful version of MathSolve for early pruning calls. Specifically, in the $\mathbb{R}$ domain, handling disequalities requires an extra solver that is often time-consuming (see Section 5). As disequalities in $\mathbb{R}$ are typically very low-constraining, and thus very rarely cause inconsistency, during early pruning calls MathSolve ignores disequalities, which are instead considered when checking complete search branches.

In the $\mathbb{Z}$ domain, as the theory of linear arithmetic on $\mathbb{Z}$ is much harder, in theory and in practice, than that on $\mathbb{R}$ [9], during early pruning calls MathSolve looks for a solution on the reals only.

4.6. STATIC LEARNING

Before starting the actual MathDpll search, the problem can be preprocessed by adding some basic mathematical relationships among the math-atoms as Boolean constraints to the problem. As the added constraints are consequences of the underlying theory, the satisfiability of the problem is preserved. The new constraints may significant help to prune the search space in the *Boolean level*, thus avoiding some LAL-unsatisfiable models and calls to the more expensive MathSolve. In other words, before the search, we learn, at low cost, some basic facts that most often would have to be discovered, at a much higher cost, by the math solver during the search.

The simplest case of static learning is based on (in)equalities between math-terms and constants. Assume that ϕ contains a set of math-atoms of form $S_t = \{(t \bowtie_1 c_1), \ldots, (t \bowtie_n c_n)\}$, where t is a math-term $\bowtie_i \in \{<, \leq, =, \geq, >\}$, and c_i are constant. First, ϕ is conjoined with a set of constraints over the equality atoms of form $(t = c_i)$ in S_t, ensuring that at most one of them can be true. This can be achieved with pairwise mutual exclusion constraints of form $\neg(t = c_i) \lor \neg(t = c_j)$. Second, the math-atoms in S_t are connected with a linear number of binary constraints that compactly encode the obvious mathematical (in)equality relationship between them. For instance, if $S_t = \{(t \leq 2), (t = 3), (t > 5), (t \geq 7)\}$, then ϕ is conjoined with the constraints $(t = 3) \rightarrow \neg(t > 5)$, $(t = 3) \rightarrow \neg(t \leq 2)$, $(t \leq 2) \rightarrow \neg(t > 5)$, and $(t \geq 7) \rightarrow (t > 5)$. Now $(t \geq 7)$ implies $(t > 5)$, $\neg(t = 3)$ and $\neg(t \leq 2)$ in the *Boolean level*.

Furthermore, some facts among difference constraints of the form $t_1 - t_2 \bowtie c$, $\bowtie \in \{<, \leq, =, \geq, >\}$, can be easily derived and added. First, mutually exclusive pairs of difference constraints are handled. E.g., if $(t_1 - t_2 \leq 3), (t_2 - t_1 < -4) \in$ *MathAtoms* (ϕ), then the clause $\neg (t_1 - t_2 \leq 3) \lor \neg (t_2 - t_1 < -4)$ is conjoined to ϕ. Second, clauses corresponding to triangle inequalities and equalities between difference constraints are added. For example, if $(t_1 - t_2 \leq 3), (t_2 - t_3 < 5), (t_1 - t_3 < 9) \in$ *MathAtoms* (ϕ), then $(t_1 - t_2 \leq 3) \land t_3 < 5) \rightarrow (t_1 - t_3 < 9)$ is added

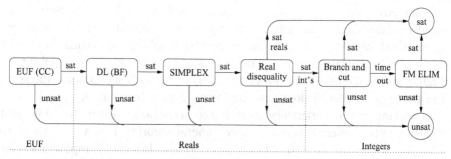

Figure 2. Control flow of MATHSOLVE.

to ϕ. Similarly, for $(t_1 - t_2 = 3)$, $(t_2 - t_3 = 0)$, $(t_1 - t_3 = 5) \in MathAtoms(\phi)$ we add the constraint $(t_1 - t_2 = 3) \wedge (t_2 - t_3 = 0) \rightarrow \neg(t_1 - t_3 = 5)$ to ϕ.

4.7. CLUSTERING

At the beginning of the search, $MathAtoms(\phi)$, that is, the set of mathematical atoms, is partitioned into a set of disjoint *clusters* $C_1 \cup \cdots \cup C_k$: intuitively, two atoms belong to the same cluster if they share a variable. If L_i is the sets of literals built with the atoms in cluster i, it is easy to see that an assignment μ is LAL-satisfiable if and only if each $\mu \cap L_i$ is LAL-satisfiable. Based on this idea, instead of having a single, monolithic solver for linear arithmetic, the mathematical solver is instantiated k different times. Each is responsible for handling the mathematical reasoning within a single cluster. A dispatcher is responsible for the activation of the suitable mathematical solver instances, depending on the mathematical atoms occurring in the assignment to be analyzed.

The advantage of this approach is manifold. First k solvers running on k disjoint problems are typically faster than running one solver monolithically on the union of the problem. Furthermore, the construction of smaller conflict sets becomes easier, and this may result in a significant gain in the overall search. Finally, when caching the results of previous calls to the linear solvers, it increases the likelihood of a hit.

5. A Layered MATHSOLVE

In this section, we discuss the structure of MATHSOLVE. We disregard the issues related to clustering, since the different instances of MATHSOLVE that result are completely independent of each other. MATHSOLVE is responsible for checking the satisfiability of a set of mathematical atoms μ and returning, as appropriate, a model or a conflict set.

In many calls to MathSolve, a general solver for linear constraints is not needed: very often, the unsatisfiability of the current assignment μ can be established in less expressive, but much easier, subtheories. Thus, MathSolve is organized in a *layered hierarchy* of solvers of increasing solving capabilities. If a higher-level solver finds a conflict, then this conflict is used to prune the search at the Boolean level; if it does not, the lower-level solvers are activated.

Layering can be understood as trying to favor faster solvers for more abstract theories over slower solvers for more general theories. Figure 2 shows a rough idea of the structure of MathSolve. Three logical components can be distinguished. First, the current assignment μ is passed to the *equational solver*, which deals only with (positive and negative) equalities (Section 5.1). Secondly, if this solver does not find a conflict, MathSolve tries to find a conflict over the reals (see Section 5.2). Third, if the current assignment is also satisfiable over the reals and the variables are to be interpreted over the integers, a solver for linear arithmetic over the integers is invoked (see Section 5.3).

5.1. EQUALITY AND UNINTERPRETED FUNCTIONS

The first layer of MathSolve is provided by the equational solver, a satisfiability checker for the logic of unconditional ground equality over uninterpreted function symbols. It is incremental and supports efficient backtracking. The solver generates conflict sets, deduces assignments for equational literals, and can provide explanations for its deductions. Thanks to the equational solver, MathSAT can be used as an efficient decision procedure for the full logic of *equality over uninterpreted function symbols* (EUF). However, in this section we focus on the way the equational solver is used to improve the performance on LAL.

The solver is based on the basic congruence closure algorithm suggested in [29]. We slightly extend the logic by allowing for *enumerated objects* and *numbers*, with the understanding that each object denotes a distinct domain element (i.e., an object is implicitly different from all the other objects and from all numbers). Similarly, different numbers are implicitly different from each other (and from all objects).

The congruence closure module internally constructs a congruence data structure that can determine whether two arbitrary terms are necessarily forced to be equal by the currently asserted constraints, and can thus be used to determine the value of (some) equational atoms. It also maintains a list of asserted *dis-equations* and signals unsatisfiability if either one of these or an implicit dis-equation is violated by the current congruence.

If two terms are equal, an auxiliary proof tree data structure allows us to extract the reason, that is, the original constraints (and just those) that forced this equality. If a disequality constraint is violated, we can return the reason (together with the violated inequality) as a *conflict set*.

Similarly, we can perform *forward deduction*: for each unassigned equational atom, we can determine whether the two sides are already forced to be equal by the current assignment, and hence whether the atom has to be asserted as true or false. Again, we can extract the reason for this deduction and use it to represent the deduction as a learned clause on the Boolean level.

There are two ways in which the equational solver can be used: as a full solver for a purely equational cluster or as a layer in the arithmetic reasoning process. In the first case, the equational solver is associated to a cluster not involving any arithmetic at all, which contains only equation of the $v_i \bowtie v_j$, $v_i \bowtie c_j$, with $\bowtie \in \{=, \neq\}$. As stated above, the equation solver implicitly knows that syntactically different constants in $\mathcal{D}$ are semantically distinct. Hence, it provides a full solver for some clusters, avoiding the need to call an expensive linear solver on an easy problem. This can significantly improve performance, since in practical examples a purely equation cluster often is present – typical examples are the modeling of assignments in a programming language, and gate and multiplexer definitions in circuits.

In the second case, the equational solver also receives constraints involving arithmetic operators. While arithmetic functions are treated as fully uninterpreted, the equational solver has a limited interpretation of $<$ and $\leq$, knowing only that $s < t$ implies $s \neq t$, and $s = t$ implies $s \leq t$ and $\neg(s < t)$. However, all deductions and conflicts under EUF semantics are also valid under fully interpreted semantics. Thus, the efficient equational solver can be used to prune the search space. Only if the equational solver cannot deduce any new assignments and reports a tentative model, does this model need to be analyzed by lower solvers.

5.2. LINEAR ARITHMETIC OVER THE REALS

To check a given assignment μ of linear constraints for satisfiability over the reals, MATHSOLVE first considers only those constraints that are in the difference logic fragment. That is, it considers the subassignment of μ consisting of all constraints of the forms $v_i - v_j \bowtie c$ and $v_i \bowtie c$, with $\bowtie \in \{=, \neq, <, >, \leq, \geq\}$. Satisfiability checking for this subassignment is reduced to a negative-cycle detection problem in the graph whose nodes correspond to variables and whose edges correspond to the constraints. MATHSOLVE uses an incremental version of the Bellman-Ford algorithm to search for a negative-cycle and hence for a conflict. See, for instance [13], for background information. In many practical cases, for instance in bounded model-checking problems of timed automata, a sizable amount or even all of μ is in the difference logic fragment. This causes a considerable speedup, since the Bellman-Ford algorithm is much more efficient than a general linear solver and generally generates much better (smaller) conflict sets.

If the difference logic fragment of μ turns out to be satisfiable, MATHSOLVE checks the satisfiability of the subassignment of μ consisting of all constraints except the disequalities by means of the simplex method. MATHSOLVE uses a variant of the simplex method, namely, the Cassowary algorithm (see [10]), that uses slack variables to efficiently allow the addition and removal of constraints and the generation of minimal conflict set.

When this also turns out to be consistent, disequalities are taken into account: the incremental and backtrackable machinery is used to check, for each disequality $\Sigma c_i v_i \neq c_j$ in μ, and separately from the other disequalities, whether it is consistent with the non-disequality constraints in μ. We do so by adding and retracting both $\Sigma c_i v_i < c_j$ and $\Sigma c_i v_i > c_j$. If one of the disequalities is inconsistent, the assignment μ is inconsistent. However, because the theory of the reals is (logically) convex, if each disequality separately is consistent, then all of μ is consistent – this follows from a dimensionality argument, basically because it is impossible to write an affine subspace A of $\mathbb{R}^k$ as a finite union of proper affine subspaces of A.

5.3. LINEAR ARITHMETIC OVER THE INTEGERS

Whenever the variables are interpreted over the reals, MATHSOLVE is done at this point. If the variables are to be interpreted over the integers, and the problem is unsatisfiable in $\mathbb{R}$, then it also is so over $\mathbb{Z}$. When the problem is satisfiable in the reals, it is possible that it is not so in the integers. The first step carried out by MATHSOLVE in this case is a simple form of branch-and-cut (see, e.g., [26]) that searches for solutions over the integers by tightening the constraints. The algorithm acts on the representation of the solution space constructed over the integers and makes use of the incremental and backtrackable machinery. Branch-and-cut also takes into account disequalities.

Branch-and-cut is complete only when the solution space is bounded, and there are practical cases when it can be very slow to converge. Therefore, if it does not find either an integer solution or a conflict within a small, predetermined amount of search, the current assignment is analyzed with the Fourier–Motzkin Elimination (FME) procedure. Since it is computationally expensive, FME is called only as a last resort.

6. The MATHSAT System

The MATHSAT system is a general solver implementing the ideas and algorithms described earlier in this paper. It also has some other features and accepts a richer input language than pure LAL, as for example, equalities over uninterpreted functions are allowed.

It is structured in three main components: (i) a preprocessor, (ii) a Boolean satisfiability solver, and (iii) the MATHSOLVE theory reasoner.

6.1. PREPROCESSOR

MATHSAT supports a rich input language, with a large variety of Boolean and arithmetic operators, including a ternary *if-then-else* construct on the term and formula level. For reasons of simplicity and efficiency, MATHDPLL, the core engine of the solver, handles a much simplified language. Reducing the rich input language to this simpler form is done by a *preprocessor* module.

The preprocessor performs some basic normalization of atoms, so that the core engine has to deal only with a restricted set of predicates. It eliminates each ternary *if-then-else* term $t = ITE(b, t_1, t_2)$ over math terms t_1 and t_2 by replacing it with a new variable v_t and adding the boolean if-then-else constraint ITE $(b, v_t = t_1, v_t = t_2)$ to the formula. Furthermore, it uses a standard linear-time, satisfiability preserving translation to transform the formula (including the remaining *if-then-else* on the Boolean level) into clause normal form.

6.2. BOOLEAN SOLVER

The propositional abstraction of the math-formula produced by the preprocessor is given to the Boolean satisfiability solver extended to implement the MATHDPLL algorithm described in Section 3. This solver is built upon the MINISAT solver [17], from which it inherits conflict-driven learning and back-jumping, restarts [8, 22, 37], optimized Boolean constraint propagation based on the two-watched literal scheme, and the VSIDS splitting heuristics [28]. In fact, if MATHSAT is given a purely Boolean problem, it behaves substantially like MINISAT, as MATHSOLVE is not instantiated.* The communication with MATHSOLVE is carried out through an interface (similar to the one in [20]) that passes assigned literals, LAL-consistency queries, and back-tracking commands and receives back answers to the queries, mathematical conflict sets, and implied literals (Section 3).

The Boolean solver has been extended to handle some options relevant when dealing with math-formulas. For instance, MATHSAT inherits MINISAT's feature of periodically discarding some of the learned clauses to prevent explosion of the formula size. However, clauses generated by theory-driven learning and forward deduction mechanisms (Section 3) are never discarded, as a default option, since they may have required a lot of work in MATHSOLVE. As a second example, it is possible to initialize the VSIDS heuristics weights of literals so that either Boolean or theory atoms are preferred as splitting choices early in the MATHDPLL search.

---

* In some experiments on some very big pure SAT formulas, which are not reported here, MATHSAT took on average 10–20% more time than MINISAT to solve the same instances.

6.3. MathSolve

The implementation of MathSolve is composed of several software modules. The equational reasoner is implemented in C/C++ and reuses some of the data structures of the theorem prover E [33] to store and process terms and atoms. The module for handling difference constraints is developed in C++. The simplex algorithm for linear arithmetic over the reals is based on the Cassowary system [5]. The branch-and-cut procedure is implemented on top of it and uses the incrementally features of Cassowary to perform the search. For the Four-ier–Motzkin elimination. MathSolve uses the Omega system [30].

A very important point is that MathSAT is able to deal with infinite-precision arithmetic. To this end, the mathematical solver handles arbitrary large rational numbers by means of the GMP library [21].

7. Experimental Evaluation

In this section we report on the experiments we have carried out to evaluate the performance of our approach. The experiments were run on a bi-processor XEON 3.0 GHz machine with 4 GB of memory (test in Section 7.2), on a 4-Processor PentiumIII 700 MHz machine with 6 GB of memory (tests in Section 7.3.1), and on a bi-processor XEON 1.4 GHz machine with 2 GB of memory (tests in Section 7.3.2), all of them running Linux RedHat Enterprise. The time limit for all the experiments was set to 300 s, and the memory limit was set to 512 MB.

An executable version of MathSAT and the source files of all the experiments performed in the paper are available at [27].

7.1. DESCRIPTION OF THE TEST CASES

The set of benchmarks we used in the experimentation, described below, involves all the suites available in the literature we are aware of. For the test on LAL, we used the following suites. The **SAL suite**, originally presented in [32], is a set of benchmarks for ground decision procedures, derived from bounded model checking of timed automata and linear hybrid systems, and from test-case generation for embedded controllers. The **RTLC suite**, provided by the authors of [31], formalizes safety properties for RTL (see [31] for a more detailed description). The **CIRC suite**, generated by ourselves, encodes the verification of certain properties for some simple circuits. The suite is composed of three kinds of benchmark, all of them being parametric in (and scaling up with) N, that is, the width of the data-path of the circuit, so that $[0..2^N - 1]$ is the range of integer variables. In the first benchmark, the modular sum of the integers is checked for inequality against the bitwise sum of their bit decomposition. The negation of the resulting formula is therefore unsatisfiable. In the second benchmark, two identical shift-and-add multipliers and two integers a and b are given; a and the bit decomposition of b (respectively b and the bit decomposition of a) are given as input to the first (respectively, the second) multiplier and the outputs of the two multiplier are checked for inequality. The negation of the resulting formula is therefore unsatisfiable. In the third benchmark, an integer a and the bitwise decomposition of an integer b are given as input to a shift-and-add multiplier; the output of the multiplier is compared with the constant integer value p^2, p being the biggest prime number strictly smaller than 2^N. The resulting formula is satisfiable, but it has only one solution, where $a = b = p$. The **TM suite** is a set of benchmark for (temporal) metric planning, provided to us by the authors of [36] (see also [41]).

The benchmark below have been used for the comparison in Section 7.3.2 and fall into the difference logic fragment of LAL. The **DLSAT suite** is provided to us by the authors of [14] (see the paper for more detail). The suite contains two different sets of benchmark: the first set formalizes the problem of finding the optimal schedule for the job shop problem, a combinatorial optimization problem; the second set is concerned with bounded model checking of timed automata that model digital circuits with delays, and formalizes the problem of finding the maximal stabilization time for the circuits. The **SEP suite** [34] is a set of benchmarks for separation logic (i.e., difference logic) derived from symbolic simulation of several hardware designs, which is maintained by O. Strichman. The **DTP suite** [1, 38] is a set of benchmarks from the field of temporal reasoning. The set of benchmark is similar in spirit to the standard random k-CNF SAT benchmark and consists of randomly generated 2-CNF difference formulas. For our tests we have selected 60 randomly generated DTP formulas with 35 numerical variables in the "hard" satisfiability transition area.

The SAL, TM, DLSAT, and DTP suites are in the domain of reals, while the RTCL, CIRC, and SEP suites are in the domain of integers. Because of the different sources of problems within one suite, the benchmark suites cannot be straightforwardly characterized in terms of structural properties of their formulas (except for the DPT suite, in which only positive difference inequalities in the form $(x - y \leq c)$ occur). Nearly all problems contain a significant quantity of Boolean atoms (e.g., control variables in circuits, actions in planning problems, discrete variables in timed and hybrid system). Nearly all problems contain many difference inequalities in the form $(x - y \leq c)$ (e.g., time constraints in scheduling problems and in timed and hybrid systems verification problems, range constraints in RTL, circuits). Some problems, such as ATPG problems in RTLC and timed and hybrid systems in SAL, contain lots of simple equalities in the form $(x = y)$ or $(x = c)$. The problems in the CIRC suite contain complex LAL atoms with very big integer constants, like $(b = \Sigma_i \, 2^i b_i)$ or $(x \leq 2^{32})$.

7.2. EVALUATING DIFFERENT OPTIMIZATIONS

In this section we evaluate the impact of several optimizations on the overall performance of MATHSAT. The experimental evaluation has been conducted in the following way. We chose a "default" option configuration for MATHSAT, that involves theory-driven backjumping and learning, theory-driven deduction, weakened early pruning, static learning, clustering, and EQ layering (that is, using the EUF solver as described in the second case of Section 5.1).

The configuration has been tested against each of the configuration obtained by switching off (or changing) different options *one at a time* (in other words, each version that has been tested differs from the default version only with respect to one of the optimizations). Specifically, the variants we considered are respectively the default version without (weekend) early pruning, with full early pruning, without clustering, without theory-driven deduction, without static learning, and without EQ layering.

The six variants of MATHSAT have been run on the following test suites: SAL, RTLC, CIRC, TM, DLSAT, SEP, DTP.

The scatter plots of the overall results are given in Figure 3. Each plot reports the results of the evaluation on each of the options. The X and Y axes show,

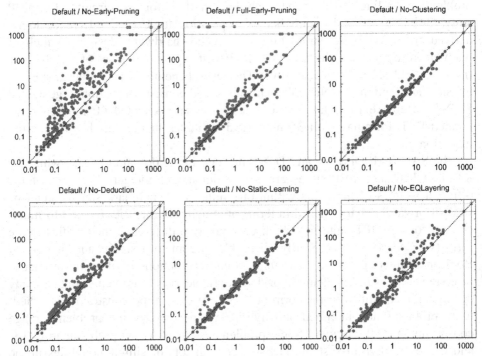

Figure 3. Scatter plots for six different variations of MATHSAT (Y axis), compared against the default version (X axis).

respectively, the performance of the default version and of the modified version of MATHSAT. A dot in the upper part of a picture, that is, above the diagonal, means that the default version performs better, and vice versa. The two uppermost horizontal lines represent benchmarks that ended in time-out (lower) or out-of-memory (higher) for the modified version of MATHSAT, whereas the two rightmost vertical lines represent time-out (left) or out-of-memory (right) for the default version. Notice that the axes are logarithmic, so that only big performance gaps are highlighted. For example, the fact that a variant is 50% faster or slower than the default on some sample (i.e., a 1.5 performance factor) is hardly discernible on these plots.

From the plots in Figure 3 we observe the following facts.

- Dropping (weakened) early pruning worsens the performances significantly, or even drastically, in most benchmarks. This is due to the fact that early pruning may allow for significant cuts to the boolean search tree, and that the extra cost of intermediate calls to MATHSOLVE is much reduced by the incrementality of MATHSOLVE. From nearly all our experiments, it turns out that early pruning causes a significant reduction of the number of branches explored in the Boolean search tree, which is proportional to the overall reduction of CPU time.

- Using full early pruning instead of its weakened version most often worsens performances, on both $\mathbb{R}$ and $\mathbb{Z}$ domains. From the experimental data, we see that full early pruning does not introduce significant reductions in the number of boolean branches explored, while the calls to MATHSOLVE require longer times on average.

  Within the $\mathbb{R}$ domian, this fact seems to suggest that ignoring disequalities in the consistency check makes MATHSOLVE faster without reducing significantly the pruning effect of the boolean search space. Within the $\mathbb{R}$ domain, this fact seems to suggest that in most cases the assignments that are consistent in $\mathbb{R}$ are consistent also in $\mathbb{Z}$ and that the overhead due to handling integers also in early pruning calls in sometimes heavy.

- Dropping clustering slightly worsens the performances in most cases, although the gaps are not dramatic. A possible explanation is that the effects of "dividing and conquering" the mathematical search space are not as relevant as those of other factors (e.g., cutting the Boolean search space). This combines with the fact that the mathematical solver is very effective in producing small conflict sets, even in presence of larger problems. In our test, only a few tests actually had more than one cluster. A more refined analysis shows that for the problems with only a single cluster the overhead is not significant.

- Dropping theory-driven deduction worsens the performance in most cases. The importance of deduction is both in the immediate effect of assigning truth values to unassigned literals, which fires Boolean constraint propagation, and in the learning of extra clauses from the deduction. From our experiments, it turns out that theory-driven deduction is most effective in problems that are rich in simpler equalities like $(x = c)$ and $(x = y)$ (e.g., the problems in the RTLC and the BMC on timed system problems in SAL), which can be easily and effectively deduced by the EUF solver.

- Static learning seems to introduce only slight improvements on average. This may be due to the fact that most benchmarks derive from the encoding of verification problems, so that short clauses that can be learned easily are already part of the encodings (see, e.g., [4]). Moreover, in general, the effect of static learning is hindered in part by theory-driven learning. From our experiments, it turns out that in some benchmarks (e.g., DTP, and partly DLSAT and CIRC) where lots of clauses can be learned off-line, static-learning is effective (e.g., more than one order magnitude faster on DTP) while on other benchmarks where very few or no clause can be learned off-line, static learning is ineffective.

- Dropping EQ layering worsens the performance in most cases. We believe this is due to the fact that many practical problems contain lots of simple equalities, from which lots of information can be deduced and learned by simply applying equality propagation and congruence closure. From our experiments, it turns out that EQ layering is most effective in problems which are rich of simpler equalities like $(x = c)$ and $(x = y)$ (e.g., the problems in RTLC and the BMC on timed system problems in SAL), which can be easily and effectively handled by the EUF solver.

Figure 4 shows the impact of switching off simultaneously all six options described above. We notice that, altogether, the six optimizations improve the performances significantly, and even dramatically in most cases.

7.3. COMPARISON WITH OTHER STATE-OF-THE-ART TOOLS

In this section we report the results of the evaluation of MATHSAT with respect to other state-of-the-art tools. We distinguish the evaluation into two parts: in

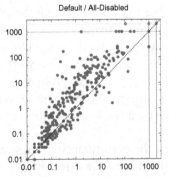

Figure 4. Scatter plots for the version of MATHSAT with all features disabled (Y axis) compared against the default version (X axis).

Section 7.3.1 we compare MATHSAT against CVC, ICS, and UCLID, which support linear arithmetic logic (LAL), whereas in Section 7.3.2 we compare MATHSAT against TSAT++ and DLSAT, which are specialized solvers for difference logic (DL).

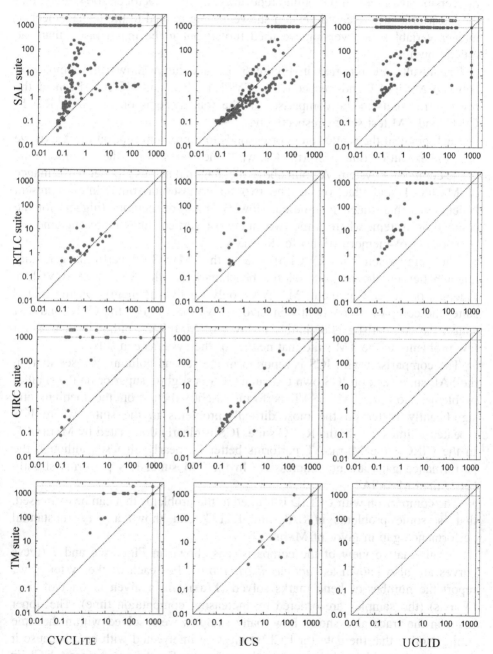

Figure 5. Execution time ratio: the X and Y axes report MATHSAT and each competitor's times, respectively.

7.3.1. Comparison on Linear Arithmetic Logic

We have compared MATHSAT with ICS [18, 23], CVCLITE [7, 15], and UCLID [35, 43]. We ran ICS version 2.0 and UCLID version 1.0. For CVCLITE, we used the version available on the online repository, as of 10 October 2004, given that the latest officially released version showed a bug related to the management of integer variables (the version we used turned out to be much faster than the official one).

The results are reported in Figure 5. Each column shows the comparison between MATHSAT and, respectively, CVCLITE, ICS and UCLID. Each of the rows corresponds to the comparison of the four systems on the SAL, RTCL, CIRC, and TM test suites, respectively.

Each point in the scatter plot corresponds to a problem run; on the X axis we have the execution time of MATHSAT, while the Y axis shows the execution time of the competitor system. A point above the diagonal means a better performance of MATHSAT and vice versa. The two uppermost horizontal lines represent benchmarks that ended in time-out (lower) or out-of-memory (higher) for the competitor system, whereas the two rightmost vertical lines represent time-out (left) or out-of-memory (right) for MATHSAT.

The comparison with CVCLITE shows that MATHSAT performs generally much better on the majority of the benchmarks in the SAL suite (CVCLITE timeouts on several of them, MATHSAT only on five of them). On the RTLC suite, the comparison is slightly in favor of MATHSAT. For the CIRC and TM suites, the comparison is definitely in favor of MATHSAT, although there are a few problems in the TM suite that neither of the systems can solve.

The comparison with ICS is reported in the second column. We see that on the SAL suite (i.e., on ICS own test suite) ICS is slightly superior on the smaller problems. However, MATHSAT performs slightly better on the medium and significantly better on the most difficult problems in the suite, where ICS repeatedly times out. In the RTLC suite, ICS is clearly dominated by MATHSAT. In the CIRC suite MATHSAT performs better on nearly all tests, although the performance gaps are not impressive. In the TM suite, ICS performs slightly better than MATHSAT.

The comparison with UCLID is limited to the problems that can be expressed, that is, some problems in SAL and RTLC, and shows a very substantial performance gap in favor of MATHSAT.

An alternative view of the comparison is shown in Figures 6 and 7 (these curves are also known as *runtime distributions*). For each of the systems, we report the number of benchmarks solved (Y axis) in a given amount of time (X axis) (the samples are ordered by increasing computaion time). The upper point in the trace also shows how many samples were solved within the time limit. (Notice that the data for UCLID must be interpreted with care because it was confronted only with a subset of the problems. For the same reason, UCLID is not reported in the totals).

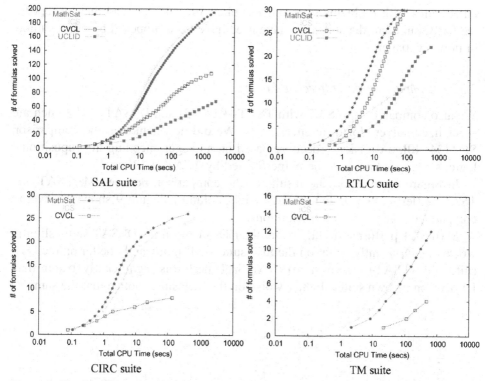

Figure 6. Number of benchmarks solved (*Y* axis) *versus* time (*X* axis) for each suite.

The curves highlight that UCLID is the worst scorer except for the RTLC suite, where it performs better than ICS, that MATHSAT and ICS perform globally better than CVCLITE, and that MATHSAT is sometimes slower on the smaller problems than ICS, but more powerful when it comes to harder problems.

One potential criticism to every empirical comparison is that the choice of the test cases may bias the results. For our tests, however, we remark that we have run *all the test cases* used by the ICS team in [16], that we have also introduced

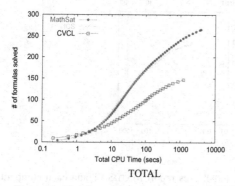

Figure 7. Number of benchmarks solved (*Y* axis) *versus* time (*X* axis) (all suites).

other suites with problems from other application domains, and that, except for the CIRC suite, all the suites we have used have been proposed by other authors in previous papers.

7.3.2. *Comparison on Difference Logic*

We also compared MathSAT with TSAT++ [2, 42] and DLSAT [14], which are specialized solvers for difference logics. We did not include in the comparison SEP [34, 40], a decision procedure based on an eager encoding in propositional logic, since it is known to be outperformed by TSAT++ [2].

In Figure 8 we report the results of the comparison between MathSAT and TSAT++ (left column), and DLSAT (right column). Figure 9 shows an overall comparison using runtime distributions.

MathSAT performs slightly better than TSAT++ on the DLSAT suite, slightly worse or equivalently better on the SEP suite, and significantly better on the DTP suite (i.e., TSAT++ own suite). MathSAT performs significantly better than DLSAT on its own suite, slightly worse on the SEP suite (notice that the samples

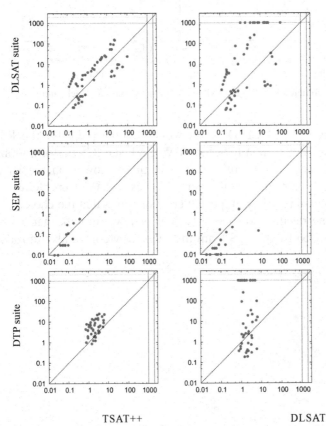

Figure 8. Execution time ratio: the *X* and *Y* axes report MathSAT and each competitor's times, respectively.

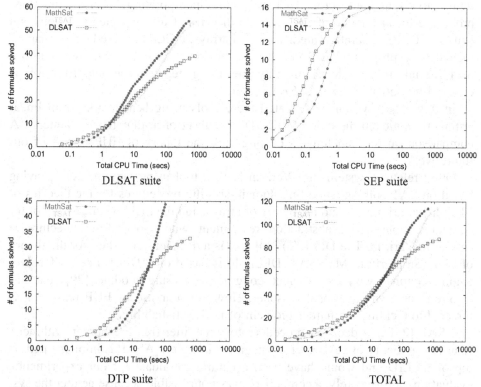

Figure 9. Number of benchmarks solved (*Y* axis) *versus* time (*X* axis) for each suite.

here are much fewer and much simpler) and significantly better in the DTP suite. On the whole, we can see that MATHSAT and TSAT++ both outperform DLSAT. Interestingly, MATHSAT exhibits on these problems a behavior that is comparable to or even better than TSAT++, which is a highly specialized solver, despite its ability to deal with a larger class of problems.

8. Related Work

In this paper we have presented a new decision procedure for linear arithmetic logic. The verification problem for LAL is well known and has received a lot of interest in the past. In particular, decision procedures are the ones considered in Section 7.3, namely, CVCLITE [7, 15], ICS [18, 23], and UCLID [35, 43].

CVCLITE is a library for checking validity of quantifier-free first-order formulas over several interpreted theories, including real and integer linear arithmetic, arrays, and uninterpreted functions. CVCLITE replaces the older tools SVC and CVC [15]. ICS is a decision procedure for the satisfiability of formulas in a quantifier-free, first-order theory containing both uninterpreted function symbols and interpreted symbol from a set of theories including arithmetic, tuples, arrays, and bit vectors. UCLID is a tool incorporating a decision functions procedure for arithmetic of counters, the theories of uninterpreted functions and equality (EUF), separation predicates, and arrays. UCLID is based on an "eager" reduction to propositional SAT; that is, the input formula is translated into a SAT formula in a single satisfiability-preserving step, and the output formula is checked for satisfiability by a SAT solver.

In this paper, we have compared these tools using benchmarks from linear arithmetic logic (in the case of UCLID the subset of arithmetic of counters). A comparison on the benchmarks dealing with the theory of EUF is part of our future work.

Other relevant systems are Verifun [19], a tool using lazy-theorem proving based on SAT-solving, suporting domain-specific procedures for the theories of EUF, linear arithmetic and the theory of arrays, and the tool ZAPATO [6], a tool for counterexample-driven abstraction refinement whose overall architecture is similar to Verifun. The DPLL(T) [20] tool is a decision procedure for the theory of EUF. Similarly to MATHSAT, DPLL(T) is based on a DPLL-like SAT-solver engine coupled with an efficient congruence closure module [29] that has inspired our own equational reasoner. However, our use of EUF reasoning is directed to tackling the harder problem of LAL satisfiability.

ASAP [25] is a decision procedure for quantifier-free Presburger arithmetic (that is, the theory of LAL over nonnegative integers). ASAP is implemented on top of UCLID and would have been a natural candidate for our experimental evaluation; unfortunately, a comparison was not possible because neither the system nor the benchmarks described in [25] have been made available.

We mentioned HDPLL, a decision procedure for LAL, specialized for the verification of circuits at the RTL level [31]. The procedure is based on DPLL-like Boolean search engine integrated with a constraint solver based on Fourier-Motzkin elimination and finite domain constraint propagation. According to the experimental results in [31], HDPLL seems to be very effective for its application domain. We are very interested in incorporating some of the ideas into MATHSAT and in performing a thorough experimental comparison. However, HDPLL is not publicly available.

Concerning the fragment of difference logic, other related tools are the ones considered in Section 7.3.2, namely, TSAT++ [2, 42], and DLSAT [14]. While TSAT++ and DLSAT implemented an approach similar to MATHSAT, they are specialized to dealing with difference logics and do not implement any form of layering. In general, TSAT++ appears to be much more efficient than DLSAT, based on a lean implementation that tightly integrates the theory solver with a state-of-the-art library for SAT. An alternative approach is implemented in SEP [34, 40], that is based on a eager approach that reduces satisfiability of the difference logic to the satisfiability of a purely propositional formula.

Concerning the very different domain of constraint logic programming, we notice that some ideas related to the mathematical solver(s) presented in this paper (i.e., layering, stack-based interfaces, theory-deduction) are to some extent similar to those presented in [24].[*]

9. Conclusions and Future Work

In this paper we have presented a new approach to the satisfiability of linear arithmetic logic. The work is carried out within the (known) framework of integration between off-the-shelf SAT solvers, and specialized theory solvers. We proposed several improvements. In the top level algorithm, we exploit theory learning and deduction, theory-driven backjumping, and we adopt a stack-based interface that allows for an incremental and backtrackable implementation of the mathematical solver. We also use static learning and clustering. We heavily exploit the idea of layering: the satisfiability of theory constraints is evaluated in theories of increasing strength (equality, linear arithmetic over the reals, and linear arithmetic over the integers). The idea is to prefer less expensive solvers (for weaker theories), thus reducing the use of more expensive solvers. We carried out a thorough experimental evaluation of our approach: our MATHSAT solver is able to tackle effectively a wide class of problems, with performance comparable with and often superior to the state-of-the-art competitors, both on LAL problems and against specialized competitors on the subclass of difference logics.

As future work, we plan to enhance MATHSAT by investigating different splitting heuristics and the integration of other boolean reasoning techniques, that are complementary to DPLL. An extension of MATHSAT to nonlinear arithmetics is currently ongoing, based on the integration of computer-algebraic methods. Further extensions include the development of specialized modules to deal with memory access, bit-vector arithmetic, and the extension to the integration of EUF and LA. On the side of verification, we envisage MATHSAT as a back-end for lifting SAT-based model checking beyond the Boolean case, to the verification of sequential RTL circuits and of hybrid systems.

References

1. Armando, A., Castellini, C. and Giunchiglia, E.: SAT-based procedures for temporal reasoning, in *Proc. European Conference on Planning, CP-99*.
2. Armando, A., Castellini, C., Giunchiglia, E. and Maratea, M.: A SAT-based decision procedure for the boolean combination of difference constraints, in *Proc. Conference on Theory and Applications of Satisfiability Testing (SAT'04)*, 2004.
3. Audemard, G., Bertoli, P., Cimatti, A., Kornilowicz, A. and Sebastiani, R.: A SAT based approach for solving formulas over boolean and linear mathematical propositions, in *Proc. CADE'2002*, Vol. 2392 of *LNAI*, 2002.
4. Audemard, G., Cimatti, A., Kornilowicz, A. and Sebastiani, R.: SAT-based bounded model checking for timed systems, in *Proc. FORTE'02*, Vol. 2529 of *LNCS*, 2002.

---

[*] We are grateful to an anonymous reviewer for pointing out this fact to us.

5. Badros, G. and Borning, A.: The Cassowary linear arithmetic constraint solving algorithm: interface and implementation. Technical Report UW-CSE-98-06-04, University of Washington, 1998.

6. Ball, T., Cook, B., Lahiri, S. and Zhang, L.: Zapato: Automatic theorem proving for predicate abstraction refinement, in *Proc. CAV'04*, Vol. 3114 of *LNCS*, 2004, pp. 457–461.

7. Barrett, C. and Berezin, S.: CVC Lite: A new implementation of the cooperating validity checker, in *Proc. CAV'04*, Vol. 3114 of *LNCS*, 2004, pp. 515–518.

8. Bayardo, Jr., R. J. and Schrag, R. C.: Using CSP look-back techniques to solve real-world SAT instances, in *Proc. AAAI/IAAI'97*, 1997, pp. 203–208.

9. Bockmayr, A. and Weispfenning, V.: Solving numerical constraints, in *Handbook of Automated Reasoning*, MIT, 2001, pp. 751–842.

10. Borning, A., Marriott, K., Stuckey, P. and Xiao, Y.: Solving linear arithmetic constraints for user interface applications, in *Proc. UIST'97*, 1997, pp. 87–96.

11. Bozzano, M., Bruttomesso, R., Cimatti, A., Junttila, T., van Rossum, P., Schulz, S. and Sebastiani, R.: An incremental and layered procedure for the satisfiability of linear arithmetic logic, in *Proc. TACAS 2005*, Vol. 3440 of *LNCS*, 2005, pp. 317–333.

12. Brinkmann, R. and Drechsler, R.: RTL-Datapath verification using integer linear programming, in *Proc. ASP-DAC 2002*, 2002, pp. 741–746.

13. Cherkassky, B. and Goldberg, A.: Negative-cycle detection algorithms, *Math. Program.* **85** (1999), 277–311.

14. Cotton, S., Asarin, E., Maler, O. and Niebert, P.: Some progress in satisfiability checking for difference logic, in *Proc. FORMATS-FTRTFT 2004*, 2004.

15. CVC. CVC, CVCLITE and SVC. http://verify.stanford.edu/{CVC, CVCL, SVC}.

16. de Moura, L. and Ruess, H.: An experimental evaluation of ground decision procedures, in R. Alur and D. Peled (eds.), *Proc. 15th Int. Conf. on Computer Aided Verification-CAV04*, Vol. 3114 of *LNCS*. Boston, Massachusetts, 2004, pp. 162–174.

17. Eén, N. and Sörensson, N.: An extensible SAT-solver, in *Theory and Applications of Satisfiability Testing (SAT 2003)*, Vol. 2919 of *LNCS*, 2004, pp. 502–518.

18. Filliâtre, J.-C., Owre, S., Ruess, H. and Shankar, N.: ICS: Integrated canonizer and solver, in *Proc. CAV'01*, Vol. 2102 of *LNCS*, 2001, pp. 246–249.

19. Flanagan, C., Joshi, R., Ou, X. and Saxe, J.: Theorem proving using lazy proof explication, in *Proc. CAV'03*, Vol. 2725 of *LNCS*, 2003, pp. 355–367.

20. Ganzinger, H., Hagen, G., Nieuwenhuis, R., Oliveras, A. and Tinelli, C.: DPLL(T): fast decision procedures, in *Proc. CAV'04*, Vol. 3114 of *LNCS*, 2004, pp. 175–188.

21. GMP. GNU Multi Precision Library. http://www.swox.com/gmp.

22. Gomes, C., Selman, B. and Kautz, H.: Boosting combination search through randomization, in *Proc. of the Fifteenth National Conf. on Artificial Intelligence*, 1998, pp. 431–437.

23. ICS. ICS. http://www.icansolve.com.

24. Jaffar, J., Michaylov, S., Stuckey, P.J. and Yap, R.H.C.: The CLP(R) languages and systems, *ACM Trans. Program. Lang. Syst. (TOPLAS)* **14**(3) (1992), 339–395.

25. Kroening, D., Ouaknine, J., Seshia, S. and Strichman, O.: Abstraction-based satisfiability solving of Presburger arithmetic, in *Proc. CAV'04*, Vol. 3114 of *LNCS*, 2004, pp. 308–320.

26. Land, H. and Doig, A.: An automatic method for solving discrete programming problems, *Econometrica* **28** (1960), 497–520.

27. MATHSAT. MATHSAT. http://mathsat.itc.it.

28. Moskewicz, M. W., Madigan, C. F., Zhao, Y., Zhang, L. and Malik, S.: Chaff engineering an efficient SAT solver, in *Proc. DAC'01*, 2001, pp. 530–535.

29. Nieuwenhuis, R. and Oliveras, A.: Congruence closure with integer offset, in *Proc. 10th LPAR*, 2003, pp. 77–89.

30. Omega. Omega. http://www.cs.umd.edu/projects/omega.

31. Parthasarathy, G., Iyer, M., Cheng, K.-T. and Wang, L.-C.: An efficient finite-domain constraint solver for circuits, in *Proc. DAC'04*, 2004, pp. 212–217.
32. SAL. SAL Suite. http://www.csl.sri.com/users/demoura/gdp-benchmark.html.
33. Schulz, S.: E-A Brainiac theorem prover, *AI Commun.* **15**(2/3) (2002), 111–126.
34. SEP. SEP Suite, http://iew3.technion.ac.il/~ofers/smtlib-local/benchmarks.html.
35. Seshia, S., Lahiri, S. and Bryant, R.: A hybrid SAT-based decision procedure for separation logic with uninterpreted function, in *Proc. DAC'03*, pp. 425–430.
36. Shin, J.-A. and Davis, E.: Continuous time in a SAT-based planner, in *Proc. AAAI-04*, 2004, pp. 531–536.
37. Silva, J. P. M. and Sakallah, K. A.: GRASP – A new search algorithm for satisfiability, in *Proc. ICCAD'96*, 1996, pp. 220–227.
38. Stergiou, K. and Koubarakis, M.: Backtracking algorithms for disjunctions of temporal constraints, *Artif. Intell.* **120**(1) (2000), 81–117.
39. Strichman, O.: On solving presburger and linear arithmetic with SAT, in *Proc. of Formal Methods in Computer-Aided Design (FMCAD 2002)*, 2002.
40. Strichman, O., Seshia, S., Bryant, R.: Deciding separation formulas with SAT, in *Proc. of Computer Aided Verification, (CAV'02)*.
41. TM. TM-LPSAT. http://csl.cs.nyu.edu/~jiae/.
42. TSAT. TSAT++. http://www.ai.dist.unige.it/Tsat.
43. UCLID.UCLID. http://www-2.cs.cmu.edu/~uclid.
44. Zhang, L. and Malik, S.: The quest for efficient boolean satisfiability solves, in *Proc. CAV'02*, 2002, pp. 17–36.